The Inflation Accounting
Steering Group's

# Guidance Manual
## on
## Current
## Cost Accounting
including the Exposure Draft

Published on behalf of the
**Inflation Accounting Steering Group,**
a Committee of the Accounting Standards Committee,
the governing bodies of which are:

**The Institute of Chartered Accountants in England and Wales**

**The Institute of Chartered Accountants of Scotland**

**The Institute of Chartered Accountants in Ireland**

**The Association of Certified Accountants**

**The Institute of Cost and Management Accountants**

**The Chartered Institute of Public Finance and Accountancy**

by
TOLLEY PUBLISHING COMPANY LIMITED
and
THE PUBLICATIONS DEPARTMENT OF THE
INSTITUTE OF CHARTERED ACCOUNTANTS
IN ENGLAND AND WALES
1976

This manual was written for
The Inflation Accounting Steering Group
by
David Gilbert

ISBN 0 510 49349 1

First Published in December 1976 for
The Inflation Accounting Steering Group
by
Tolley Publishing Company Ltd, 44a High Street, Croydon, CR9 1UU
and
The Publications Department of The Institute of Chartered Accountants in England and
Wales, PO Box 433, Chartered Accountants' Hall, Moorgate Place, London, EC2P 2BJ

Text set in 11 pt Photon Times, printed by photolithography,
and bound in Great Britain at The Pitman Press, Bath

# Contents

# Acknowledgements

The Inflation Accounting Steering Group gratefully acknowledges the assistance of all concerned in the publication of this book. They include The Working Party, under whose direction the book was written, consisting of Ian Hay Davison (Chairman), David Cairns, to whom particular thanks is due for his assistance in the preparation of the Birchwood examples, Philip Grindell, Wouter Poldervaart, Stanley Thomson, and Michael Inwards who acted as adviser to the Working Party. The Working Party is grateful to all those who have considered earlier drafts of this book and made valuable suggestions for improvements in both the text and the examples. It is not possible to mention all those who helped in the production of this book but special mention should be made of the work of Haydn Everitt, Lawrie Lee, Michael Lockyer, Sheila Masters, Christopher and Pamela Morgan, who prepared the index, Nick Temple and Dick Wilkins. The Working Party is also grateful for the assistance of The Steering Group Secretariat: Chris Westwick (Secretary), Colin Archer, Nigel Davey, John Foyle, Bob Francis, and David Stevenson.

It is acknowledged that amendments will be required in subsequent editions to take account of changes between the Exposure Draft on CCA and the Statement of Standard Accounting Practice. Further suggestions for improvement from readers will be welcome and will be considered for incorporation in subsequent editions of this book. Suggestions, comments and queries should be sent to:

The Secretary
The Inflation Accounting Steering Group
6th Floor, First National House
119 Finsbury Pavement
London EC2P 2HJ

# Introduction

1     Current Cost Accounting (CCA) has been developed to correct the deficiencies of historical cost accounting which fails to provide much of the information primarily required by the users of accounts. In recommending its introduction, The Inflation Accounting Committee (The Committee) set up by the Government under the chairmanship of Mr (now Sir) Francis Sandilands described CCA as 'evolutionary rather than revolutionary' and stated that it involves 'no more than an extension in degree of principles already established in modern accounting conventions'. The Committee also recognised the need to provide practical guidance in the form of detailed instruction manuals to assist individual companies in preparing accounts using CCA principles. This book has been written to meet that need.

2     The Committee published its report on 4th September 1975* since when its recommendations have been considered at length by the accounting profession and a wide range of individuals, companies and organisations representing industry and commerce throughout the United Kingdom. The Inflation Accounting Steering Group (The Steering Group), set up by the accounting profession in response to The Committee's recommendation to co-ordinate the introduction of CCA, has developed the CCA system described in this book in the light of the suggestions put forward by all those who commented on the original proposals contained in The Committee's report.

3     The most frequent comment on the CCA system envisaged by The Committee was that it failed to recognise the effects on company accounts of what has been described as 'the debasement of the monetary unit'. The Consultative Committee of Accountancy Bodies (CCAB), representing the accounting profession, was one of the principal exponents of this point of view and its initial reactions to the report of The Committee have led to The Steering Group's proposal that the accounts should include a statement, by way of note, setting out prominently the gain or loss for the period of account in the shareholders' net equity interest after allowing for the change in the value of money during the period.

4     The Steering Group's proposals for a system of CCA, endorsed by the

* *The Report of the Inflation Accounting Committee* (HMSO, Cmnd 6445)

1

Accounting Standards Committee (ASC), were published as Exposure Draft Number 18 by the ASC on 30th November 1976. That Exposure Draft, on which this book is based, is reproduced at Appendix A.

## The aims of this book

5  For CCA to become the generally accepted system of accounting in this country it must have the ability to form the basis of a complete accounting system embracing all forms of financial reporting, particularly those designed for management. It must be more than just a means of presenting financial information in the published accounts of companies. This can be achieved only if the basic records and books of account of all business enterprises can be maintained on a basis consistent with the principles of CCA. In writing this book therefore the aim has been to provide guidance not just on the preparation of published accounts using CCA principles, but also on the implementation and operation of a complete CCA system.

6  The complexities of present day trade and the wide range of industries and services currently undertaken by the business community make it impossible for any book seeking to describe a system of accounting to deal with every problem that might be encountered in practice. The aim has been to deal with those problems which it is believed will arise most frequently and which are common to the widest range of organisation. In this respect The Steering Group is indebted to the many companies and representative bodies who took part in the field testing of CCA and who brought to its notice not only many of the problems but also many of the solutions described in this book. Whilst every effort has been made to make the examples in this book realistic, there has been the need, in order to demonstrate clearly the solutions to problems, to use examples which although they illustrate the principles involved, are simpler than will be found in reality.

7  Systems for recording financial information range from the simplest cash book and ledger system for small businesses to the complex computer based systems of the largest companies. Inevitably a book of this kind must aim at a level somewhere between the two and in the majority of cases the view has been taken that the level should be closer to the former than the latter. The aim has been, however, also to recognise the more important matters which will be mainly of relevance to the larger companies. The term *company* is used throughout this book to denote all forms of business enterprise.

## The status of the book

8  It was mentioned above that this book is based on the Exposure Draft on CCA issued by the ASC which is reproduced at Appendix A. Exposure Drafts of proposed Statements of Standard Accounting Practice are

issued by the ASC so that all interested parties have an opportunity to comment on the proposals contained therein before they are finalised. At the end of the exposure period the comments received are considered and, if agreed, are incorporated into a revised version of the proposed accounting standard. Once it is approved, the accounting standard is issued by the accountancy bodies as a Statement of Standard Accounting Practice (SSAP) to be complied with by their members with effect from a specified date. This book has been prepared by The Steering Group as a guide to the accounting procedures required by the proposed accounting standard on CCA. It is not therefore part of the Exposure Draft on CCA. The views expressed in this book are those of The Steering Group and are not necessarily those of the ASC or of the accountancy bodies which it represents. The methods of calculation and presentation described in this book are put forward only as suggestions. Those companies which find that their particular circumstances necessitate methods of calculation or presentation different from those described are free to use whichever methods seem most appropriate having regard to the objectives and principles of CCA and the intentions of the proposed standard.

## Management accounting

9  In recent years the rapid increase in the rate of inflation has led many companies to incorporate elements of either CCA or replacement cost accounting into their accounting systems and to develop methods of assessing performance and of forecasting which take account of the effects of cost changes. Management accounting systems take many months if not years to develop and even relatively minor changes should be made only after an extensive review of their effect. The Steering Group firmly believes that the introduction of CCA will lead to an improvement in the information available to management but it recognises that fully operational CCA systems will take time to develop and that their introduction should not be hurried. Consequently it would be premature for the first edition of this book to include recommendations on how to convert long standing historical cost management accounting techniques onto a CCA basis; the subject requires more research than there has been time for at this stage in the introduction of CCA. The second edition of this book which, it is planned, will be published at the same time as the Statement of Standard Accounting Practice on CCA will be revised and much expanded and will include a discussion of CCA techniques for management written in the light of practical experience.

## The need for current cost accounting

10  The historical cost accounting convention has traditionally been used as the basis for preparing accounts because of its underlying simplicity and certainty, derived from original bookkeeping records. It has always contained the inherent inadequacy that changes in price levels over a period of years would result in accounts not reflecting current conditions, but

3

given that such changes were sufficiently gradual, the inadequacy has been accepted, or partly dealt with by some companies which have revalued some or all of their fixed assets. In recent years, changes in price levels have accelerated to the extent that the inadequacy and lack of comparability between the accounts of those organisations that have revalued and those that have not has reached the point where accounts prepared under the historical cost convention lose their usefulness because:

(a) not all balance sheets reveal the real value of all the assets;
(b) depreciation is inadequate to replace the assets consumed during the year;
(c) the charge for the cost of stock consumed is inadequate to replace it because stock is charged at the cost of purchase and not at the cost of replacement;
(d) the effects of holding monetary assets or owing monetary liabilities are ignored.

As a result of these inadequacies:

(e) growth is exaggerated because no allowance is made for the fall in the value of the money used to measure the results;
(f) their uncritical use may lead to the situation where capital, although maintained in money terms, may not be maintained in real terms and may be distributed to shareholders, employees, customers or the Inland Revenue to the detriment of the long term viability of the business.

11   CCA seeks:

(a) to remedy these defects;
(b) to minimise the extra work load placed on the community as a whole and on producers of accounts in particular; and
(c) not to increase the opportunity to manipulate published results.

The proposed Standard is, therefore, a compromise between the above three conflicting forces. It is described as an initial Standard because the ASC recognises that it will almost certainly require modification in the light of experience of its operation. Comments from the producers and users of accounts will, therefore, be welcome.

### Summary of CCA

12   In summary, CCA as described in the proposed Statement of Standard Accounting Practice attempts to deal with the criticisms made of historical cost accounting in the following ways:

(a) fixed assets are to be shown in the balance sheet at their value to the business and not at their depreciated original cost; stocks are to be shown in the balance sheet at their value to the business and not at the lower of their original cost and net realisable value;

4

(b) depreciation for the year is to be calculated on the value to the business of the fixed assets concerned;

(c) the cost of stock consumed during the year is to be calculated on the value to the business of the stock at the date of consumption and not at the date of purchase;

(d) the effects of the loss or gain from holding monetary assets or owing liabilities will be shown in the 'statement of the gain or loss in the value of the shareholders' net equity interest after allowing for the change in the value of money';

(e) the distinction between real and apparent growth insofar as the equity interest is concerned is made clear in the 'statement on the gain or loss in the value of the shareholders' net equity interest after allowing for the change in the value of money';

(f) directors may appropriate to a revaluation reserve amounts required to maintain the scale of the business. The main components of this appropriation are likely to be:

(i) increased replacement cost of fixed assets and stock;
(ii) increased requirements for monetary working capital;
(iii) depreciation underprovided in the past on fixed assets because prices have risen since the depreciation was provided.

# 1 The Main Features of Current Cost Accounting

1.1    Current Cost Accounting is concerned principally with ensuring that realistic costs are charged against revenue.

The two main costs concerned are depreciation calculated as the proportion of the value to this business of fixed assets consumed during the year, and the value to the business of stock and work in progress consumed during the year.

1.2    In order to arrive at these costs it is necessary to value fixed assets and stocks on the basis of 'value to the business', which is defined as the amount the company would lose if it were deprived of the asset. A substantial proportion of the work involved in CCA is therefore this process of valuation.

1.3    The value of any asset can be related to a value expressed in money in one of only three ways. Firstly, the asset can be sold or exchanged for money; examples would be the sale of trading stock or the 'exchange' of a debt for money when the debt is settled. Secondly, the asset can be bought for a sum of money. Thirdly, and lastly, the asset can be held and used to earn money, either directly, in the form of interest, rent or dividends, or indirectly by using the asset to produce goods which can be sold. Thus any asset can be only bought, sold or held.

1.4    The following information is in respect of a machine, Machine A, owned by a manufacturing company:

(a) The machine's net replacement cost is             £4,000
(b) The machine's net realisable value is             £2,000
(c) The present value of the net income that will be earned from using the machine during the rest of its life (i.e. its 'use value') is             £5,000

1.5    The net replacement cost is the money now required to buy a new machine of the same type as Machine A, *less* an amount of depreciation that recognises the fact that a true replacement for Machine A would not be a new machine but a machine that has the same remaining useful life as Machine A.

1.6    The net realisable value is the net cash proceeds that would be received if Machine A were sold now.

1.7    The 'use value' of £5,000 is the *present value* of future cash flows to be derived from the asset.

This figure is arrived at by calculating the net cash inflow (less attributable cash outgoings) from the sale of Machine A's production over its remaining useful life, adding the net cash proceeds that will be received on disposal at the end of its life, and discounting the resulting amount to recognise that the cash inflow will be received at discrete points in the future.

1.8    It will be seen that the net replacement cost, the net realisable value and the 'use value' are the only money amounts that can be associated with the value of Machine A. They represent respectively the asset's purchase, sale and holding value.

1.9    In order to establish which of the three values is the value to the business, the full amount of money that would be lost by the company if it were deprived of the machine must be established.

1.10    The lowest value, the net realisable value, is clearly not the full amount that would be lost since the company would not sell the asset if it could earn more by using it.

1.11    In the example the use value, more formally, the '*economic*' *value*, is the highest of the three values and therefore might seem to represent the full loss. However this value is in fact greater than the full loss. True, the company would lose income of £5,000 if it did nothing to mitigate its loss. However, it can replace machine A with a similar machine for £4,000 and this would restore its ability to earn £5,000. The full loss therefore is:

|  | £ |
|---|---|
| Loss of income from Machine A | 5,000 |
| Net replacement cost | 4,000 |
|  | 9,000 |
| Income from replacement | 5,000 |
|  | £4,000 |

As the income which is lost and the income from the replacement cancel each other, the value to the business is represented by the net replacement cost.

1.12    In comparison with Machine A, the following information relates to Machine B owned by the same company:

7

(a) The net replacement cost (NRC) is              £6,000
(b) The net realisable value (NRV) is          £1,000
(c) The economic value (EV) is               £2,000

Machine B is different from Machine A in the previous example in that NRC is higher than both NRV and EV. The full loss that the company would suffer if it were deprived of Machine B is £2,000 (the EV) not £6,000 (the NRC) as in the case of Machine A. This is because the company cannot mitigate the loss of the machine by replacing it because the cost of replacement, £6,000, is higher than the income, £2,000, that would be earned from it. Once again the NRV is not the value to the business because the company has been deprived of more than just the likely proceeds of sale.

1.13    Table 1.1 shows six machines including Machines A and B from the examples above.

The valuations of each machine are ranked in order of magnitude. Table 1.2 shows the amount of each valuation. It will be seen that each machine is representative of one of the only six ways in which the three bases of valuation can be ranked in order of magnitude. The columns headed 'value to the business' in Tables 1.1 and 1.2 show which of the three bases of valuation represents the value to the business of the machine in each case.

**Table 1.1**

| Machine | | | | | | Value to the business |
|---------|-----|---|-----|---|-----|-----------------------|
| A | EV | > | NRC | > | NRV | NRC |
| B | NRC | > | EV | > | NRV | EV |
| C | NRC | > | NRV | > | EV | NRV |
| D | EV | > | NRV | > | NRC | NRC |
| E | NRV | > | EV | > | NRC | NRC |
| F | NRV | > | NRC | > | EV | NRC |

> = greater than

**Table 1.2**

| Machine | NRC | NRV | EV | Value to the business |
|---------|--------|--------|--------|-----------------------|
| A | £4,000 | £2,000 | £5,000 | £4,000 (NRC) |
| B | £6,000 | £1,000 | £2,000 | £2,000 (EV) |
| C | £6,000 | £2,000 | £1,000 | £2,000 (NRV) |
| D | £6,000 | £7,000 | £8,000 | £6,000 (NRC) |
| E | £6,000 | £8,000 | £7,000 | £6,000 (NRC) |
| F | £6,000 | £8,000 | £5,000 | £6,000 (NRC) |

8

1.14 Machines A and B have already been considered. By going through the same procedure for the other machines it will be seen that Machine C is the only machine, other than Machine B, whose value to the business is not NRC. It will be noted that Machines B and C are the only ones for which NRC is higher than both NRV and EV; in all other cases the value to the business is NRC.

1.15 It is clear that the company would not lose NRC, £6,000, if it were deprived of Machine B or C since it would not replace an asset for £6,000 from which the most it could gain, either from its use or by selling it, was only £2,000. Therefore the most a company will lose if deprived of an asset whose NRC is higher than both NRV and EV is NRV or EV whichever is the higher.

### The CCA concept of value

1.16 Three formal statements can now be made based on the foregoing discussion regarding the basic concept of value used in CCA.

1 **The CCA concept of value is that of 'value to the business'.**
2 **The value to the business of a company's assets is identical in amount with the adverse value of the entire loss, direct and indirect, that the company might expect to suffer if it were deprived of those assets (i.e. the value to the business is equal to its deprival value).**
3 **The value to the business of an asset is its written down current replacement cost (NRC) except in situations where NRC is greater than both net realisable value (NRV) and economic value (EV) in which case the value of the asset to the business is NRV or EV whichever is the greater.**

### The valuation of liabilities

1.17 It would be inconsistent with the underlying concepts of CCA if liabilities were valued on a basis different from that used for assets. Therefore, in principle, liabilities should be valued at their negative value to the business in just the same way as assets. It is more difficult to visualise how, say, the NRC of a liability should be assessed but nevertheless the principle is exactly the same for liabilities as it is for assets. It will be seen however that in practice CCA, at least initially, will not require liabilities to be shown other than at their historical cost except by way of note in certain specific cases (e.g. quoted debentures).

### The usual valuation basis for fixed assets

1.18 As we have seen there are only six ways in which valuations of an asset on the three bases (NRC, NRV and EV) can be ranked in order of magnitude. If the occurrence of each order of magnitude arose purely by chance NRC would be the value to the business in four out of every six cases and NRV and EV would be the value to the business once each in every six cases. Valuations however are not dictated by chance; they depend on the market factors surrounding the particular business in question. The order of magnitude in which valuations under the three bases are likely to be ranked therefore depends on economic reality. Assets which can be replaced for £6,000 but sold for less and also earn less for their owner are, one hopes, few and far between. The sort of assets which may fall into this category might be large items of specialised plant or purpose built factories in industries which are now less profitable than when the assets were originally purchased. In practice, however, we believe that Machine A in our example probably represents the situation which will occur most frequently with regard to fixed assets; that is, in the majority of cases, EV is likely to be higher than NRC which in turn is likely to be higher than NRV. We believe therefore that the occurrence of circumstances similar to those depicted by Machines B and C is substantially less than in one third of cases and that in the great majority of cases NRC will correctly represent the value of a fixed asset to a business.

### The valuation of trading stock

1.19    The valuation of trading stock is carried out in the same way as for fixed assets. The only variation, which in no way alters the principle, is that EV and NRV are effectively the same: the present value of all future net cash flows is effectively the same as the current net realisable value of any asset whose future net cash flows are represented only by the net proceeds of its sale, as in the case of trading stock. The value to the business of trading stock therefore, can be stated simply as the *lower of replacement cost and net realisable value*. This is analagous to the historical cost accounting basis of 'the lower of cost and net realisable value'.

### The measurement of total gains

1.20    The increase (or decrease) in the value of an individual asset over a period of time may be arrived at by measuring the value of the asset at the beginning and end of the period and computing the difference between the two values. The same process is applied to arrive at the increase in the total value of a company's net assets. A company's total gain in the year is defined as the difference between the value to the business of net assets at the beginning and end of the year, after making allowance for new capital put in and dividends paid out. It should be noted that 'total gain' as used here does not (because of the difficulty of objective measurement) include a change in the value of the company's goodwill, nor does it include changes in other intangible assets where assessment of their value to the business is not practicable.

### Losses

1.21    In this and following chapters we have generally assumed that all changes in value result in a gain and that the result of all transactions is

10

always a gain. We recognise that this is not always the case but we believe that it would unnecessarily complicate the presentation of the principles of CCA if, in each instance, we described the effect of suffering losses as well as earning gains. It will be clear that losses occur when there is a fall in the value to the business of its net assets or when assets are sold at less than their value to the business. The treatment of all such losses in most cases is the opposite of that for gains and therefore, unless the occurrence of losses requires particular comment, we shall treat losses as negative gains which, as such, require no special mention.

### The analysis of total gain

1.22 The total gain earned by a company in a year can be summarised as follows:

(a) Gains can arise from value added by productive activity involving the use or sale of a company's assets, so that the amounts received or receivable exceed the value to the business of the assets used up.

(b) Gains can arise merely because of increases in the value to the business of a company's net assets as a result of changing prices leading in turn to changes in the amount of the NRC, NRV, or EV of the net assets.

It should be noted that productive activity can include the transfer of assets to where they are needed.

1.23 The gains arising under (a) can be subdivided between:

(i) gains arising from normal manufacturing or trading activity, called 'operating gains';

(ii) gains not in the normal course of the company's business called 'extraordinary gains'.

1.24 Gains arising under (b) are called 'holding gains' or 'revaluation surpluses', to recognise that they arise merely because the company is holding the asset or liability when prices are rising, so that while there is a money value gain, there is no gain in terms of the asset in question.

### Realised and unrealised gains

1.25 Gains under (a) normally arise when an asset is acquired or a liability settled and therefore both operating gains and extraordinary gains are normally realised gains.

1.26 Holding gains need not involve the consumption or disposal of the particular asset or liability to which the gain is attached so that holding gains can be realised or unrealised. For example: a company values its stock of sheet steel at its value to the business on 1st January at £50,000, based on its replacement cost. On 30th June the replacement cost increases to

£60,000. The company has made a gain of £10,000 which is an unrealised holding gain. If the company sells all its sheet steel on 1st July for £60,000 it turns the unrealised holding gain into a realised holding gain. If it had recorded the unrealised gain of £10,000 on 30th June the company would record no further gain on 1st July as a result of the sale.

1.27 It will be seen that the total gain earned by a company in any period can be analysed as follows:

$$\text{Total gain} = \begin{cases} \text{Operating gains} \\ \text{Extraordinary gains} \\ \text{Realised holding gains} \\ \text{Unrealised holding gains} \end{cases}$$

1.28 The following are examples of different types of gain (all costs other than for materials have been ignored).

### Example 1.1

A company which manufactures copper pipes purchases a quantity of copper on 1st January for £10,000. During January the company uses all the copper to manufacture pipes which it sells on 1st February for £15,000. At 1st February the company assesses the value to the business of the copper in the pipes at £10,000 (the replacement cost). The whole gain of £5,000 (£15,000 − £10,000) is an operating gain.

### Example 1.2

The same company as in Example 1.1 purchases another quantity of copper for £10,000 on 1st February and sells the pipes made out of the copper for £15,000 on 1st March, at which date the company assesses the value of the copper in the pipes at £12,000 (the replacement cost). The total gain of £5,000 (£15,000 − £10,000) is made up of a realised holding gain (revaluation surplus) of £2,000 (£12,000 −£10,000) and an operating gain of £3,000 (£15,000 − £12,000).

### Example 1.3

A company owns a factory which it no longer needs. It sells the factory for £150,000. The factory originally cost £80,000, but the company has since assessed the value to the business at £120,000. The total gain since the factory was bought of £70,000 (£150,000 − £80,000) is made up of a realised holding gain (revaluation surplus) of £40,000 (£120,000 − £80,000) and an extraordinary gain of £30,000 (£150,000 − £120,000).

### Example 1.4

A shipping company purchases a number of ships and either leases or disposes of the ships according to the conditions of the market. In any accounting year the company normally finds that it sells some ships and buys others. On each sale the company computes the revaluation surplus which arises by deducting the original cost plus any revaluation surplus previously recorded from the value to the business at the date of sale. The remainder of the gain, if any, the difference between the sale proceeds and the value to the business at the date of sale, is either an operating gain or an extraordinary gain depending on the view taken as to the nature of the company's business and on whether gains from the sale of ships are likely to continue to be a regular feature of the company's business in the future.

1.29   It will be seen from Example 1.4 that the distinction between operating gains and extraordinary gains may be blurred in practice.

### Which gains are profits?

1.30   The Inflation Accounting Committee wrote in its Report: " 'Profit for the year' is a practical business concept used as a guide for prudent decision making by companies. It may usefully be defined as the amount of the total gains arising in the year that may prudently be regarded as distributable. It is thus a subjective concept, since inevitably there will be differences of opinion on how far gains arising in any given year may prudently be distributed. Gains that are legitimately regarded as profit by a company in a given set of circumstances might not be regarded as profit by another company operating in different circumstances."

1.31   CCA recognises the subjective nature of the concept of profit outlined in this quotation and accepts that no reasonably objective accounting system can arrive at a profit that will in all cases be regarded by the management as distributable. Its main aim, therefore, is to correct the failure of the historical cost method of accounting to bring into the profit calculation the current cost of the consumption of the stocks, plant and equipment, and other physical assets used up in generating the revenue of the business. CCA in computing profit attempts to deduct from that revenue the amount needed to restore the productive capacity so consumed.

### Example 1.5

A   A printer produces 10,000 copies of a book during a week. Historical production costs are as follows:

|                               | £      |
| ----------------------------- | ------ |
| Paper ink and binding material | 2,000  |
| Labour                        | 500    |
| Overheads                     | 200    |
| Depreciation                  | 50     |
| Total cost of production      | £2,750 |

The price charged by the printer to the publisher is £3,500 therefore the total gain is £750 (£3,500 − £2,750).

B  At the date of sale:
   (a) The replacement cost of material is                                    £2,200
   (b) The replacement cost of machinery is 10% higher than the
       value on which the depreciation charge has been based.

C  The value to the business of assets consumed in generating the income of
   £3,500 is arrived at as follows:

|  |  | £ |
|---|---|---:|
| Materials: | | |
| | Replacement cost | 2,200 |
| | Labour | 500 |
| | Overheads | 200 |
| Depreciation: | | |
| | The value to the business used up, represented by depreciation based on the net replacement cost of the asset | 55 |
| Total value to the business of assets consumed in production | | £2,955 |

D  Current cost operating profit is arrived at by deducting from income the
   value to the business of assets consumed in generating that income.
   Therefore current cost operating profit is:

|  | £ |
|---|---:|
| Income | 3,500 |
| Value to the business of assets consumed | 2,955 |
| Current cost operating profit | £545 |

The remainder of the total gain of £205 (£750 − £545) is a realised holding gain
(revaluation surplus) being the difference between the historical cost of assets
consumed and their value to the business at the date of consumption, and will
not be credited to profit.

No adjustment to labour or overheads was made to arrive at their value to the
business because the actual cost of labour and overheads in the example were the
same as their value to the business at the date of consumption of the stock to which
they related. If the cost of labour and overheads had increased between the date the
costs of production had been incurred and the date of sale of the products, an adjustment would have been necessary to eliminate from the current cost operating profit
the resulting holding gain on the stock consumed.

1.32   It will have been observed that the concept underlying the calculation of
       current cost operating profit in Example 1.5 is the same as that used to
       calculate the operating gain in Example 1.2. The current cost operating
       profit of a company for the year is the same as the total of that described in
       paragraph 1.23 as the company's operating gains for the year and is
       calculated by deducting from income the value to the business of assets con-
       sumed in generating that income, at the dates on which the income is earned.
       Similarly, extraordinary profits are the same as those described in paragraph
       1.23 as extraordinary gains.

1.33   CCA does not, for reasons which are outlined in ED 18 make provision
       in the profit calculation for the effect of inflation on monetary assets and

liabilities, or for the fact that this can affect the amount that the directors consider it appropriate to distribute as dividend. (As indicated in the Introduction to this book, and at greater length in Chapter 19, provision is however made for a note to the accounts for the benefit of those who regard the overall effect of inflation on the shareholders' interest, and on the monetary balances of the company, as significant).

1.34 The concepts and methods of CCA therefore need to be borne in mind when interpreting the current cost profit figure. The current cost profit is not to be regarded as a measure of what should be distributed in a given year, though it will normally be a relevant factor in determining that distribution. Nor can the current cost profit be regarded in all cases as an indicator of the level of distribution that could be maintained. It will however be a much better indicator of the economic resources used up in earning the revenue than is provided by historical cost accounting.

1.35 It will remain, as at present, for the directors to decide how much it is appropriate to distribute. This will depend on a number of factors, not least of which will be the company's cash planning, including the financing aspects of the plans for future expansion and the working capital requirements. The law relating to distributions (which at present in effect largely depends upon the net balance sheet position) will remain an overall constraint.

**The appropriation account**

1.36 Under CCA, revaluation surpluses arising from the adjustment of asset balances to their value to the business are in general credited to a Revaluation Reserve Account. However, for the reasons explained above, it does not follow that the amount of the revaluation surplus in a given year coincides with the amount which the directors consider should be appropriated for the continuing needs of the business. It is therefore for the directors to indicate the extent, if any, by which the holding gains fall short of, or exceed, the amount needed to be retained for the maintenance of the business at the level they consider appropriate, augmenting or restricting the appropriation to Revaluation Reserve accordingly, and explaining the reasons behind the decision. To ensure that the discretionary nature of such appropriations and of the appropriations to dividends and free reserves are apparent to users of the accounts, they are shown in an Appropriation Account. This account brings together the current cost profit for the year from the profit and loss account, the revaluation surplus for the year, the appropriation to the Revaluation Reserve, and the dividend. The balance is a transfer to, or from, free reserves.

**The difference between CCA and historical cost accounting**

1.37 We have now surveyed the fundamental concepts of CCA. For convenience they are summarised below:

15

1   The unit of measurement is money.
2   Assets are recorded at their current value to the business.
3   Current cost profit is struck after charging the current value to the business, as at the date of consumption, of assets consumed during the period, excluding revaluation surpluses. Extraordinary gains are shown separately.

If we were similarly to summarise the fundamental concepts of historical cost accounting the summary would be something like:

1   The unit of measurement is money.
2   Assets are recorded at their historical cost although fixed assets are sometimes recorded at a valuation where that valuation is considered to be materially different from historical cost. Assets are shown at the net amount which is expected to be recovered from their normal use when this is lower by a material amount than the historical cost. (Although short term fluctuations in fixed asset values are usually ignored.)
3   Historical cost profit is struck after charging the cost of assets consumed during the period where 'cost' is calculated as explained in 2, i.e. on an historical basis. Extraordinary gains, and surpluses and deficiencies arising from any revaluation of fixed assets, are shown separately.

1.38    This summary does scant justice to the intricacies of modern day historical cost accounting conventions, but it is sufficient for the purpose of comparison with CCA.

1.39    Standard accounting policies are being developed by the accountancy profession to minimise the differences in the treatment of similar situations by different companies but these policies have often led to departures from the basic concepts of historical cost accounting, producing together an accounting system which is neither theoretically sound nor wholly consistent in its approach.

1.40    The fundamental failing of historical cost accounting, however, is not the inconsistencies or complexities which have been introduced, but the basic concept of historical cost accounting itself. By recording only the historical cost of assets, information required by users on the current value and changes in value of those assets will never be shown in historical cost accounts, except by chance, so that the economic and business reality is suppressed. The recognition of this fact has led to the introduction of some of the accounting policies which have made historical cost accounting complex and internally inconsistent and yet have still failed to provide adequately the information required by users.

1.41    The following table sets out the main differences between accounts drawn up using CCA and historical cost accounting (HCA) principles.

**Profit and Loss Account**

| | CCA | HCA |
|---|---|---|
| -Cost of sales | Current value to the business of stock consumed | Historical cost (or, if lower, the net realisable value) of stock consumed |
| -Depreciation | Current value to the business of fixed assets consumed | Time allocation of historical cost (or of revaluation, where made) |

**Balance Sheet**

| | CCA | HCA |
|---|---|---|
| -Fixed assets | Value to the business | Normally historical cost less depreciation. Sometimes a valuation less depreciation |
| -Stock | Value to the business | Lower of historical cost and net realisable value |

1.42   In the following two chapters we consider in more detail the information contained in the current cost balance sheet and profit and loss account in comparison with the information contained in the historical cost accounts. In certain cases the information will be the same as that shown in the historical cost accounts but this is due not to departures from CCA principles, but to CCA principles and historical cost accounting principles, in these cases, providing the same information.

# 2 The Balance Sheet

2.1    This chapter deals with the general principles involved in arriving at the value to the business of some individual classes of asset and liability that are commonly found in company balance sheets. Each item in the balance sheet is considered only in general terms with the aim that when, in later chapters, specific CCA principles and their practical application are considered in detail, the general concepts underlying these principles will be seen with clarity. The theory of CCA requires that all assets and liabilities are recorded in the balance sheet at their value to the business. As a matter of practicality, however, liabilities are normally recorded at face value.

2.2    **Birchwood Limited is the hypothetical company that will be used throughout this book to demonstrate the preparation of current cost accounts and the conversion of historical cost accounts to current cost accounts on the introduction of CCA. Each stage of the preparation will be recorded on a columnar CCA Worksheet.**

2.3    Table 2.1 sets out the balance sheet of Birchwood Limited at 31st December 1978 drawn up using CCA principles in column 1 and historical cost principles in column 2. Both column 1 and column 2 represent the same underlying physical quantities; the differences in the figures are the result of using different accounting conventions.

2.4    The CCA Worksheet is set out initially in Table 2.2 and is repeated throughout the book each time entries are made. The first two columns of the Worksheet are to record the opening historical cost (HC) balance sheet and these have been completed with Birchwood's HC balance sheet from Table 2.1. Columns 3 and 4 headed 'Opening Balance Sheet Journal' will be completed by entering the journal entries required to convert the opening HC balance sheet to current cost and columns 5 and 6 will record the completed current cost opening balance sheet shown in Table 2.1, once the necessary journal entries have been made. Columns 7 and 8 will record the income and expenditure for 1979 and a summary is set out in Table 2.3 in conventional form. In the Worksheet the corresponding double-entry is shown, i.e. debtors are credited with £295,290, fixed assets debited with £6,036 and so on. Columns 9 and 10 will record the journal entries required to arrive at the current cost accounts for 1979;

18

columns 11 and 12 will record the completed current cost profit and loss account for 1979 and columns 13 and 14 will record the current cost balance sheet at the end of 1979.

## Table 2.1

BIRCHWOOD LIMITED

|  | Balance sheet as at 31.12.78 | |
|---|---|---|
|  | 1 | 2 |
|  | CC | HC |
|  | £'000 | £'000 |
| ASSETS EMPLOYED: | | |
| Fixed assets | 26,690 | 19,596 |
| Investment in subsidiaries and associated company | 18,364 | 13,984 |
| Quoted and unquoted investments | 1,523 | 1,147 |
| Current assets | | |
| Stock and work in progress | 52,873 | 51,313 |
| Debtors | 32,727 | 32,727 |
| Cash | 465 | 465 |
|  | 86,065 | 84,505 |
| Current liabilities | | |
| Creditors | 23,011 | 23,011 |
| Current tax | 3,582 | 3,582 |
| Bank overdraft | 6,481 | 6,481 |
| Dividend | 5,700 | 5,700 |
|  | 38,774 | 38,774 |
| Net current assets | 47,291 | 45,731 |
| ACT recoverable | 3,070 | — |
|  | 96,938 | 80,458 |
| FINANCED BY: | | |
| Ordinary share capital | 32,185 | 32,185 |
| General reserve | 37,248 | 14,051 |
| Revaluation reserve | 13,505 | — |
| Shareholders funds | 82,938 | 46,236 |
| Preference share capital | 4,000 | 4,000 |
| 10% Debenture stock 1990/93 | 10,000 | 10,000 |
| Deferred tax | — | 20,222 |
|  | 96,938 | 80,458 |

19

**Table 2.2**

## BIRCHWOOD LIMITED
## CCA Worksheet

| | 1 | 2 | 3 | 4 | 5 | 6 |
|---|---|---|---|---|---|---|
| | Opening balance sheet historical cost | | Opening balance sheet journal | | Opening balance sheet current cost | |
| | Dr £'000 | Cr £'000 | Dr £'000 | Cr £'000 | Dr £'000 | Cr £'000 |
| Land and buildings | 4,719 | 569 | | | | |
| Plant and machinery | 15,446 | | | | | |
| Investment in subsidiaries and associates | 13,984 | | | | | |
| Quoted and unquoted investments | 1,147 | | | | | |
| Stock and work in progress | 51,313 | | | | | |
| Debtors | 32,727 | | | | | |
| Cash | 465 | | | | | |
| Creditors | | 23,011 | | | | |
| Current tax | | 3,582 | | | | |
| Bank overdraft | | 6,481 | | | | |
| Dividend | | 5,700 | | | | |
| Deferred tax | | 20,222 | | | | |
| Ordinary share capital | | 32,185 | | | | |
| Reserves – general | | 14,051 | | | | |
| Reserves – revaluation | | | | | | |
| Preference share capital | | 4,000 | | | | |
| 10% Debentures | | 10,000 | | | | |
| Realisation of fixed assets | | | | | | |
| Revenue income | | | | | | |
| Revenue expenditure | | | | | | |
| Depreciation | | | | | | |
| Interest | | | | | | |
| Tax expense | | | | | | |
| Dividends received | | | | | | |
| Revenue surplus | | | | | | |
| | 119,801 | 119,801 | | | | |

| 7 | 8 | 9 | 10 | 11 | 12 | 13 | 14 |
|---|---|---|---|---|---|---|---|
| Income and expenditure for 1979 | | Journal entries | | Profit and loss account for 1979 | | Closing balance sheet | |
| Dr £'000 | Cr £'000 | Dr £'000 | Cr £'000 | Dr £'000 | Cr £'000 | Dr £'000 | Cr £'000 |
| 6,036 | | | | | | | |
| 139 | | | | | | | |
| | 295,290 | | | | | | |
| 1,319 | 465 | | | | | | |
| 283,487 | | | | | | | |
| 3,582 | | | | | | | |
| 6,481 | 3,430 | | | | | | |
| 5,980 | | | | | | | |
| | 8,000 | | | | | | |
| | 238 | | | | | | |
| 1,319 | | | | | | | |
| | 920 | | | | | | |
| 308,343 | 308,343 | | | | | | |

21

**Table 2.3**

BIRCHWOOD LIMITED

INCOME AND EXPENDITURE 1979

|  | £'000 | £'000 |
|---|---|---|
| Balance brought forward-cash | 465 | |
|       -bank overdraft | | 6,481 |
| RECEIPTS | | |
| Debtors | 295,290 | |
| Sale of fixed assets | 238 | |
| Rights issue | 8,000 | |
| Dividends received | 920 | |
| PAYMENTS | | |
| Creditors and wages | | 283,487 |
| Tax | | 3,582 |
| Dividends | | 5,980 |
| Amounts owing to subsidiaries (net) | | 139 |
| Purchase of fixed assets | | 6,036 |
| Interest | | 1,319 |
| Balance carried forward-cash | | 1,319 |
|       -bank overdraft | 3,430 | |
| | 308,343 | 308,343 |

2.5　The journal entries required to prepare the current cost balance sheet of Birchwood Limited at 31st December 1978 and 31st December 1979 are considered in subsequent chapters. The figures in column 1 of Table 2.1 are considered in the remainder of this chapter in general terms only.

**Fixed assets**

2.6　The figure for fixed assets in Birchwood's HC balance sheet at 31st December 1978 is made up as follows:

| | Land and buildings | Plant and machinery | Total |
|---|---|---|---|
| | £'000 | £'000 | £'000 |
| Cost | 4,719 | 23,899 | 28,618 |
| Accumulated depreciation | 569 | 8,453 | 9,022 |
| Net book value | 4,150 | 15,446 | 19,596 |

2.7　To arrive at the figure for fixed assets in the current cost balance sheet the figure for net book value has been replaced by the amount which represents the value to the business of the company's fixed assets at the balance sheet date.

22

### Plant and machinery

2.8      It was stated in Chapter 1 that in the large majority of cases the value to the business of fixed assets will be their written down current replacement cost (net current replacement cost) and this has been assumed to be the case in this example with regard to plant and machinery.

2.9      The net current replacement cost of plant and machinery is arrived at as follows:

|  | £'000 |
|---|---|
| Gross current replacement cost of plant and machinery | 34,160 |
| Accumulated depreciation | 12,810 |
| Net current replacement cost | 21,350 |

2.10      The gross current replacement cost is normally the cost that would have to be incurred to obtain and install at the date of the valuation a substantially identical replacement asset in new condition.

2.11      The accumulated depreciation in the current cost balance sheet in respect of plant and machinery represents the proportion of the gross current replacement cost that corresponds to the proportion of the assets' expired service potential since their acquisition. In other words it is the accumulated depreciation based on gross current replacement cost instead of historical cost. It follows that the net current replacement cost of an asset is the current value of its unexpired service potential.

### Land and buildings

2.12      The value to the business of land and buildings in owner occupation and held by a non-property company will normally be the open market value for their existing use plus estimated attributable acquisition costs.

2.13      Unlike the situation with plant and machinery there cannot be an identical replacement for a property (unless the existing building is actually demolished and rebuilt in its existing state). On the other hand there is usually a fairly active market for comparable replacements, and the market probably provides a better indication of the current value to a business of its property than would the net replacement cost of the existing property.

2.14      The open market value of a property, plus acquisition costs can therefore be regarded as equivalent to the net replacement cost of the property. Similarly the net realisable value of the property is equivalent to its open market value less costs of disposal.

Furthermore, with regard to commercial and industrial property the open market value can probably be regarded as being equivalent to its economic value because it is often by reference to the value from use by potential users that the open market value is determined.

2.15 The open market value of property is a 'net' figure and it would be meaningless to show in the balance sheet 'gross open market value less depreciation'. Consequently, although depreciation should be charged on buildings and on the interest in leasehold land (but not normally on freehold land) the amount of the depreciation charge is deducted before arriving at the open market value in the balance sheet.

2.16 Whilst open market value will be the normal method of valuation for property there will be some properties for which no open market value can be established because, for example, their special nature or location is such that no market, or only a severely restricted market, exists for them. For example, in the case of an office building in the centre of a large industrial complex no open market value may be established for the building, although an open market value for the associated land could be established based on its value as bare land. For such properties the value to the business will be the lower of (a) the depreciated replacement cost of the building plus the open market value of the bare land for its existing use and (b) the economic value of the land and building. The depreciated replacement cost of a building is similar to the net current replacement cost of plant and machinery but, as with the open market value of property, it is notified as a net figure and is not shown 'gross less depreciation'. In all cases in which a property is valued at economic value the associated plant and machinery will also be valued on an economic value basis because the flow of income from the plant and machinery and the land and buildings cannot be distinguished separately.

2.17 The current cost balance sheet of Birchwood includes land and buildings at their value to the business as follows:

|  | Open market value | Depreciated replacement cost | Total |
|---|---|---|---|
|  | £'000 | £'000 | £'000 |
| Value to the business | 2,630 | 2,710 | 5,340 |

**Investment in subsidiaries and associated companies**

2.18 The figure in the HC balance sheet is made up as follows:

|  | £'000 |
|---|---|
| Share in subsidiaries at cost | 11,342 |
| Shares in associated company at cost | 444 |
| Amounts owing from subsidiaries | 2,198 |
|  | 13,984 |

2.19    In the current cost balance sheet shares in subsidiaries and associated companies and amounts owing from subsidiaries are shown at their value to the business as follows:

|                                             | £'000  |
|---------------------------------------------|--------|
| Shares in subsidiaries at valuation         | 15,713 |
| Shares in associated company at valuation   | 453    |
| Amounts owing from subsidiaries             | 2,198  |
|                                             | 18,364 |

**Shares in subsidiaries**

2.20    The figure in the current cost balance sheet of a holding company in respect of shares in its subsidiary companies is the cost of the shares plus post-acquisition movements in reserves less amounts written off in respect of goodwill. The subsidiaries' accounts will have been prepared applying CCA principles and movements in reserves will therefore reflect all revaluation surpluses and deficits.

2.21    It could be argued that the above method of including shares in subsidiaries in the holding company's balance sheet does not strictly accord with the concept of showing the shares at their value to the business of the holding company. Nevertheless, on practical grounds, the proposed treatment is considered to be the most appropriate.

**Shares in associated companies**

2.22    The general principles involved in the valuation of shares in associated companies are similar to those employed in the valuation of shares in subsidiaries. The only differences are practical ones and arise from the fact that, by definition, a majority of the share capital of an associated company is not held by the holding company. Shares in associated companies therefore should be valued in the holding company's balance sheet at cost plus attributable post-acquisition movements in reserves, less amounts written off in respect of goodwill.

2.23    The treatment of subsidiaries and of associated companies in the consolidated accounts is considered fully in Chapter 14.

**Amounts owing from subsidiary companies**

2.24    Amounts owing from subsidiary companies in the HC balance sheet are shown at their net realisable value. In most cases this will be the full amount of the debts due. The value to the business of a debt fixed in money terms is the realisable value of that debt and consequently it is shown in the current cost balance sheet at that value. The net realisable value represents the full amount of the loss that would be suffered by the company if it were to be deprived of the debtor at the balance sheet date.

### Quoted and unquoted investments

2.25   Quoted and unquoted investments in the HC balance sheet in our example are shown at cost. If, however, the net realisable value of the investments had been materially lower than cost a provision for the diminution in value would have been made if it was considered that the diminution in value was of a permanent nature.

2.26   In the current cost accounts, investments are shown at their value to the business, regardless of whether that value is higher or lower than the original cost or of whether the investments are held as long term or current assets. The value to the business for all practical purposes, unless a closer approximation to the value to the business can be made, is arrived at as follows:

Quoted investments   —Stock Market mid-price
Unquoted investments—At a directors' valuation based on the CCA net asset value of the company and/or the value of a stream of income from the investment.

2.27   In the exceptional circumstances that they consider mid-market price to be unrealistic the directors may use another method of valuing quoted investments normally using the valuation criteria applicable to unquoted investments. In Birchwood's case all its quoted investments have been valued at mid-market price.

### Stock and work in progress

2.28   The figure for stock and work in progress in Birchwood's HC balance sheet is based on the historical cost of stock calculated using the first in first out (FIFO) method. If any item in stock was considered to have a net realisable value that was below FIFO cost then that item of stock would be shown at its net realisable value.

2.29   The figure for stock in the current cost balance sheet is the value to the business of that stock at the balance sheet date. The value to the business of a company's stock is the lower of the *replacement cost* of that stock and its net realisable value. This is analogous with the historical cost concept of lower of *cost* and net realisable value. In this example, the replacement cost of stock has increased during the period up to the balance sheet date which represents the company's stock holding period and is therefore higher than the FIFO cost of the stock.

If there had been no increase in replacement costs during the period that the company held the stock on hand at the balance sheet date, the FIFO cost and the value to the business would have been the same.

### Debtors

2.30   Debtors, which in the example are assumed all to be realisable within one year of the balance sheet date, are shown in the HC balance sheet at their net realisable value, i.e. the full amount of the debts due to the company, less any provision for doubtful debts.

2.31    Debtors in the current cost balance sheet are shown at their value to the business which, in the case of current debtors, is their net realisable value; the same figure as that appearing in the HC balance sheet. The net realisable value represents the full amount of the loss that would be suffered if the company were to be deprived of the debtors at the balance sheet date.

### Cash

2.32    The value to the business of cash held at the balance sheet date is the amount of that cash. The full loss that the company would suffer if deprived of the cash is the full amount of that cash. The figure for cash therefore is the same in both the HC balance sheet and the current cost balance sheet.

### Current liabilities

2.33    By now it will be apparent that 'monetary items', those assets and liabilities that are fixed in amount in terms of money, are shown in the current cost balance sheet at their monetary amount.

2.34    The value to the business of current liabilities therefore is the monetary amount of these liabilities. In the example current liabilities are made up of creditors, current tax, bank overdraft and dividend. Each of these items is shown in the current cost balance sheet at the same amount as in the HC balance sheet.

### Deferred tax

2.35    Historical cost conventions require that provision be made for deferred tax whenever a material saving in current tax has resulted from the granting of capital or other tax allowances which defer but do not forgive the tax saved. Such allowances are said to give rise to 'originating timing differences'.

2.36    Deferred tax in Birchwood's HC balance sheet represents tax at the rate of 50% on stock relief and on the difference between the net book value of qualifying fixed assets and the tax written down value of those assets which, because of the application of 100% first year allowances, is nil. Therefore the amount of deferred tax in the HC balance sheet in the example relating to qualifying fixed assets represents 50% of the written down value of such assets.

2.37    The principle underlying the amount of deferred tax in the current cost balance sheet is that deferred tax should be provided for, using the

27

liability method, in respect of material tax savings arising from all originating timing differences other than the tax savings which can be seen with reasonable probability to continue for the foreseeable future either by reason of recurring timing differences or, in the case of revalued assets, by the continuing use of the assets or the postponement of liability on their sale. The practical effect of this principle is that deferred tax need only be provided if the liability to the tax is likely to become payable in the foreseeable future. In the case of fixed assets for example, if it is considered that roll over relief will be available or if the asset will continue in use no deferred tax need be provided as long as originating timing differences arising in the future are at least equal to the historical cost depreciation charge. The full amount of deferred tax, however, will need to be shown by way of note as a contingent liability. It will be appreciated that for most companies much of the deferred tax liability in the HC balance sheet will become a contingent liability to be shown by way of note rather than a liability, albeit deferred, to be included in the balance sheet.

2.38    In Birchwood's case it is considered that none of the historical cost deferred tax liability will become payable in the foreseeable future and therefore the full amount shown in the HC balance sheet has been released to general reserve. The result is that Birchwood's current cost balance sheet shows a nil deferred tax liability and an amount recoverable in respect of Advance Corporation Tax which, in the HC balance sheet, is netted off against the deferred tax figure.

### Intangible assets (excluding goodwill)

2.39    Patents, licences and other separable intangible assets are recorded, if at all, in the HC balance sheet either at a nominal amount or at cost less any amounts written off. Birchwood has no intangible assets. The concept of CCA would require that all intangible as well as tangible assets be included in the balance sheet at their value to the business whether that value is higher or lower than historical cost. It will be appreciated, however, that the difficulties of establishing values for intangible assets are considerable. With this in mind ED 18 takes the view that it is better to exclude intangible assets from the balance sheet than to show them at values which cannot be readily established. Consequently, unless values can be readily established for separable intangible assets they should not be included in the CCA balance sheet.

### Debenture stock

2.40    Birchwood's 10% debenture stock 1990/93, is a monetary liability and is therefore shown in the current cost balance sheet at its full face value. Whilst it is recognised that long term liabilities could be regarded as having a current value to the business of a lesser (or greater) amount than face value, depending on the money rate of interest payable and expected

28

inflation, it is considered on practical grounds that the liability should be shown at face value in the balance sheet. However, where the liability takes the form of a listed security the mid-market value should be shown by way of a note to the accounts.

### Preference share capital

2.41 Preference share capital and all other forms of non-equity share capital are best regarded as monetary liabilities. As such they are shown in the current cost balance sheet at their paid up par value.

### Ordinary share capital

2.42 Birchwood's paid up ordinary share capital is shown in the current cost balance sheet and the HC balance sheet at its nominal amount. A company's share capital designates (together with any share premium account) the amount of the shareholders' original capital before the accretion of any income and as such has certain legal connotations. No question arises of showing it at its 'value to the business'; its value is reflected in the figure for the net equity interest.

### Reserves

2.43 Reserves in the HC balance sheet in our example consist only of the balance on profit and loss account. The reserves in the current cost balance sheet are made up of the following amounts:

|  | £'000 |
|---|---|
| General reserve | 37,343 |
| Revaluation reserve | 13,410 |
|  | 50,753 |

### General reserves

2.44 The next chapter deals with the differences between the historical cost and current cost profit and loss account in more detail. The general reserve in the current cost balance sheet is analogous with the profit and loss account balance in the HC balance sheet.

2.45 In Table 2.1 Birchwood's general reserve in the current cost balance sheet is higher than the profit and loss account balance in the HC balance sheet by the amount of deferred tax transferred to general reserve on the introduction of CCA (£23,292,000) less an amount of £95,000 representing a fall in subsidiaries' general reserves.

29

**Revaluation reserve**

2.46    In Table 2.1 the balance on the revaluation reserve is made up as follows:

|                                                          | £'000  |
|----------------------------------------------------------|--------|
| Fixed assets                                             | 7,094  |
| Stock                                                    | 1,560  |
| Investments (including subsidiaries and associated company) | 4,851  |
|                                                          | 13,505 |

It is not appropriate at this point to explain in any detail the movements on revaluation reserve. The accounting entries required to record revaluation surpluses and other movements on revaluation reserve are considered fully in the following chapters.

## SUMMARY

2.47    All the items in Birchwood's balance sheet in Table 2.1 have now been considered. The general principles involved in showing assets and liabilities at their value to the business can be summarised as follows.

**Plant and machinery** are shown at their written down replacement cost unless this is higher than both their economic value and their net realisable value, in which case they are shown at economic value or net realisable value, whichever is the higher.

**Land and buildings** are shown at open market value for existing use plus acquisition costs. If no open market valuation can be made of a building it should be shown at the lower of depreciated replacement cost and economic value.

**Investments in subsidiaries and associated companies** are shown at cost plus post-acquisition movements in reserves less amounts written off in respect of goodwill.

**Stock and work in progress** are shown at the lower of current replacement cost and net realisable value.

**Intangible assets** are either not included or shown at a valuation.

**Monetary assets** are shown at their net realisable value.

**Monetary liabilities** are shown at the full amount required to settle the liability.

**Unquoted investments** are shown at a valuation.

**Quoted investments** are shown normally at mid-market price.

**Tax** (deferred or current as appropriate) is provided in full unless the liability is not likely to be payable in the foreseeable future.

**Share capital** is shown at its paid up nominal value.

**Reserves** are analysed between general reserves and revaluation reserves.

# 3 The Profit and Loss Account

3.1    In this chapter the profit and loss account is considered in much the same manner as the balance sheet was considered in the previous chapter. Table 3.1 shows the items in the current cost profit and loss account and the related figures appearing in the HC profit and loss account. The figures set out in Table 3.1 are in respect of Birchwood Limited's financial year ended 31st December 1979. Column 1 shows figures using CCA principles and column 2 shows figures using HC principles. The under-lying transactions are the same in each case; differences in the figures arise from using different accounting principles.

**Table 3.1**

BIRCHWOOD LIMITED

Profit and loss account
for the year ended 31.12.79

|  | 1 CC | | 2 HC | |
|---|---|---|---|---|
|  | £'000 | £'000 | £'000 | £'000 |
| Sales |  | 309,895 |  | 309,895 |
| Cost of sales | 262,464 |  | 251,399 |  |
| Administration and selling expenses | 32,643 | 295,107 | 32,643 | 284,042 |
| Operating profit |  | 14,788 |  | 25,853 |
| Interest |  | 1,319 |  | 1,319 |
|  |  | 13,469 |  | 24,534 |
| Dividend received |  | 920 |  | 920 |
| Current cost profit before tax |  | 14,389 |  |  |
| Profit before tax |  |  |  | 25,454 |
| Taxation—corporation tax | 3,678 |  | 3,678 |  |
|        —deferred tax | — |  | 9,082 |  |
|  |  | 3,678 |  | 12,760 |
| Current cost profit/profit after tax |  | 10,711 |  | 12,694 |

31

**Sales**

3.2    The figure for sales is the same in both the HC accounts and current cost
accounts. It represents the total revenue from the sale of the company's
products. It will be clear that no change in the historical cost figure for
sales revenue is required in the current cost accounts. The value to the
business of sales revenue at the date of sale is clearly the actual amount
receivable as a result of the sale.

**Cost of sales**

3.3    Birchwood Limited use the first in, first out, (FIFO) convention for accounting for stock in its HC accounts, i.e. Birchwood assumes that the
items longest in stock will be the first to be sold. The HC figure for cost of
sales in Table 3.1 is arrived at as follows:

|  | £'000 | £'000 |
|---|---|---|
| Opening stock (FIFO) |  | 51,313 |
| Input: |  |  |
| Material | 93,001 |  |
| Labour | 90,780 |  |
| Overheads | 82,962 |  |
|  | 266,743 |  |
|  |  | 318,056 |
| Less closing stock (FIFO) |  | 66,657 |
| Cost of sales |  | 251,399 |

3.4    The cost of sales figures therefore is made up of a mixture of stock on
hand at the beginning of the year and input during the year. The use of
the FIFO convention ensures that each item of stock consumed is included in cost of sales at its original cost.

3.5    The aim of CCA is to charge against sales revenue the value to the
business of the stock consumed at the date that it is consumed. The date
of consumption of stock is normally the date of sale and to arrive at the
current cost of sales therefore it is necessary to substitute the current
replacement cost (the value to the business) of stock sold at the date of
sale for the historical cost of stock sold. The cost of stock sold at the date
it is purchased by the company is therefore irrelevant to the determination of current cost of sales.

**Example 3.1**

A company sells detergent which it buys in bulk. On 1st March, the company
sells 10 gallons of detergent for £10. The cost of detergent to the company at 1st
January, the last date at which the company purchased any detergent prior to

the sale was 50p per gallon and the company's whole stock of detergent is recorded in its books at that price. The replacement cost of detergent at 1st March is 70p per gallon. Historical cost accounting would match the cost of detergent at 1st January of 50p per gallon with the sale price at 1st March of £1 per gallon and show a profit of £5 on the sale of 10 gallons. Current cost accounting matches the purchase price at 1st March with the sales price at 1st March and shows a current cost profit of £3 and a realised revaluation surplus of £2.

The total gain recorded is the same in both cases. However CCA recognises that if 50p per gallon is shown as profit, and distributed, only approximately 7 gallons out of the 10 gallons of detergent sold could be replaced unless additional capital is found. In other words the company could not distribute 50p profit and still be as well off as it was before the sale. Therefore, although the total surplus is £5, the current cost operating profit is £3. The remaining £2 is a realised revaluation surplus (the difference between original cost and value to the business at the date of sale) which may need to be retained by the company if the value to the business of its physical assets is to be maintained.

### The cost of sales adjustment (COSA)

3.6 Not all companies will be in a position to ascertain the replacement cost of stock at the date at which it makes each individual sale during the year. This may be because such information is not available or because the company does not have the necessary resources to obtain such a volume of information. Such companies may continue to use their existing accounting procedures and make an adjustment to their historical cost of sales figure to arrive at the current cost of sales figure required by CCA. This adjustment is called, unimaginatively, the cost of sales adjustment (COSA).

3.7 The mechanics of the COSA will be described in a later chapter (Chapter 8). In this chapter we are concerned only with its object, which is to adjust the cost of sales figure arrived at using HC conventions by an amount which represents the realised revaluation surpluses or deficits between the date of purchase of the stock sold and the date of its consumption.

3.8 Birchwood Limited does not have the means to obtain the necessary information to record current cost of sales in its books at the date of sale and therefore has made a COSA to the historical cost of sales (already adjusted for increased current cost depreciation). The cost of sales figure in the current cost accounts is made up as follows:

|  | £'000 | £'000 |
|---|---|---|
| Opening stock | | 51,313 |
| Input: | | |
| Material | 93,001 | |
| Labour | 90,780 | |
| Overheads | 85,880 | 269,661 |
| | | c/f 320,974 |

|  | £'000 |
|---|---|
|  | b/f 320,974 |
| Less closing stock | 66,657 |
|  | 254,317 |
| Cost of sales adjustment | 8,147 |
| Current cost of sales | 262,464 |

The historical cost opening stock is used because the adjustment to current cost is included in the COSA. The adjustment to closing stock is taken directly to revaluation surplus.

3.9   Each element of cost of sales must be charged against sales revenue at its value to the business at the date of consumption. Therefore the COSA may consist of adjustments to the material, labour and overhead elements of cost of sales. There is no difference in principle between the different elements of the COSA but the methods used to arrive at each element may differ depending on the availability of information and the company's accounting system. The methods used to calculate Birchwood's COSA are considered in Chapter 8.

**Depreciation**

3.10   Included in the overhead element of cost of sales is a charge for depreciation on the company's fixed assets. In the HC profit and loss account depreciation is based on the historical cost of fixed assets. In the current cost profit and loss account the depreciation charge is based on the value to the business of fixed assets and to be consistent with other charges against current cost operating profit the depreciation charge should be based on the value to the business of fixed assets at the time the revenue against which the depreciation can be charged accrues to the company. It would clearly be impracticable however to calculate a depreciation charge each time a sale is made by the company and therefore the depreciation charge for the year may normally be based on the average value to the business during the year of the fixed assets.

**Example 3.2**

A company purchases a machine on 30th June which rises in value between the date of acquisition and the financial year end from a cost of £10,000 to £12,000. The value on which the depreciation charge for the period should be based is £11,000, (£10,000 + £12,000) ÷ 2.

3.11   It will be recalled from the previous chapter that the balance sheet value of fixed assets is determined with reference to the value and unexpired service potential of the asset *at the balance sheet date*. The depreciation charge against current cost operating profit however is based on the

34

*average value* of the asset for the period before calculating the charge for depreciation for the year. Consequently if the gross value of the asset has increased during the period the depreciation charge against current cost operating profit will, when added to the accumulated depreciation brought forward, be insufficient to reduce the gross value of the asset at the balance sheet date to its value to the business at that date. Therefore to the extent that the accumulated depreciation at the balance sheet date is deficient further depreciation must be deducted from the value of the asset. This additional depreciation is called 'backlog depreciation' and must be charged against the revaluation surplus and not against current cost operating profit which has already been correctly charged with the value to the business of the fixed assets consumed during the period.

## Example 3.3

Holly Limited owns equipment which has a gross value of £9,000 and accumulated depreciation of £2,700 at the start of the year. At the end of the financial year the gross value is £11,000 and the remaining life is 6 years. To arrive at the average value of the asset for the period before calculating the charge for depreciation the opening value must be adjusted to account for the increase in value during the year:

|  | Opening | Adjusted value |
|---|---|---|
|  | £ | £ |
| GRC | 9,000 | 11,000 |
| Depreciation 30% | 2,700 | 3,300 |
| NRC 70% | £6,300 | £7,700 |

The increase in the accumulated depreciation of £600 is that part of backlog depreciation which relates to prior years.

The depreciation charge for this year can now be calculated:

Average value before charging depreciation $\dfrac{6,300 + 7,700}{2} = £7,000$

The unexpired service life at the end of the year was 6 years and therefore was 7 years at the beginning of the year. The depreciation charge is therefore:

$$1/7 \times £7,000 = £1,000$$

Further backlog depreciation is required because the depreciation charge is based on the average value for the year rather than the year-end value.

|  | £ |
|---|---|
| Depreciation based on year-end value—1/7 × £7,700 | 1,100 |
| Depreciation based on average value— 1/7 × £7,000 | 1,000 |
| Additional backlog depreciation required | £100 |

35

At the year end the value to the business is thus £6,600, made up as follows:

|  | £ | £ |
|---|---|---|
| NRC at beginning of the year | | 6,300 |
| Change in GRC | 2,000 | |
| *Less* backlog depreciation: | | |
| for prior years | 600 | |
| for current year | 100 | |
| | 700 | |
| | | 1,300 |
| | | 7,600 |
| Depreciation charge for the year | | 1,000 |
| NRC at the end of the year | | £6,600 |

This figure represents the unexpired service potential of the asset i.e. $6/10 \times £11,000$.

## Administration and selling expenses

3.12    In this chapter administration and selling expenses include all labour, overhead and other expenses, except interest, which are not included in cost of sales. They include such expenses as general management salaries and marketing and promotion expenses. By its nature such expenditure cannot be directly related to particular sales and it would be incorrect to do so, even on an apportionment basis, because administration and selling expenditure is largely incurred independently of the value of sales. Consequently it would be meaningless to attempt to arrive at current cost at the date of consumption of any particular goods sold. Administration and selling expenditure therefore is charged against current cost operating profit as it is incurred. The charge for such expenditure in the current cost profit and loss account and the HC profit and loss account is therefore the same.

## Interest

3.13    The figure for interest is the same in both the current cost profit and loss account and the HC profit and loss account. Interest represents the cost to the company of operating at a level above that which has not been financed by means other than specific borrowing. Many companies 'borrow' from their creditors but generally creditors do not charge for this service. (Although increasingly, interest charges are being levied by suppliers on balances which are not promptly settled).

3.14    Interest is a charge for the use of the money to finance assets which earn the company's trading revenue. Interest therefore is normally to be regarded as a trading expense and should be deducted in arriving at current cost profit.

3.15 An exception to the treatment of interest as a trading expense may arise in circumstances, familiar to property and development companies, in which specified assets being financed by interest bearing loans are in the course of construction and therefore are not earning revenue. In such circumstances interest may be added to the cost of the asset before any revaluation surplus is determined, and need not be written off against current cost profit as soon as it is incurred.

3.16 It will be noted that if interest is capitalised as a part of the cost of an asset in the way suggested, it will be charged against revenue over the life of the asset as part of the depreciation charge. Interest will therefore be correctly treated as a charge against revenue at the dates at which that revenue is earned.

## Example 3.4

A manufacturing company pays interest on its bank overdraft. The bank overdraft finances, in part, the company's stock, plant and machinery.

**Treatment of interest**
The interest is charged against current cost operating profit as it is incurred.

## Example 3.5

A development company pays interest on a loan which has been raised from its bankers to finance the development of a housing estate. It is the company's normal policy to charge interest as a development cost.

**Treatment of interest**
1  As interest is paid it is added to the cost of the development.
2  As houses are completed and sold the value to the business of each house (including interest at current rates) is assessed at the date of sale. The difference between the value to the business including interest at the date of sale and the sale proceeds is an operating gain, i.e. part of current cost operating profit.
3  The difference between the historical cost, including interest, and the value to the business at the date of sale, including interest, is a realised revaluation surplus.

## Example 3.6

A newly formed company pays interest on finance it has obtained to build the processing plant that it needs to carry on its business.

**Treatment of interest**
1  Until manufacture commences, interest is charged as a building cost.
2  When manufacture commences:

    (a) Interest is charged to profit and loss account as it is incurred.
    (b) Depreciation is charged as a cost of manufacture based on the value to the business of the processing plant. The interest which had been

charged as a cost of building the plant, adjusted as necessary to arrive at the current cost of borrowing, will be charged as a cost of manufacture, being part of the depreciation charge, over the life of the plant.

### Dividends received

3.17 During 1979 Birchwood received dividends of £920,000. As with all types of income this amount is shown in the current cost profit and loss account at the same figure as in the HC profit and loss account.

### Profit before tax

3.18 All the constituent parts of Birchwood Limited's current cost profit for the year before tax have now been considered. It will be seen that the difference between the current cost profit before tax and the historical cost profit before tax is made up of two elements, as follows:

|  | £'000 | £'000 |
|---|---|---|
| Historical cost profit before tax |  | 25,454 |
| *Less*: |  |  |
| (a) The cost of sales adjustment | 8,147 |  |
| (b) Additional depreciation on fixed assets | 2,918 | 11,065 |
| Current cost profit before tax |  | 14,389 |

### Corporation tax

3.19 The charge for corporation tax in the current cost profit and loss account must be arrived at based on the taxable income, allowable expenditure and capital and other allowances which the present taxation legislation require to be used for the assessment of tax. Thus the cost of sales adjustment is not an allowable deduction from taxable income and the depreciation charge, however calculated, is to be replaced by capital allowances based on historical cost. The charge for corporation tax therefore is the same in both the current cost accounts and the historical cost accounts. In the current cost accounts any tax (deferred or otherwise) provided in respect of revaluation surpluses on non-current assets or extraordinary items would be netted off against the gross amounts to which the tax relates.

### Deferred tax

3.20 In the HC profit and loss account deferred tax is provided in respect of all timing differences, i.e. all those allowances which defer but do not forgive the payment of tax.

As explained in the previous chapter, deferred tax is provided in the current cost accounts only if it is considered that it is likely to be payable in the foreseeable future. Birchwood considers that it will continue to receive sufficient capital allowances, roll over relief and stock relief to make provision for deferred tax unnecessary in the current cost accounts.

## SUMMARY

### Profit after tax

3.21 To summarise the principles discussed in this chapter the sources of difference between the historical cost profit after tax and the current cost profit of Birchwood Limited are set out below:

|  | £'000 |
|---|---|
| Historical cost profit after tax | 12,694 |
| *Less:* |  |
| (a) Cost of sales adjustment | (8,147) |
| (b) Additional depreciation on fixed assets | (2,918) |
| (c) Deferred tax write-back | 9,082 |
| Current cost profit after tax | 10,711 |

# 4 Indices and Current Cost Accounting

4.1    Indices are used in CCA to obtain approximate values of certain fixed assets and stocks when their value to the business is based on replacement costs and when their replacement cost cannot be determined more accurately by other means. In this chapter we consider how indices are applied in CCA, what published indices are available, and how in-house indices may be compiled. Firstly, however, we consider briefly just what an index number seeks to represent.

## What is a price index?

4.2    Price indices are ratios expressed as percentages. They measure the average changes between points in time in the prices of a defined group of goods and services.

4.3    The idea of using percentages is simply to avoid awkward decimals. Thus if a commodity cost £2 in January 1975 and now costs £2·20 the related index number, assuming January 1975 as the starting point, moves from 100 in January 1975 to 110. The index number 110 is arrived at by dividing the current price by the price at the starting point, the base date, and expressing the result as a percentage of the price at the base date thus:

$$\frac{\text{Current price}}{\text{Base date price}} \times \frac{100}{1} = \frac{2\cdot20}{2\cdot00} \times \frac{100}{1} = 110$$

## The need for index numbers

4.4    In the above example there was in fact no need to convert the prices to index numbers in order to determine the percentage price rise. If, however, one wanted some means of expressing the average increase in price of a group of items it would be necessary to construct an index. Consider the following hypothetical price information:

| Item no. | Description | Price at 1.1.75 | Price at 1.1.76 |
|---|---|---|---|
| 1 | 1lb flour | 20p | 30p |
| 2 | 1 gallon petrol | 60p | 75p |
| 3 | House contents insurance premium per £1,000 cover | £3·00 | £3·60 |
| 4 | 1 reel of cotton thread | 20p | 15p |
| | | £4·00 | £4·80 |

4.5 It is clear that the total price increase of the various items between January 1975 and January 1976 has been 80p but no meaningful figure for the average price increase can be arrived at by merely adding up the mixture of prices for pounds, gallons, etc. If, however, the price for each item at 1st January 1976 was expressed as an index number, called for individual items, a *price relative*, these price relatives could be added and averaged to arrive at an index number for the group. The calculation might proceed as follows:

| 1 | 2 | 3 | 4 | 5 |
|---|---|---|---|---|
| Item | Price at 1.1.75 (base date) | Price at 1.1.75 as a price relative (1.1.75 = 100) | Price at 1.1.76 | Price at 1.1.76 as a price relative (1.1.75 = 100) |
| 1 | 20p | 100 | 30p | 150 |
| 2 | 60p | 100 | 75p | 125 |
| 3 | £3·00 | 100 | £3·60 | 120 |
| 4 | 20p | 100 | 15p | 75 |
| Total | | 400 | | 470 |
| Index | | 100 | | 117·5 |

4.6 Columns 1, 2 and 4 merely repeat information contained in paragraph 4.4. Column 3 states the prices in column 2 as price relatives and, as 1.1.75 is taken as the base date, these are all 100. The price relatives are added to arrive at the total and divided by the number of items to arrive at the index number. Column 5 expresses the prices in column 4 as price relatives, using 1.1.75 as the base date, and these are added and averaged in the same way as those in column 3 to arrive at the index number at 1.1.76.

4.7 The index number 117·5 shows that price increase percentages of the four items averaged $17\frac{1}{2}$% between 1st January 1975, the base date, and 1st January 1976. This figure of $17\frac{1}{2}$% does not correspond to the percentage price increase of any one of the four individual items. An index number is a precise measure only of the change in price of the group of items to which it relates *as a whole*, and not of the individual items in the group.

**Weighting**

4.8 In the simplified example above it was assumed that each item was equally important. Thus it was assumed that house contents insurance was purchased just as frequently as flour and that a price change in one would have exactly the same impact as a similar percentage price change

41

in the other. Clearly this would not be the case. What was missing from the example was some mechanism to adjust the index to take account of the relative importance of each item. This mechanism is called weighting.

4.9      The purpose of weighting is to establish the index as a model of a particular spending pattern or of a particular collection of items. For example the Index of Retail Prices ('the RPI') is weighted to represent the basket of goods purchased by the average household.

4.10      Weighting may be achieved by applying a factor to the price relative of each item in the index, to reflect the importance of that item. For example, suppose the value of purchases of item A in the base period is twice the value of purchases of item B in the same period. To calculate a price index for A and B the price relatives for A and B would be multiplied respectively by 2 and 1 and the sum of the two weighted price relatives would be divided by 3 to obtain the index number. The principle is demonstrated in Example 4.1.

**Example 4.1**

| 1<br>Item | 2<br>Weight | 3<br>Unit price at base date (year 0) | 4<br>Weighted price relative at base $(2 \times (3 \div 3)\%)$ | 5<br>Unit price at year 1 | 6<br>Weighted price relative at year 1 $2 \times (5 \div 3)\%$ |
|---|---|---|---|---|---|
| A | 2 | £1 | 200 | £1·10 | 220 |
| B | 1 | £3 | 100 | £4·50 | 150 |
| Total | 3 | £4 | 300 | £5·60 | 370 |

$$\text{Index at base date:} \qquad \frac{300}{3} = 100$$

$$\text{Index at Year 1:} \qquad \frac{370}{3} = 123 \cdot 3$$

It should be noted that if no weights were applied in Example 4.1 the index number at Year 1 would have been 130 ((110 + 150) ÷ 2).

4.11      Indices may be weighted with reference to the relative importance of the items they cover either (a) at the base, called 'base weighted' or (b) in the period or at the date covered by the current index number, called 'current weighted'.

**The use of index numbers in CCA**

4.12      Although an index number was needed to ascertain the average price increase in the foregoing example it was not needed to arrive at the price increases of the individual items, since these were all known. In practice many companies would not have the resources necessary to obtain the current price of all the items they purchase or of the assets they own and will therefore use index numbers to arrive at approximate current costs. Later in this chapter the availability and the construction of indices suitable for this purpose are considered. At this point it is necessary only to bear in mind that in the absence of more accurate information the application of a suitable index number will result in an approximation, but this will normally be sufficiently accurate for CCA purposes.

4.13    Index numbers may be used in a CCA system in the following cases:

1    To ascertain the gross replacement cost of:

   (a) plant and machinery
   (b) trading stock

2    To calculate the COSA
3    To prepare the Statement of Net Change (see Chapter 19).

4.14    In the above cases index numbers are used either:

   (a) to ascertain approximate values at specific dates, e.g. at the date of the balance sheet, or
   (b) to ascertain average values during a period, e.g. the average current cost of sales during a year for the COSA.

### Using indices to arrive at values at specific dates

4.15    To arrive at a value at a particular date, when the value or cost is known at some other date, the procedure is:

   (a) *multiply* the known value by the index number for the date at which the valuation is *required*, and
   (b) *divide* by the index number for the date at which the value is *known*.

### Example 4.2

A motor car cost £1,000 when the index number for motor cars was 115. Current cost accounts are being prepared to a date at which the index number for motor cars had risen to 130. The gross replacement cost of the motor car at that date for the current cost balance sheet would therefore be:

$$£1,000 \times 130 \div 115 = £1,130 \text{ (rounded)}.$$

4.16    In some cases it can simplify the procedure if the division is carried out first. This is demonstrated in Example 4.3.

**Example 4.3**

A company is preparing its annual accounts using CCA principles for the first time. In order to arrive at the surplus for the year it needs to ascertain the value to the business of its net assets at the beginning and at the end of the year. In respect of its plant and machinery the appropriate index number was 120 at the beginning of the year and 135 at the end of the year. For a machine purchased for £1,000 when the index number was 110 the calculation can be carried out as follows:

(i) Divide by the index number at the date of the known value (in this case the date of acquisition).

$$1000 \div 110 \cdot 0 = 9 \cdot 09 \text{ (rounded)}$$

(ii) Value at the beginning of the year is

$$9 \cdot 09 \times 120 \cdot 0 = £1,091 \text{ (rounded)}$$

(iii) Value at the end of the year is

$$9 \cdot 09 \times 135 \cdot 0 = £1,227 \text{ (rounded)}$$

If the company wanted to arrive at comparative figures of revaluation surpluses for the previous year it would need to ascertain the value to the business of the machine at the beginning of the previous year. Assuming the index number at that date was 115 the calculation would be

$$9 \cdot 09 \times 115 \cdot 0 = £1,045 \text{ (rounded)}.$$

## Using indices to arrive at average current costs

4.17    To arrive at the average current cost for a period, when the historical cost or valuation at a particular date is known, the procedure is:

(a) *multiply* the known value by the average index number for *the period under review*; and
(b) *divide* by the index number for the date at which the value is *known*.

**Example 4.4**

A company purchases stock valued at £10,000 at 31st March at which date the appropriate index number was 125. The company sells all the stock evenly during the next two months and the index moves to 150 after one month and to 175 by the end of the second month. The average index number for the two months is therefore 150. The calculation of the current cost of sales in respect of the stock is:

$$£10,000 \times 150 \div 125 = £12,000$$

## Date indices and period indices

4.18    Some published indices reflect price levels at a particular date (usually in the middle of a month) and some reflect the average price level for a period. If an index number is required for a date which falls between two index numbers of a date type index, the required index number will need

44

to be estimated. Except in rare circumstances it will be sufficient to use the index number closest to the required date or the simple average of the index numbers either side of the date, as appropriate.

4.19 A similar procedure will be necessary when an index number for a date is required when using a period type index. For example, to arrive at an index number for 31st December using a monthly period type index it may be necessary to calculate the simple average of the index numbers for December and January if this would produce an index number materially different from that for the month of December.

4.20 To obtain an average index number for a period when a date type index is being used the procedure is to calculate the arithmetic average of the index numbers for the beginning and end of the period, and for all intermediate dates for which index numbers are available.

## Factors

4.21 Where a large number of calculations are needed using the same two index numbers, e.g. the index number at the opening balance sheet date and the index number at the closing balance sheet date, the two index numbers can be expressed as a 'factor' to facilitate calculation. The factor is calculated by dividing the later index number by the earlier index number. The values at the earlier date are then multiplied by the factor to arrive at the values at the later date.

### Example 4.5

A company has produced current cost accounts for a number of years. For a particular category of plant and machinery the index number at the beginning of the current accounting period was 125 and it was 155 at the end of the period. The company will therefore update the gross replacement cost of the plant and machinery in the category (and the accumulated depreciation for backlog purposes) by multiplying by the factor:

$$\frac{155}{125} = 1 \cdot 24$$

### The availability of published indices

4.22 It is not possible in this book to list all the indices which are available in the United Kingdom or abroad and which are suitable for CCA.

The most useful publication for those who wish to use United Kingdom official indices for CCA is *Price Index Numbers for Current Cost Accounting* which is published by Her Majesty's Stationery Office (HMSO) and contains all of the indices compiled by the Government Statistical Service (GSS) which are presently available, as well as describing briefly how the indices are compiled. For the moment this booklet is published at intervals of several months, but in due course a monthly publication is planned. Meanwhile the latest indices can be obtained from the Central Statistical Office (CSO). All the index numbers contained in the publication are also available from the CSO in the form of computer punched cards.

### Choosing appropriate published indices

4.23    It must be remembered that CCA is at present only in the introductory stage and that the published indices available have not been prepared specifically for CCA purposes.* Consequently in certain cases it will be necessary to consider carefully the construction of a particular index before it is used for CCA purposes. It should also be remembered that the Exposure Draft recommends that published indices should be used only if a more relevant method of valuation is impractical. Also, as pointed out in paragraph 4.7, an index measures the average change in price of a defined group of items, and may not be an accurate measure of price changes for individual items within the group. In the specific circumstances of a particular company it may be that an index is inappropriate although it is suitable for other companies in the same industrial category. For example, a company which purchases all of its materials at prices fixed by long term contracts may find that a published index of material prices for its industry as a whole might not be particularly relevant.

4.24    Choosing the published indices which are likely to be most appropriate for a company's current cost accounts is an important task which fortunately in almost all cases, will not need to be performed very often. Once appropriate indices have been chosen they will be used in all relevant calculations until the company changes the nature of its business, and thereby the type of assets it owns, and the type of costs it incurs, or until more appropriate indices are produced, either externally or in-house, or until more specific sources of price data are employed.

4.25    Before a company values its assets by reference to published indices it should first establish that more precise means of valuation are not available. For example, plant and machinery should only be valued using published indices if a better approximation is not available, or approximation by any other means is considered by the directors to be impractical.

4.26    Published indices which may be used for CCA purposes are:

(a) those published by the GSS, and
(b) other published indices approved for use by the Accounting Standards Committee.

* The GSS is currently preparing further indices for specific categories of plant and machinery which will be included in the third issue of *Price Index Numbers for Current Cost Accounting* to appear in December 1976, and in subsequent issues.

46

4.27   Those companies which decide that published indices need to be used should analyse their plant and machinery and stocks into categories which are covered by published indices, either by type or by industry. This means that to some extent a knowledge of the indices available should be obtained *before* any analysis is attempted.

4.28   Once the necessary analysis has been carried out the respective indices can be applied to each asset category as appropriate and it is only necessary from time to time to review the applicability of the various indices being used. *Price Index Numbers for Current Cost Accounting* will provide details of new official indices and of amendments to existing official indices.

### The construction of in-house indices

4.29   The construction of indices is a complex subject on which much has been written. In the remainder of this chapter we describe some of the techniques involved in compiling an index suitable for use in CCA and we indicate some of the problems which may be encountered. A full discussion of the subject is outside the scope of this book.

4.30   The factors to be considered in the construction of an index are as follows:

(a) The purpose of the index
(b) The scope of the index
(c) The base
(d) The type of index
(e) The choice of a representative sample
(f) Obtaining price data
(g) Weighting
(h) Choice of a suitable average
(i) Review and revision of the index

Each factor is considered in turn in the following paragraphs.

### The purpose of the index

4.31   The purpose of the indices required for CCA has already been considered. Other than the RPI, which is used for the statement of the gain or loss in the value of the shareholders' net equity interest after correction has been made for the change in the value of money, the indices are required to convert historical costs into current costs.

### The scope of the index

4.32   The scope of the index is the range of goods or services that the index covers, sometimes referred to as the 'population' or the 'universe'. Clearly the population for an index which is required to convert all of a company's stock from historical cost to current cost will be all of the company's stock. It may be, however, that the range of items in stock is so great as to make it desirable to categorise the stock and construct a separate index for each category. For example a general import/export company which deals in a large variety of goods might construct one index covering all its stock on hand at a particular date but it might find that the index would quickly lose touch with reality if the composition of its stock varied significantly from that at the base date.

4.33   In practice it will always be preferable to construct separate indices for different categories of stock wherever the categories can be identified at every relevant date.

4.34   The decision to be taken therefore is whether assets need to be categorised and, if so, how the categories should be structured. We suggest that categories should be made up of assets whose prices can be expected to move together. Thus a company should categorise stocks for example, as 'plastics', 'iron and steel' 'copper' etc., rather than as 'body parts', 'accessories', 'engine parts' etc; it is the nature of the stock not its *use* which most affects its price.

## Choosing the base

4.35   The base is the date or period to which all price movements are related and, for a base weighted index, on which the weighting is fixed. If the index is to be base weighted (as will usually be the case) it is important to choose a base at which the population is at a level and composition that is representative of the normal situation and at which sufficient data is available to establish the weights. At the base date the index will stand at 100.

4.36   When a number of indices are being constructed there is no need for all the indices to have the same base date although in many cases it may be convenient to choose as the base date the first day of the financial year in which CCA is to be introduced.

## The type of index

4.37   As explained in paragraph 4.11 it is possible to construct index numbers both for dates and for periods.

Period type indices are useful when the index is to be used to determine average current costs during a period (see paragraph 4.17). Date indices, however, are easier to construct than period indices because price data is needed only at specified dates whereas to construct period indices the dates of price changes are also required.

48

### Choosing a representative sample

4.38 Once the relevant items have been placed in the categories for which indices are to be compiled the next task is to choose the items from each
category whose prices are to be used to construct an index.

4.39 One method of selecting a sample is as follows:

(a) The population (i.e. all the items to be covered by the index) is broken
down into closely defined sub-groups.
(b) One or more items which are expected to be representative (as
regards price movements) of the sub-group as a whole, are selected
from each sub-group.

4.40 It is important that each sub-group is closely defined so that items from
each sub-group can be chosen which will be representative (as regards
price movements) of the sub-group as a whole. Nevertheless on practical
grounds it is desirable to have as few sub-groups as possible.

The general rule is the more sub-groups the more accurate the index but
the more work involved.

### Obtaining price data

4.41 For each item in the sample it will be necessary to collect price data at
each date for which an index number is required, i.e. monthly, quarterly,
etc. As mentioned above, if the index is to cover a period it is also
necessary to obtain the dates at which any price changes take place. It is
important to be able to obtain price data regularly for every item in the
sample. As with all sampling techniques, once the sample has been
selected it is most important that information collected about the sample
is accurate and complete; the smaller the sample in relation to the population the more important this becomes.

4.42 The price data to be obtained is the price for each item in the sample for
delivery of a quantity normally ordered by the company on normal
terms as to trade or bulk discounts and method, place and timing of
delivery. Problems may be encountered when identical items are no
longer available; this is considered below in paragraphs 4.51 to 4.52. It is
suggested to ensure consistency that discounts for prompt payment
should not be taken into account. If VAT is recoverable by the purchaser
it should be excluded from the price but it should be included where it is
irrecoverable. Other irrecoverable taxes and duties should be included.
The price required will normally be that ruling for deliveries made on the
date to which the index number relates.

### Weighting

4.43 The purpose for which the index is being designed will be an important factor in determining the weighting. In most cases, for CCA purposes, indices will be used as a means of obtaining an approximate valuation of the group of items covered by the index. In such cases the weighting needs to be based on the composition, by value, of the group of items.

4.44    It should be noted that with regard to stock the weighting applicable to the valuation of stock for Balance Sheet purposes may not be the same as the weighting applicable to the calculation of the COSA. Most companies will be able to use one index but a minority will need to decide the extent to which the weighting needs to be altered to cover both applications.

4.45    For CCA purposes the most accurate results would be achieved if the index could be current weighted (see paragraph 4.11) since the object is to value assets or determine costs as they are currently, not as they were at the base date or period. Unfortunately current weighting necessitates re-weighting the index at each date an index number is required. While this may not be too time consuming if the weights are easily determined, such as if sales values are used for weights, it could be a considerable burden if this is not the case. Indeed if companies are able to prepare current weighted indices they are probably able to identify the current cost of sales without the need for an index.

4.46    In many cases little difference in the index numbers would result if the index was base weighted instead of current weighted and in practice the weights need only be revised occasionally (see paragraphs 4.48 to 4.52 below). For example an index calculated monthly should, at most, need rebasing only annually.

### The average to be used

4.47    To arrive at the required index number the prices for the items in the sample must be averaged. The average used should be the weighted arithmetic mean.

The procedure to arrive at the weighted arithmetic mean is simply to add the relevant weighted price relatives for the items and to divide the result by the sum of the weights.

### Review and revision of the index

4.48    We have now covered briefly all the factors to be considered in the construction of a new index. For the index to continue to be useful however, it needs to be regularly monitored to ensure that:

(a) The sample remains representative of the population.
(b) The items in the sample continue to have the same specifications, i.e. they remain the same items.

## Monitoring the sample

4.49 Technological advance and relative price changes may increase the usage of certain materials and decrease the usage of others. For example a shift away from oil-based fuels was noticeable after the recent oil crisis, and on a smaller scale, there has been a steady decline over a number of years in the use of woven labels by clothing manufacturers and a corresponding increase in the use of less expensive printed labels. The effect of changes such as these may render unrepresentative the original weighting of a sample. One method of overcoming this problem is to use current weights but this fails when completely new materials replace existing ones and the whole structure of the sample thereby becomes unrealistic. Another method is to re-base the index at short intervals, but this is a time consuming process. A solution which is often the best is to use a simplified 'chain-base system'. Instead of using a fixed base, the system involves the calculation of the index for one period using the previous period as the base.

### Example 4.6

(i) A price index is constructed based on average 1970 = 100.

(ii) The average index number in 1971 based on average 1970 = 100, is 125.

(iii) During 1971 one item in the index ceased to be purchased and was replaced by another item, the sample is adjusted accordingly (for example by adding the new item to the sample with an appropriate weight and adjusting the weight for the sub-group containing the item no longer purchased) and forms the base for the index number for 1972 (based on average 1971 = 100) which was 110.

(iv) The series is now 'chained' by relating the index for 1972 to a base of average 1970 = 100 as follows:

$$\text{Price index for } 1972 \,(1970 = 100) = \frac{125 \times 110}{100} = 137 \cdot 5.$$

(v) The same procedure is followed in 1973 when the index based on average 1972 = 100 was 120. The chaining for 1973 is:

$$\text{Price index for } 1973 \,(1970 = 100) = \frac{137 \cdot 5 \times 120}{100} = 165.$$

(vi) The series with 1970 = 100 is therefore:

| | |
|---|---|
| 1970 | 100 |
| 1971 | 125 |
| 1972 | 137·5 |
| 1973 | 165 |

4.50 It can be seen from Example 4.6 that the main advantage of the chain-base system is that new items can be introduced and obsolete items dropped quite simply without the need for a completely new and revised base.

## Specification changes

4.51 The second factor which needs to be monitored is the specification of items included in the sample. Specification changes are unlikely to cause many problems with regard to indices for stock, but they are a considerable problem with regard to indices for plant and machinery; the pace of modern technology is such that many types of machinery do not stay unchanged for any length of time. Increased productive capacity, savings in running and maintenance costs and an increased useful life are all improvements which will affect the comparability of the current purchase price of machines over a period of time. When obtaining price data it is essential, therefore, to obtain information about the benefits (or otherwise) that will be derived from specification changes. It is then a matter of judgement to determine how much of a price increase can be attributed to the additional benefits to be obtained from such changes. It may be that a steady price coupled with specification changes may in fact represent a price increase or reduction. The normal method of adjusting for specification changes is before calculating the price relative to deduct from (or add to) the current price of the item the amount that, it is considered, represents the cost of the increased (or decreased) benefit to be derived from any specification changes made since the last price relative was calculated. Example 4.7 is an illustration of how this might be achieved in practice. It should be noted that no single method can be used in all circumstances, and that it will not be possible in all cases to obtain a suitable adjusted price, particularly if the specification changes have been extensive.

### Example 4.7

A company constructs an in-house index for its machinery. The representative item included in the sample for its stamping machine sub-group is manufactured by ABC Limited and is known as Model 124 Series A. On 1st February 1976 ABC Limited began selling Model 124 Series B which is superior to the Series A model.

The company's index is based on 1st January 1976 as 100 at which date the cost of the Series A model was £30,000. At 1st February 1976 the Series A machine was quoted at £33,000 and the Series B machine was quoted at £40,000. On 1st March 1976 the Series B machine was quoted at £41,200 and the Series A machine was no longer quoted.

It must be remembered that the purpose of the index is to value the company's existing machinery, i.e. including the Series A machine not the Series B machine. As no current price is available for Series A the Series B price must be adjusted in order to estimate what the Series A price *would be* if it was still available.

After establishing that the prices at 1st February 1976 of both machines are realistic (i.e. in particular that Machine A is not being sold off cheaply to clear the stock), the company would estimate a price for the Series A machine for 1st March 1976 as follows:

Series A machine price relative at 1st February:

$$\text{(1st January} = 100) \qquad = \frac{£33,000}{£30,000} \times 100 = 110 \cdot 0$$

Series B machine price relative at 1st March:

$$\text{(1st February} = 100) \qquad = \frac{£41,200}{£40,000} \times 100 = 103 \cdot 0$$

Estimated price relative for Series A machine at 1st March:

$$\text{(1st January} = 100) \qquad = 103 \cdot 0 \times \frac{110 \cdot 0}{100 \cdot 0} = 113 \cdot 3$$

Estimated price of Series A machine at 1st March 1976:

$$£30,000 \times 113 \cdot 3\% = £33,990$$

4.52   The GSS when using the above method of adjusting for specification changes would in fact require a longer period of parallel availability than one month. Nevertheless the principles employed are the same.

There are other ways of adjusting for specification changes than that used in Example 4.7 but these usually involve obtaining additional information from suppliers, which they may be unwilling or unable to supply. In all cases in which the specification changes are so great as effectively to change the nature of the item it should be treated as a different item and the sample and weighting should be adjusted accordingly.

**Periods prior to the base date**

4.53   When compiling an index it must be remembered that in many cases an index number will be required prior to the base date. For example, a company compiling an index for machinery needs to obtain an index number, at least at annual intervals, for each year in which machinery on hand was purchased prior to the base date. Otherwise, short of valuing each item individually, the company will have no way of calculating the value of its machinery at the base date. A company which is unable to value its fixed assets at the base date, either by use of its own index or on an individual basis may nevertheless be able to value its fixed assets at the base date using some index other than its own, say the most suitable official index, and use the values thus calculated as the starting values for its own index. In the first few periods this procedure may give rise to some unsatisfactory valuations but for many companies it provides a practical means of starting in-house indices without the need to go back what could be, for some companies, a considerable period of time. Example 4.8 demonstrates the procedure. In practice companies should attempt to analyse their fixed assets by date or month of acquisition rather than by year of acquisition. Also, if required, average indices for periods should be calculated using all the available intermediate index numbers and not, as in the example, just the index number for the beginning and end of the period.

## Example 4.8

A company wishes to compile an in-house index for its machinery with a base date of 1.1.76. The company's machinery on hand at 1.1.76 was purchased during the period 1969 to 1975 and the company does not have the data either to compile index numbers going back to 1969 or to individually value each item of machinery at 1.1.76.

The company decides to value its machinery at 1.1.76 using the most suitable official index available and to compile its own index from that date forward. The official index at the relevant dates was as follows:

| Date | Index Number |
|------|--------------|
| 1.1.69 | 105 |
| 1.1.70 | 115 |
| 1.1.71 | 125 |
| 1.1.72 | 120 |
| 1.1.73 | 130 |
| 1.1.74 | 145 |
| 1.1.75 | 155 |
| 1.1.76 | 160 |

The historical cost of assets on hand at 1.1.76 analysed by year of acquisition was as follows:

| Year of acquisition | Cost |
|---------------------|------|
| 1969 | £2,000 |
| 1970 | £4,500 |
| 1971 | £6,800 |
| 1972 | £9,400 |
| 1973 | £11,500 |
| 1974 | £18,000 |
| 1975 | £21,700 |

The assets are valued as follows, based on the average index number for each year of purchase:

| Year of acquisition | Cost £ | Index Beginning | Index End | Average | Factor 160 ÷ Average | Value at 1.1.76 £ |
|---------------------|--------|-----------|-----|---------|---------------------|------------------|
| 1969 | 2,000 | 105 | 115 | 110 | 1·45 | 2,900 |
| 1970 | 4,500 | 115 | 125 | 120 | 1·33 | 5,985 |
| 1971 | 6,800 | 125 | 120 | 122·5 | 1·31 | 8,908 |
| 1972 | 9,400 | 120 | 130 | 125 | 1·28 | 12,032 |
| 1973 | 11,500 | 130 | 145 | 137·5 | 1·16 | 13,340 |
| 1974 | 18,000 | 145 | 155 | 150 | 1·07 | 19,260 |
| 1975 | 21,700 | 155 | 160 | 157·5 | 1·02 | 22,134 |
| | £73,900 | | | | | £84,559 |

Having arrived at a valuation of its assets at 1.1.76, the company constructs an in-house index by selecting a sample of assets on hand at 1.1.76 and expressing the average value of the sample as 100. The prices of the assets in the sample are monitored and index numbers are compiled for subsequent dates. Assuming that the in-house index stands at 115 at 31.12.76, to arrive at a valuation for the assets on hand at 31.12.76 which were also on hand at 1.1.76, the company can either:

(a) apply the factor $\frac{115}{100} = 1 \cdot 15$ to the values at 1.1.76, or

(b) link the official index and the in-house index back to 1969 and apply a factor to the historical cost based on the linked index. Both methods will arrive at the same result.

For example, for assets purchased in 1972 the result using method (a) is calculated as follows:

$$£12,032 \times 1 \cdot 15 = £13,837$$

Using method (b) the calculation is:

(i) Convert the official (average) index number for 1972 to an index number using the in-house index base of 100 at 1.1.76. The formula is:

$$125 \times \frac{100}{160} = 78 \cdot 125$$

(ii) The factor is therefore:

$$\frac{115}{78 \cdot 125} = 1 \cdot 472$$

(iii) The valuation is therefore:

$$£9,400 \times 1 \cdot 472 = £13,837.$$

4.54　Method (b) in Example 4.8 may seem more complicated but it should be remembered that the linkage is a one-off exercise; once it has been performed the procedure is no different from that for method (a). However, on the grounds of simplicity, method (a) is preferred.

## CONCLUSION

4.55　In this chapter we have been able to provide only a brief guide to the use and construction of indices, and we would not expect that those wishing to compile indices would rely solely on the information contained herein. Nevertheless, the methods of construction described in this chapter are those most commonly used at present and are suitable for all the indices which may be required for the operation of a CCA system. As practical experience is gained in running CCA systems the use of indices will become increasingly familiar and the availability of suitable published indices will no doubt increase.

# 5 Fixed Assets— Plant and Machinery

5.1 In Chapters 2 and 3 the general principles regarding the valuation of fixed assets and the calculation of depreciation in current cost accounts were considered briefly. This chapter deals with how these principles are applied in practice for plant and machinery in normal circumstances. Land and buildings are covered in Chapter 6 and some special cases are dealt with in Chapter 7. The recording of fixed assets and depreciation information in the accounting books and records is considered in Chapter 15.

## NET CURRENT REPLACEMENT COST

5.2 A fixed asset may be valued for CCA purposes on one of a number of valuation bases depending on the particular circumstances and nature of the asset concerned. Fixed assets, however, will most frequently be valued on the basis of their net current replacement cost, land and buildings being a significant exception. The accounting entries required to record asset valuations and depreciation on a net current replacement cost basis differ in certain respects from those applicable to all other valuation bases. Nevertheless, because of the importance of the net current replacement cost basis of valuation, the basic accounting entries required to record assets on this basis are described below, before we consider particular fixed asset categories in any detail.

5.3 Net current replacement cost is distinguished from the other valuation methods because, unlike values accorded by other valuation bases, the net current replacement cost of an asset is made up of two elements which are recorded separately. The net current replacement cost of an asset is the amount which it would be necessary to spend to replace the asset in its existing condition and location. The two elements are therefore the gross cost of purchasing the asset as new, and a deduction for depreciation to reflect the expiry of a proportion of the asset's service potential. This split of gross value and depreciation will be familiar to all readers.

5.4 As will be seen later, the other bases of valuation do not distinguish between the gross value and the net value of assets because, although depreciation is charged to the profit and loss account, the accumulated depreciation is not separately identified. Nevertheless the importance of determining an asset's remaining useful life is a major feature of CCA which is relevant for all types of fixed asset and all bases of valuation.

## RECORDING NET CURRENT REPLACEMENT COST

### Revaluations

5.5    Throughout this section it is generally assumed that replacement costs will increase. Thus only the treatment of revaluation surpluses will be explained in detail. Revaluation deficits are generally treated in the same manner, although the accounting entries are, of course, reversed.

For revaluations resulting in a surplus the basic accounting entry is:

Dr   Asset account
Cr   Revaluation surplus account
        with the gain on revaluation.

It will be recalled from Chapter 3 that on a revaluation the accumulated depreciation at the date of revaluation must be adjusted so that it bears the same relationship to the gross current replacement cost after the revaluation as it did immediately prior to the revaluation. This adjustment to the accumulated depreciation is one element of the adjustment to net book value known as 'backlog depreciation'. To distinguish this element from the other element of backlog depreciation explained in paragraph 5.9 below the element calculated on a revaluation will be referred to as 'prior year backlog depreciation'. The net book value, after adjusting for this element of backlog depreciation, is known as 'the adjusted value'. To record the prior year backlog depreciation arising on revaluation the accounting entry is:

Dr   Revaluation surplus account
Cr   Accumulated depreciation account
        with the backlog depreciation.

The calculation of prior year backlog depreciation should be regarded as part of the valuation procedure in that it adjusts the carrying value to account for the expiry of service potential up to the valuation date.

The revaluation and resulting adjustment for prior year backlog depreciation can be recorded in one accounting entry for example as follows:

|  |  | £ | £ |
|---|---|---|---|
| Dr | Asset account | 1,000 | |
| Cr | Accumulated depreciation account | | 500 |
| Cr | Revaluation surplus account | | 500 |
|  |  | £1,000 | £1,000 |

### Deferred tax

5.6    It was noted in Chapter 2 that in certain circumstances revaluations may give rise to deferred tax charges or credits. The circumstances in which deferred tax might arise are discussed fully in Chapter 10. The accounting entry required to record a deferred tax charge arising on a revaluation is:

Dr   Revaluation surplus account
Cr   Deferred tax provision
       with the deferred tax based on the surplus.

5.7      Where deferred tax has been provided in respect of capital allowances the adjustment for prior year backlog depreciation will give rise to a deferred tax adjustment as follows:

Dr   Deferred tax provision
Cr   Revaluation surplus account
       with deferred tax on prior year backlog depreciation.

5.8      Example 5.1 demonstrates the accounting entries required in respect of the revaluation of plant and machinery for a company that is required to make full provision for deferred tax. It will be noted that each pair of entries (A and B, C and D) could be netted off but as in all examples they have been shown in full to ensure clarity.

**Example 5.1**

ABC Limited revalues its fixed assets annually for CCA purposes. At the beginning of year 6 the gross replacement cost of the company's plant and machinery was recorded at £20,000 and accumulated depreciation was recorded at £10,000. At the end of year 6 the gross replacement cost of the company's plant and machinery was estimated to be £22,000. There were no acquisitions or disposals during the year. Tax has been assumed at the rate of 50% and capital allowances have been assumed at 100% of historical cost. Thus at the beginning of year 6 the balance on the deferred tax account represents 50% of the opening net value of fixed assets on which 100% capital allowances had been claimed in the year of acquisition. The accounting entries to record the revaluation are:

|   |    |                                                           | £     | £     |
|---|----|-----------------------------------------------------------|-------|-------|
| A | Dr | Fixed assets                                              | 2,000 |       |
|   | Cr | Revaluation surplus account                               |       | 2,000 |
|   |    | with the revaluation surplus                              |       |       |
| B | Dr | Revaluation surplus account                               | 1,000 |       |
|   | Cr | Deferred tax provision account                            |       | 1,000 |
|   |    | with deferred tax on the revaluation surplus at the rate of 50% |       |       |
| C | Dr | Revaluation surplus account                               | 1,000 |       |
|   | Cr | Accumulated depreciation account                          |       | 1,000 |
|   |    | with prior year backlog depreciation                     |       |       |
| D | Dr | Deferred tax provision account                            | 500   |       |
|   | Cr | Revaluation surplus account                               |       | 500   |
|   |    | with deferred tax on prior year backlog depreciation     |       |       |

The figure of £1,000 in journal entry C is the amount required to maintain the same relationship between net replacement cost and gross replacement cost as that which obtained immediately prior to the revaluation and before charging depreciation for the year. After recording the accounting entries listed above the relevant ledger accounts would appear as follows (the letters in brackets refer to the journal entries above):

### Fixed Assets

| | | | |
|---|---|---|---|
| Year 6 | Opening balance | 20,000 | |
| | Revaluation | 2,000 (A) | |

### Accumulated Depreciation

| | | | |
|---|---|---|---|
| | Year 6 | Opening balance | 10,000 |
| | | Backlog depreciation | 1,000 (C) |

### Revaluation Surplus

| | | | | |
|---|---|---|---|---|
| Year 6 | Deferred tax on revaluation | 1,000 (B) | Year 6 | Revaluation | 2,000 (A) |
| | Backlog depreciation | 1,000 (C) | | Deferred tax on backlog depreciation | 500 (D) |

### Deferred Tax

| | | | | |
|---|---|---|---|---|
| Year 6 | Backlog depreciation | 500 (D) | Year 6 | Opening balance | 5,000 |
| | | | | Revaluation | 1,000 (B) |

### The depreciation charge for the year

5.9     It will be recalled from Chapter 3 that the depreciation charge for the year will normally be based on the average depreciable value of fixed assets. The average depreciable value is the average of the opening net value and the adjusted value (i.e. it is an amount calculated before charging depreciation for the year). The average depreciable value in Example 5.1 is £10,500, i.e.:

$$\frac{(£10,000 + £11,000)}{2}$$

5.10    In times of rising prices, the amount charged to the Profit and Loss Account for depreciation will not be sufficient to accumulate a total provision for depreciation equal to the gross current replacement cost of the asset at the end of its useful life. The required total provision would only be achieved if the accumulated depreciation at each accounting date were based on the value of the asset at that date. Backlog depreciation, consisting of two elements, is charged against the revaluation surplus for this purpose. The first element has already been calculated and recorded on revaluation and the second element, relating to the year under review (called 'current year backlog depreciation' in this book), is the difference between the actual depreciation charge for the year, based on the average depreciable value, and a theoretical charge based on the adjusted value at the year-end (i.e. gross replacement cost at the year-end less accumulated depreciation before charging depreciation for the year).

5.11    The accounting entries to record the depreciation charge for the year and the current year backlog depreciation are:

Dr    Profit and loss account*
Cr    Accumulated depreciation account
        with the depreciation charge for the year.
Dr    Revaluation surplus account
Cr    Accumulated depreciation account
        with current year backlog depreciation.

When deferred tax is being accounted for additional accounting entries are required as follows:

Dr    Deferred tax provision account
Cr    Profit and loss account
        with deferred tax on the depreciation charge for the year.
Dr    Deferred tax provision account
Cr    Revaluation surplus account
        with deferred tax on current year backlog depreciation.

**Example 5.2**

Continuing Example 5.1, ABC Limited charges depreciation based on the expected remaining useful life of its fixed assets on a straight line basis. At the end of year 6 the expected future useful life of the company's plant and machinery is estimated as 4 years. The depreciation charge for the year is calculated as follows:

Expected remaining useful life at end of year 6:                            4 years
Therefore the expected remaining useful life at beginning of year 6 is:    5 years

Therefore the depreciation charge for year 6 is:
1/5 × average depreciable value for year 6:

$$1/5 \times \frac{10,000 + 11,000}{2} = £2,100$$

The accounting entries to record the depreciation charge for the year are:

|   |    |                                                                 | £     | £     |
|---|----|-----------------------------------------------------------------|-------|-------|
| E | Dr | Profit and loss account                                         | 2,100 |       |
|   | Cr | Accumulated depreciation account                                |       | 2,100 |
|   |    | with the depreciation charge for the year                       |       |       |
| F | Dr | Deferred tax provision account                                  | 1,050 |       |
|   | Cr | Profit and loss account                                         |       | 1,050 |
|   |    | with deferred tax on the depreciation charge for the year at the rate of 50% |       |       |

* Profit and loss account is used here and elsewhere in similar cases to denote charges against current cost profit.

60

The theoretical depreciation charge based on the adjusted value at the year-end is:

$$1/5 \times £11,000 = £2,200$$

Current year backlog depreciation is therefore:

$$£2,200 - £2,100 = £100$$

The accounting entries to record the current year backlog depreciation are:

|  |  |  | £ | £ |
|---|---|---|---|---|
| G | Dr | Revaluation surplus account | 100 | |
|  | Cr | Accumulated depreciation account | | 100 |
|  |  | with current year backlog depreciation | | |
| H | Dr | Deferred tax provision account | 50 | |
|  | Cr | Revaluation surplus account | | 50 |
|  |  | with deferred tax on current year backlog depreciation at the rate of 50% | | |

The ledger accounts will now appear as follows:

**Fixed Assets**

| Year 6 | Balance (from Example 5.1) | 22,000 | | | |
|---|---|---|---|---|---|

**Revaluation Surplus**

| Year 6 | Backlog depreciation | 100 (G) | Year 6 | Balance (from Example 5.1) | 500 |
|---|---|---|---|---|---|
| | | | | Deferred tax on backlog depreciation | 50 (H) |

**Deferred Tax Provision**

| Year 6 | Depreciation | 1,050 (F) | Year 6 | Balance (from Example 5.1) | 5,500 |
|---|---|---|---|---|---|
| | Backlog depreciation | 50 (H) | | | |

**Accumulated Depreciation**

| | | | Year 6 | Balance (from Example 5.1) | 11,000 |
|---|---|---|---|---|---|
| | | | | Charge for the year | 2,100 (E) |
| | | | | Backlog for the year | 100 (G) |

**Profit and Loss Account**

| Year 6 | Depreciation | 2,100 (E) | Year 6 | Deferred tax | 1,050 (F) |
|---|---|---|---|---|---|

At the end of year 6 ABC Limited's accounts will include, *inter alia*, the following amounts:

61

Profit and loss account:

|  | £ |
|---|---|
| Depreciation | (2,100) |
| Deferred tax credit | 1,050 |
|  | £(1,050) |

Fixed assets:

|  | £ |
|---|---|
| Gross current replacement cost | 22,000 |
| Less: accumulated depreciation | 13,200 |
| Net current replacement cost | £8,800 |
| Deferred tax | £4,400 |
| Revaluation surplus | £ 450 |

5.12    The preceding paragraphs provide an overall view of the accounting treatment to be adopted when fixed assets are valued on the basis of their net current replacement cost. In the following paragraphs the treatment of plant and machinery and the concept of net current replacement cost is considered in detail.

5.13    The treatment of categories of fixed assets such as 'fixtures and fittings', 'furniture and equipment', etc., is the same as that for plant and machinery. So, too, is the treatment of motor vehicles. The term 'plant and machinery' in this book will therefore be used to cover all such categories of fixed asset.

## The normal basis of valuation for plant and machinery

5.14    Plant and machinery will normally be valued on the basis of its net current replacement cost, i.e. gross current replacement cost less accumulated depreciation. In some exceptional cases it will be necessary to value plant and machinery with reference to its economic value or its net realisable value. These bases of valuation are considered in Chapter 7.

## GROSS CURRENT REPLACEMENT COST (GRC)

5.15    The gross current replacement cost (GRC) of plant and machinery is either (a) the cost to be incurred to obtain and install at the date of the valuation a substantially identical replacement in new condition or (b) the cost of a modern equivalent asset, whichever is the lower. The cost of a modern equivalent asset is the GRC of a modern piece of plant or machinery adjusted by the present value of any material differences in operating costs over its whole life, for material differences in output capacity, provided that any additional output is usable by the company, and for material differences in the total expected useful life of the modern machine compared with that of a substantially identical replacement.

5.16    It will be seen from the above definition that the GRC will not always be the actual replacement cost of an existing item of plant and machinery. It is recognised also that it may not always be practicable to arrive at GRCs for items of plant and machinery on an item by item basis.

### The cost of a substantially identical asset

5.17 There are a number of methods of estimating the cost of a substantially identical asset. The most usual methods are listed below in descending order of preference; that is, a method higher on the list will normally provide a closer approximation to the required figure than one lower down. Companies should use the best estimate they can, having regard to materiality and the cost of obtaining the data.

1 Suppliers' official price lists, catalogues, etc., with appropriate deductions for normal trade discounts.
2 The company's own replacement cost estimates based on expert opinion.
3 An index compiled by the company from its own purchasing (or manufacturing) experience.
4 Authorised external price indices analysed by asset type.
5 Authorised external price indices analysed by using industry.

5.18 The appropriate source of data in each particular case will depend on the circumstances. Nevertheless, whichever source of data is used there must be a means of independently verifying the resulting GRCs. A company may wish to employ the services of external valuers to determine GRCs, but whether or not external valuers are used will not change the sources of data available. External valuers are bound by the above list just as the company's own staff as can be seen from the Draft Guidance Note: *Current Cost Accounting, the Valuation of Fixed Assets* prepared by the Assets Valuation Standards Committee of The Royal Institution of Chartered Surveyors (RICS) which is reproduced at Appendix B.

5.19 As far as possible GRCs should be obtained on a consistent basis. Nevertheless it is recognised that it may not be possible to use the same method of valuation each year. Companies may, for example, obtain expert valuations on a rotational basis and use authorised indices in intermediate years to avoid the expense of annual expert valuations. Similarly, official price lists can be used without adjustment as the basis of GRCs only so long as substantially identical assets are available.

5.20 Whichever source of price data is used the GRC should be based on the replacement cost of the item for delivery on the date of valuation. When using official indices, however, the index number applicable to the valuation date should be used even though this means that, strictly, the index number for *orders* at the date of valuation is being used.

5.21 The following is an example of a situation in which various sources of data might be used.

## Example 5.3

Elmtree Limited is a large electrical engineering company which manufactures domestic appliances from electric irons to washing machines. Much of its plant and machinery consists of relatively cheap individual machines of various types but some items are large, expensive pieces of specialised plant and there are some other items of expensive machinery which are easily identifiable.

Elmtree Limited decides to value its plant and machinery by the following methods:

| | |
|---|---|
| Specialised plant | Company's own estimate based on engineers' expert opinion. |
| Individual items with original cost of more than £15,000 | Suppliers' price lists (adjusted as necessary by engineers if substantially identical assets are no longer available). |
| Other plant and machinery | Official price index for engineering and allied industries other than vehicles (reference 1070). |

### Suppliers' price lists, etc.

5.22   Suppliers' price lists, catalogues, etc., should be used to value plant and machinery whenever it is practical to do so as they will normally provide the most accurate source of replacement costs. It would not normally be sufficient to obtain prices from the supplier orally or in writing specifically for CCA purposes unless there was some other evidence available to show that the prices so obtained were those generally available to the supplier's customers. Normal trade discounts should be taken into account as should bulk discounts if the items in question would normally be purchased in bulk (e.g. a fleet of vehicles). Discounts for cash or prompt payment, however, should be ignored. If VAT is recoverable by the purchaser it should be excluded, but it should be included where it is irrecoverable. Other irrecoverable taxes and duties should be included. The price required is that ruling for deliveries on the valuation date. It would not normally be appropriate to use prices at which the item could be ordered at the valuation date for delivery at some subsequent date.

### Replacement cost estimates

5.23   Replacement cost estimates may appropriately be used in the following circumstances:

(a) Where an identical asset is no longer available and the GRC is arrived at by adjusting the price of a comparable asset in respect of differences in operating costs, rate of output and life to arrive at the GRC of a modern equivalent asset.

(b) Where the asset is manufactured by the company for its own use rather than purchased from outside suppliers.

(c) Where the existing asset is not fully utilised, in which case the required GRC should be based on an asset that would be fully utilised at the present or expected rate of production (see paragraph 5.31).

5.24 Replacement cost estimates should be based on the expert opinion either of suitably qualified staff or of external professionally qualified valuers.

### Modern equivalent asset

5.25 Whether or not an existing asset is still being sold by suppliers there may be on sale a modern equivalent asset whose performance is similar to that of the existing asset. Where there is a modern equivalent asset the GRC of the existing asset, as explained in paragraph 5.15, will be the lower of the GRC of the modern equivalent asset and the GRC of the existing asset.

5.26 Where there is an alternative replacement which is not equivalent to the existing asset, a discounted value of any anticipated cost savings over the estimated useful life of the alternative replacement and an amount to take account of any increased production (providing it is usable) should be deducted from the GRC of the alternative replacement to arrive at the GRC of a modern equivalent asset. The lower of this GRC and the GRC of the existing asset should be used as the GRC for CCA purposes.

5.27 Where there is a modern equivalent asset, or an alternative replacement the cost of which can be adjusted to arrive at the cost of a modern equivalent asset, but the existing asset is no longer available, an estimated notional replacement cost for the existing asset can be obtained by the application of a suitable price index to the last known GRC of the existing asset. The estimate so obtained should be compared with the cost of the modern equivalent asset and the lower of the two values should be used as the GRC. Where no reasonable estimate can be made of the potential cost savings to be obtained by the use of an alternative replacement, the indexed GRC of the existing asset should be used as the GRC for CCA purposes.

5.28 The following examples demonstrate the various alternatives discussed in the preceding paragraphs:

(a) GRC of identical replacement £10,000
GRC of modern equivalent replacement £12,000
GRC for CCA purposes is £10,000

(b) GRC of identical replacement £12,000
GRC of modern equivalent replacement £10,000
GRC for CCA purposes is £10,000

(c) GRC of identical replacement £12,000
GRC of alternative replacement £18,000

| | |
|---|---|
| Estimated current value of anticipated benefits from using the alternative replacement | £10,000 |
| GRC for CCA purposes is (£18,000–£10,000) = | £8,000 |

(d) GRC of identical replacement £12,000
GRC of alternative replacement £20,000
Estimated current value of anticipated benefits from
using the alternative replacement £5,000
GRC for CCA purposes is £12,000

(e) Identical replacement no longer available but the
application of an appropriate index to the last known
GRC for the existing asset produces a GRC of £12,000
GRC of alternative replacement £18,000
Value of anticipated benefits from using the alternative
replacement cannot be reasonably estimated.
GRC for CCA purposes is £12,000

(f) If an identical replacement was not available in cases (a) to (d) above but an index adjusted GRC of £11,000 had been calculated, the GRC for CCA purposes would have been £11,000 in each case except (c) for which the GRC would remain at £8,000.

## Adjustments to arrive at the cost of a modern equivalent asset

5.29 Adjustments to the cost of an alternative replacement asset may be required to arrive at the cost of a modern equivalent asset in respect of three factors as follows:

(a) Operating costs
(b) Productive output
(c) Service potential.

A material difference between the existing asset and the alternative asset in respect of any one of the above factors will necessitate an adjustment to the capital cost of the alternative asset to arrive at a cost for a modern equivalent replacement for the existing asset. Example 5.4 demonstrates an adjustment in respect of an improvement in operating costs and productive output. The general method of approach is:

(a) Ascertain the annual benefit at expected costs and prices over the life of the alternative asset.
(b) Discount the figures arrived at in (a) by a factor based on the company's present money rate of interest on borrowings (on the assumption that any borrowings would be made currently at a fixed interest rate).

### Example 5.4

Willowtree Ltd estimates that the expected benefits from an alternative replacement machine, which has a GRC of £250,000, over its estimated useful life of 5 years, at expected money values, is as follows:

| | Years | | | | |
|---|---|---|---|---|---|
| | 1 | 2 | 3 | 4 | 5 |
| | £ | £ | £ | £ | £ |
| Increased useable production | 12,000 | 15,000 | 16,500 | 17,500 | 19,000 |
| Reduced operator time | 4,000 | 4,400 | 5,000 | 5,500 | 6,000 |
| Reduced overheads: | | | | | |
| power | 1,000 | 1,200 | 1,500 | 1,900 | 2,300 |
| floor space | 500 | 500 | 500 | 700 | 700 |
| | £17,500 | £21,100 | £23,500 | £25,600 | £28,000 |

Present money rate of
interest on 5 year loans
= 15% per annum

| Present value of future savings discounted at 15% per annum (assuming that the savings are made on the last day of each year) | £15,217 | £15,955 | £15,452 | £14,637 | £13,920 |
|---|---|---|---|---|---|

The present value of expected future benefits is therefore £75,181, say £75,000.

The GRC of a modern equivalent asset to replace the existing asset is therefore
£250,000 − £75,000 = £175,000.

5.30    It will be appreciated that Example 5.4 has been simplified to demonstrate clearly the principles involved. In practice the calculation could be quite complicated.

## The treatment of existing assets with excess productive capacity

5.31    Excess productive capacity may arise where a decline in the market for the output of a machine (or a group of machines) being valued has led to a fall in the profitable volume of production to a level below that anticipated when the machine was purchased. If the directors consider that the reduced level of production will continue indefinitely the NRC of the existing machine will be an unrealistic assessment of its deprival value. In these circumstances the existing machine should be valued at the NRC of the machine which would provide the business with the productive capacity which is justified by market conditions foreseeable over the remaining life of the existing machine. If no machine small enough to be fully utilised by the company is available the directors should consider whether they will replace the existing machine at the end of its useful life. If the machine will not be replaced the directors should consider valuing the machine on the basis of its economic value (see Chapter 7 paras 7.7 to 7.9). If the machine will be replaced (i.e. the excess capacity will continue indefinitely) the method of adjusting for excess capacity should be that illustrated in Example 5.5.

5.32    It is not necessary to value plant and machinery with excess productive capacity in the manner described above if the excess productive capacity is expected to be temporary or if the asset is held in the expectation of increased future production.

### Example 5.5

The directors of Widget Limited consider that there is an annual market for 100,000 left-handed widgets and the company purchases a machine that can produce this quantity. In the first year of production, sales of left-handed widgets run only at an annual level of 50,000. The directors, however, decide that the low level of sales can be attributed to the fact that the product is newly introduced and in the annual accounts the machine is recorded at its full net replacement cost.

In the second year left-handed widget sales reach an annual level of 75,000 and there is no indication that they will reach a higher level in future. As there is no prospect of reaching the anticipated annual sales level of 100,000 in the foreseeable future, the directors consider that the left-handed widget machine should be valued at an amount to take account of the lower level of production. The GRC of the machine therefore is estimated as being that of an alternative replacement with three-quarters of the capacity of the existing machine.

5.33    In certain circumstances it may be appropriate to consider the cost of a modern piece of machinery which has similar capacity to that of a battery of existing assets, or, more unusually, to consider the cost of a group of modern machines which together would replace the capacity of an existing one. In such cases a comparison should be made, in the manner described above for individual assets, between the GRC of the alternative machinery, adjusted as necessary to arrive at a modern equivalent of the existing machinery, and the current replacement cost of the existing machinery.

### Documentary evidence of expert estimates

5.34    Where an expert estimate is made of the cost of a modern equivalent asset the necessary documentary evidence should include details in respect of the calculation of operating cost savings and any differences in output and working lives as well as evidence of the cost of the alternative asset used as the basis of the calculation. Where estimates are made of the cost of replacing plant constructed by the company for its own use, documentary evidence should be produced of materials required and their current cost, labour rates and the estimated number of hours of production and any attributable overheads. In all cases the costs to be used should be those ruling at the balance sheet date.

### The use of indices

5.35    As explained in the previous chapter, changes in an index will never, except by chance, be a precise measure of changes in the replacement

68

cost of individual items covered by the index. Consequently the use of an index will probably provide less precise results than if estimates of replacement costs were made in respect of individual items of plant and machinery. On the other hand, an in-house index, because it is based on the experience of the company itself, will, if soundly constructed, be more relevant than a widely based published index.

### Using official indices

5.36 The CSO expects ultimately to publish monthly indices (normally period type indices) for fixed assets as follows:

(i) '**First provisional**' indices, approximately three weeks after the end of the month to which they relate (except that indices may not be available at this stage for some of the more detailed categories of assets);

(ii) '**Second provisional**' indices, approximately seven weeks after the end of the month to which they relate; and

(iii) '**Firm**' indices. These will usually be available about 12 weeks after the end of the month to which they relate, but in some cases the delay may be sixteen weeks. In such cases a '**third provisional**' index will be published after twelve weeks.

5.37 Ideally the 'firm' indices should be used but it is appreciated that tight accounting timetables at the accounting date may not allow companies to wait for the publication of 'firm' indices. In such circumstances it is permissible to use, in the absence of more up-to-date indices, either:

(a) The first provisional index for the month preceding the month in which the accounting date falls, or, where the accounting date falls in the first half of a calendar month, the first provisional index that relates to the next preceding month; or

(b) The directors' estimate of the index at the accounting date.

5.38 If by the time the accounts are prepared, but before the accounts are signed, more relevant official indices have been published and the directors are of the opinion that the application of such indices would result in a materially different figure for the Balance Sheet value of fixed assets and/or the charge for depreciation, the accounts should be adjusted to take account of the differences.

5.39 The nature (e.g. 'first provisional for November 1979', 'directors' estimate of year-end official index for . . .') of the index number used to arrive at the figures in the accounts should be disclosed in the notes to the accounts. To avoid changes necessitated by the publication of more relevant indices it is suggested that a directors' estimate of the year-end indices should be used thus minimising the likelihood of any material differences requiring adjustment.

5.40    There is no need to revise accounts prepared using provisional indices when the figures are displayed as comparative figures in the succeeding year. Similarly, when preparing the accounts for the succeeding year the index to be used as the denominator in the updating factor should be the index that was used as the numerator at the previous balance sheet date.

### Example 5.6

Public Company Limited makes up its accounts to 31st December annually. The Accounts Department is required to submit the 1976 accounts to the Board for approval and signature three weeks after the year-end and, once signed, the accounts are to be published at the end of February.

The most up-to-date official index available at the time the Accounts Department prepare the fixed asset and depreciation information for the accounts is the first provisional for November, published about 21st December, and this index is used for the accounts. By the time the Board meets to sign the accounts the second provisional for November and the first provisional for December are published. The Directors consider that had the first provisional for December been used instead of the first provisional for November, the depreciation charge for the year and the value of fixed assets would have been materially higher and they decide that the accounts must be adjusted to reflect these facts, before they are signed.

For the 1977 accounts the comparative figures will be those that appeared in the final 1976 accounts. The December 1976 asset values will be converted to December 1977 values by applying a factor using the first provisional for December 1976 as the denominator.

### Other published indices

5.41    Published indices from sources other than the United Kingdom Government Statistical Service may be used for revaluing assets in the same way as official indices, if they have been approved for use by the Accounting Standards Committee.

## DEPRECIATION

5.42    The general method of providing for depreciation using the net current replacement cost basis of valuation was described in paragraphs 5.9 to 5.11. The principle is that the charge for depreciation of plant and machinery in the Profit and Loss Account should equal the value to the business of plant and machinery consumed during the year. The annual charge may be based on:

(i) the sum of the monthly charges for depreciation made during the year where these are based on a monthly up-dating of asset values;

(ii) the average depreciable value for the year calculated before charging depreciation for the current period (see paragraph 5.45); or

(iii) the sum of the charges for periods in excess of a month (e.g. quarterly or half-yearly) if these charges have been based on the average depreciable value for the period.

### Management accounts

5.43    Where monthly management accounts are prepared and the charges for depreciation in those accounts are based on a monthly up-dating of asset values, the aggregate of the monthly charges will closely approximate to the theoretically correct charge for depreciation for the year. It makes little difference if the monthly depreciation charges are based on average for the month, beginning or end of the month asset values.

5.44    Where accounts are produced for longer than monthly periods (e.g. quarterly, half-yearly) depreciation charges should be based on average asset values and, except in the circumstances described in paragraph 5.48 below, it will not normally be appropriate in such cases to base the depreciation charge on values at the beginning or end of the period.

### Average depreciable values

5.45    In order to arrive at the average depreciable value of an asset for a period it is necessary first to obtain an adjusted value at the end of the period. The adjusted value is obtained by increasing the opening accumulated depreciation in the same proportion as the GRC has been increased during the period. This increase in the accumulated depreciation is the prior year backlog depreciation (see paragraph 5.5). The adjusted value is obtained by deducting the adjusted accumulated depreciation from the GRC at the end of the period.

### Example 5.7

At the beginning of the period:

|  | £ |
|---|---|
| Gross current replacement cost | 20,000 |
| Accumulated depreciation | 10,000 |
| Net current replacement cost | £10,000 |

During the period the GRC increases by 20%.

At end of period:

|  | £ |
|---|---|
| Gross current replacement cost £20,000 + 20% | 24,000 |
| Accumulated depreciation £10,000 + 20% | 12,000 |
| Adjusted value at the year-end (i.e. before depreciation for the year) | £12,000 |

5.46    The average depreciable value will normally be arrived at by averaging the net replacement cost at the beginning of the period and the adjusted value at the end of the period. If accounts are prepared annually it may exceptionally be necessary to calculate weighted averages where there have been material and uneven price changes during the year. This, however, would require the determination of GRCs at intervals (e.g. quarterly) during the year.

**Example 5.8**

(a) Change in value occurs evenly through the year

| | |
|---|---:|
| Net current replacement cost at beginning of year | £20,000 |
| Adjusted value at end of year | £30,000 |

Average depreciable value $\dfrac{(£20,000 + £30,000)}{2}$ = £25,000

(b) Change in value occurs at end of first quarter.

| | |
|---|---:|
| Net current replacement cost at beginning of year | £20,000 |
| Adjusted value at end of year | £30,000 |

Average depreciable value $\dfrac{(£20,000 \times 1) + (£30,000 \times 3)}{4}$ = £27,500

## Depreciation on additions

5.47 The depreciation charge for additions should be based on the average of the cost of the additions and their gross current replacement cost at the end of the period. (Exceptionally, however, it may be necessary to weight the average in a manner similar to that demonstrated in Example 5.8.)

**Example 5.9**

| | |
|---|---:|
| Additions at cost | £8,000 |
| GRC at year-end | £9,000 |
| Average depreciable value: | |

$\dfrac{£8,000 + £9,000}{2}$ = £8,500

## Depreciation based on year-end values

5.48 The charge for depreciation may be based on end-of-year values instead of average depreciable values if the calculation is considered to be easier in practice and is not likely to produce a materially different charge for depreciation from that based on the average depreciable value.

## Different methods for calculating depreciation

5.49 Throughout this book it has been assumed that the value of fixed assets is depreciated over the estimated remaining useful life of the assets on a straight line basis. Thus, if the GRC of an asset does not change throughout its life the depreciation charge to the Profit and Loss Account would be the same each year.

5.50 In an historical cost accounting system, the straight line method of calculating depreciation is not the only method of calculation available. Depreciation may be calculated for example on the declining balance method or, less frequently, on the sum of the digits method.

5.51 Methods of calculating depreciation other than the straight line method are not prohibited under CCA. It is necessary only to ensure that the method of calculation chosen produces a depreciation charge that fairly represents the value to the business of assets consumed during the year.

5.52    Whichever basis is adopted for calculating the charge for depreciation it should be disclosed in the notes to the accounts and should be consistently applied.

### The depreciation charge for the year

5.53    The depreciation charge for the year is calculated by apportioning the average depreciable value over a period equal to the expected remaining working life of the asset at the Balance Sheet date plus the period under review, i.e. the remaining useful life at the beginning of the accounting period.

### Example 5.10

| | |
|---|---|
| Average depreciable value | £18,000 |
| Estimated remaining useful life at year-end | 5 years |

Depreciation charge for the year:

$$\frac{£18,000}{(5 + 1)} = £3,000$$

### The remaining useful life of assets

5.54    The estimated remaining useful life of assets should be reviewed regularly, for major assets preferably annually, to enable physical wear and tear, changes in the commercial environment, and technology to be taken into account. It should be noted that, on the introduction of CCA, all assets still in use should be attributed a realistic value in the balance sheet. The treatment of fully depreciated assets still in use on the introduction of CCA is considered in paragraphs 7.25 and 7.26.

5.55    The requirement to calculate the charge for depreciation with reference to the estimated remaining useful life and net value of fixed assets is of particular relevance when there is a change (other than because of the lapse of time) in the estimate of remaining useful life. Where there is no change, the depreciation charge will be the same whether calculated with reference to remaining lives and net values or total lives and gross values. Thus, where no change in asset life is envisaged the practice of calculating depreciation as a fixed percentage of the gross value of the asset may continue, so long as the percentage represents a realistic proportion of the asset's total life.

### Changes in asset lives

5.56    The method used to calculate the charge for depreciation described in paragraph 5.53 above ensures that the correct charge for depreciation is made whether or not the estimate of the remaining useful life of the asset has changed during the year.

**Example 5.11**

At 31st December 1977 an asset is estimated to have a remaining useful life of 5 years and its net current replacement cost at that date is £25,000.

At 31st December 1978 the same asset is estimated as having a remaining useful life of 8 years because of a delay in the development of a new product that would have replaced the output of the existing machine.

The adjusted value of the existing machine at 31st December 1978 is £29,000.

The average depreciable value for 1978 is:

$$\frac{(£25,000 + £29,000)}{2} = £27,000$$

The depreciation charge for 1978 is:

$$\frac{£27,000}{(8 + 1)} = £3,000$$

**Backlog depreciation for the year**

5.57    As explained in paragraph 5.10, current year backlog depreciation is required to ensure that accumulated depreciation equals the gross current replacement cost of an asset at the end of its useful life.

5.58    The current year backlog depreciation is the difference between the actual depreciation charge for the year and a theoretical charge based on the adjusted value at the year-end.

**Example 5.12**

| | |
|---|---:|
| Net current replacement cost at 1st January | £18,000 |
| Adjusted value at 31st December | £22,000 |
| Estimated remaining useful life at 31st December | 3 years |

Average depreciable amount:

$$\frac{(£18,000 + £22,000)}{2} = £20,000$$

Depreciation charge for the year:

$$\frac{£20,000}{(3 + 1)} = £5,000$$

Current year backlog depreciation:

(i) Theoretical charge:

$$\frac{£22,000}{(3 + 1)} = £5,500$$

(ii) Current year backlog depreciation

$$£5,500 - £5,000 = £500$$

The accounting entry to record the current year backlog depreciation is:

Dr Revaluation Surplus £500
Cr Accumulated Depreciation £500

## ACQUISITIONS AND DISPOSALS

5.59 The accounting entries required to record the acquisition of fixed assets are the same both for a current cost system and for an historical cost system. With regard to the disposal of fixed assets, however, there is some difference between CCA and historical cost accounting resulting from the recording of unrealised surpluses on revaluations.

5.60 In an historical cost system the profit or loss on disposal is the difference between the sale proceeds, if any, and the historical net book value.

5.61 The procedure on disposal in a current cost system is the same as that in an historical cost system except that the asset is transferred to the Realisation Account on disposal at its value to the business at the previous accounting date rather than at its historical cost.

### Example 5.13

ABC Limited sells a machine at the beginning of its financial year for £2,000. The amounts recorded in the books of account in respect of the machine immediately prior to the sale were:

|  | £ |
|---|---|
| Gross current replacement cost (historical cost £6,000) | 10,000 |
| Accumulated depreciation | 9,000 |
| Net current replacement cost | £1,000 |

The accounting entries to record the disposal are:

|  |  |  | £ | £ |
|---|---|---|---|---|
| A | Dr | Realisation account | 10,000 | |
|  | Cr | Fixed asset account | | 10,000 |
|  |  | with the gross current replacement cost | | |
| B | Dr | Accumulated depreciation account | 9,000 | |
|  | Cr | Realisation account | | 9,000 |
|  |  | with accumulated depreciation on the asset sold | | |
| C | Dr | Cash/debtors | 2,000 | |
|  | Cr | Realisation account | | 2,000 |
|  |  | with the sale proceeds | | |

The Realisation Account will appear as follows:

Realisation Account

| | £ | | £ |
|---|---|---|---|
| Gross current replacement cost (A) | 10,000 | Accumulated depreciation (B) | 9,000 |
| | | Proceeds of sale (C) | 2,000 |
| Balance— | | | |
| Surplus on disposal | 1,000 | | |
| | £11,000 | | £11,000 |

75

5.62     Example 5.13 shows that a surplus of £1,000 has arisen at the date of disposal based upon the NRC at that date. This surplus can be regarded as being either the result of incorrectly valuing the machine at an NRC of £1,000 instead of £2,000 or the difference between the value to the business of the selling company and the value to the business of the purchasing company. The treatment of this surplus is considered below.

### Depreciation on disposals

5.63     In principle, when an asset is sold or scrapped, depreciation where applicable should be charged from the previous accounting date to the date of disposal. In practice this depreciation may not be material and can often be ignored and the balance on the realisation account can be credited or charged, as appropriate, to the profit and loss account as part of the charge for depreciation for the year. If, however, the depreciation for the period from the previous accounting date to the date of disposal is material, depreciation should be calculated for the period to the date of disposal and consideration should be given as to the appropriate treatment of the remaining balance on the realisation account.

This should normally be charged or credited to the profit and loss account, disclosed if appropriate as an exceptional or extraordinary item, but if the profit or loss can clearly be shown to have resulted from a movement in the replacement cost of the asset in the period since its previous revaluation it should be treated as a revaluation surplus or deficit.

### Example 5.14

(a) An asset with a net current replacement cost at 1st January of £1,000 is sold on 30th September for £900. Depreciation between 1st January and 30th September is treated as immaterial and the loss on sale of £100 is treated as part of the total depreciation charge for the year.

(b) A chemical plant valued at £150,000 at 1st January is sold on 30th June for £200,000. At the date of sale the plant had an estimated remaining useful life of 39 years, and its adjusted value at that date (estimated by the company's engineers) was £160,000.
Depreciation charge for the period up to the date of sale is:

$$\frac{(£150,000 + £160,000)}{2} \times \frac{1}{(39 + 1)} \times \frac{1}{2} = £1,937 \text{ say } £2,000$$

The directors consider that the balance on the Realisation Account of £52,000 (£50,000 + £2,000) should be treated as an extraordinary item because in their view the sale proceeds reflect the alternative use value of the asset attributed by the purchaser and the gain cannot be considered to have arisen through the normal operation of the business.

76

# ECONOMIC VALUE AND NET REALISABLE VALUE

5.64  In exceptional cases, the net current replacement cost of a group of assets taken together may be significantly in excess of the present value of those assets' future potential earning power (i.e. economic value). In such cases it would be appropriate to estimate the assets' economic value by reference to the present value of expected future cash flows and record the assets in the accounts at that value and not at their NRC. Similarly there will be occasions on which the value to the business of a fixed asset is its net realisable value rather than its NRC. The limited circumstances in which economic value or net realisable value may be regarded as the value of fixed assets in current cost accounts are considered in Chapter 7.

## BIRCHWOOD'S PLANT AND MACHINERY

5.65  The normal situations likely to be found by companies adopting CCA in respect of plant and machinery and similar asset categories have all now been covered. Certain special situations are considered in Chapter 7. Paragraphs 5.66 to 5.89 below, using the hypothetical company, Birchwood Limited, as an example, demonstrate the procedure required to convert plant and machinery from an historical cost basis to a current cost basis and the accounting procedure once CCA has been introduced.

**The CCA worksheet**

5.66  The Worksheet that is used throughout this book to prepare Birchwood's current cost accounts for the year ended 31st December 1979 is set out in Table 6.1 at the end of Chapter 6 with the HC Balance Sheet at 31st December 1978 in columns 1 and 2 of the Worksheet and the adjustments to convert fixed assets at 31st December 1978 to a CCA basis entered in columns 3 and 4. The accounting entries explained below in respect of plant and machinery as at 31st December 1978 have been entered in these columns against the relevant headings. The accounting entries in respect of land and buildings are considered in Chapter 6.

5.67  Birchwood's plant and machinery at 31st December 1978 is made up, in the HC Balance Sheet, as follows:

|  | £'000 |
|---|---|
| Cost | 23,899 |
| Accumulated depreciation | 8,453 |
| Net book value | 15,446 |

5.68  Birchwood's plant and machinery consists mainly of machines of low individual value but it also owns four specialised machines of high value. The directors decide that the four specialised machines should be valued based on the GRC estimated by the company's engineers. The other plant and machinery is to be valued by reference to official indices.

77

5.69  The company's engineers estimate the GRC and future working life of the specialised machines as follows:

|  | GRC £'000 | Future useful life at 31.12.1978 |
|---|---|---|
| Machine 1 | 340 | 1 year |
| Machine 2 | 410 | 4 years |
| Machine 3 | 400 | $4\frac{1}{4}$ years |
| Machine 4 | 445 | $4\frac{1}{2}$ years |
|  | 1,595 | |

5.70  The remainder of the company's plant and machinery is to be valued by reference to the official index of capital expenditure for the engineering and allied industries (ref. 1070). Before the index can be applied, however, the assets must be analysed by date of acquisition. This analysis produces results as follows:

|  | Cost £'000 | Accumulated Depreciation at 31.12.1978 £'000 |
|---|---|---|
| 1974 | 2,280 | 1,538 |
| 1975 | 4,222 | 2,249 |
| 1976 | 6,219 | 2,352 |
| 1977—1st quarter | 1,887 | 566 |
| 2nd quarter | 1,982 | 520 |
| 3rd quarter | 1,499 | 337 |
| 4th quarter | 1,118 | 210 |
| 1978—1st quarter | 824 | 123 |
| 2nd quarter | 1,013 | 114 |
| 3rd quarter | 368 | 28 |
| 4th quarter | 1,188 | 45 |
|  | 22,600 | 8,082 |

5.71  The appropriate index number for 31st December 1978 is 172·1 and the plant and machinery is updated by a factor calculated by using that number as the numerator and the average index number for the period of acquisition as the denominator as follows:

|  | (1) Historical Cost | (2) Historical Depn. | (3) Index at 31.12.78 | (4) Index on acquisition | (5) Factor (3) ÷ (4) | (6) Current (1) × (5) GRC | (7) Current (2) × (5) Depn. |
|---|---|---|---|---|---|---|---|
|  | £'000 | £'000 |  |  |  | £'000 | £'000 |
| 1974 | 2,280 | 1,538 | 172·1 | 100·0 | 1·721 | 3,924 | 2,647 |
| 1975 | 4,222 | 2,249 | 172·1 | 109·5 | 1·572 | 6,637 | 3,535 |
| 1976 | 6,219 | 2,352 | 172·1 | 115·9 | 1·485 | 9,235 | 3,493 |

| | (1) Historical Cost | (2) Historical Depn. | (3) Index at 31.12.78 | (4) Index on acquisition | (5) Factor (3) ÷ (4) | (6) Current GRC (1) × (5) | (7) Current Depn. (2) × (5) |
|---|---|---|---|---|---|---|---|
| 1977—1 | 1,887 | 566 | 172·1 | 120·1 | 1·433 | 2,704 | 811 |
| —2 | 1,982 | 520 | 172·1 | 123·9 | 1·389 | 2,753 | 722 |
| —3 | 1,499 | 337 | 172·1 | 127·8 | 1·347 | 2,019 | 454 |
| —4 | 1,118 | 210 | 172·1 | 131·2 | 1·312 | 1,467 | 276 |
| 1978—1 | 824 | 123 | 172·1 | 136·1 | 1·265 | 1,042 | 156 |
| —2 | 1,013 | 114 | 172·1 | 147·7 | 1·165 | 1,180 | 133 |
| —3 | 368 | 28 | 172·1 | 157·9 | 1·090 | 401 | 31 |
| —4 | 1,188 | 45 | 172·1 | 169·9 | 1·013 | 1,203 | 46 |
| | 22,600 | 8,082 | | | | 32,565 | 12,304 |

5.72 A similar procedure is followed to arrive at the net current replacement cost of the specialised machines at 31st December 1978 as follows:

| | (1) Historical Cost | (2) Historical Depn. | (3) GRC | (4) Depn. conversion factor (3) ÷ (1) | (5) Current depn. (2) × (4) |
|---|---|---|---|---|---|
| | £'000 | £'000 | £'000 | | £'000 |
| Machine 1 | 216 | 151 | 340 | 1·574 | 238 |
| Machine 2 | 309 | 124 | 410 | 1·327 | 165 |
| Machine 3 | 384 | 57 | 400 | 1·042 | 59 |
| Machine 4 | 390 | 39 | 445 | 1·141 | 44 |
| | 1,229 | 371 | 1,595 | | 506 |

5.73 The figures for total plant and machinery are therefore:

| | Historical Cost | Historical Depn. | Current GRC | Current Depn. |
|---|---|---|---|---|
| | £'000 | £'000 | £'000 | £'000 |
| Indexed Assets | 22,600 | 8,082 | 32,565 | 12,304 |
| Specialised Machines | 1,299 | 371 | 1,595 | 506 |
| Total | 23,899 | 8,453 | 34,160 | 12,810 |

5.74 The required accounting entries (A and B) to convert the historical cost Balance Sheet at 31st December 1978 to a CCA basis are therefore:

|  |  |  | £'000 | £'000 |
|---|---|---|---|---|
| A | Dr | Plant and machinery | 10,261 | |
| | Cr | Revaluation surplus | | 10,261 |

with the difference between the gross replacement cost of plant and machinery and their historical cost (34,160—23,899)

|  |  |  | £'000 | £'000 |
|---|---|---|---|---|
| B | Dr | Revaluation surplus | 4,357 | |
| | Cr | Accumulated depreciation | | 4,357 |

with prior year backlog depreciation being the difference between CCA depreciation and historical cost depreciation (12,810—8,453)

5.75    The above journal entries have been entered in columns 3 and 4 of the Worksheet (Table 6.1)

5.76    Birchwood considers that it will not, in the foreseeable future, sell its fixed assets in a situation that would result in a tax liability. Consequently no provision is made for deferred tax on the revaluation (see Chapter 10).

### Additions and disposals of Birchwood's plant and machinery

5.77    The next step is to record additions and disposals of plant and machinery during 1979. During this year Birchwood's purchases and sales of plant and machinery are as follows:

|  | £'000 |
|---|---|
| **Purchases**: 30th June | 6,036 |
| **Sales** at net current replacement cost: | |
|     Assets purchased in 1974 | 258 |
|     Assets purchased in 1975 | 117 |
| | 375 |
| **Sale proceeds** | 238 |

5.78    The purchases have been recorded in the expenditure column (column 7) in the Worksheet.

5.79    The Realisation Account in respect of the sales will appear as follows:

#### Realisation Account

| | £'000 | | £'000 |
|---|---|---|---|
| GRC of assets sold | 1,002 | Accumulated depreciation on asset sold | 627 |
| | | Sale proceeds | 238 |
| | | Balance—loss on disposal | 137 |
| | 1,002 | | 1,002 |

80

The relevant journal entries to eliminate the assets disposed of (journal entry a) have been entered in columns 9 and 10 in the Worksheet and the receipt of the sale proceeds is shown in column 8. The loss on sale (journal entry b in columns 9 and 10) not being a material amount, is treated as part of the depreciation charge for the year.

### Revaluation at 31st December 1979

5.80   The revaluation at 31st December 1979 is performed, so far as the assets valued with reference to the official index is concerned, by up dating the GRC and accumulated depreciation at the beginning of the year by reference to the movement in the index. The index number at 31st December 1978 used to value assets at that date was 172·1 and the equivalent index number at 31st December 1979 was 209·6. The up-dating factor is therefore:

$$\frac{209 \cdot 6}{172 \cdot 1} = 1 \cdot 218$$

and for non-specialised machines the revaluation amounts are:

| (1) | (2) | (3) | (4) | (5) | (6) | (7) | (8) | (9) |
| --- | --- | --- | --- | --- | --- | --- | --- | --- |
| | | | | | | | 31.12.79 | |
| 31.12.78 | | Disposals | | | | Updating Factor | GRC | Depn. before charge for the year |
| GRC | Depn. | GRC | Depn. | (1)–(3) | (2)–(4) | | (5) × (7) | (6) × (7) |
| £'000 | £'000 | £'000 | £'000 | £'000 | £'000 | | £'000 | £'000 |
| 32,565 | 12,304 | 1,002 | 627 | 31,563 | 11,677 | 1·218 | 38,444 | 14,223 |

5.81   The index number at the date of acquisition of the additions during the year was 195·6. The updating factor in respect of these assets is therefore:

$$\frac{209 \cdot 6}{195 \cdot 6} = 1 \cdot 072$$

and the revaluation amounts are therefore in £'000s

$$\text{Cost} \times \text{Factor} = \text{GRC}$$
$$6,036 \times 1 \cdot 072 = 6,471$$

5.82   The specialised assets on hand at 31st December 1979 are again valued by the company's engineers with the following results:

| Machine | 31.12.78 GRC | Depn. | Future Life | 31.12.79 GRC | Depn. (before charge for the year) | Future Life |
|---|---|---|---|---|---|---|
|  | £'000 | £'000 |  | £'000 | £'000 |  |
| 1 | 340 | 238 | 1 | 380 | 266 | – |
| 2 | 410 | 165 | 4 | 510 | 205 | 3 |
| 3 | 400 | 59 | $4\frac{1}{4}$ | 490 | 72 | 4 |
| 4 | 445 | 44 | $4\frac{1}{2}$ | 615 | 51 | 4 |
|  | 1,595 | 506 |  | 1,995 | 594 |  |

5.83   The figures for total plant and machinery are therefore:

| | 31.12.78 (after disposals) GRC | Depn. | 31.12.79 GRC | Depn. (before charge for the year) |
|---|---|---|---|---|
| | £'000 | £'000 | £'000 | £'000 |
| Indexed assets | 31,563 | 11,677 | 38,444 | 14,223 |
| Specialised machines | 1,595 | 506 | 1,995 | 594 |
| | 33,158 | 12,183 | 40,439 | 14,817 |
| Additions | 6,036 | — | 6,471 | — |
| Total | 39,194 | 12,183 | 46,910 | 14,817 |

5.84   The journal entries (c and d) required to record all the above revaluations are set out below and have been entered into the journal columns (columns 9 and 10) of the Worksheet (Table 6.1)

|  |  |  | £'000 | £'000 |
|---|---|---|---|---|
| c | Dr | Plant and machinery | 7,716 | |
|  | Cr | Revaluation surplus | | 7,716 |
| d | Dr | Revaluation surplus | 2,634 | |
|  | Cr | Provision for depreciation | | 2,634 |

with revaluation surpluses (46,910–39,194) and prior year back-log depreciation (14,817–12,183) arising on the revaluation at 31st December 1979.

**Depreciation charge for the year**

5.85   The first step in the calculation of the annual depreciation charge for the year is to establish estimates of the remaining useful lives at the end of the year. For this purpose assets must be analysed by reference to the year in which it is expected they will be scrapped. The period over which the assets are to be depreciated will then be from the beginning of the year under review to the end of the year in which the asset is expected to be scrapped (i.e. equivalent to the expected remaining useful life of the asset at the year end plus the year under review). The analysis of Birchwood's plant and machinery by expected year of retirement is set out in Table 5.1.

5.86 Once the remaining useful lives of the assets being depreciated have been established the next step is to calculate the average depreciable value for the year. That amount, for assets on hand at the beginning of the year (when calculating depreciation annually), is the simple arithmetic average of the net current replacement cost at the beginning of the year and the adjusted value at the year end. For additions in the year the average depreciable value is the simple arithmetic average of the cost of the asset and its GRC at the year end. (As noted in paragraph 5.46 exceptionally it may be necessary to calculate a weighted average.) The necessary calculations for Birchwood are shown in Table 5.1.

5.87 The depreciation charge for the year and the current year backlog depreciation can now be calculated as indicated in Table 5.1. The depreciation charge is arrived at by dividing the average depreciable value by the depreciable life shown in column 5. (For simplicity, a full year's depreciation has been charged in respect of additions.) The current year backlog depreciation is the difference between the actual depreciation charge and a depreciation charge based on the adjusted value of the asset at the year end calculated in the same way as the actual depreciation charge.

5.88 Birchwood's journal entries (e and f) to record the depreciation charge for the year and the current year backlog depreciation are:

|  |  |  | £'000 | £'000 |
|---|---|---|---|---|
| e | Dr | Profit and loss account | 6,626 | |
| | Cr | Accumulated depreciation | | 6,626 |
| | | with the depreciation charge for the year. | | |
| f | Dr | Revaluation surplus | 595 | |
| | Cr | Accumulated depreciation | | 595 |
| | | with the current year backlog depreciation. | | |

5.89 The above journal entries are recorded in columns 9 and 10 of the Worksheet (Table 6.1) and are the final entries needed to account for Birchwood's plant and machinery in the 1979 accounts. A summary of Birchwood's plant and machinery for 1979 is set out in Table 5.2.

**Table 5.1**

**BIRCHWOOD'S PLANT AND MACHINERY SCHEDULE FOR 1979**

| | (1) Year of retirement | (2) Net current replacement cost (after disposals) 31.12.78 | (3) Adjusted value 31.12.79 | (4) Average depreciable value for 1979 | (5) Depreciable life | (6) Depreciation charge (4) ÷ (5) | (7) Depreciation on adjusted value (3) ÷ (5) | (8) Current year backlog depreciation (7) − (6) |
|---|---|---|---|---|---|---|---|---|
| | | £'000 | £'000 | £'000 | | £'000 | £'000 | £'000 |
| Specials | | | | | | | | |
| 1 | 1979 | 102 | 114 | 108 | 1 | 108 | 114 | 6 |
| 2 | 1982 | 245 | 305 | 275 | 4 | 69 | 76 | 7 |
| 3 | 1983 | 341 | 418 | 380 | 5 | 76 | 84 | 8 |
| 4 | 1983 | 401 | 564 | 483 | 5 | 97 | 113 | 16 |
| Others | 1980 | 1,019 | 1,242 | 1,130 | 2 | 565 | 621 | 56 |
| | 1981 | 2,985 | 3,636 | 3,311 | 3 | 1,104 | 1,212 | 108 |
| | 1982 | 5,742 | 6,993 | 6,368 | 4 | 1,592 | 1,748 | 156 |
| | 1983 | 6,680 | 8,136 | 7,408 | 5 | 1,482 | 1,627 | 145 |
| | 1984 | 3,460 | 4,214 | 3,837 | 6 | 640 | 702 | 62 |
| | | 20,975 | | | | | | |
| Additions: | | | | | | | | |
| | 1985 | 6,036 | 6,471 | 6,254 | 7 | 893 | 924 | 31 |
| | | 27,011 | 32,093 | | | 6,626 | 7,221 | 595 |

**Table 5.2**

BIRCHWOOD LIMITED
PLANT AND MACHINERY
YEAR ENDED 31st DECEMBER 1976

|  | £'000 |
|---|---|
| Gross replacement cost at 1st January 1979 | 34,160 |
| Additions | 6,036 |
|  | 40,196 |
| *Less* disposals | 1,002 |
|  | 39,194 |
| Revaluation | 7,716 |
| Gross replacement cost at 31st December 1979 | 46,910 |
| Accumulated depreciation at 1st January 1979 | 12,810 |
| *Less* disposals | 627 |
|  | 12,183 |
| Backlog depreciation (2,634 + 595) | 3,229 |
| Depreciation charge | 6,626 |
| Accumulated depreciation at 31st December 1979 | 22,038 |
| Net current replacement cost at 1st January 1979 | 21,350 |
| Net current replacement cost at 31st December 1979 | 24,872 |

# 6 Fixed Assets— Land and Buildings

6.1   As explained in Chapter 1, the value to the business of assets is their deprival value. In the case of land and buildings the method used to estimate deprival value will depend to a large extent on the reason why the land and buildings are owned by the company. Principally this chapter deals only with land and buildings held by non-property companies for the purpose of carrying on their business, although, unless specifically excluded, the general rules also apply to property companies (as defined in ED 18). Land and building held by property companies are considered further in Chapter 7.

## FREEHOLD LAND AND BUILDINGS

### The normal basis of valuation

6.2   The value to the business of freehold land and buildings will normally be their open market value for their existing use plus estimated attributable acquisition costs, which should be taken to include stamp duty, legal costs and any agents' fees.

6.3   The terms 'open market value', and 'existing use' have the meanings given by The Royal Institution of Chartered Surveyors' Draft Guidance Note: *Current Cost Accounting: The Valuation of Fixed Assets* which is reproduced at Appendix B.

## OPEN MARKET VALUE

6.4   Open market value is a valuation after taking into account the degree of wear and tear at the date of the valuation. It is therefore a 'net value' (i.e. net of depreciation). A gross value will therefore not be available and consequently the normal accounting entries in respect of land and buildings are different from those for plant and machinery valued with reference to their net current replacement cost. The accounting entries are considered in paragraphs 6.13 and 6.14 below.

6.5   Open market values, or estimates thereof, should be determined, at least annually either by professional valuers or by the directors. In years when a professional valuation of particular properties is not undertaken, the directors should estimate values for the properties after consultation with their professional valuers.

### Frequency of professional valuations

6.6 Professional valuations should be carried out at intervals of not more than five years. The frequency of professional valuations will depend on the relative importance of freehold land and buildings in the accounts. Intervals of between three and five years will be normal but valuations should be made more frequently if:

(a) the relevant assets represent a major proportion of the company's gross assets; or
(b) there have been considerable market variations or major changes in the property assets since the previous professional valuation.

6.7 In addition to the considerations outlined in the preceding paragraph the period between professional valuations should be decided by the directors in the light of:

(a) the number of properties to be valued and their value individually;
(b) the significance of the depreciation charge on buildings in the profit and loss account.

6.8 It is not intended that the interval between professional valuations should be fixed in any way except that it may not exceed five years. Within this limit the interval can be increased or decreased at the discretion of the directors although it is suggested that any proposal to increase the interval should be discussed with the company's auditors.

### Professionally qualified valuers

6.9 The valuation of land and buildings should be carried out by professionally qualified valuers who have post-qualification valuation experience and have knowledge of valuing properties in the location and category of the company's properties. In the United Kingdom such persons will be corporate members of one or more of the following professional bodies:

(a) The Royal Institution of Chartered Surveyors
(b) The Incorporated Society of Valuers and Auctioneers
(c) The Rating and Valuation Association.

Members of these professional bodies are aware of the valuation requirements of CCA and will normally be prepared to issue valuation certificates for the purpose and to provide a figure for the 'depreciable amount' (see paragraph 6.17 below).

### The cost of valuations

6.10 Whilst no guidance can be given as to the likely cost of employing the services of external professional valuers, it is worth noting that the Inland Revenue have confirmed to the IASG that the practice of allowing as a deduction from taxable income the cost of valuations for the purposes of Section 16(1)(a) of the Companies Act 1967 will be extended to cover the cost of valuations for inclusion in published current cost accounts. Also, it will often be possible to negotiate with the valuers for substantial reductions from scale fees for large jobs and for repeat valuations.

### Intermediate valuation procedures

6.11 In the years between professional valuations the directors should estimate, in consultation with their professional valuers, the value to the business of their land and buildings. These intermediate estimates should take into account:

(a) Variations in market prices.
(b) Additional properties acquired.
(c) Additions to and the refurbishment of existing buildings.
(d) Disposals.
(e) Changes in usage.
(f) Increases in construction costs.

6.12 Intermediate valuation estimates will be subject to audit by the company's auditors. It is therefore important to ensure that the estimates are prepared on a reasonable and consistent basis and that they are supported by documentary evidence. For example, the company's professional valuers may be able to provide the directors with information on local property values and on construction costs. They might also be prepared to provide the directors with an estimate of the increase in the value of a property resulting from improvements to the property during the year.

### Accounting treatment on revaluation

6.13 As explained above, the value placed on land and buildings will always be a 'net value', i.e. the valuation will always recognise the current condition of the property. Consequently a separate depreciation provision account is not maintained and there is no question of providing for backlog depreciation on a revaluation. The amount debited or credited to the asset account on a revaluation is therefore simply the difference between the current value (which will be after depreciation for the period) and the previously recorded value. If depreciation up to the date of valuation has not been previously recorded (as will normally be the case except on the first introduction of CCA as in Example 6.1) the journal entry in the case of a valuation resulting in a surplus will be:

(a) Dr Land and buildings
with the increase in value
(b) Dr Profit and loss account
with depreciation up to the date of valuation

(c) Cr   Revaluation surplus
        with the surplus on valuation (a) + (b).

The calculation of the depreciation charge is considered in paragraphs 6.15 to 6.21 below.

6.14   An accumulated depreciation account is not maintained in respect of land and buildings in a CCA system. Therefore, on the introduction of CCA, any balance on such an account should be closed and the balance transferred to the appropriate asset account as follows:

Dr   Provision for depreciation
Cr   Land and buildings
        with the accumulated depreciation at the date of the introduction of CCA.

### Example 6.1

PQR Limited adopted a CCA system on 1st January 1978. At that date the balances in the books in respect of freehold land and buildings were:

|  | £ |
|---|---|
| Cost | 150,000 |
| Depreciation (buildings) | 20,000 |
| | £130,000 |

The company's valuers who were asked to value the company's property at 1st January 1978 reported that freehold land and buildings had a value at that date of £200,000.

The accounting entries on the introduction of CCA are therefore:

|  | £ | £ |
|---|---|---|
| Dr   Provision for depreciation | 20,000 | |
| Cr   Freehold land and buildings | | 20,000 |
| Dr   Freehold land and buildings | 70,000 | |
| Cr   Revaluation surplus | | 70,000 |

The ledger accounts will appear as follows:

### Provision for Depreciation

| 1.1.78 | Transfer to asset account | £20,000 | 1.1.78 | Balance | £20,000 |
|---|---|---|---|---|---|

### Freehold Land and Buildings

| 1.1.78 | Balance brought forward | 150,000 | 1.1.78 | Transfer from depreciation | 20,000 |
|---|---|---|---|---|---|
| 1.1.78 | Revaluation | 70,000 | 1.1.78 | Revised balance carried forward— value | 200,000 |
| | | £220,000 | | | £220,000 |

### Revaluation Surplus

| | | | 1.1.78 | Freehold land and buildings | £70,000 |
|---|---|---|---|---|---|

## DEPRECIATION OF FREEHOLD LAND AND BUILDINGS

### Land

6.15 Depreciation will not normally be provided on freehold land except in special circumstances such as in the case of a mine or quarry, or where it has a high existing use value for a limited period of time such as a chemical waste dump.

### Freehold buildings

6.16 Depreciation should be provided on all freehold buildings based on their future economic useful life.

For years in which a professional valuation is carried out the future economic useful life will be estimated by the valuers in consultation with the directors. In the intervening years the directors may assume, unless there is evidence to the contrary, that the future economic useful life reduces evenly with the passage of time. Thus, if the valuers estimate that a building has a future economic useful life of 40 years at the date of valuation it can normally be assumed that one year later the building's future economic useful life will be 39 years.

### The depreciable amount

6.17 The nature of an open market valuation is such that it is not possible to arrive at a valuation for buildings as distinct from the site on which the buildings are situated. There is need, however, for a value of the buildings on which to base the charge for depreciation. Such value will be advised by the valuers for CCA purposes. This value, or the open market value of the land and buildings if lower, is called '*the depreciable amount*'. The difference, if any, between the depreciable amount and the open market value of the land and buildings is called '*the residual amount*'.

6.18 In years between professional valuations the directors should calculate an estimated depreciable amount by the application of an index of construction costs to the depreciable amount advised by the valuers on the occasion of the last professional valuation. The GSS compiles such an index which is published in *Price Index Numbers for Current Cost Accounting* (see paragraph 4.22).

### Example 6.2

At the end of year 6 the depreciable amount advised by the valuers was £50,000, and the official index of construction costs was 110.

A professional valuation was not carried out at the end of year 7 at which date the official index of construction costs stood at 120.

The depreciable amount at the end of year 7 is calculated as:

$$\frac{120}{110} \times £50,000 = £54,500 \text{ (approx)}.$$

### The charge for depreciation in the profit and loss account when there is a professional valuation

6.19    In years at the end of which a professional valuation of property has been carried out, the charge for depreciation on buildings in the profit and loss account is arrived at by dividing the depreciable amount at the balance sheet date by the remaining economic useful life of the buildings at the year end rather than the remaining life at the beginning of the year as for plant and machinery. This life is appropriate because the depreciable amount is already net of the depreciation for the year. Also it should be noted that because of practical difficulties it is not considered necessary to calculate an average depreciable value as in the case of plant and machinery.

6.20    Example 6.3 demonstrates the procedure on revaluation and the calculation of the depreciation charge in a year in which a professional valuation is made.

### Example 6.3

ABC Limited owned freehold land and buildings at 31st December 1977 which were recorded on the company's accounts at that date at an open market value of £500,000. The depreciable amount at 31st December 1977 was estimated at £360,000. At 31st December 1978 the company's valuer placed a value on the land and buildings of £575,000 and estimated the depreciable amount at £390,000. The valuer considered that at 31st December 1978 the remaining economic useful life of the building was 40 years.

The depreciation charge therefore is to be based on 40 years (i.e. $2\frac{1}{2}$%).

|                                                   | £  | £       |
|---------------------------------------------------|----|---------|
| The depreciation charge for the year is therefore:|    |         |
| £390,000 × $2\frac{1}{2}$%                         |    | 9,750   |
| The valuation at 31st December 1977 was           |    | 500,000 |
| The valuation at 31st December 1978 was           |    | 575,000 |
| The movement during the year was therefore        |    | 75,000  |

Made up of:

|                    |    |        |
|--------------------|----|--------|
| Depreciation       | Dr | 9,750  |
| Revaluation surplus| Cr | 84,750 |

91

The accounting entry is therefore:

|    |                           | £      | £      |
|----|---------------------------|--------|--------|
| Dr | Freehold land and buildings | 75,000 |        |
| Dr | Profit and loss account    | 9,750  |        |
| Cr | Revaluation surplus        |        | 84,750 |

## Depreciation in years between professional valuations

6.21    In years between professional valuations the charge for depreciation on buildings in the profit and loss account is arrived at by dividing the directors' estimated depreciable amount at the balance sheet date by the remaining economic useful life of the building *at the date of the last professional valuation*. The reason for this is that the directors' estimated depreciable amount, unlike the professional valuers' depreciable amount, does not take into account depreciation since the last valuation. (If it does the procedure is the same as if there has been a professional valuation.)

### Example 6.4

Continuing Example 6.3 the directors' estimate that the depreciable amount (before depreciation) at 31st December in the years 1979 to 1981 are:

|      | £       |
|------|---------|
| 1979 | 400,000 |
| 1980 | 420,000 |
| 1981 | 450,000 |

The depreciation charge in these years is calculated as follows:

| 1979 | £400,000 ÷ 40 = £10,000 |
| 1980 | £420,000 ÷ 40 = £10,500 |
| 1981 | £450,000 ÷ 40 = £11,250 |

In 1982 a professional valuation is carried out the results of which are that the depreciable amount at 31st December 1982 is £400,000 and the remaining economic useful life of the building at that date is 36 years.

The depreciation charge for 1982 is therefore:

$$£400,000 ÷ 36 = £11,111$$

## OTHER METHODS OF VALUATION OF FREEHOLD LAND AND BUILDINGS

### Depreciated replacement cost

6.22    It may not be possible for a valuer to arrive at an open market value for land and buildings if there are no comparable market transactions. This may be because of the specialised nature of the building, its particular use, its location or otherwise. A large works complex, a sports stadium or a specialised chemical processing factory may be cases where no open market valuation could be made. In such circumstances the value of the building should be calculated on a 'depreciated replacement cost' (drc) basis.

6.23 The drc for a building is its estimated current gross replacement cost reduced by an amount to take account of the physical wear and tear of the existing building and its obsolescence. The drc is therefore notified as a 'net' value. When the valuation is to be made on a drc basis it is important that the valuer consults the directors in order to arrive at the amount to be deducted to take account of depreciation because the future economic useful life of the building may depend not only on its physical life but also on the length of time the building can be profitably employed for its existing use. For example, the building housing a chemical processing plant may have a physical life of 10 years but the directors may consider that the profitable sale of the product being manufactured at the plant may only be able to continue for a further 5 years. When buildings are valued on a drc basis depreciation should be based on the drc at the year end.

6.24 When buildings are valued on a drc basis the associated land will be valued on the basis of its open market value as a vacant site for its existing use, plus acquisition costs.

**Example 6.5**

ABC Chemicals Limited owns a freehold factory which the company's valuers are unable to value on an open market value basis. The valuers therefore value the factory on a drc basis at £100,000 and value the related land at open market value for existing use, plus acquisition costs, at £20,000. They estimate that the building has a future physical life of 40 years but the directors consider that the factory's products will only be sold profitably for a further 20 years and that it has no alternative use.

The factory and site will be shown on the accounts at a value of £120,000 and the depreciation charge for the year will be £5,000 (£100,000 ÷ 20).

6.25 When buildings are valued on a drc basis the value, in years for which a professional valuation is performed, should be arrived at in the same way as the depreciable amount is arrived at for properties valued with reference to their open market value (see paragraph 6.17). Similarly, the depreciation charge for years in which no professional valuation is carried out should be based on the estimated remaining economic useful life of the building at the date of the last professional valuation (see paragraph 6.21).

## LEASEHOLD LAND AND BUILDINGS

6.26 Leasehold land and buildings should be valued in the same way as freehold land and buildings. There may be circumstances, however, in which a lease could have a negative value, for example, because of:

(a) market variations whereby the current rent payable becomes above the open market rent;

(b) the provisions of full repairing leases when the maintenance expenditure or other obligations are expected to be particularly onerous.

6.27    Where the negative value arises because of market variations in property rents the negative value should either be deducted from the positive value of other leases or shown as a liability.

6.28    Where the negative value of the lease is the result of onerous obligations under the lease a provision for the relevant expenditure should be set up by debiting profit and loss account and crediting a suitably titled provision account.

6.29    When provisions are made for commitments under leases, expenditure incurred in meeting the commitments should be charged against the provision and not against the profit and loss account.

### Depreciation of leasehold land and buildings

6.30    A depreciable amount will be advised by the valuer of leasehold property in the same way as for freehold property. Both the depreciable amount and the residual amount, if any, should be depreciated, however, since the leaseholder's interest in both the buildings and the land may be limited by the term of the lease. The lease should be depreciated as follows:

(a) **the depreciable amount**—over the shorter of the remaining economic useful life of the building and the remaining period of the lease, and

(b) **the residual amount**—over the remaining period of the lease.

### Example 6.6

Forest Properties Ltd. has a number of leasehold properties. The majority of these leases involve rents at market values and have, therefore, no value.

The lease for a property in Copse Road gives the company the benefit of a rental below market rates and the company's valuers have placed a value of £100,000 on it at 31st December 1977. The lease is included in the balance sheet at that amount and the year's depreciation is calculated by dividing the amount by the remaining term of the lease (8 years).

Depreciation in 1976 is:

$$\frac{100,000}{8} = £12,500$$

94

The value at the beginning of the year was £95,000 and the following entries are made:

|  |  | £ | £ |
|---|---|---|---|
| Dr | Depreciation | 12,500 | |
| Dr | Leasehold property | 5,000 | |
| Cr | Revaluation surplus | | 17,500 |

The Leasehold Property account will appear as follows:

Leasehold Property—Copse Road

| | £ | | £ |
|---|---|---|---|
| 1.1.77 Balance brought forward | 95,000 | 31.12.77 Depreciation | 12,500 |
| 31.12.77 Revaluation | 17,500 | Balance carried forward | 100,000 |
| | £112,500 | | £112,500 |

## IMPROVEMENTS TO PROPERTIES

6.31   Where expenditure is incurred on the improvement to property such expenditure should be debited to the relevant fixed asset account and not to profit and loss account. The next valuation of the property after the improvements have been made will take account of the increased value of the property as a result of the improvements. It should be noted that the increase in the value of the property as a result of improvement may not be as great as the cost of those improvements.

### Example 6.7

Beechtree Limited owns the freehold of a property which had a value of £200,000 in the balance sheet at the 31st December 1978. During June 1979 it carried out and paid for improvements to the property costing £70,000. At the end of the year the company's valuers place a value on the improved property of £250,000 of which £200,000 was the depreciable amount and assessed its remaining economic useful life as 50 years.

The accounting entries are:

|  |  | £ | £ |
|---|---|---|---|
| Dr | Freehold property | 70,000 | |
| Cr | Cash/Creditors | | 70,000 |

with the cost of improvements.

(The above entry is made at time improvements are made)

|  |  | £ | £ |
|---|---|---|---|
| Dr | Revaluation surplus | 16,000 | |
| Dr | Profit and loss account | 4,000 | |
| Cr | Freehold property | | 20,000 |

with the revaluation of property at the year-end and depreciation for the year.

The ledger account for the freehold property will appear as follows:

Freehold Property

| | £ | | £ |
|---|---|---|---|
| 1.1.79 Balance brought forward | 200,000 | 31.12.79 Revaluation | 20,000 |
| 30.6.79 Cost of improvements | 70,000 | 31.12.79 Balance carried forward | 250,000 |
| | £270,000 | | £270,000 |

## LAND AND BUILDINGS THAT ARE NOT OWNER OCCUPIED

6.32    A company's land and buildings may not all be owner occupied. In such circumstances the valuer will arrive at an open market value with reference to any potential use. If, however, the company plans to occupy the property it should be valued as owner occupied land and buildings with reference to its planned use. Any land and buildings which have become surplus to the company's requirements and for which there is an intention to sell, should be valued at their net realisable value. This is discussed further in the following chapter.

## ALTERNATIVE USE VALUE

6.33    Alternative use value should not be used as the basis of valuation for land and buildings unless there is an intention to sell them, in which case the alternative use value may be the net realisable value. The alternative use value should be reported in the directors' report, however, if it materially exceeds the existing use value.

## BIRCHWOOD'S LAND AND BUILDINGS

6.34    The procedure adopted in respect of plant and machinery in the previous chapter will now be continued and the principles involved in accounting for land and buildings will be demonstrated by continuing the preparation of Birchwood's current cost accounts for the year ended 31st December 1979.

6.35    Birchwood's historical cost balance sheet at 31.12.1978 as set out in Table 3.1 includes an amount for land and buildings made up as follows:

| | Cost | Depreciation | Net |
|---|---|---|---|
| | £'000 | £'000 | £'000 |
| Freehold land and buildings | 3,296 | — | 3,296 |
| Leasehold land and buildings | 1,423 | 569 | 854 |
| | 4,719 | 569 | 4,150 |

In addition to the leasehold property included in the balance sheet, Birchwood also held three leasehold properties for which no premium was paid and on which no subsequent capital expenditure has been incurred.

6.36 Birchwood's first full current cost accounts are in respect of the year ended 31st December 1979 and professional valuations were prepared at that date by the company's valuers. The directors, in consultation with the valuers, estimated the value of the company's property at 31st December 1978 as follows:

|  | Value | Depreciable amount | Residual amount |
|---|---|---|---|
|  | £'000 | £'000 | £'000 |
| Freehold—owner occupied |  |  |  |
| Open market value existing use | 1,020 | 840 | 180 |
| Depreciated replacement cost | 2,710 | 2,710 | — |
| Freehold—unoccupied |  |  |  |
| Open market value | 490 | 490 | — |
|  | 4,220 | 4,040 | 180 |
| Leasehold—owner occupied |  |  |  |
| Open market value existing use | 1,140 | 1,140 | — |
| Open market value existing use (negative) | (20) | (20) | — |
|  | 1,120 | 1,120 | — |
| Total | 5,340 | 5,160 | 180 |

The land associated with the buildings valued at depreciated replacement cost is included in the residual amount of £180,000 as it is valued as bare land at open market value for existing use. The negative value of £20,000 for leasehold property is in respect of a lease which commenced in 1965 on which the annual rent is now in excess of current market rates.

### Adjusted opening balances

6.37 The accounting entries to adjust the opening historical cost figures to a CCA basis are set out in the following paragraphs but the first accounting entry (Journal entry C in Table 6.1 columns 3 and 4) on the introduction of CCA is:

|  | £'000 | £'000 |
|---|---|---|
| Dr Depreciation | 569 |  |
| Cr Leasehold land and buildings with the accumulated depreciation at the date of change to CCA |  | 569 |

6.38 It will be recalled from paragraph 6.4 that only net values will be available once CCA is introduced and this first entry closes the depreciation provision accounts which will no longer be required.

6.39 The historical cost opening value is now adjusted to current value as follows:

|  | CCA value | HC | Increase |
|---|---|---|---|
|  | £'000 | £'000 | £'000 |
| Freehold | 4,220 | 3,296 | 924 |
| Leasehold | 1,120 | 854 | 266 |
| Total | 5,340 | 4,150 | 1,190 |

Birchwood does not intend to sell any of its property in the foreseeable future and therefore no deferred tax provision is required (see Chapter 10). The accounting entry (Journal entry D in Table 6.1, columns 3 and 4) is therefore:

|  |  | £'000 | £'000 |
|---|---|---|---|
| Dr | Freehold property | 924 |  |
| Dr | Leasehold property | 266 |  |
| Cr | Revaluation surplus with the increase in value |  | 1,190 |
|  |  | 1,190 | 1,190 |

**Valuations at 31st December 1979**

6.40 The results of the professional valuation at 31st December 1979 were as follows:

|  | Value | Depreciable amount | Residual amount | Remaining economic useful life |
|---|---|---|---|---|
|  | £'000 | £'000 | £'000 |  |
| Freehold-owner occupied |  |  |  |  |
| Open market value existing use | 1,150 | 770 | 380 | 40 years |
| Depreciated replacement cost | 3,560 | 3,560 | — | 35 years |
| Freehold-unoccupied |  |  |  |  |
| Open market value | 400 | 400 | — | 20 years |
|  | 5,110 | 4,730 | 380 |  |

|  | £'000 | £'000 | £'000 | |
|---|---|---|---|---|
| Leasehold-owner occupied | | | | |
| Open market value | | | | |
| existing use | 580 | 580 | — | 9 years |
| | 450 | 450 | — | 16 years |
| | (20) | (20) | — | 3 years |
| | 30 | 30 | — | 5 years |
| | 25 | 25 | — | 12 years |
| | 1,065 | 1,065 | — | |
| Total | 6,175 | 5,795 | 380 | |

### Depreciation charge for the year

6.41 The depreciation for the year is calculated by dividing the depreciable amount by the number of years of remaining economic useful life. The results are as follows:

| | | Depreciation | |
|---|---|---|---|
| | | £'000 | £'000 |
| Freehold: | | | |
| Open market value | | | |
| —owner occupied | 770 ÷ 40 | 19 | |
| —unoccupied | 400 ÷ 20 | 20 | |
| | | | 39 |
| Depreciated replacement cost | 3,560 ÷ 35 | | 101 |
| | | | 140 |
| Leasehold: | | | |
| | 480 ÷ 9 | 64 | |
| | 450 ÷ 16 | 28 | |
| | (20) ÷ 3 | (7) | |
| | 30 ÷ 5 | 6 | |
| | 25 ÷ 12 | 2 | |
| | | | 93 |
| | | | 233 |

### Recording the revaluation at the year-end and the depreciation for the year

6.42 The revaluation at the year-end and the depreciation for the year for each category of land and buildings is recorded in journal entry (g) in Table 6.1, columns 9 and 10 as follows:

| | | £'000 | £'000 | £'000 |
|---|---|---|---|---|
| Dr | Freehold land and buildings (5,110 − 4,220) | 890 | | |
| Cr | Leasehold land and buildings (1,120 − 1,065) | (55) | 835 | |
| Dr | Profit and loss account—depreciation | | 233 | |
| Cr | Revaluation surplus | | | 1,068 |
| | | | 1,068 | 1,068 |

# Table 6.1

**BIRCHWOOD LIMITED**
CCA Worksheet

| | 1 | 2 | 3 | 4 | 5 | 6 |
|---|---|---|---|---|---|---|
| | Opening balance sheet historical cost | | Opening balance sheet journal | | Opening balance sheet current cost | |
| | Dr £'000 | Cr £'000 | Dr £'000 | Cr £'000 | Dr £'000 | Cr £'000 |
| Land and buildings | 4,719 | 569 | C 569<br>D 1,190 | C 569 | 5,340 | |
| Plant and machinery | 15,446 | | A 10,261 | B 4,357 | 21,350 | |
| Investment in subsidiaries and associates | 13,984 | | | | | |
| Quoted and unquoted investments | 1,147 | | | | | |
| Stock and work in progress | 51,313 | | | | | |
| Debtors | 32,727 | | | | | |
| Cash | 465 | | | | | |
| Creditors | | 23,011 | | | | |
| Current tax | | 3,582 | | | | |
| Bank overdraft | | 6,481 | | | | |
| Dividend | | 5,700 | | | | |
| Deferred Tax | | 20,222 | | | | |
| Ordinary share capital | | 32,185 | | | | |
| Reserves – general | | 14,051 | | | | |
| Reserves – revaluation | | | B 4,357 | A 10,261<br>D 1,190 | | |
| Preference share capital | | 4,000 | | | | |
| 10% Debentures | | 10,000 | | | | |
| Realisation of fixed assets | | | | | | |
| Revenue income | | | | | | |
| Revenue expenditure | | | | | | |
| Depreciation | | | | | | |
| Interest | | | | | | |
| Tax expense | | | | | | |
| Dividends received | | | | | | |
| Revenue surplus | | | | | | |
| | 119,801 | 119,801 | | | | |

100

| 7 | 8 | 9 | 10 | 11 | 12 | 13 | 14 |
|---|---|---|---|---|---|---|---|
| Income and expenditure for 1979 | | Journal entries | | Profit and loss account for 1979 | | Closing balance sheet | |
| Dr £'000 | Cr £'000 | Dr £'000 | Cr £'000 | Dr £'000 | Cr £'000 | Dr £'000 | Cr £'000 |
| | | g 835 | | | | | |
| 6,036 | | a 627 ⎫ c 7,716 ⎭ | a 1,002 ⎫ d 2,634 ⎪ e 6,626 ⎬ f 595 ⎭ | | | | |
| 139 | | | | | | | |
| | 295,290 | | | | | | |
| 1,319 | 465 | | | | | | |
| 283,487 | | | | | | | |
| 3,582 | | | | | | | |
| 6,481 | 3,430 | | | | | | |
| 5,980 | | | | | | | |
| | 8,000 | | | | | | |
| | | d 2,634 ⎫ f 595 ⎭ | c 7,716 ⎫ g 1,068 ⎭ | | | | |
| | 238 | a 1,002 | b 137 ⎫ a 627 ⎭ | | | | |
| | | e 6,626 ⎫ b 137 ⎬ g 233 ⎭ | | | | | |
| 1,319 | | | | | | | |
| | 920 | | | | | | |
| 308,343 | 308,343 | | | | | | |

6.43 Birchwood's land and buildings may be summarised on a CCA basis as follows:

|  | Freehold land and buildings | | Leasehold land and buildings | Total |
|---|---|---|---|---|
|  | At open market value | At depreciation replacement cost | At open market value |  |
|  | £'000 | £'000 | £'000 | £'000 |
| At 1.1.79 | 1,510 | 2,710 | 1,120 | 5,340 |
| Depreciation charge for the year | 39 | 101 | 83 | 233 |
|  | 1,471 | 2,609 | 1,027 | 5,107 |
| Revaluation | 79 | 951 | 38 | 1,068 |
| At 31.12.79 | 1,550 | 3,560 | 1,065 | 6,175 |

# 7 The Treatment of Special Cases— Fixed Assets

7.1    This chapter deals with a number of matters relating to fixed assets and depreciation which, it is believed, will be of relevance only in a limited number of cases. For the convenience of the reader the matters dealt with in this chapter are listed below, together with the relevant paragraph numbers:

|  | Paragraphs |
|---|---|
| Economic value | 7.2–7.12 |
| Net realisable value | 7.13–7.20 |
| Changes in the basis of valuation | 7.21 |
| The treatment of changes in value | 7.22 |
| Disclosure of the effects of introducing CCA | 7.23 |
| Changes in asset lives | 7.24 |
| Fully depreciated assets | 7.25–7.26 |
| Leased assets other than land and buildings | 7.27–7.37 |
| Fixed assets in the course of construction | 7.38–7.41 |
| The treatment of capital based Government grants | 7.42–7.44 |
| Special provisions relating to property companies | 7.45–7.46 |

## ECONOMIC VALUE

7.2    It is appropriate to value assets at their economic value when that value is less than the net current replacement cost but higher than the net realisable value of the assets concerned. It is expected that this situation will arise only infrequently. Nevertheless there may be occasions on which the directors should consider whether economic value is the appropriate basis of valuation for fixed assets in the current cost Balance Sheet.

### Land and buildings

7.3    The economic value of land and buildings valued with reference to their open market value need not be considered since the open market value of land and buildings is not materially affected by the activities currently undertaken by the owner. Thus, except in the case of a forced sale, the fact that the owner of a property is carrying on business at an uneconomical rate of return will have no significant effect on the open market value of the property. In such circumstances, therefore, it is not appropriate to write-down land and buildings to economic value, even if an economic value could be determined.

7.4 When an open market value is not available buildings will normally be valued on the basis of their depreciated replacement cost. In such cases the situation is analogous to that for plant and machinery and if the building is part of an unprofitable operation it, together with all the fixed assets associated with that operation, including the land, may need to be valued on the basis of economic value.

### Example 7.1

XYZ Limited owns a Paper Mill for which no open market value can be established. The company's valuers have estimated that the depreciated replacement cost of the building is £150,000 but the directors consider that the Mill, which currently runs at a loss, will never achieve an adequate rate of return.

The directors consider that a value of £150,000 is excessive and that the economic value of the Mill as a whole, based on expected future earnings, is £100,000 and it is included in the accounts at this figure.

7.5 In Example 7.1 it is worth noting that although the Mill was currently in a loss making situation the operation still had some value because the directors foresaw some return in the future.

7.6 A similar situation arises when, although a company is currently achieving an inadequate rate of return, the directors consider that an improved rate of return is likely. In such cases, although there is *prima facie* evidence that an adequate rate of return is not being made, the directors must decide whether the full depreciated replacement cost can be justified by the **potential** profitability of the operation or whether a write-down of the operation as a whole to its economic value should be made to reflect the lower level of profitability currently being achieved.

### Plant and machinery

7.7 Plant and machinery should be valued on the basis of economic value only where, because cash flows to be derived from the use of the assets are inadequate, there is no economic justification for replacing the existing assets at the end of their useful life.

7.8 In such circumstances, and only for groups of assets for which the cash flow can be separately identified, the directors should use as the economic value of assets the discounted present value of the estimated future cash flows.

7.9 In calculating the present value of estimated future cash flows, regard should be paid to the following guidelines:

104

(i) The cash flow has to be reasonably foreseeable both as to amount and timing and should include appropriate allowances for expected price changes.

(ii) An appropriate rate of discount to be applied in arriving at the present value of future cash flows would be the particular company's money cost of capital, i.e. the estimated or actual rate at which the company could raise finance for the same period as the cash flow is anticipated.

(iii) Cash flows and the cost of capital should normally be calculated before taking into account the incidence of taxation. This treatment will produce values on a basis consistent with that of assets valued at their NRC or NRV.

**Example 7.2**

Grommit Limited runs an operating unit which produces 200,000 grommits per annum. The company has found that the grommit market is price sensitive and the directors consider that it will never be possible to increase sufficiently the selling price of grommits to earn a reasonable rate of return. Consequently the directors have decided that at the end of the physical life of the plant, or earlier if it proves economical to do so, the company's grommit business will be terminated.

The grommit operating unit will be valued for CCA purposes at its estimated economic value.

The estimate of the economic value might proceed as follows:

| | |
|---|---|
| Expected remaining useful life of the operating unit | 8 years |
| But period over which amount and timing of cash flow can be reasonably foreseen | 5 years |

| | Year | | | | |
|---|---|---|---|---|---|
| | 1 | 2 | 3 | 4 | 5 |
| | £'000 | £'000 | £'000 | £'000 | £'000 |
| Estimated income (i.e. cash receipts) from sale of grommits for 5 years at 200,000 grommits per annum | 2,000 | 2,200 | 2,350 | 2,500 | 2,600 |
| Less: Estimated operating costs (i.e. cash payments) | 1,800 | 1,990 | 2,130 | 2,260 | 2,345 |
| | 200 | 210 | 220 | 240 | 255 |
| Company's money rate of interest 15% | | | | | |
| Present value of future net cash flows (assuming net receipts are received on the last day of each year) | 174 | 159 | 145 | 137 | 127 |

Therefore the total present value of future net cash flows is £742,000, which the directors consider to be the economic value.

105

## Depreciation of economic value

7.10 The depreciation charge for assets valued at economic value is calculated by dividing the average of the estimated economic value at the beginning and end of the accounting period by the estimated remaining life at the middle of the period. The middle of the period is appropriate because the average value for the period is being depreciated. For example:

| | | |
|---|---|---|
| 1st January | economic value | £20,000 |
| 31st December | economic value | £16,000 |

Average depreciable value $\dfrac{(£20,000 + £16,000)}{2} = £18,000$

Estimated future useful life at 31 December = 4 years.

Depreciation charge £18,000 $\times \dfrac{1}{(4 + \frac{1}{2})} = £4,000$

7.11 Any amount by which the economic value at the end of the period differs from the economic value at the beginning of the period, less the depreciation charge for the period, should be charged or credited as appropriate, to the profit and loss account, disclosed if material as either an exceptional or extraordinary item depending on whether or not the change in value is the result of the normal operations of the company.

## Accounting for economic value

7.12 The accounting treatment for assets valued with reference to their economic value is similar to the accounting treatment for land and buildings.

This is because, like land and buildings, assets valued with reference to their economic value are recorded only at a net valuation.

## Example 7.3

Watnot Limited owns a plant that is valued at its economic value. The economic value of the plant at 31st December 1977 and 31st December 1978 respectively was £50,000 and £60,000. At 31st December 1978 the plant had an estimated remaining useful life of 5 years.

For 1978:

Average depreciable value $\dfrac{(£50,000 + £60,000)}{2} = £55,000$

Depreciation charge $£55,000 \times \dfrac{1}{(5 + \frac{1}{2})} = £10,000$

Revaluation surplus £60,000 − (£50,000 − £10,000) = £20,000

Journal entries:

|  |  | £ | £ |
|---|---|---|---|
| Dr | Profit and loss account | £10,000 | |
| Cr | Plant and machinery with the depreciation | | |
| | charge for the year | | £10,000 |
| Dr | Plant and machinery | £20,000 | |
| Cr | Profit and loss account with the revaluation | | |
| | surplus for the year | | £20,000 |

The plant and machinery account for 1978 will appear as follows:

### Plant and Machinery

| | £ | | £ |
|---|---|---|---|
| 1.1.78 Balance b/f | 50,000 | 31.12.78 Depreciation | 10,000 |
| 31.12.78 Profit and loss | | | |
| account | 20,000 | 31.12.78 Balance c/f | 60,000 |
| | £70,000 | | £70,000 |

The directors consider that the revaluation surplus is material and has arisen through increased productivity. Consequently the surplus is disclosed as an exceptional item rather than an extraordinary item.

## NET REALISABLE VALUE

7.13 It is appropriate to value an asset on the basis of its net realisable value when this value exceeds its economic value but is below its net current replacement cost.

7.14 The net realisable value of a fixed asset is the estimated proceeds from its sale on the open market, less all costs expected to be incurred in realising the proceeds.

### Land and buildings

7.15 The open market value of a property less costs of disposal is that property's net realisable value. It is appropriate to use net realisable value as the value to the business of land and buildings only in limited circumstances (e.g. when there is an intention to sell). Property companies will need to consider which of their properties should be valued at net realisable value and which should be valued at open market value plus acquisition costs.

7.16 Property which is valued on the basis of the depreciated replacement cost of the building and the open market value of the bare land is so valued because an existing use open market value for the whole property cannot be ascertained. If a net realisable value can be ascertained for such buildings it is likely to be low.

### Plant and machinery

7.17 Plant and machinery might be valued on the basis of its net realisable value in circumstances when:

(a) the asset has reached the end of its useful life, in which case the net realisable value will be its scrap value;

(b) there is a decision to dispose of an asset before the end of its useful life.

### Depreciation of net realisable value

7.18     Assets at the end of their useful life will be valued at their scrap value. Any change in the net realisable value during an accounting period should be charged or credited, as appropriate, to the profit and loss account.

7.19     Assets valued at their net realisable value which are not at the end of their useful life should be depreciated in exactly the same way as assets valued at their economic value (see paragraph 7.10). Any difference between the net realisable value at the end of the period and the net realisable value at the beginning of the period, less depreciation for the period, should be charged or credited, as appropriate, to the profit and loss account and disclosed, if material, as either an exceptional or extraordinary item depending on the circumstances.

7.20     The accounting treatment for assets valued at their net realisable value is the same as for assets valued at their economic value.

## CHANGES IN THE BASIS OF VALUATION

7.21     On a change in the basis of valuation from net current replacement cost to either economic value or net realisable value, the procedure is as follows:

1   Transfer the accumulated depreciation in respect of the asset at the beginning of the year to the asset account.
2   Calculate the depreciation charge to the profit and loss account for the year, based on the average depreciable value, assuming an adjusted value at the year end on a net replacement cost basis.
3   Calculate the further write-down required, being the difference between the opening net current replacement cost less the depreciation charge for the year, and the closing valuation. (The treatment of this write-down is considered further in paragraph 7.22.)

### Example 7.4

A machine is valued on 1st January as follows:

|  | £ |
|---|---|
| Gross current replacement cost | 20,000 |
| Depreciation | 10,000 |
| Net current replacement cost | £10,000 |

108

At 31st December it is decided that the machine should be valued on an economic value basis at £5,000 and that its estimated remaining useful life is 3 years. The index used to estimate the GRC at 1st January moved from 110 to 120 during the year.

The adjusted value at the year end is:

$$£10,000 \times \frac{120}{110} = £10,900 \text{ (approx.)}$$

The depreciation charge for the year is:

$$\frac{(£10,000 + £10,900)}{2} \times \frac{1}{(3 + 1)} = £2,612$$

The further write-down required is:

$$(£10,000 - £2,612) - £5,000 = £2,388$$

The accounting entries are:

|  |  | £ | £ |
|---|---|---|---|
| Dr | Accumulated depreciation | 10,000 | |
| Cr | Plant and machinery with the opening accumulated depreciation | | 10,000 |
| Dr | Profit and loss account | 2,612 | |
| Cr | Plant and machinery with the depreciation for the year | | 2,612 |
| Dr | Profit and loss account | 2,388 | |
| Cr | Plant and machinery with the further write-down required | | 2,388 |

The Plant and Machinery Account will appear as follows:

Plant and Machinery

| | £ | | | £ |
|---|---|---|---|---|
| 1st January Balance: GRC | 20,000 | 1st January Balance: Depreciation | | 10,000 |
| | | 31st December | Depreciation for the year | 2,612 |
| | | 31st December | Write-down to economic value | 2,388 |
| | | 31st December | Economic value carried forward | 5,000 |
| | £20,000 | | | £20,000 |

# THE TREATMENT OF CHANGES IN VALUE

7.22 Where the value of an item of plant and machinery has changed for any reason other than depreciation or a movement in the gross replacement cost the movement should be reflected in the profit and loss account. The directors should consider whether the change has arisen in the normal course of operation of the business. If it has, it should be reflected in the operating profit and disclosed if appropriate as an exceptional item. Alternatively, it may be more appropriate to treat the change as an extraordinary item. Such changes in value may arise, for example, as a result of:

(a) a change in the basis of valuation, e.g. a write-down from net current replacement cost to economic value,
(b) a change in economic value.

Changes resulting from movement in gross replacement cost (including backlog depreciation) should be treated as revaluation surpluses or deficits.

In the case of land and buildings held as fixed assets changes in value should be treated as revaluation surpluses or deficits except where:

(a) The change is a result of depreciation; in which case the depreciation is charged to profit and loss account.
(b) There has been a change in the basis of valuation to open market value for any potential use; in which case the change should be treated as an extraordinary item in the profit and loss account.
(c) There has been a change in basis of valuation to economic value (together with all associated fixed assets) in which case the write-down should be charged to profit and loss account.

## DISCLOSURE OF THE EFFECTS OF INTRODUCING CCA

7.23  On the introduction of CCA depreciation will normally be based on the estimated remaining useful life of fixed assets and on net asset values. For some companies (e.g. property companies) this may constitute a material change in accounting policy and present accounting practice would require that the effect of such change should be disclosed in the audited accounts. For such companies, however, it will not be necessary on the introduction of CCA to identify separately the effect of the change in accounting policy and the effect of asset revaluations, changes in asset lives, etc.; only the total effect of introducing CCA need be disclosed. For example the amount of backlog depreciation in respect of prior years need not be split between the amount arising on revaluation and the amount arising on changes in the estimated remaining useful lives of assets.

## CHANGES IN ASSET LIVES

7.24  As explained in Chapter 5, the basis of calculating depreciation in a CCA system is such that changes in asset lives are automatically taken into account in the normal depreciation calculations (see paragraph 5.49).

## FULLY DEPRECIATED ASSETS

7.25    The principles of CCA require that all assets in use are attributed a value until the end of their useful lives. Only if asset values are immaterial will nil values be acceptable.

7.26    On the introduction of CCA there may be assets still in use which have been fully written off and other assets for which the book value does not reflect the current estimate of the remaining useful life. In such cases values should be established, on the appropriate basis of valuation, which reflect, *inter alia*, the estimated remaining useful life of the asset at the date of the introduction of CCA. If a net current replacement cost valuation basis is appropriate, the net current replacement cost should be determined by:

(i) estimating the gross current replacement cost;
(ii) estimating the future and therefore the total useful working life of the asset;
(iii) calculating that proportion of the gross current replacement cost that relates to the future useful working life.

The requisite net adjustment to the gross value of the asset and its accumulated depreciation should be treated as a revaluation surplus.

### Example 7.5

Nutbolt Limited introduces CCA on 1st January 1977. At 31st December 1976 the Balance Sheet included plant and machinery that had cost £10,000 but was fully depreciated, and further plant and machinery that had cost £10,000 that was 90% depreciated. All this plant and machinery is estimated to have a remaining useful life of 4 years at 1st January 1977. The plant and machinery was purchased as follows:

| Year of acquisition | Cost | Accumulated depreciation |
|---|---|---|
| | £ | £ |
| 1966 | 10,000 | 10,000 |
| 1968 | 10,000 | 9,000 |
| | £20,000 | £19,000 |

The GRC and the total useful life of the plant and machinery at 1st January 1977 is estimated as follows:

| Assets acquired in | £ | Total life |
|---|---|---|
| 1966 | 24,000 | 15 years (1966 to 1976 plus 4 years) |
| 1968 | 26,000 | 13 years (1968 to 1976 plus 4 years) |
| | £50,000 | |

111

The undepreciated proportion of the GRC at 1st January 1977 therefore should be:

|  |  | £ |
|---|---|---:|
| 1966 | £24,000 × 4/15 = | 6,400 |
| 1968 | £26,000 × 4/13 = | 8,000 |
|  |  | £14,400 |

and accumulated depreciation should be:

|  |  | £ |
|---|---|---:|
| 1966 | 11/15 × £24,000 = | 17,600 |
| 1968 | 9/13 × £26,000 = | 18,000 |
|  |  | £35,600 |

At 1st January 1977 the accounting entries are:

|  |  | £ | £ |
|---|---|---:|---:|
| Dr | Plant and machinery | 30,000 | |
| Cr | Revaluation surplus | | 30,000 |
| | with the surplus on revaluation (£50,000–£20,000) | | |
| Dr | Revaluation surplus | 16,600 | |
| Cr | Accumulated depreciation | | 16,600 |
| | with backlog depreciation on the revaluation (£35,600–£19,000) | | |

# LEASED ASSETS OTHER THAN LAND AND BUILDINGS

7.27 There are two types of lease distinguished by the proposed accounting standard:

(a) Operating leases
(b) Financing leases (or full pay-out leases).

## Operating leases

7.28 Operating leases are those under which the rentals payable by the lessee in the primary rental period are not expected to be sufficient to amortise the lessor's capital outlay. The lessor is therefore dependent for his profit on re-leasing the asset or disposing of it to realise its residual value at the end of the lease. No special treatment is considered necessary for operating leases. The asset acquired by the lessor should be revalued each year and depreciated in the normal way. The lessee should charge against his operating profit as an expense the rental payments under the terms of the lease.

## Finance leases

7.29 Under a finance lease an asset is leased for a period considered to be the whole useful life of the asset. During the period of the lease the rentals payable by the lessee are sufficient to amortise the lessor's capital outlay and to show a return on that capital. Finance leases, for the lessee, are effectively a method of purchasing an asset on credit terms and the proposed accounting treatment in the lessee's books reflects this point of view.

### The lessee's books

7.30 The accounting treatment of finance leases in CCA is based on the assumption that the reality of the situation so far as the lessee is concerned is that:

(a) He has purchased an asset.
(b) He has a commitment to pay for the asset over its useful life.

There are two elements therefore to be accounted for; the asset and the liability.

7.31 The asset should be accounted for in exactly the same way as any other fixed asset. It should be valued at net current replacement cost, economic value or net realisable value as appropriate and it should be depreciated over its expected useful life, backlog depreciation being debited against revaluation surplus in the case of assets valued at net current replacement cost.

7.32 The liability to be included in the balance sheet is the discounted value of the payments under the lease. The discount rate to be used will normally be the implicit rate of interest payable by the lessee in respect of the lease.

### Example 7.6

Chestnut Limited, the lessee, enters into a leasing agreement whereby the lessor acquires a machine for £335 on 31st December 1979 and agrees to lease it to Chestnut Limited from 1st January 1980 for an annual rental of £100 payable on 31st December each year for five years, starting in 1980. The useful life of the machine is expected to be five years. Chestnut Limited is aware that the cost to the lessor of the machine is £335 and calculates that a discount factor of 15% will produce a discounted value of £335 for a stream of payments of £100 per annum for five years. Fifteen per cent is therefore the implicit rate of interest payable by Chestnut Limited in respect of the lease.

7.33 The amount of the liability and the current replacement cost of the asset will be the same figures on the first day of the lease so long as the money rate of interest implicit in the lease is used. Thus the initial accounting entry to account for the lease is:

$$\begin{array}{ll} \text{Dr} & \text{Fixed Assets} \\ \text{Cr} & \text{Liabilities} \end{array}$$

with the current replacement cost of the asset.

7.34 Once the asset has been recorded the accounting entries for changes in value and depreciation are the same as for any other fixed asset.

7.35    The liability reduces year by year as the rental payments are made; the reduction in the discounted value of the liability should be credited to the profit and loss account, thereby reducing the rental payments to a figure which represents an annual interest charge.

**Example 7.7**

Continuing Example 7.6, the liability will be reduced as follows:

|          | Discount rate | Discounted value of liability | Reduction: credit to profit and loss account |
|----------|---------------|-------------------------------|----------------------------------------------|
|          |               | £                             | £                                            |
| 31.12.80 | 15%           | 335                           | —                                            |
| 31.12.81 | 15%           | 285                           | 50                                           |
| 31.12.82 | 15%           | 228                           | 57                                           |
| 31.12.83 | 15%           | 162                           | 66                                           |
| 31.12.84 | 15%           | 87                            | 75                                           |
| 31.12.85 | 15%           | —                             | 87                                           |

In each year the profit and loss account will be debited with the rent payable and credited with the reductions shown above.

**The lessor's books**

7.36    It follows that an asset subject to a finance lease, if regarded as being purchased by the lessee, should not also be regarded as being owned by the lessor. In substance, if not in form, the asset of the lessor is a right to a stream of income represented by the rental payments determined by the lease agreement, the value of which is the current value of the income stream—i.e. its economic value—calculated using as the discount rate the rate of return implicit, so far as the lessor is concerned, in the lease. It should be appreciated that the rate of discount implicit in the lease will not necessarily be the same for the lessor and the lessee since the incidence of tax relief, and, possibly, government grants may be very different for each.

7.37    The reduction year by year in the economic value should be determined by the rate of discount used and should be charged against the rental income received. The rate of discount may be changed by the lessor during the course of the lease in that he may use either the original rate of discount or a rate of discount which is the rate of return implicit in leases currently being negotiated. Any change in the economic value as a result of using a different rate of discount from that previously applied should be treated as a revaluation surplus or deficit.

**Example 7.8**

Continuing Example 7.7 the asset in the lessor's books will be reduced as follows assuming that in 1982 the rate of interest implicit in current leases changed from 15% to 18%:

| | Discount rate | Economic value | Reduction: debit to revaluation surplus | Reduction: debit to operating profit |
|---|---|---|---|---|
| | | £ | £ | £ |
| 31.12.80 | 15% | 335 | — | — |
| 31.12.81 | 15% | 285 | — | 50 |
| 31.12.82 | 15%/18% | 218 | 10 | 57 |
| 31.12.83 | 18% | 157 | — | 61 |
| 31.12.84 | 18% | 85 | — | 72 |
| 31.12.85 | 18% | — | — | 85 |

In each year the profit and loss account is credited with the rent receivable and debited with the reductions shown above. The reduction of £10 resulting from the change in the discount rate from 15% to 18% is debited as a revaluation surplus. The amount of £10 is the difference at 31.12.82 between the balance using a discount rate of 18% and the balance using a discount rate of 15%. In the year in which the discount rate changes the rate to be used for calculating the debit to profit and loss account is the rate applicable prior to the change and the rate used to calculate the end of year economic value is the rate applicable after the change. The resulting difference is a revaluation surplus or deficit.

## FIXED ASSETS IN THE COURSE OF CONSTRUCTION

### Plant and machinery

7.38 Plant and machinery in the course of construction by a company for its own use should be valued at the current replacement cost of the work completed at the date of the valuation. If there is evidence indicating that on completion the value of the asset will be considerably less than its gross current replacement cost, consideration should be given to writing down the current cost of the work completed in anticipation of the write-down required on completion. Where plant and machinery in the course of construction is represented only by the amount of progress payments made to the contractor, the progress payments should be regarded as monetary assets and not as construction work in progress.

### Land and buildings

7.39 Land and buildings in the course of development should be valued at the lower of:

(a) the aggregate of the open market value plus acquisition costs of the bare land and the current replacement cost of construction work completed at the date of the valuation, and

(b) the estimated open market value at the date of the valuation, plus acquisition costs, of the land and buildings as if the development were complete, less the estimated costs, current at the date of the valuation, required to complete the development.

As with plant and machinery, if the cost of construction work is represented only by the amount of progress payments made to the contractor, the progress payments should be regarded as monetary assets and not as construction work in progress.

7.40 Where, because of the nature of the building, the land and buildings when completed will not have an open market value, (b) above will not be applicable and the land and buildings in the course of construction should be valued as in (a).

7.41 When land and buildings in the course of construction are to be valued as in (a) above, regard should be had to the overall profitability of the activity in which they are to be employed and, if appropriate, an amount should be written off in anticipation of the write-down to economic value that will be required on completion. The write-down to economic value should follow the normal rules (see paragraphs 7.3 to 7.5).

## THE TREATMENT OF CAPITAL BASED GOVERNMENT GRANTS

7.42 The general principles to be applied in respect of capital based government grants are:

(a) The grant potentially receivable at the date of valuation should be taken into account in arriving at the value to the business of relevant assets at that date.

(b) Either method allowed by SSAP4 of accounting for Government grants may be used under CCA (but see below).

7.43 The deferred credit method of accounting for Government grants, although permissible under CCA, creates practical problems and is not recommended. If the method were used, the deferred credit would need to be treated effectively as a negative fixed asset. The transfer to profit and loss account each year would be equivalent to the depreciation charge and 'negative backlog depreciation' would also need to be calculated.

7.44 Accounting for Government grants by reducing the gross replacement cost of the related asset by the amount of the grant potentially receivable at the date of valuation involves no more work than if a discount on the replacement cost of the assets had been granted by the supplier. If the rate of grant is say 25% the GRC at the valuation date is simply reduced by 25%. If at the next valuation date the rate of grant is changed to 30%, the GRC at that date is simply reduced by 30%. The depreciation charge, backlog depreciation, revaluation surpluses or deficits and the NRC are calculated in the normal manner based on the reduced GRC.

## SPECIAL PROVISIONS RELATING TO PROPERTY COMPANIES

7.45   A company which is substantially engaged in holding land and buildings:

(a) as an investment to earn rental income at arms' length; and/or

(b) for development and resale or holding after development to earn rental income at arms' length,

is defined for the purpose of the proposed accounting standard as a 'property company'.

7.46   Except where specifically excluded, the general rules relating to the valuation and depreciation of land and buildings also apply to the land and buildings owned by property companies. The value of a property company's land and buildings however is particularly significant and for this reason a full professional valuation of all the land and buildings owned by a property company should be carried out every year on a consistent basis and as close as is practicable to the year end. At least every third year the valuation should be carried out by external professionally qualified valuers. In the years between full external valuations, the property portfolio should be valued by the company's internal professional qualified valuers and in such years at least a sample of the land and buildings will be required to be valued by external professionally qualified valuers in order to substantiate the internally prepared valuation.

# 8 Stock and Cost of Sales

8.1     To many companies the purchase, manufacture and sale of trading stock represents the essence of their business. The design of the whole accounting system of such companies is often the result of the management's requirements for information with regard to transactions involving stock and work in progress.

8.2     It is envisaged therefore that on the introduction of CCA many companies will not wish to depart from long established accounting routines designed to meet the particular requirements of management and which may already incorporate elements of CCA or replacement cost accounting. In many cases companies will continue to use their existing stock accounting systems making only the adjustments necessitated by the introduction of CCA. In certain circumstances the adjustments required to existing systems could be minimal, for example where a standard costing system is in operation (see Chapter 17), and will not necessarily be the same for all companies. The wide range of accounting techniques that has been developed to account for stock and work in progress makes it impossible in this book to do more than suggest general methods of converting existing accounting systems on to a CCA basis.

## GENERAL PRINCIPLES

8.3     The general principles of CCA applicable to stock and work in progress are essentially straightforward. Nevertheless the wide variety of stocks held and the number of methods of trading employed by industry have led to the need for special provisions in certain circumstances in order to produce a suitable and practicable system.

8.4     The general principles relating to stock and work in progress are consistent with those applicable to other items in financial statements prepared using CCA principles:

(a) Stock and work in progress should be stated in the balance sheet at its value to the business at the balance sheet date.
(b) The charge for cost of sales in the profit and loss account should include the value to the business, at the date of consumption, of stock and work in progress consumed during the period.

8.5      This chapter deals with how the general principles may be applied in practice by most trading and manufacturing companies in normal circumstances. Some special cases are dealt with in Chapter 9 and the recording in the accounting books and records of current cost information relating to stock and work in progress is considered in Chapter 16. Certain methods of adjusting stock and work in progress to current cost are applicable only to companies which operate a standard costing system and these are considered in Chapter 17.

### The value to the business of stock and work in progress

8.6      The value to the business of stock and work in progress is the lower of current replacement cost and net realisable value. This compares with the historical cost convention of 'the lower of (historical) cost and net realisable value'.

8.7      Economic value is not normally appropriate as a separate criterion for the value to the business of stock and work in progress because it is not normally used in the business over a period of time to generate a flow of income but is held for sale or for incorporation into a finished product to be sold at a future date. The net realisable value, therefore, will normally represent the economic value.

### The lower of current replacement cost and net realisable value

8.8      Where it is necessary to compare current replacement cost and net realisable value in order to determine the value to the business of stock and work in progress the comparison should be made in respect of each item of stock and work in progress separately but where this is impracticable, groups or categories of similar items may be taken together. The reason for this provision will be familiar to most readers and is no different from the comparison required to be made under existing HC conventions (see SSAP 9, paragraph 2); if the comparison is made in total, an unacceptable setting off of shortages and surpluses may result. This can be seen from the following simple example.

### Example 8.1

|  | Product A | Product B | Total |
|---|---|---|---|
|  | £ | £ | £ |
| (a) Current replacement cost | 5 | 10 | 15 |
| (b) Net realisable value | 10 | 5 | 15 |
| (c) Value to the business (lower of (a) and (b)) | £5 | £5 | £15 |

It can be seen that if the comparision of current replacement cost and net realisable value is made in total a value to the business of £15 is produced instead of the correct figure of £10.

119

### Current replacement cost of stock and work in progress

8.9      The current replacement cost of stock and work in progress will normally be the cost at which it was or could have been replaced at the date concerned by the normal method of operation of the company. The current replacement cost will therefore comprise the current cost of purchased items together with the current cost of manufacture, processing and other expenses incurred in the normal course of business in bringing the product or service to its present location and condition. Such current costs will include all related production overheads even though these may accrue on a time basis.

8.10     It should be stressed that current cost in the preceding paragraph in all cases refers to current cost at the valuation date, i.e. the balance sheet date or the date of consumption of the stock. This implies the following:

(a) The current cost of purchased items is to be based on replacement cost at the valuation date.

(b) The current cost of labour is to be based on labour rates and the normal level of labour efficiency at the valuation date.

(c) The current cost of manufacturing overheads such as light, heat, power and other establishment charges is to be based on their cost at the valuation date.

(d) The current cost of depreciation is to be based on the value to the business of fixed assets at the valuation date.

## STOCK AND WORK IN PROGRESS IN THE BALANCE SHEET

8.11     For the purpose of discussing the treatment of stock and work in progress in the balance sheet in this chapter stock and work in progress is analysed between the following categories. A reference simply to 'stock' should be taken to mean the total of a company's stock and work in progress.

(a) **Raw materials and components**
Comprising raw materials and components purchased for incorporation into products for sale.

(b) **Work in progress**
Comprising products and services in intermediate stages of completion, including labour and overhead costs.

(c) **Finished goods**

(d) **Goods purchased for resale**

### Accounting entries

8.12     Assuming a period of generally rising prices the accounting entry required to increase the figure for stock in the balance sheet to its value to the business is normally:

Dr   Stock
Cr   Revaluation surplus
with the excess of the value to the business over the historical cost or previous value.

Such an accounting entry should be made on the introduction of CCA, so that at the beginning of the first period for which current cost accounts are to be prepared the opening stock is recorded at its value to the business.

### Example 8.2

Oaktree Ltd adopts CCA on 1st January 1977. The company's balance sheet at 31st December 1976 included stock on a FIFO basis at £1,500,000. The company calculates that the value to the business of stock at 31st December 1976 is £2,000,000. The accounting entry is therefore:

|  |  |  | £ | £ |
|---|---|---|---|---|
| 31.12.76 | Dr | Stock | 500,000 | |
|  | Cr | Revaluation surplus | | 500,000 |

8.13   As explained in the opening paragraphs of this chapter companies may wish to continue using their existing accounting methods preparatory to arriving at the current cost of stock. In Chapter 17 some of the advantages in this respect of using a standard costing system are discussed and at the end of this chapter the Birchwood example shows how current cost of sales and the balance sheet value of stock might be arrived at after initially using a FIFO method of accounting for stock, i.e. one which assumes that the items longest in stock are the first to be sold. A Base Stock method of accounting, i.e. one which assumes that all input to stock in a period is sold in that period might be useful to companies whose volume of stock remains fairly constant and in such circumstances will provide a sufficiently accurate current cost of sales figure because cost of sales when the volume of stock remains constant is equal to the cost of purchases. The Last In First Out method (LIFO) which assumes the items last input to stock are the first to be sold may also be useful in arriving at current cost of sales but has serious disadvantages when the volume of stock falls during a period of rising prices, and therefore should be used only where the volume of stock is constant.

8.14   Whichever method of accounting for stock is used preparatory to arriving at current cost of sales, whether it be a standard costing system, or some other system, using conventions such as FIFO, Base Stock, or LIFO, the book value of stock at the end of the accounting period may need to be adjusted to arrive at its value to the business at that date. No adjustment may be required, however, in the following cases:

(a) Where the replacement cost of stock has not changed materially since purchase or, if later, the previous balance sheet date.

(b) Where the FIFO convention is being used and there have been no material price increases in the normal stock holding period (see Example 8.3).

(c) Where the company has adopted a full CCA system and adjusts the carrying value of stocks each time there is a change in the current replacement cost.

8.15  In the above cases the only adjustment that might be required to adjust the book value of stocks to their value to the business at the balance sheet date would be a write down to net realisable value.

**Example 8.3**

Pinewood Ltd assembles tractors from bought-in components and accounts for stock on a FIFO basis. The reliability of the supply of components is such that Pinewood Ltd's stock of them never represents more than is needed for two weeks production so that on a FIFO basis stock is input to work in progress two weeks after it is purchased. The following is a summary of movements of components for the last quarter of 1976, a purchase price increase from £200 to £300 per unit having occurred in the middle of November.

VOLUME
(expressed in terms of tractors)

|  | October | November | December |
|---|---|---|---|
| Opening balance | 200 | 200 | 200 |
| Purchases | 400 | 400 | 400 |
|  | 600 | 600 | 600 |
| Input to work in progress | 400 | 400 | 400 |
| Closing balance | 200 | 200 | 200 |

UNIT PRICE

|  | October | November | December |
|---|---|---|---|
|  | £ | £ | £ |
| Opening balance | 200 | 200 | 300 |
| Purchases | 200 | 250 | 300 |
| Input to work in progress | 200 | 200 | 300 |
| Closing balance | 200 | 300 | 300 |

VALUE

|  | October | November | December |
|---|---|---|---|
|  | £ | £ | £ |
| Opening balance | 40,000 | 40,000 | 60,000 |
| Purchases | 80,000 | 100,000 | 120,000 |
|  | 120,000 | 140,000 | 180,000 |
| Input to work in progress | 80,000 | 80,000 | 120,000 |
| Closing balance | £40,000 | £60,000 | £60,000 |

It can be seen that Pinewood Limited's closing balance fully reflects the increase in the replacement cost of components because the purchase price increase occurred prior to the period in which the stock on hand at the end of the period was purchased. Consequently no adjustment is required to arrive at the value to the business of the stock of components for balance sheet purposes at the end of 1976.

## RAW MATERIALS AND COMPONENTS

### Determination of current replacement cost

8.16    Although it is recognised that companies may often find it impracticable either to obtain or to use the current replacement cost of each item in stock in order to determine the replacement cost of materials on an item by item basis, wherever it is practicable to do so the replacement cost of materials should be determined with reference to prices current at the balance sheet date. Many companies with a limited range of items in stock may in fact find it easier to value stocks by reference to their replacement cost than, say, to their FIFO cost.

8.17    The price to be used is that for delivery of a quantity normally ordered by the company on normal terms as to trade or bulk discounts and method, place and timing of delivery. It is suggested that to ensure consistency all discounts for prompt payment should be ignored. If VAT is recoverable by the purchaser it should be excluded from the price but it should be included where it is irrecoverable. Other irrecoverable taxes and duties should be included. Delivery charges made by the supplier should be included, so too should any other transportation costs incurred by the company in bringing the materials to their present location.

8.18    Where it is not practicable for companies to obtain the current replacement cost of individual items in stock they may update the total materials balance (or such part of that balance as cannot be updated on an item by item basis) to current cost levels by using suitable indices based on material costs currently being incurrd by the company or, failing that, by using suitable authorised external indices.

### Example 8.4

Ashdown Limited has a wide variety of raw materials and bought in components. It decides to adopt different methods of calculating replacement cost depending on the availability of information and the significance of items involved. It decides to analyse items into three categories, A, B, and C.

A items are those which have high individual values and will be valued on an item by item basis. This category includes certain major raw materials and commodities and the more important bought-in components. They represent about 60% of stocks by value.

B items are those which do not fall into category A and which are bought frequently and have individual values which range from a few pence each to about £100. These form about 30% of the total value of stock. Ashdown believes it can construct an in-house index for these goods and will value them by reference to it.

C items cover all other types of stock and include a wide variety of consumables, paint, fasteners and so on. They are usually held in fairly large quantities but have low individual values and only account for about 10% of total stock by value. They will be valued using the most suitable index published by the CSO.

### Determination of net realisable value

8.19    The net realisable value of an item of stock is the estimated proceeds of sale less all further costs to completion and less all costs to be incurred in marketing, selling and distribution directly related to the item in question. Net realisable value is discussed in Chapter 9; it need only be considered where there is *prima facie* evidence that it is lower than current replacement cost.

## WORK IN PROGRESS

8.20    Contract work in progress is considered in Chapter 9, and this chapter deals only with work in progress of a general nature. The method of calculating the value to the business of work in progress for balance sheet purposes will depend on the accounting system and the extent to which current replacement cost can be determined on an item by item basis. In general work in progress should be analysed into its different elements—i.e. material, labour and overheads—and the current replacement cost of each element should then be calculated separately. Net realisable value, as with stock of raw materials and components, need only be considered where there is *prima facie* evidence that it is lower than current replacement cost.

### Materials

8.21    The material content of work in progress may be valued at its value to the business using methods which are essentially the same as those used to value raw materials and components. Many companies, however, even if they are able to value raw materials and components on an item by item basis before they are input to work in progress may be unable to do so once they form part of work in progress. Companies which find it impracticable to recalculate each item of material in work in progress at current replacement cost should update the total material content to current cost levels using where possible in-house indices based on current material costs or, failing that, suitable authorised external indices.

### Labour

8.22    In this chapter we consider both productive and non-productive (or indirect) labour under the general heading of 'labour'. It is appreciated that many companies treat non-productive labour as an overhead when including it as part of cost of sales but the general principles discussed herein apply equally to non-productive labour and productive labour. The labour element of work in progress, like all other elements of the balance sheet stock figure, should be shown at its value to the business at the balance sheet date, i.e. using labour rates current at the balance sheet date and the number of hours that would have been spent had the stock in question been produced on or about the balance sheet date. No adjustment will be necessary where there has been no change in labour rates or labour efficiency during the stock holding period because in such circumstances labour will already be included in work in progress at current cost. Where there has been a change however, an adjustment to all or some of the labour content of work in progress will be required. The extent of the adjustment will depend on the date or dates on which changes in labour rates have occurred during the stock holding period and/or when changes in labour efficiency occurred. Changes just before the balance sheet date will have a greater effect than earlier ones.

## Example 8.5

A company whose year end is 31st December has a stock holding period of three months in respect of work in progress. From 1st November, all workers received a pay increase of 10%. There were no changes in labour rates or labour efficiency after that date. Before any adjustment to current value is made the labour content of work in progress is accounted for on a FIFO basis. Before the pay increase the monthly input of labour to work in progress was £100,000. Similarly the transfer to finished goods each month included £100,000 of labour. The movement of the labour content of work in progress for the last quarter of the year was as follows:

|  | October | November | December |
|---|---|---|---|
|  | £ | £ | £ |
| Opening balance | 300,000 | 300,000 | 310,000 |
| Input | 100,000 | 110,000 | 110,000 |
|  | 400,000 | 410,000 | 420,000 |
| Transfer to finished goods | 100,000 | 100,000 | 100,000 |
| Closing balance | £300,000 | £310,000 | £320,000 |

It can be seen that because the pay increase occurred two months before the year end, only two months increase is included in the closing balance. Therefore, to arrive at current cost an adjustment to one month's stock is required as follows:

|  |  | £ | £ |
|---|---|---|---|
| Dr | Work in progress | 10,000 |  |
| Cr | Revaluation surplus |  | 10,000 |

with the amount required to increase the labour content of work in progress to current cost at the balance sheet date.

The transfer to finished products reflects none of the increase in labour costs and therefore a comparable adjustment will be required to the closing balance of stock of finished products to the extent that they have not been sold by the end of December. For those that have been sold a COSA to the historical cost of sales will be required.

8.23 It is worth noting that the circumstances described in Example 8.5 imply that the company's production cycle is three months; i.e. the company's products are 'on the production line' for three months from start to finish. For many companies the production cycle will be much shorter, possibly only a few days, and in such circumstances it may often be unnecessary to make any adjustment to the labour content of work in progress for balance sheet purposes.

8.24 Companies should calculate the current cost of labour by the most accurate means available. Where the number of hours charged is known these should be recosted at current labour rates. Where a large number of different labour rates are in operation it will often be possible to arrive at a suitably weighted average labour rate for all labour. Those companies which do not know the number of hours represented by the labour content of work in progress will need to apply an index to the historical cost of labour. Where labour efficiency has changed significantly during the stock holding period prior to the valuation date the number of hours to which current labour rates are to be applied should be adjusted accordingly.

## Overheads

8.25 It is not possible in this book to deal with all the methods that may be used to account for overheads or to describe all the various methods of charging overheads into work in progress. However, the two methods which are believed to be the most generally used will be discussed. These are called 'the machine-hour rate method' and 'the percentage up-lift method'. As noted above, non-productive labour included in overheads should be treated in the same way as productive labour. Depreciation when treated as an overhead follows the same general rules as other overheads but certain special considerations with regard to depreciation are discussed in paragraphs 8.35 to 8.38 below.

## The machine-hour rate method of charging overheads to work in progress

8.26 In general terms the machine-hour rate method of charging overheads to work in progress in an historical cost system involves the establishment of:

(a) Actual or standard times for each job (expressed in machine-hours).
(b) The total number of machine-hours expected to be used.
(c) The total overheads expected to be charged to work in progress.

The machine-hour rate is (c) divided by (b) and the charges made to work in progress made in respect of work done will be the number of (actual or standard) hours taken multiplied by the machine-hour rate. A labour hour rate may be used in a similar manner by substituting labour hours for machine-hours. A job may be a particular stage of production or the manufacture of a complete item.

8.27    For CCA purposes it is necessary to recalculate machine-hour rates at the balance sheet date in respect of all cost increases since the rates were established and adjust the value of overheads included in work in progress with reference to the recalculated rates.

8.28    Machine-hour rates may need correction at the balance sheet date for all or some of the following reasons:

(a) The total number of machine-hours actually used was different from the estimate of total machine-hours.
(b) The actual (historical) cost of overheads incurred was different from the estimate of total overheads.
(c) The level of costs current at the balance sheet date was different from the level of (historical) costs actually incurred.
(d) The level of efficiency at the balance sheet date was different from the average for the accounting period (e.g. if there was more productive output in the same number of hours).

Under historical cost conventions adjustments would be made to the value of work in progress in respect of any over or under absorption of overheads resulting from (a), (b) and that part of (d) which the company considers reflects the 'normal' level of efficiency at the time the work in progress was produced.

8.29    To adjust the overhead element of work in progress to a CCA basis at the balance sheet date two adjustments are required. The first adjustment is that made under historical cost conventions as described above and has the effect (on the assumption of increasing costs) of up-lifting work in progress to FIFO cost. If this adjustment is not made and costs are increasing the operating profit will be understated and the whole up-lift to current cost will be reflected as a revaluation surplus.

8.30    The second adjustment (assuming rising costs) is to up-lift work in progress from FIFO cost to current cost and is the adjustment for (c) of paragraph 8.28 and for part of (d). It is achieved by adjusting the FIFO value of work in progress to a value calculated with reference to a recalculated year end machine-hour rate. The recalculated machine-hour rate should take into account both the level of costs and the 'normal' level of efficiency *at the balance sheet date*. The difference between the FIFO value and the value using the recalculated machine-hour rate is debited to work in progress and credited to revaluation suplus.

### Example 8.6

Elm Limited calculates an overhead rate based on machine-hours. In 1975 it had based its calculations on overheads of £200,000 per month and likely machine-hours of 50,000 per month giving an hourly rate of £4. During December 1976 overheads were running at a rate of £240,000 and hours had increased to 55,000 per month. For the purposes of the historical cost accounts Elm recognised that it had unrecovered overheads as follows:

|  | £ |
|---|---|
| Actual overheads in December | 240,000 |
| Charged to work in progress 55,000 hours at £4 | 220,000 |
| Under-recovery | £20,000 |

Elm decided therefore to revalue work in progress in its historical cost accounts and, having one month's work in progress, made an entry debiting work in progress and crediting cost of sales with £20,000.

The actual overheads for December did not, however, reflect fully the current costs at the end of 1976 and Elm calculated that if all overheads were based on end of 1976 costs the total would have been £275,000, which gives rise to a machine-hour rate of £5. For its current cost accounts, therefore, Elm needs to increase stock values by a further £35,000 as follows:

|  |  | £ | £ |
|---|---|---|---|
| Dr | Work in progress | 35,000 | |
| Cr | Revaluation surplus | | 35,000 |

8.31    Having completed the adjustments required to arrive at current cost at the balance sheet date the only under or over absorption of overheads not adjusted for when arriving at the current value of work in progress will be those that have arisen as a result of 'abnormal' production or expenditure. Such over or under absorptions will have correctly been charged or credited as part of cost of sales as they represent cost savings or otherwise resulting from the year's activities.

### The percentage uplift method of charging overheads to work in progress

8.32    Under this method, in an historical cost system, total overheads for the year are estimated and expressed as a percentage of labour or materials (or both) and the input to work in progress is uplifted by this percentage to account for overheads. The percentage uplift method provides a simple and sufficiently accurate method of charging overheads to work in progress for many companies but for some companies the method is too imprecise. As with the machine-hour rate method underabsorbed overheads arising because of cost increases, to the extent that they relate to work in progress on hand, are commonly added to the balance sheet value of work in progress to arrive at a FIFO cost.

8.33    In a CCA system any increases in costs after the percentage uplift has been calculated need to be added to the balance sheet value of work in progress to the extent that the increases relate to work in progress on hand at the balance sheet date. In some cases there may be no need to make any adjustment to the uplift percentage because the cost of the material or labour content to which the percentage is applied may have increased in the same proportion as the cost of overheads. On the other hand when the cost of material or labour has increased proportionally more or less than the cost of overheads the uplift percentage will need to be reduced or increased as appropriate.

### Example 8.7

Yewtree Limited operates two factories for which costings are calculated separately. Both factories use the percentage uplift method of charging overheads. The historical cost estimates for the year were:

|  | Factory | |
| --- | --- | --- |
|  | 1 | 2 |
|  | £ | £ |
| Estimated materials | 450,000 | 260,000 |
| Estimated overheads | 45,000 | 39,000 |
| Percentage uplift | 10% | 15% |

On a current cost basis the following results were obtained:

|  | £ | £ |
| --- | --- | --- |
| Actual materials at prices current at the year end | 510,000 | 270,000 |
| Actual overheads at prices current at the year end | 51,000 | 54,000 |
| Percentage uplift | 10% | 20% |

In factory 1 stock can be valued by applying the original percentage uplift to the current cost of materials. In factory 2 however the percentage uplift needs increasing to 20%.

8.34 As in the case of the machine-hour rate system there are two parts to the necessary adjustment. Firstly any 'normal' underabsorption of incurred overheads (assuming rising costs) should be debited to the balance sheet value of stock and credited to operating profit to the extent that it relates to work in progress on hand at the balance sheet date.

Secondly the difference between the overhead content of work in progress arrived at after accounting for the first part of the adjustment as above and the overhead content of work in progress arrived at using the recalculated uplift percentage at the year end (assuming rising costs) should be debited to work in progress and credited to stock revaluation reserve.

### Example 8.8

Using again the information for factory 2 in Yewtree Limited (Example 8.7) the following is applicable:

|            | Historical cost estimate | Historical cost actual | Current cost actual |
|------------|--------------------------|------------------------|---------------------|
|            | £                        | £                      | £                   |
| Materials  | 260,000                  | 270,000                | 270,000             |
| Overheads  | 39,000                   | 43,000                 | 54,000              |
| Uplift     | 15%                      | 16%                    | 20%                 |

If the estimated uplift is applied to the actual materials there is an under-recovery of overheads of 1% and for the purposes of the historical cost accounts these under-recovered overheads need to be added back to work in progress. A further 4%, however, needs to be added in the current cost accounts.

If, therefore, the work in progress in the original accounts was, say:

|                    | £       |
|--------------------|---------|
| Materials          | 80,000  |
| Overheads at 15%   | 12,000  |
|                    | £92,000 |

In order to adjust this to historical cost FIFO overheads need to be increased to 16% of materials.

|                    | £       |
|--------------------|---------|
| Materials          | 80,000  |
| Overheads at 16%   | 12,800  |
|                    | £92,800 |

The accounting entry for the adjustment is:

|    |                   | £   | £   |
|----|-------------------|-----|-----|
| Dr | Work in progress  | 800 |     |
| Cr | Cost of sales     |     | 800 |

with the difference between the amount calculated using revised (FIFO) overhead uplift percentage and the amount calculated using the original overhead uplift percentage (£12,800–£12,000).

In order to adjust to current costs a further entry is required because the work in progress valuation for CCA should be:

|                    | £       |
|--------------------|---------|
| Materials          | 80,000  |
| Overheads at 20%   | 16,000  |
|                    | £96,000 |

Therefore:

|    |                    | £     | £     |
|----|--------------------|-------|-------|
| Dr | Work in progress   | 3,200 |       |
| Cr | Revaluation surplus|       | 3,200 |

with the amount required to increase overheads on a FIFO basis to a CCA basis (£16,000–£12,800).

## Depreciation

8.35 Depreciation on production plant and machinery, factory buildings and other fixed assets which form part of a company's production facilities is

130

normally included in production overheads but is considered separately here for convenience.

8.36   It will be appreciated that to arrive at the depreciation charge to be included in stock at the year end it would theoretically be necessary to calculate depreciation with reference to asset values at the year end. In Chapter 5, however, it was stated that depreciation should be charged on the average value of plant and machinery during the year and not normally on its year end value, and that any difference between depreciation based on average values and on year end values is not charged to the profit and loss account but is deducted from revaluation surplus as current year backlog depreciation.

8.37   To arrive at the correct valuation of stock at the year end it would be necessary to:

(a) Debit stock and credit operating surplus with that part of the depreciation charge for the year that relates to stock on hand at the balance sheet date; and

(b) Debit stock and credit revaluation surplus with that part of the current year backlog depreciation for the year that relates to stock on hand at the balance sheet date.

8.38   It is desirable that wherever the depreciation charge for the year is material the adjustment at (a) above should be made but on practical grounds and, because the adjustment is unlikely to be material, it will not normally be necessary to make the adjustment at (b). That adjustment has no effect on operating profit and is only likely to be material if the stock holding period is long and if the value to the business of fixed assets has risen steeply during the year.

### Example 8.9

When Pine Limited's plant and machinery was valued the following results were obtained:

|  | £'000 |
|---|---|
| Plant and machinery |  |
| Historical cost depreciation | 3,713 |
| Current cost depreciation | 6,326 |
| Depreciation based on end of year adjusted value | 6,403 |

The difference between current cost and historical cost depreciation is £2,613,000 and is likely to have a material effect on either operating profit or the value of stock.

The difference between depreciation on the end of year adjusted value and the current cost charge is current year backlog depreciation of only £77,000 and is not likely to be material in relation to the total value of stock, particularly when it is remembered that only a small proportion of the current year backlog depreciation is applicable to stock on hand at the balance sheet date.

## FINISHED GOODS

8.39 Finished goods should be valued at current replacement cost or net realisable value, whichever is the lower. In so far as they can be analysed between materials, labour and overheads, finished goods should be treated in the same way as work in progress. Where finished goods cannot be analysed into their constituent elements they may be adjusted to current replacement cost in total by applying a suitable index or percentage uplift calculated with reference to current cost levels at the balance sheet date.

**Example 8.10**

Hawthorn Limited is able to determine from its total input records over a period of time the material, labour and overhead mix of finished goods. For the six months prior to the year end the following were input to work in progress at historical cost:

|  | £ | % |
|---|---|---|
| Materials | 240,000 | 48·8 |
| Labour | 163,000 | 33·1 |
| Overheads | 89,000 | 18·1 |
|  | £492,000 | 100·0 |

The year end value of finished goods is £160,000 when valued at historical FIFO cost. Using the percentages above Hawthorn estimates the following analysis:

|  | £ (rounded) | % |
|---|---|---|
| Material | 78,000 | 48·8 |
| Labour | 53,000 | 33·1 |
| Overhead | 29,000 | 18·1 |
|  | £160,000 | 100·0 |

Using appropriate indices to calculate the current value of finished goods, Hawthorn applies, to each element, the updating factor appropriate for the stockholding period.

## GOODS PURCHASED FOR RESALE

8.40 Goods purchased for resale should be valued at the lower of current replacement cost and net realisable value. So far as possible current replacement cost should be determined using methods similar to those applicable to raw materials and components.

8.41 It is recognised that practical difficulties may be encountered where there is a large number of rapidly changing individual items, for example, goods purchased for resale held by merchants or retailers. In such cases it may be acceptable to continue the practice adopted under historical cost conventions for balance sheet purposes of deducting the normal gross profit margin from the current selling price. The (historical cost) gross profit margin used should be that applicable to the stock holding period immediately prior to the balance sheet date so that it represents the closest approximation to the difference between selling price and FIFO cost. The FIFO cost thus calculated may then be increased to current cost by the application of a suitable index.

### Example 8.11

Woods Stores Limited has for historical cost purposes always valued stocks at selling price less the normal gross profit margin. Under CCA it needs to reduce this deduction in a time of rising prices and decides to do this by applying an index. Stock at retail price in department A at the end of December amounted to £140,000 and represented two months purchases. The normal gross profit margin in this department is 20% and for historical cost purposes stock would be valued as follows:

|  | £ |
|---|---|
| Stock at retail price | 140,000 |
| 20% gross profit margin | 28,000 |
| Stock at historical cost | £112,000 |

The index applicable to this kind of stock was 108 at the end of the year and averaged 106 over the stockholding period. In order to express stock at current costs, therefore the adjustment is as follows:

$$£112,000 \times \frac{108}{106} = £114,100 \text{ (rounded)}$$

## THE COST OF SALES

8.42    The charge for cost of sales in the profit and loss account under CCA should be the value to the business, at the date of consumption, of stock consumed. It is therefore necessary, theoretically, to calculate the value to the business of each item sold at the time it is consumed.

8.43    The date of consumption of stock and work in progress is the date at which the stock or work in progress becomes specific to the requirements of a particular customer as a result of a contract and will therefore usually be the date of delivery to a customer.

8.44    It is recognised that it is clearly impracticable for many companies to determine current values accurately at the time of consumption. Most companies will therefore need to develop methods of arriving at an acceptable approximation to current cost of sales and in such cases there are a number of courses of action available depending on the circumstances of the company.

8.45    Companies which have a relatively low sales volume may be able to identify sales on an item by item basis but may not be able to determine accurately the current cost of sales at the date of consumption. Such companies may nevertheless be able to determine current value with sufficient accuracy by using information available within the company such as an in-house index of current prices based on the company's purchasing and manufacturing experience.

### Example 8.12

Firtree Tools Limited produces a wide variety of machine tools some of which are for stock and others to order. For those produced for stock it needs to ascertain the current value of the machine tool at the date of sale. There is a job card for each tool which records materials, labour and overhead charged to the job. It would be a lengthy task to revalue each item on the card and Firtree decides that reliable estimates can be obtained by uplifting the three major elements (material, labour and overhead) by appropriate indices. For one particular job the following had been charged to it according to the job card:

|  | £ |
|---|---|
| Materials and components | 4,800 |
| Labour | 3,060 |
| Overheads | 1,980 |
| Total historical cost | £9,840 |

The materials and components were entered on the job card over the period April to June when the company's in-house index averaged 110. At the date of delivery the index was 121. The revalued materials and components figure is:

$$£4,800 \times \frac{121}{110} = £5,280$$

Labour was incurred during the period June to August. Firtree calculates from its wages rates an index which was 100 throughout the period of manufacture but had increased to 115 by the date of delivery. Thus

$$£3,060 \times \frac{115}{100} = £3,519$$

Firtree also recalculates an hourly overhead rate each month and from it an index. The index was 110 during the period of manufacture and subsequently fell to 108 at the date of delivery. Thus

$$£1,980 \times \frac{108}{110} = £1,944$$

The total current value of the machine tool at the date of sale is:

|  | £ |
|---|---|
| Materials and components | 5,280 |
| Labour | 3,519 |
| Overheads | 1,944 |
| Total current value | £10,743 |

8.46    Where companies do not have the resources to compile in-house indices they may use authorised external price indices either for the costs of each type of stocks used by the company or for the cost of stocks of companies in the relevant industrial category.

8.47　Companies with a large volume of sales will often find it impracticable to determine cost of sales on an item by item basis and will probably calculate current cost of sales on a periodic basis (e.g. monthly). Such companies may calculate current cost of sales for a period either by direct reference to current replacement costs during the period or by adjusting the historical cost of sales figure (e.g. FIFO cost) to current cost of sales by means of a cost of sales adjustment (COSA).

8.48　To use the first method companies will need to be able to ascertain the following information:

(a) The pattern of sales during the period.
(b) The average current replacement cost of stock.

8.49　Companies with a fairly regular sales pattern may be able, where price levels have increased (or decreased) steadily during the year, to calculate current cost of sales for relatively long periods, e.g. quarterly or even annually. Nevertheless whatever system a company chooses should be flexible enough to account for any likely pattern of sales and price levels. Companies should recognise that their chosen system, if circumstances require it, may call for more frequent calculations than originally envisaged.

### Example 8.13

Larch Limited sells three products, 'Steady', 'New Steady' and 'Seasonal'. Sales of the three products for each quarter of 1976 were as follows:

| | Volume | | | | |
|---|---|---|---|---|---|
| | 1 | 2 | 3 | 4 | Total |
| Steady | 10,000 | 10,000 | 10,000 | 10,000 | 40,000 |
| New Steady | 5,000 | 5,000 | 5,000 | 5,000 | 20,000 |
| Seasonal | 4,000 | 2,000 | 4,000 | 10,000 | 20,000 |

It is assumed that for all products the volume of sales is evenly spread throughout each quarter.

Average unit replacement costs for each product in each quarter and at the beginning and end of the year were as follows:

| | Unit price | | | | | |
|---|---|---|---|---|---|---|
| | Opening price | Average during quarter | | | | Closing price |
| | | 1 | 2 | 3 | 4 | |
| | £ | £ | £ | £ | £ | £ |
| Steady | 1 | 2 | 4 | 6 | 8 | 9 |
| New Steady | 1 | 2 | 3 | 5 | 8 | 9 |
| Seasonal | 1 | 2 | 4 | 6 | 8 | 9 |

The current cost of sales of Steady can be determined for a whole year by one calculation because both price increases and sales occurred evenly. Thus current cost of sales for Steady can be calculated as follows:

$$40,000 \times \frac{(£1 + £9)}{2} = £200,000$$

The current cost of sales of New Steady, despite there being an even sales volume, cannot be calculated in total for the year in the same way as for Steady because of the uneven pattern of price increases. The calculation is therefore:

$$(5,000 \times £2) + (5,000 \times £3) + (5,000 \times £5) + (5,000 \times £8) =$$
$$20,000 \times \frac{(£2 + £3 + £5 + £8)}{4} = £90,000$$

If the calculation had been performed on total sales for the year in the same way as for Steady the calculation would have produced an incorrect cost of sales figure of £100,000.

The current cost of sales of Seasonal cannot be determined on a total basis (unless a weighting factor is applied) because of the uneven sales pattern. Current cost of sales for Seasonal is therefore:

$$(4,000 \times £2) + (2,000 \times £4) + (4,000 \times £6) + (10,000 \times £8) = £120,000$$

not £100,000, which would be the result if calculated in the same way as for Steady, or New Steady.

### The cost of sales adjustment (COSA)

8.50    Companies which find it impracticable or undesirable to calculate current cost of sales in the manner described above will usually need to adjust their figure of historical cost of sales to current cost of sales by means of a COSA. For example a company may wish to continue to use a FIFO system of determining cost of sales during the year and make an adjustment at the year end to determine the current cost of sales.

8.51    There are two basic methods of arriving at the required COSA as follows:

(a) determine the current cost of sales by methods similar to those described above (see Example 8.12 and 8.13) and deduct the book figure from the amount so determined to arrive at the COSA; or

(b) the averaging method.

8.52    It will be appreciated that method (a) is in essence no different from the methods described in the preceding paragraphs. It may simply be easier for companies to make an adjustment to historical cost figures rather than directly to record current cost amounts. Both methods (a) and (b) arrive at a COSA which is the difference between the book historical cost of sales and the current cost of sales.

### The averaging method of calculating the COSA

8.53    The effect of using the averaging method to calculate the COSA is to produce a cost of sales figure which, after making the COSA, consists of:

**The historical cost of input to stock during the period** (referred to as 'purchases' but which includes labour and overheads as well as materials)

either increased by
>the average current cost of the decrease in stock volume during the period

or decreased by
>the average current cost of the increase in stock volume during the period.

### Example 8.14

| | | |
|---|---|---:|
| Cost of input to stock | | £150,000 |
| Decrease in stock volume: | | |
| Opening stock | 10,000 units at £8 each | |
| Closing stock | 8,000 units at £12 each | |
| Decrease | 2,000 units | |

Average current cost of stock per unit during period

$$\frac{(£8 + £12)}{2} = £10$$

| | |
|---|---:|
| Average current cost of the decrease in stock volume over the period: £10 × 2,000 units | £20,000 |
| Current cost of sales | £170,000 |

8.54   The averaging method used in this way will arrive at the correct figure for current cost of sales only in certain circumstances and should therefore be used with caution. It relies on two assumptions holding true throughout the accounting period and, therefore, where the averaging method is used, the COSA should be calculated for the shortest accounting periods practicable, for example, each month (see paragraph 8.61).

8.55   The two assumptions are:

1   Any increase or decrease in stock volume occurs evenly during the period.
2   Any change in replacement costs occurs evenly during the period and therefore the average current cost of stock can be obtained by averaging the current cost at the beginning and end of the period.

8.56   An even increase or decrease in stock volume can occur either because purchases and sales during the period occur evenly or because any fluctuation in the level of sales is matched by similar fluctuations in the level of purchases. In exceptional circumstances, if it is known that there were material uneven stock volume or price changes during the period chosen for the COSA calculation it may be necessary to calculate weighted average current unit costs. If changes in stock volume have occurred evenly but replacement cost increases have been uneven the averaging

137

method can be used but the average current unit price for the period should be calculated by averaging price observations at regular intervals during the period.

8.57   The averaging method is demonstrated in Example 8.15 below. The steps involved are as follows:

Step 1    Divide the closing book value of stock by the unit price of stock held at the end of the year to arrive at the closing stock 'volume'.

Step 2    Divide the opening book value of stock by the unit price of stock held at the beginning of the year to arrive at the opening stock 'volume'.

Step 3    Deduct the opening stock volume from the closing stock volume to arrive at the increase or decrease in stock volume during the year.

Step 4    Multiply the change in stock volume calculated in Step 3 by the average current unit price for the period to arrive at the average current value of the movement in stock volume.

Step 5    Ascertain the historical cost of purchases and either deduct the average current value of any increase in stock or add the average current value of any decrease in stock, arrived at in Step 4. The resulting figure is the current cost of sales.

Step 6    The COSA is the difference between the amount arrived at in Step 5 and the book figure of cost of sales before making the COSA.

8.58   The stock 'volumes' arrived at using the averaging method will be hypothetical volumes where the 'unit price' used is an index or some other form of average.

Unit prices may however be actual unit costs, for example the hourly labour rates for the labour content of work in progress and finished goods. The average current replacement cost per unit used to evaluate the change in stock volume is the average current unit cost for the period which again can be expressed either in terms of specific items or as an index. In all cases the main point to bear in mind is that the same unit of measurement must be used for the beginning, end and average unit costs for the period.

**Example 8.15**

Craeglea Limited had in 1976 purchases of £960,000, opening stock at current cost of £150,000 and closing stock at current cost of £228,000. The cost of sales before the COSA therefore was £882,000. The index applicable to Craeglea's stock holding at the beginning of the year was 100, at the end of the year was 120 and averaged 110. The cost of sales adjustment is calculated as follows:

| Step 1 | $\dfrac{£228,000}{120}$ | = | 1,900 indexed units |
|---|---|---|---|
| Step 2 | $\dfrac{£150,000}{100}$ | = | 1,500 indexed units |
| Step 3 | Step 1 − Step 2 | = | 400 increase in indexed units |
| Step 4 | 400 × £110 | = | £44,000 |
| Step 5 | £960,000 − £44,000 | = | £916,000 current cost of sales |

| Step 6 | | £ |
|---|---|---|
| | CC cost of sales | 916,000 |
| | HC cost of sales | 882,000 |
| | Cost of sales adjustment | £ 34,000 |

8.59 Where the company's own accounting system can be used to arrive at current unit costs this should be used. For example the company may be able to compile an in-house index based on its purchasing and manufacturing experience. Current unit costs may be determined by reference to the most suitable authorised external index where a company finds it impracticable to use other means.

8.60 Companies may not wish to revalue stock in the balance sheet as frequently as they calculate COSAs. In such cases the increase or decrease in stock volume during a period will need to be arrived at (in Steps 1 and 2) by dividing the opening and closing values of stock by unit prices calculated with reference to the particular accounting convention being used. For example where a FIFO system is used to arrive at cost of sales before making a COSA, the unit prices to be used will be those applicable to the dates on which stock on hand at the beginning and end of the period would be assumed, on a FIFO basis, to have been purchased. The average current unit cost to be applied to the stock *movement* for the period (in Step 4) however in all cases should be calculated based on current unit costs at the beginning and end of the period (weighted if necessary), regardless of whether stock at the beginning or end of the period is valued on the basis of current cost, FIFO cost or any other basis.

### Example 8.16

Drift Limited had in 1978 purchases of £840,000, opening stock at FIFO historical cost of £105,000 and closing stock at FIFO historical cost of £215,000. The historical cost of sales therefore was £730,000. Opening stock represented two months purchases whereas closing stock is equal to the last three months purchases. The index applicable to Drift's stocks was as follows:

| 1977 | | |
|---|---|---|
| Mid-November | 104 | average for period = 106 |
| Mid-December | 108 | |

139

|  | 1978 |  |  |
|---|---|---|---|
|  | Mid-October | 124 | ⎫ |
|  | Mid-December | 132 | ⎬ average for period = 128 |
|  | Average for 1978 | 120 | ⎭ |

Step 1    $\dfrac{£215,000}{128}$      = 1,680 indexed units

Step 2    $\dfrac{£105,000}{106}$      =  991 indexed units

Step 3    Step 1 − Step 2      =  689 increase in indexed units

Step 4    689 × £120      = £  82,680

Step 5    £840,000 − £82,680      = £757,320 current cost of sales

|  |  | £ |
|---|---|---|
| Step 6 | Current cost of sales | 757,320 |
|  | Historical cost of sales | 730,000 |
|  | Cost of sales adjustment | £ 27,320 |

8.61    As with the other methods of arriving at current cost of sales, the averaging method should be applied to each category of stock individually and, where applicable, to each constituent part of a category (e.g. material, labour and overhead). This is of particular relevance where the cost of the different elements of stock changes at materially different rates during a period. To minimise the margin of error where the assumptions upon which the averaging method is based do not hold true the current cost of sales should be calculated at the most frequent intervals practicable, for example monthly. Example 8.17 shows the degree of inaccuracy that may result where replacement cost increases arise irregularly and where stock movements do not occur evenly.

**Example 8.17**

Variations Limited calculated the cost of sales adjustment both quarterly and annually during 1978 with the following results:

|  | Quarter | | | | Year |
|---|---|---|---|---|---|
|  | 1 | 2 | 3 | 4 |  |
|  | £ | £ | £ | £ | £ |
| Opening stock | 40,000 | 55,968 | 11,040 | 18,975 | 40,000 |
| Purchases | 131,968 | 74,072 | 145,935 | 163,965 | 515,940 |
| Closing stock | (55,968) | (11,040) | (18,975) | (47,940) | (47,940) |
| Cost of sales | 116,000 | 119,000 | 138,000 | 135,000 | 508,000 |
| Stock index: |  |  |  |  |  |
|   beginning of period | 100 | 106 | 115 | 115 | 100 |
|   average for period | 103 | 110·5 | 115 | 128 | 120·5 |
|   end of period | 106 | 115 | 115 | 141 | 141 |

| | Quarter 1 | Quarter 2 | 3 | 4 | Year |
|---|---|---|---|---|---|
| Step 1 Closing volume | 528 | 96 | 165 | 340 | 340 |
| Step 2 Opening volume | 400 | 528 | 96 | 165 | 400 |
| Step 3 Volume increase/(decrease) | 128 | (432) | 69 | 175 | (60) |
| Step 4 Current cost of increase/(decrease) | 13,184 | (47,736) | 7,935 | 22,400 | (7,230) |
| Step 5 Current cost of sales | 118,784 | 121,808 | 138,000 | 141,565 | 523,170 |
| Step 6 COSA | £2,784 | £2,808 | — | £6,565 | £15,170 |

£12,157

On a quarterly basis the cost of sales adjustment for the year is £12,157 compared with the more inaccurate figure of £15,170 on an annual basis.

### Alternative application of the average method

8.62    The application of the averaging method described above is based on an adjustment to the input to stock for changes in the volume of stock during the period.

Some companies may find it more convenient to apply the averaging method to cost of sales (i.e. input plus opening stock, less closing stock) rather than to the input stock, and the following paragraph describes the application of the averaging method in such cases. The matters considered in paragraphs 8.55, 8.56 and 8.58 to 8.61 are relevant whichever application of the averaging method is adopted. The application of the averaging method described below is that contained in the *Sandilands Report* (paragraphs 596 and 597).

8.63    To arrive at current cost of sales, using the averaging method, based on the historical cost of sales, the procedure is as follows. It is important to use as the historical cost of sales the figure arrived at after taking into account the closing book value of stock used in the COSA calculation:

Step 1    Multiply the closing book value of stock in the balance sheet ('the unadjusted closing value') by the average current unit cost during the period and divide by the unit cost applicable to the closing book value of stock.

Step 2    Multiply the opening book value of stock in the balance sheet ('the unadjusted opening value') by the average current unit cost during the period and divide by the unit cost applicable to the opening book value of stock.

Step 3    Deduct the amount arrived at in Step 2 ('the adjusted opening stock') from the amount arrived at in Step 1 ('the adjusted closing stock').

Step 4    Deduct the unadjusted opening value of stock from the un-adjusted closing value of stock.

Step 5    Deduct the (adjusted) amount arrived at in Step 3 from the (unadjusted) amount arrived at in Step 4 to arrive at the COSA.

**Example 8.18**

Using the Craeglea Limited information again from Example 8.15 the alternative calculation of the cost of sales adjustment is:

|        |                                   | £          |
|--------|-----------------------------------|------------|
| Step 1 | $£228,000 \times \dfrac{110}{120}$ | = 209,000 |
| Step 2 | $£150,000 \times \dfrac{110}{100}$ | = 165,000 |
| Step 3 | Step 1 – Step 2                   | = 44,000   |
| Step 4 | £228,000 – £150,000               | = 78,000   |
| Step 5 | Step 4 – Step 3                   | = £34,000  |

8.64    It can be seen from a comparison of Examples 8.15 and 8.18 that both applications of the averaging method produce the same result in the same circumstances. It is purely a matter of preference and ease of calculation that will determine which application is adopted by companies. A further discussion of the averaging method is contained in Appendix 3 to ED 18.

## BIRCHWOOD'S STOCK AND COST OF SALES

8.65    The procedure adopted in previous chapters will now be continued and the principles covered in this chapter will be applied to the stock and cost of sales of Birchwood Limited. The accounting entries for inclusion in the CCA Worksheet are dealt with at the end of the example in paragraph 8.103.

### Opening balance sheet

8.66    Birchwood's opening balance sheet at 31.12.78 includes stock at FIFO cost as follows:

|                   | £'000  |
|-------------------|--------|
| Raw materials     | 19,216 |
| Work in progress  | 12,444 |
| Finished goods    | 19,653 |
|                   | 51,313 |

8.67    The first step in the preparation of Birchwood's current cost accounts for 1979 is to value the stock at 1st January 1979 at current cost.

### Materials

8.68    Although Birchwood began the compilation of an in-house index for raw materials at the beginning of 1979 it had to use an official index at 1st January 1979 to value the raw material content of stock at that date.

8.69   The stock holding period for the materials content of each category of stock at 31st December 1978 was as follows:

|  |  |
|---|---|
| Raw materials | 3 months |
| Work in progress | 1 month |
| Finished goods | 1 month |

The appropriate index stood at 178·6 at 31st December 1978, being the average of the published December and January indices.

The factors to be used to update the raw material content of each category of stock will therefore be calculated using 178·6 as the numerator and using the index numbers for the mid point of the stock holding period as the denominators as follows:

(a) **Raw materials**
    Stock holding mid-point 15th November
    Index number at 15th November 172·7

$$\text{Factor } \frac{178\cdot6}{172\cdot7} = 1\cdot034$$

(b) **Work in progress—raw materials content**
All raw materials are input to work in progress at the start of manufacture, the longest held raw materials being input first. Consequently, the raw material included in work in progress at 31st December 1978 can be assumed to have been purchased in September 1978. The stock holding mid-point is therefore 15th September.
    The index number for 15th September is 169·1

$$\text{The factor is therefore } \frac{178\cdot6}{169\cdot1} = 1\cdot056.$$

(c) **Finished goods—raw materials content**
If the raw material content of work in progress can be assumed to have been purchased in September it follows that the raw material content of finished goods can be assumed to have been purchased in August. The stockholding mid point for the raw material content of finished goods is therefore 15th August.
    The index number for 15th August is 167·7

$$\text{The factor is therefore } \frac{178\cdot6}{167\cdot7} = 1\cdot065.$$

8.70   Birchwood is able to calculate that work in progress at 31st December 1978 consists of raw materials, labour and overhead in the following proportions:

|  |  |
|---|---|
| Raw materials | 50% |
| Labour | 25% |
| Overheads | 25% |

Similarly finished goods can be analysed as follows:

| | |
|---|---|
| Raw materials | 30% |
| Labour | 35% |
| Overheads | 35% |

8.71 The current cost of the raw material content of stock can therefore be calculated as follows (in £'000):

|  |  | Increase over historical cost £'000 |
|---|---|---|
| Raw materials | £19,216 × 1·034 = £19,869 | 653 |
| Work in progress—<br>Raw material<br>content | (12,444 × 50%) × 1·056 = 6,570 | 348 |
| Finished goods—<br>Raw material<br>content | (19,653 × 30%) × 1·065 = 6,279 | 383 |
| | | 1,384 |

### Labour

8.72 Birchwood treats both productive and applicable non-productive labour as 'labour'. Birchwood did not increase wage rates during its work in progress and finished goods stock holding periods and the level of efficiency has remained constant. Consequently no adjustment is required to the value of the labour content of stock.

### Overheads excluding depreciation

8.73 After reviewing overhead levels excluding depreciation Birchwood decides that price changes within the stock holding period have been immaterial and consequently no adjustment has been made to the overhead content of work in progress and finished goods.

### Depreciation

8.74 As Birchwood is adopting CCA for the first time on 1st January 1979 the depreciation included in stock at 31st December 1978 amounting to £312,000 for work in progress and £690,000 for finished goods is based on the historical cost of fixed assets. To arrive at the opening value of stock for CCA purposes the depreciation element of overheads should be recalculated with reference to the current value of fixed assets at 31st December 1978 as calculated in Chapters 5 and 6.

Birchwood estimates that based on the current costs at the 31st December 1978 the depreciation included in stock should be £367,000 for work in progress and £811,000 for finished goods; increases of £55,000 and £121,000 respectively.

### Summary of opening stock

8.75 The CCA value of opening stock at 1st January 1979 was as follows:

| | Historical cost | | | | Adjustments | | Current cost |
|---|---|---|---|---|---|---|---|
| | Raw materials | Labour | Overheads | Total | Raw materials | Deprecn. | |
| | £'000 | £'000 | £'000 | £'000 | £'000 | £'000 | £'000 |
| Raw materials | 19,216 | — | — | 19,216 | 653 | — | 19,869 |
| Work in progress | 6,222 | 3,111 | 3,111 | 12,444 | 348 | 55 | 12,847 |
| Finished goods | 5,896 | 6,879 | 6,878 | 19,653 | 383 | 121 | 20,157 |
| | 31,334 | 9,990 | 9,989 | 51,313 | 1,334 | 176 | 52,873 |

### Cost of sales for 1979

8.76 Birchwoods historical (FIFO) cost of sales for 1979 is as follows:

| | £'000 | £'000 |
|---|---|---|
| Opening stock | | 51,313 |
| Input to stock | | |
| Raw materials | 93,001 | |
| Labour | 90,780 | |
| Overheads (including depreciation based on current cost) | 85,880 | |
| | | 269,661 |
| | | 320,974 |
| Closing stock | | 66,657 |
| Cost of sales | | 254,317 |

### Raw materials

8.77 As mentioned above Birchwood began maintaining an in-house raw materials price index on 1st January 1979. That index, the official index and the cost of purchases and the raw material content of cost of sales for each month of 1979 are shown below:

| | Official index | In-house index (average for the month) | Purchases | Historical (FIFO) cost of sales |
|---|---|---|---|---|
| | | | £'000 | £'000 |
| January | 182·7 | 100·0 | 6,355 | 5,833 |
| Feburary | 187·9 | 103·1 | 6,872 | 6,184 |
| March | 192·5 | 105·3 | 7,416 | 6,573 |

145

|           | Official index | In-house index (average for the month) | Purchases | Historical (FIFO) cost of sales |
|-----------|----------------|----------------------------------------|-----------|----------------------------------|
| April     | 194·8          | 105·9                                  | 7,166     | 6,350                            |
| May       | 196·1          | 107·2                                  | 7,078     | 6,266                            |
| June      | 197·5          | 108·3                                  | 7,579     | 6,998                            |
| July      | 200·3          | 109·5                                  | 7,623     | 5,989                            |
| August    | 200·3          | 110·6                                  | 8,458     | 6,314                            |
| September | 203·5          | 110·9                                  | 9,006     | 7,202                            |
| October   | 206·1          | 114·0                                  | 8,217     | 6,919                            |
| November  | 208·5          | 117·1                                  | 8,444     | 6,532                            |
| December  | 210·4          | 117·9                                  | 8,787     | 6,453                            |
|           |                |                                        | 93,001    | 77,613                           |

8.78    During 1979 Birchwood continued to account for stock on a FIFO basis and therefore, at the end of the year, a COSA needs to be calculated to arrive at current cost of sales. As Birchwood has monthly figures available it can calculate the COSA on a monthly basis by using current prices for the month or by using either application of the averaging method as appropriate. In fact it will be seen that the information available to Birchwood makes it unnecessary to resort to the averaging method.

8.79    In paragraph 8.69 it was explained that based on the year end stock holdings the raw material content of Birchwood's cost of sales in any month represents raw materials purchased five months previously. This will hold true throughout the year so long as the volume of stocks does not fluctuate materially. A brief review of the purchases and FIFO cost of sales figures in paragraph 8.77 however makes it clear that there must have been some material fluctuation of stock balances at least during the last six months of the year. Consequently, it is not appropriate to calculate a COSA for the year as a whole.

8.80    Taking each month separately a COSA is required as follows:

(a) For months where the volume of stock has not fluctuated materially, current cost of sales will approximate to the cost of purchases. The COSA will therefore be the difference between FIFO cost of sales and purchases for the month.

(b) For months where the volume of stock has changed materially between the beginning and end of the month, the current cost of sales will approximate to purchases for the month, plus or minus the stock movement valued at average current replacement cost for the month. This can be calculated either by applying current unit costs to FIFO cost sales or by using the averaging method.

146

### The COSA where stock volume is steady

8.81   There are a number of ways in which to determine whether the volume of stock has remained reasonably steady. Clearly if stock quantities are known stock movements can be determined easily but in other circumstances some calculation may be necessary. In such cases there are two basic methods of calculating the stock movement:

1 Determine stock 'volumes' at the beginning and end of the period as if the averaging method was to be adopted (see paragraph 8.57).
2 Determine the 'volume' of purchases and cost of sales by:

   (a) dividing purchases by the average current cost per unit
   (b) dividing FIFO cost of sales by the average FIFO cost per unit.

8.82   In each case the stock movement will be the difference between the two 'volumes'. If this figure is immaterial it can be assumed that there has been no material stock movement during the period. Birchwood decides to use method 2 above to determine whether material stock movements have occurred. As Birchwood's in-house index was not being compiled prior to January 1979 it cannot be used for any months for which the raw materials content of cost of sales was purchased prior to 1st January. This is because the unit of measurement used to determine the volume of sales and the volume of purchases must be the same. Consequently, as the material content of cost of sales represents goods purchased five months prior to sale, Birchwood needs to use the official index, the only unit of measurement common to both purchases and cost of sales, for the first five months of 1979 and may use its own index thereafter.

| Month | Official index | | Purchases £'000 | Volume | Official index | | Historical cost of sales £'000 | Volume |
|---|---|---|---|---|---|---|---|---|
| Jan. 79 | Jan. 79 | 182·7 | 6,355 | 3,478 | Aug. 78 | 167·7 | 5,833 | 3,478 |
| Feb. 79 | Feb. 79 | 187·9 | 6,872 | 3,657 | Sept. 78 | 169·1 | 6,184 | 3,657 |
| Mar. 79 | Mar. 79 | 192·5 | 7,416 | 3,852 | Oct. 78 | 170·6 | 6,573 | 3,853 |
| Apr. 79 | Apr. 79 | 194·8 | 7,166 | 3,679 | Nov. 78 | 172·7 | 6,350 | 3,677 |
| May 79 | May 79 | 196·1 | 7,078 | 3,609 | Dec. 78 | 173·6 | 6,266 | 3,609 |
| | In-house index | | | | In-house index | | | |
| June 79 | June 79 | 108·3 | 7,579 | 6,998 | Jan. 79 | 100·0 | 6,998 | 6,998 |
| | | | 42,466 | | | | 38,204 | |
| July 79 | July 79 | 109·5 | 7,623 | 6,962 | Feb. 79 | 103·1 | 5,989 | 5,809 |

8.83   It can be seen that until June 1979 there was no stock movement but that a material movement must have occurred in July because purchases materially exceeded sales. It should be noted that as soon as a significant stock movement occurs the assumption that there is a 5 month time lag between the purchase of raw materials and their sale as finished products becomes invalid and it is pointless continuing to the end of the year.

8.84    The cost of sales adjustment for the first six months of the year in respect of raw materials can now be calculated. It is simply the difference between purchases and the FIFO raw material content of cost of sales as follows (from paragraph 8.77):

|  | £'000 |
|---|---|
| Purchases for first six months | 42,466 |
| HC cost of sales first six months | 38,204 |
| COSA for first six months | 4,262 |

### The COSA where stock volume changes

8.85    For the second half of the year it is not possible to use the purchases figure as the current cost of sales because the 'volume' of purchases does not approximate to the volume of sales. Nevertheless the volume of sales and the average current cost of purchases per unit can be determined so there will be no need to resort to the averaging method.

8.86    After the first 5 months of the year the company's in-house index number can be used as the average current cost of purchases per unit. The FIFO cost of sales divided by the index number for the month in which the material content of cost of sales was purchased will give the sales 'volume'.

8.87    Continuing the calculations begun in paragraph 8.82 it can be established that the raw material content of cost of sales in July was less than one month's purchases and therefore some of February's purchases related to June and August's cost of sales, as follows:

|  | £'000 |  |
|---|---|---|
| Material content of July cost of sales | 5,989 | (from paragraph 8.82) |
| February purchases used in first half of year | 515 | (see below) |
| February purchases used in August | 368 | (balance |
| Total February purchases | 6,872 | (from paragraph 8.82) |

The £515,000 used in the first half of the year can be calculated as follows:

|  | £'000 |  |
|---|---|---|
| Materials content of historical cost opening stock | 31,334 | (from paragraph 8.75) |
| January purchases | 6,355 | (from paragraph 8.82) |
|  | 37,689 |  |
| January to June cost of sales | 38,204 | (from paragraph 8.82) |
| February purchases (balance) | 515 |  |

The £515,000 arises because the opening stock was not quite sufficient to cover the volume of sales in January to May.

8.88 Similar calculations show that the cost of sales for the remainder of the year included purchases for months as follows (in £'000):

**Purchases**

|  | Feb. | Marcl | April | May | June | July | Aug. | Sept. | Total |
|---|---|---|---|---|---|---|---|---|---|
| Cost of sales | 5,989 | | | | | | | | 5,989 |
| July | 368 | 5,946 | | | | | | | 6,314 |
| August | | 1,470 | 5,732 | | | | | | 7,202 |
| September | | | 1,434 | 5,485 | | | | | 6,919 |
| October | | | | 1,593 | 4,939 | | | | 6,532 |
| November | | | | | 2,640 | 3,813 | | | 6,453 |
| December | | | | | | | | | |
|  | 6,357 | 7,416 | 7,166 | 7,078 | 7,579 | 3,813 | | | 39,409 |
|  | 515 | | | | | | | | 515 |
| 1st half of year | | | | | | 3,810 | 8,458 | 9,006 | 21,274 |
| Closing stock | | | | | | | | | |
|  | 6,872 | 7,416 | 7,166 | 7,078 | 7,579 | 7,623 | 8,458 | 9,006 | 61,198 |

Thus it will be seen that February's purchases were sold mainly in July and partly in August and so on through the period. It can be seen that part of July's purchases and all of August to December's purchases were in stock at the end of 1979 (October to December's purchases are not shown for this reason).

8.89 It is now possible to compute current cost of sales and the COSA in respect of raw materials for the second half of 1979 as follows, in £'000:

**Purchases**

|  |  | Feb. | March | April | May | June | July | Aug. | Sept. | Total |
|---|---|---|---|---|---|---|---|---|---|---|
| In house index | | 103·1 | 105·3 | 105·9 | 107·2 | 108·3 | 109·5 | 110·6 | 110·9 | |
| **Cost of sales** | | | | | | | | | | |
| July | 109·5 | 6,361 | | | | | | | | 6,361 |
| Aug. | 110·6 | 395 | 6,245 | | | | | | | 6,640 |
| Sept. | 110·9 | | 1,548 | 6,003 | | | | | | 7,551 |
| Oct. | 114·0 | | | 1,544 | 5,833 | | | | | 7,377 |
| Nov. | 117·1 | | | | 1,740 | 5,340 | | | | 7,080 |
| Dec. | 117·9 | | | | | 2,874 | 4,106 | | | 6,980 |
|  | | 6,756 | 7,793 | 7,547 | 7,573 | 8,214 | 4,106 | | | 41,989 |

The figures above are derived from the table shown in paragraph 8.88 by dividing the figures shown therein by the purchases index numbers and multiplying by the cost of sales index numbers. For example, the figure of £4,106 is calculated as:

$$£3,813 \times \frac{117·9}{109·5} = £4,106$$

The cost of sales adjustment for the second six months can therefore be calculated as follows:

149

|  | £'000 |
|---|---|
| Current cost of sales | 41,989 |
| Historical cost of sales | 39,409 |
| Cost of sales adjustment | 2,580 |

and the cost of sales adjustment for the whole year is therefore:

|  | £'000 |
|---|---|
| First six months (paragraph 8.84) | 4,262 |
| Second six months (as above) | 2,580 |
|  | 6,842 |

**Labour**

8.90 Although there is a time lag of up to five months between the purchase of raw materials and their sale as part of finished products the time lag in respect of labour is much shorter. This is apparent from the following figures of Birchwood's input to work in progress and transfers to finished goods and cost of sales:

|  | Work in progress | Finished goods | Historical cost of sales |
|---|---|---|---|
|  | £'000 | £'000 | £'000 |
| 1st January balance | 3,111 | 6,879 | — |
| INPUT |  |  |  |
| Jan. | 6,800 | 6,924 | 6,805 |
| Feb. | 6,800 | 6,915 | 7,215 |
| March | 6,800 | 6,272 | 7,669 |
| April | 7,820 | 7,310 | 7,408 |
| May | 7,820 | 7,803 | 7,310 |
| June | 7,820 | 7,698 | 8,164 |
| July | 7,820 | 7,715 | 6,987 |
| Aug. | 7,820 | 7,653 | 7,366 |
| Sept. | 7,820 | 7,741 | 8,402 |
| Oct. | 7,820 | 7,592 | 8,072 |
| Nov. | 7,820 | 7,608 | 7,620 |
| Dec. | 7,820 | 7,420 | 7,529 |
|  | 90,780 | 88,651 | 90,547 |
| 31st December balance | 5,240 | 4,983 | — |

8.91 The input to work in progress in each case is the month's wages. The labour content of work in progress and finished goods at 1st January can be seen to represent respectively approximately half and one month's labour. It can also be seen that the only increase in labour rates occurred in April (15%) and that the year end balances for both work in progress

150

and finished goods represent about 65% of one month's labour. The year-end balances can be calculated as follows:

|  | Work in progress | Finished goods |
|---|---|---|
|  | £'000 | £'000 |
| Balance at 1st January | 3,111 | 6,879 |
| Wages | 90,780 | — |
| Transfer to finished goods | (88,651) | 88,651 |
| Transfer to cost of sales | — | (90,547) |
| Balance at 31st December | 5,240 | 4,983 |

8.92 For the period January to March there was no change in the cost of labour. The cost of sales figures for those months therefore reflect the current value of labour. In April, however, wage rates increased by 15% and cost of sales for a period thereafter will be based on the old labour rates and therefore a COSA is required to increase it to current cost. A simple way to do this is to calculate the effect of a 15% increase on the labour element of stock at the end of March, i.e. immediately before the wage increase. The calculation is as follows:

|  | Work in progress: Labour | Finished goods: Labour |
|---|---|---|
|  | £'000 | £'000 |
| 1st January balance (paragraph 8.75) | 3,111 | 6,879 |
| Wages for three months to March | 20,400 |  |
| Transfer to finished goods | (20,111) | 20,111 |
| Transfer to cost of sales | | (21,689) |
| 31st March balance | 3,400 | 5,301 |

Increase to current cost at 31st March:

$$£'000\,(3,400 + 5,301) \times 15\% = £1,305,000$$

8.93 After April there are no further wage rate increases and therefore, except for the opening balance of labour at the beginning of April, all input to historical cost of sales will have been made at current cost.

The whole of the balance of labour at the beginning of April will have been input to cost of sales well before the year end and therefore the amount of £1,305,000 represents the amount by which historical cost of sales falls short of current cost of sales, i.e. £1,305,000 is the COSA for the labour content of cost of sales.

### Overheads

8.94 Birchwood charges overheads into work in progress based on the percentage uplift method. A review of overheads during the year has shown that

151

there had been no increases in overheads in any month which would give rise to a material COSA. Consequently, on the grounds of immateriality Birchwood makes no adjustment to the FIFO cost of sales in respect of overheads.

**Current cost of sales**

8.95   The current cost of sales for the year is as follows:

|  | £'000 | £'000 |  |
|---|---|---|---|
| FIFO cost of sales | | 254,317 | (paragraph 8.76) |
| Add COSA in respect of: | | | |
| Material | 6,842 | | (paragraph 8.89) |
| Labour | 1,305 | 8,147 | (paragraph 8.92) |
| Current cost of sales | | 262,464 | |

**Year end stock valuation**

8.96   The method of arriving at the current value of stock at the year end is similar to that used at the beginning of the year. One difference however is that Birchwood uses its in-house index at the year end instead of the official index used at the beginning of the year. The only other variation is that because the overhead charge to work in progress is assumed to have included current cost depreciation no adjustment to the overhead content of stock is required in that respect.

8.97   Closing stocks at historical cost are made up as follows:

|  | Material | Labour | Overheads | Total |
|---|---|---|---|---|
|  | £'000 | £'000 | £'000 | £'000 |
| Raw materials | 25,448 | — | — | 25,448 |
| Work in progress | 17,011 | 5,240 | 4,978 | 27,229 |
| Finished goods | 4,263 | 4,983 | 4,734 | 13,980 |
|  | 46,722 | 10,223 | 9,712 | 66,657 |

No adjustment to either labour or overheads is necessary there having been no material price changes during the stockholding period. From paragraph 8.88 it can be seen that the material element of closing stocks comprises half July's purchases plus all the purchases for August to December. The index numbers in paragraph 8.77 are the average index numbers for the months in question and can be used as the denominator for the purpose of revaluing the materials content of stocks at current cost at the end of December. The numerator is the index at 31st December which is 118·5. The revaluation is carried out as follows:

| Month of purchase | Purchases in stock | Multiply by | Divide by | Stock at December prices |
|---|---|---|---|---|
| | £'000 | | | £'000 |
| July | 3,810 | 118·5 | 109·8[1] | 4,112 |
| August | 8,458 | 118·5 | 110·6 | 9,062 |
| September | 9,006 | 118·5 | 110·9 | 9,623 |
| October | 8,217 | 118·5 | 114·0 | 8,541 |
| November | 8,444 | 118·5 | 117·1 | 8,545 |
| December | 8,787 | 118·5 | 117·9 | 8,832 |
| | 46,722 | | | 48,715 |

[1] the July denominator is one quarter of the difference between the July and August indices added to the July index. This is due to only the purchases in the second half of July being valued.

8.98   The increase in the value of the material element of stock is therefore £1,993,000 (48,715 − 46,722) and this gives a closing stock figure as follows:

| | £'000 |
|---|---|
| Total stock as historical cost | 66,657 |
| *Add* adjustment to material element | 1,993 |
| Total stock at current cost | 68,650 |

8.99   The increase in the value of the materials element of total stocks can be analysed over raw materials, work in progress and finished goods. Assuming stocks move on a FIFO basis raw material stocks will have been the last to be purchased and do, in fact, equal the October, November and December purchases. Therefore the adjustment to raw material stocks is, from paragraph 8.97:

| | Purchases | Stock at December prices | Difference |
|---|---|---|---|
| | £'000 | £'000 | £'000 |
| October | 8,217 | 8,541 | 324 |
| November | 8,444 | 8,545 | 101 |
| December | 8,787 | 8,832 | 45 |
| | 25,448 | 25,918 | 470 |

8.100   Similarly the materials element of work in progress represents all the September purchases plus over ninety per cent of August's purchases. Revalued at December prices these are:

153

|  | Purchases | Stock at December prices | Difference |
|---|---|---|---|
|  | £'000 | £'000 | £'000 |
| August | 8,005 | 8,577 | 572 |
| September | 9,006 | 9,623 | 617 |
|  | 17,011 | 18,200 | 1,189 |

8.101 In revaluing the August purchases the August index (110·6) was used because any adjustment for the fact that not all the month's purchases are involved is likely to be immaterial.

8.102 On the same basis the materials element of finished goods is revalued as follows:

|  | Purchases | Stock at December prices | Difference |
|---|---|---|---|
|  | £'000 | £'000 | £'000 |
| July | 3,810 | 4,112 | 302 |
| August | 453 | 485 | 32 |
|  | 4,263 | 4,597 | 334 |

8.103 The total adjustment to the materials element of stock is therefore analysed as follows:

|  | £'000 |  |
|---|---|---|
| Raw materials | 470 | (paragraph 8.99) |
| Work in progress | 1,189 | (paragraph 8.100) |
| Finished goods | 334 | (paragraph 8.102) |
|  | 1,993 |  |

**The CCA Worksheet**

8.104 The CCA Worksheet is completed in respect of stock and cost sales as follows:

The Worksheet is shown in Table 8.1 after the entries below have been recorded:

(a) **Adjustment to opening stock** (e) is entered in columns 3 and 4 as follows:

|  | £'000 | £'000 |
|---|---|---|
| Dr Stock and work in progress | 1,560 |  |
| Cr Revaluation surplus |  | 1,560 |

Being the difference between the current cost of stock (52,873) and the FIFO cost of stock (51,313) at the beginning of the year. (see paragraph 8.75)

154

(b) **The COSA**

Care must be taken to avoid double counting the adjustment to opening stock. In Birchwood's case the COSA is an adjustment to a FIFO cost of sales figure which will have already been charged with the FIFO cost of opening stock. In such cases the COSA *includes the opening stock adjustment* (i.e. the opening current cost of stock includes some unrealised revaluation surplus which becomes realised as it is charged to cost of sales through the COSA). The adjustment to opening stock will be reflected in the profit and loss account when the worksheet is cross-cast. It is therefore necessary when recording the COSA in the worksheet only to account for the difference between the COSA and the adjustment to opening stock. The accounting entry (h) to be entered in columns 9 and 10 is therefore:

|  |  | £'000 | £'000 |
|---|---|---|---|
| Dr | Cost of sales | 6,587 | |
| Cr | Revaluation surplus | | 6,587 |
| | being the difference between the | | |
| | COSA (8,147 paragraph 8.95) and | | |
| | the opening stock adjustment (1,560 as above) | | |

(c) **The Adjustment to Closing Stock**

The adjustment to closing stock (j) is entered in columns 9 and 10 as follows:

|  |  | £'000 | £'000 |
|---|---|---|---|
| Dr | Stock and work in progress | 1,993 | |
| Cr | Revaluation surplus | | 1,993 |
| | being the difference between the | | |
| | current cost of stock (68,650, | | |
| | paragraph 8.98) and the FIFO cost | | |
| | of stock (66,657, paragraph 8.97) | | |
| | at the end of the year. | | |

# Table 8.1

## BIRCHWOOD LIMITED
## CCA Worksheet

| | 1 | 2 | 3 | 4 | 5 | 6 |
|---|---|---|---|---|---|---|
| | Opening balance sheet historical cost | | Opening balance sheet journal | | Opening balance sheet current cost | |
| | Dr £'000 | Cr £'000 | Dr £'000 | Cr £'000 | Dr £'000 | Cr £'000 |
| Land and buildings | 4,719 | 569 | C 569 } D 1,190 | C 569 | 5,340 | |
| Plant and machinery | 15,446 | | A 10,261 | B 4,357 | 21,350 | |
| Investment in subsidiaries and associates | 13,984 | | | | | |
| Quoted and unquoted investments | 1,147 | | | | | |
| Stock and work in progress | 51,313 | | E 1,560 | | 52,873 | |
| Debtors | 32,727 | | | | | |
| Cash | 465 | | | | | |
| Creditors | | 23,011 | | | | |
| Current tax | | 3,582 | | | | |
| Bank overdraft | | 6,481 | | | | |
| Dividend | | 5,700 | | | | |
| Deferred tax | | 20,222 | | | | |
| Ordinary share capital | | 32,185 | | | | |
| Reserves – general | | 14,051 | | | | |
| Reserves – revaluation | | | B 4,357 | A 10,261 } D 1,190 } E 1,560 | | |
| Preference share capital | | 4,000 | | | | |
| 10% Debentures | | 10,000 | | | | |
| Realisation of fixed assets | | | | | | |
| Revenue income | | | | | | |
| Revenue expenditure | | | | | | |
| Depreciation | | | | | | |
| Interest | | | | | | |
| Tax expense | | | | | | |
| Dividends received | | | | | | |
| Revenue surplus | | | | | | |
| | 119,801 | 119,801 | | | | |

| 7 | 8 | 9 | 10 | 11 | 12 | 13 | 14 |
|---|---|---|---|---|---|---|---|
| Income and expenditure for 1979 | | Journal entries | | Profit and loss account for 1979 | | Closing balance sheet | |
| Dr £'000 | Cr £'000 | Dr £'000 | Cr £'000 | Dr £'000 | Cr £'000 | Dr £'000 | Cr £'000 |
| | | g 835 | | | | | |
| 6,036 | | a 627 ⎫<br>c 7,716 ⎭ | a 1,002 ⎫<br>d 2,634<br>e 6,626<br>f 595 ⎭ | | | | |
| 139 | | | | | | | |
| | | j 1,993 ⎫<br>h 6,587 ⎭ | | | | | |
| | 295,290 | | | | | | |
| 1,319 | 465 | | | | | | |
| 283,487 | | | | | | | |
| 3,582 | | | | | | | |
| 6,481 | 3,430 | | | | | | |
| 5,980 | | | | | | | |
| | 8,000 | | | | | | |
| | | d 2,634 ⎫<br>f 595 ⎭ | c 7,716 ⎫<br>g 1,068<br>h 6,587<br>j 1,993 ⎭ | | | | |
| | 238 | a 1,002 | b 137 ⎫<br>a 627 ⎭ | | | | |
| | | e 6,626 ⎫<br>b 137<br>g 233 ⎭ | | | | | |
| 1,319 | | | | | | | |
| | 920 | | | | | | |
| 308,343 | 308,343 | | | | | | |

# 9 The Treatment of Special Cases—Stock and Cost of Sales

9.1 The matters considered in this chapter are listed below, together with the relevant paragraph numbers:

| | Paragraphs |
|---|---|
| Net realisable value | 9.2–9.7 |
| Goods purchased for resale which are turned over rapidly | 9.8–9.10 |
| Contract work in progress | 9.11–9.21 |
| Purchased seasonal agricultural produce | 9.22–9.25 |
| Consumable stores | 9.26 |
| Profits from dealing and other similar activities | 9.27–9.32 |
| Stocks of land and constructions | 9.33–9.36 |

## NET REALISABLE VALUE

### Stock sold at below replacement cost

9.2 The charge to cost of sales in respect of goods sold is the value to the business, at the date of consumption of the stock and work-in-progress sold. The date of consumption is normally the date of sale. Therefore, when stock is sold at below current replacement cost the value to the business of the stock at the date of consumption is the price at which it is sold—its net realisable value. This is analogous to the situation in an historical cost system when stock is sold at below its historical cost. Any write-down of stock to net realisable value should be charged to profit and loss account, disclosed if appropriate as an exceptional or extraordinary item.

### Net realisable value in the balance sheet

9.3 The balance sheet value of stock held should be stated at the lower of current replacement cost and net realisable value. The determination of net realisable value should be carried out in the same way as in an historical cost system. (See SSAP9 Appendix I, paragraph 5.)

### Accounting for net realisable value at the balance sheet date

9.4 A fall in net realisable value or an increase in current replacement cost

158

may give rise to circumstances in which the value to the business of stock becomes its net realisable value. The accounting entries required to account for a change to net realisable value differ depending on the company's method of accounting.

9.5    A company which accounts for stock movements during the year on a FIFO basis and adjusts balance sheet values to a CCA basis at the year end may do so in two ways:

1    It may increase the value of stock to current replacement cost and then make a deduction for items whose value to the business is their net realisable value; or

2    It may increase the value of stock to its value to the business with reference to current replacement cost or net realisable value as appropriate.

9.6    Under method 1 it is clear that any adjustment to arrive at net realisable value will represent a reduction in stock values. Under method 2, however, the adjustment will be either an increase or decrease in stock value depending on whether net realisable value is higher or lower than historical cost (or the previously recorded replacement cost).

9.7    No problem arises in identifying the write-off to be charged in the profit and loss account where method 1 above is employed, but where method 2 is used, items of stock will be adjusted to net realisable value without first accounting for them at current replacement cost. Unless an adjusting entry is made, therefore, write-offs may be incorrectly netted off against revaluation surpluses instead of being charged against current cost profit. Where method 2 is employed therefore an adjusting entry should be made as follows:

Dr    Profit and loss account (normally cost of sales)
Cr    Revaluation reserve
        with the excess of current replacement cost over net realisable value at the balance sheet date.

Strictly, the adjusting entry should be made at the date net realisable value first represents the value to the business of the relevant stock, and the amount debited to cost of sales in that case would be the excess of current replacement cost over net realisable value at that date. It is recognised, however, that most companies will compare net realisable value and current replacement cost only at the balance sheet date and the accounting entry shown above is therefore suggested on the grounds of simplicity.

### Example 9.1

At the balance sheet date Biline Ltd's stock of finished goods includes two products, A and B. A flood just before the year end damaged most of product B

159

and it has been decided to sell off cheaply the entire year end stock of B. At the balance sheet the relevant figures for finished goods were:

|  | A | B | Total |
|---|---|---|---|
|  | £'000 | £'000 | £'000 |
| FIFO cost | 150 | 30 | 180 |
| Current replacement cost | 170 | 34 | 204 |
| Net realisable value | 190 | 20 | 210 |
| Lower of current replacement cost and net realisable value | 170 | 20 | 190 |

Biline therefore adjusts its finished goods stock with the accounting entry:

|  |  | £ | £ |
|---|---|---|---|
| Dr | Finished goods | 10,000 |  |
| Cr | Stock revaluation surplus |  | 10,000 |

Being the difference between the CCA value of stock and the FIFO value of stock (£190,000–£180,000).

This however represents a netting off of a revaluation surplus of £20,000 on A goods, (£170,000–£150,000) and a write off of £14,000 on B goods (£34,000–£20,000) and the following entry therefore is needed:

|  |  | £ | £ |
|---|---|---|---|
| Dr | Cost of sales | 14,000 |  |
| Cr | Stock revaluation surplus |  | 14,000 |

Being the difference (on B goods) between current replacement cost and net realisable value at the balance sheet date (£34,000–£20,000).

## GOODS PURCHASED FOR RESALE WHICH ARE TURNED OVER RAPIDLY

9.8 As stated in Chapter 8 the requirement to show stock in the balance sheet at the lower of current replacement cost and net realisable value may cause difficulties where there is a large number of rapidly changing individual items in stock. Consequently where, under historical cost conventions, it has been permissible to state stock in the balance sheet at current selling price less the normal gross profit margin, this approach can be continued under CCA where it is the only practicable method of arriving at a figure for balance sheet purposes which approximates to the value to the business. The gross margin to be deducted should be that based on prices current during the stock holding period during which stock held at the balance sheet date can be deemed on a FIFO basis to have been purchased.

9.9 As demonstrated in Example 8.3, the FIFO method of stock valuation may provide an adequate approximation to current purchase price where there has not, on average, been a change of price levels during the stock holding period which would be likely to result in a material difference between the FIFO value of stock and its value to the business. Therefore, for balance sheet purposes only, companies with a rapid stock turnover, and thus a short stock holding period, may find that a FIFO valuation is acceptable.

9.10 The rate of stock turnover will not affect the total revaluation surplus or deficit arising during the period because this depends upon the volume of stock held and the increase in unit values during the period and not on the rate of turnover of stock during the period. However, where there is a rapid turnover of stock so that each item of stock is held only for a short period it is unlikely that it will be practicable to attempt to calculate the revaluation surplus or deficit on each individual item of stock sold. In these circumstances it is recognised that it will usually be necessary for a COSA to be calculated using the averaging method or some other similar method using indices representative of the changes in the current value of stock. To determine the cost of sales figure that most closely approximates to the value to the business at the date of consumption of stock consumed using the averaging method, stock should be suitably categorised.

## Example 9.2

Elmers Ltd are retailers of home decorating materials. Elmers' stock falls into three categories—wallpaper, paint and equipment. The stock levels at the beginning and end of the period and purchases during the period were:

|  | Wallpaper | Paints | Equipment |
|---|---|---|---|
|  | £ | £ | £ |
| Beginning of period | 19,980 | 15,980 | 23,940 |
| Purchases | 500,000 | 320,000 | 130,000 |
| End of period | 26,000 | 16,200 | 30,000 |

During the period the Company has compiled the following indices for each category:

|  | Wallpaper | Paint | Equipment |
|---|---|---|---|
| Beginning of period | 120 | 136 | 105 |
| Average | 126 | 154 | 112 |
| End of period | 130 | 162 | 120 |

Using the averaging method the COSA for each category is computed as:

|  | £ |
|---|---|
| Wallpaper | 1,779 |
| Paint | 2,895 |
| Equipment | 3,536 |
|  | £8,210 |

161

## CONTRACT WORK IN PROGRESS

9.11 Contract work in progress is defined by the proposed accounting standard as:

Work in progress which is specific to the requirements of a particular customer as the result of a contract.

This definition of contract work in progress is substantially different from that under SSAP9 of long term contract work in progress and a careful study of the differences between ED18 and SSAP9 is recommended. Nevertheless those terms of SSAP9 in respect of long term contract work in progress which are compatible with ED18 should continue to be applied. For example, profit attributable to long term contract work in progress may be added to the value to the business of such work in progress for balance sheet purposes and recorded as part of operating profit.

9.12 Under CCA the accounting treatment is not dependent on the length of time between the commencement of work on a contract and final sale. Consequently, the proposed CCA treatment of contract work in progress will affect companies ranging from those engaged in the construction of buildings, ships, aircraft and other items for which manufacturing time could extend over many months, if not years, to companies engaged in the manufacture of items such as clothing or foods which are made to a particular customer's specific requirements but which individually can be manufactured in a few hours.

9.13 The important consideration is the point at which work in progress becomes specific to a particular customer. For example, if a printer is engaged by a publisher to print a specified book there will be a point (for example when pages are printed) after which the materials, labour and overheads incurred can be used for no other item than the particular book in question. At that point the work in progress is consumed because it can be sold only to the specific publisher who ordered the work and therefore no longer represents general trading stock. In such cases the date of consumption of the work in progress will arise before the completion of the finished product.

9.14 Some manufacturing companies produce substantial items which, although incorporating elements which may be specific to the requirements of a particular customer, conform largely to a standard pattern. Where the normal period of manufacture of such items is lengthy, it is frequently the case that the majority if not all of such work in progress has been undertaken to fulfil contracts with various customers. In such circumstances it is appropriate, on practical grounds, to treat such work in progress to the extent that it is covered by contracts with customers as contract work in progress, as described above. For example, a shipbuilder may lay down the keels of a number of similar vessels

162

each for a different purchaser. It may be that it is not until a late stage of manufacture that differences of design required by the various purchasers are reflected in the work completed.

Thus, although each keel may have been identified for a particular purchaser when it was originally laid down it is not until much later that they actually became specific to a customer's requirements. Nevertheless, on practical grounds and in view of the fact that the work in progress has been undertaken to fulfil contracts, the vessels should be treated as contract work in progress from the commencement of manufacture.

9.15 As stated above, if as a result of a contract, work in progress becomes specific to a particular customer prior to the date of sale, the date of consumption of that work in progress will be prior to the date of sale. Thus, on eventual sale of the finished item the charge to cost of sales (which will be recorded at the date of sale, not at the date of consumption) will be the value to the business at the date of consumption unadjusted for any price movements between the date of consumption and the date of sale.

### Example 9.3

Firtree Ltd designs and manufactures pumps to its customers' specific requirements. The Company carries a general components stock from which parts of each pump are drawn as required during manufacture. The job card for pump number 100 which was completed and sold in June 1978 shows that components, all of which were purchased in late December 1977, were drawn from stock as follows:

|  | Historical cost |
|---|---|
|  | £ |
| 1st January | 1,020 |
| 1st February | 630 |
| 1st March | 350 |
|  | £2,000 |

The appropriate index for the components was at the following levels during the period up to the date of sale:

| 1st January | 70 |
|---|---|
| 1st February | 73.3 |
| 1st March | 74 |
| 1st April | 77 |
| 1st May | 80 |
| 1st June | 83 |

The current cost of sales will be:

$$\frac{(£1,020 \times 70)}{70} + \frac{(£630 \times 73.3)}{70} + \frac{(£350 \times 74)}{70} = £2,050.$$

Movements in replacement costs after the date of input to contract work in progress are ignored.

163

9.16    The intention of the method of accounting for contract work in progress outlined above is to treat contract work in progress as a monetary asset from the point when it is consumed, i.e. from when it becomes specific to a particular customer, until the time of sale. The value to the business of work in progress incurred before the date of consumption is therefore determined at the date of consumption in accordance with the normal rules. Costs incurred after the date of consumption are recorded at the actual amounts incurred, i.e. they are deemed to be consumed as they are incurred. Where appropriate the total value to the business should be reduced to net realisable value.

### Fixed assets purchased for work on contracts

9.17    Where plant or machinery is purchased specifically for the purpose of undertaking a particular contract, and it is not intended by the company that the item will continue in use after completion of the contract, the historical cost of the item should be treated as a part of contract work in progress and not as a fixed asset. The effect of this treatment is to charge contract work in progress only with the historical cost of plant and machinery consumed and not with amounts based on replacement cost. Thus plant and machinery purchased specifically for a particular contract is deemed to be consumed when it is purchased.

9.18    Some construction companies at present, under historical cost accounting, treat some plant and machinery purchased specifically for particular contracts (e.g. those used on contracts in the UK) as fixed assets and therefore charge depreciation to contract work in progress on a time basis instead of charging the full cost of the asset immediately on purchase. Under CCA such companies will need to consider whether adjustments are required to this treatment in the light of the requirements of CCA in respect of fixed assets and contract work in progress. It follows that if depreciation rather than the full historical cost of the plant and machinery is to be charged to contract work in progress, the depreciation charge should be based on *historical cost*. The amount to be shown as the value to the business of fixed assets, however, is normally an amount after charging depreciation based on *replacement cost*. The difference, if any, between the depreciation charged to contract work in progress and the depreciation charged in arriving at the net replacement cost of plant and machinery shown as fixed assets will therefore need to be accounted for and it follows that the difference, apart from backlog depreciation, may need to be charged against operating profit.

### Fixed assets leased for work on contracts

9.19    Where an item of plant or machinery is not purchased but is leased specifically for the purpose of undertaking a particular contract the amount to be included as part of contract work in progress in respect of the leased item is the lease rentals paid or accrued. It would not normally be appropriate to regard such leases as finance leases.

### Maintenance of the business

9.20 Companies whose business is wholly or mainly the performance of work under contracts, e.g. construction companies, will need to consider the effect on their business of the proposed treatment of contract work in progress. If the amount shown as current cost profit by a contracting company is distributed, sufficient funds may not be retained in the business to undertake future contracts of a nature and size similar to those currently undertaken. For example, if all materials are input to the contract account at the commencement of the contract and the contract is not completed for two years, no provision will be made for increases in material costs during those two years when determining the operating profit on the contract.

9.21 One of a contractor's normal sources of finance is progress payments from customers. Where progress payments are received these may substantially cover the contracting company's investment in materials, plant and machinery and in such cases, assuming equivalent progress payments will be received in respect of future contracts, the level of business which might be undertaken should not be diminished by distributing the current cost profit. Where adequate progress payments are not received, however, and in the absence of alternative sources of finance, the directors may wish to consider the appropriation to revaluation reserve of some portion of current cost profit (see Chapter 18).

## PURCHASED SEASONAL AGRICULTURAL PRODUCE

9.22 It is frequently the case that agricultural products can be purchased only on a seasonal basis; a good example is strawberries. A whole year's crop may often be purchased in one month and then sold in processed or frozen form over the following year. Exceptionally heavy crops, once purchased when fresh, may be sold in preserved form over a period of more than a year.

9.23 It will not always be possible to determine an appropriate current replacement cost of seasonal stock at the date of consumption because in many cases replacement at the date of consumption would be impossible. In such cases it may be possible to purchase the produce at the date of consumption in a preserved form, or to purchase the produce from a later crop but these may have different characteristics or emanate from a different geographical area. If such purchases do not conform to the normal method of operation of the company the replacement cost should not be determined by reference to the cost at which such purchases could be made. The value to the business of the produce stock in such circumstances should be calculated at the lower of the unit cost of bulk purchase made from the most recent relevant harvest and net realisable value. Processing and other such costs, however, follow the normal rules and are calculated at current costs.

### Example 9.4.

Softfruit Ltd purchases home produced strawberries during June which it sells during June and July in fresh strawberry cakes and sells during the rest of the year in yoghurts. In December Softfruit imports fresh strawberries from Israel for sale at Christmas. The price Softfruit pays for Israeli strawberries cannot be regarded as an indication of the current replacement cost of the home produced strawberries which are by then held in a processed form. Consequently the cost of sales of strawberries included in yoghurts throughout the year, until the next home season, should be based on the historical price paid in the preceding June.

9.24 The above treatment of seasonal produce may not adequately reflect any changes in the cost of such produce from one crop to the next. Where this is the case the directors may wish to consider at the end of the financial year the retention of additional amounts, by appropriation to the revaluation reserve, based on estimates of replacement costs which will be incurred at the time of the next harvest.

9.25 For balance sheet purposes, the value to the business should be calculated in the same way as for the charge to cost of sales, i.e. the lower of the unit cost of bulk purchases made from the most recent relevant harvest and net realisable value.

## CONSUMABLE STORES

9.26 It is considered that the revaluation of consumable stores to current replacement cost would not normally result in a material adjustment. Therefore, unless the adjustment is likely to be material, consumable stores should be valued at cost, or net realisable value if this is likely to be lower. Where such items as consumable spares, jigs, fixtures and tools are treated as stock these should similarly be valued at the lower of cost and net realisable value. Where major items of substantial value are concerned these should be valued at their value to the business, the normal criteria being applied.

## PROFITS FROM DEALING AND OTHER SIMILAR ACTIVITIES

9.27 It is recognised that not all businesses depend for their profit, in the general sense of the word, solely on the sale of manufactured products. Profit earned by judicious buying is no less valuable and no less the result of operations than profit earned from increased sales. Equally, a company, whose business involves the purchase of assets solely with a view to gaining the benefit of an increase in their market value, is no less an operating company than a retailer who makes a profit by adding a mark-up to cost of sales. The following paragraphs describe the provisions of CCA which have been incorporated into the proposed accounting standard with the purpose of ensuring that gains such as those described above are treated as operating profits rather than as revaluation surpluses.

### Dealing in investments, commodities and similar items

9.28   Where the whole, or an identifiable part, of the business of a company involves the purchase of assets solely with a view to obtaining the benefit of an increase in market value, thereby enabling a surplus to be realised, any gain or loss on such transactions should be shown as an operating profit or loss and not as a revaluation surplus or deficit. Examples of the type of business that would be covered by this provision are investment dealing and certain commodity dealing activities.

9.29   The purpose of this provision is to ensure that companies which are in business solely to make revaluation surpluses can treat those surpluses as profits arising from operations and do not need to show them as revaluation surpluses and then restrict the appropriation to revaluation reserve in order to arrive at an amount available for distribution.

### Stock purchased in advance of normal requirements

9.30   Following the reasoning in the previous paragraph, where stock is purchased in advance of normal requirements in order to avoid an expected increase in replacement cost, the difference between the actual purchase cost and the cost ruling at the date when the stock would normally have been purchased should be shown as an operating profit and not a revaluation surplus. For a company to be able to take advantage of this provision it will need to have evidence available that the purchase was a departure from normal buying patterns. It is essential therefore that such decisions together with the date(s) on which the purchases would normally have been made should be clearly recorded by management at the time of purchase.

### Example 9.5

Pine Ltd anticipates an increase in the price of grommits and buys some for £1,000 in advance of the normal purchasing data by when the same quantity would have cost £1,200. When the stock is resold the replacement cost has increased to £1,300. Pine Ltd can record the operating profit of £200 gained from judicious buying by two methods:

Method A: *At the normal purchase date* by recording the gain as follows:

|     |               | £   | £   |
| --- | ------------- | --- | --- |
| Dr  | Stock         | 200 |     |
| Cr  | Cost of sales |     | 200 |

Method B: *At the date of sale* by calculating the revaluation surplus based on the price at the normal purchase date:

|     |                               | £     | £     |
| --- | ----------------------------- | ----- | ----- |
| Dr  | Cost of sales (operating profit) | 100   |       |
| Cr  | Revaluation surplus           |       | 100   |
| Dr  | Cost of sales                 | 1,000 |       |
| Cr  | Stock                         |       | 1,000 |

It can be seen that in Method A the cost of sales will be recorded as £1,300 at the date of consumption (i.e. current cost at the date of consumption) so that under both methods the total net charge to cost of sales is £1,100 being cost at the date of actual purchase plus revaluation surplus between the normal date of purchase and the date of consumption.

### Stock purchased at above or below the relevant market price

9.31 Where stock is purchased at a price substantially below, or above, the relevant market price at the date of purchase the difference between the actual purchase price and the market price at the date of purchase should be shown as an operating gain or loss. Thus, as in paragraph 9.30 the effects of good or bad purchasing will be reflected in the operating profit for the year and not treated as revaluation surpluses or deficits.

### Example 9.6

Broom Ltd is able to buy stock from a competitor in liquidation for £20,000. The open market price at the date of purchase is £25,000. At the date of sale the replacement cost is £26,000. As in Example 9.5 Broom Ltd may use either of two methods to record this gain:

A: At date of purchase:

|     |                  | £     | £     |
| --- | ---------------- | ----- | ----- |
| Dr  | Stock            | 5,000 |       |
| Cr  | Operating profit |       | 5,000 |

or B: At date of sale:

|     |                     | £      | £      |
| --- | ------------------- | ------ | ------ |
| Dr  | Cost of sales       | 21,000 |        |
| Cr  | Revaluation surplus |        | 1,000  |
| Cr  | Stock               |        | 20,000 |

9.32 It should be noted that if the provisions of paragraphs 9.30 and 9.31 are to be invoked by a company using the averaging method of arriving at the

168

COSA, the purchase dates and prices used should be chosen with care. The date of purchase to be used for the COSA should be the normal date of purchase, not the actual date of purchase when the provisions of paragraph 9.30 are invoked and in respect of the provisions of paragraph 9.31 the purchase prices to be used should be 'normal' market prices at the relevant dates not necessarily actual purchase prices.

## STOCKS OF LAND AND CONSTRUCTIONS

9.33    Unless they should be regarded as contract work in progress stocks of land and constructions should be treated in a manner consistent with the general principles of CCA in respect of stock, having regard to the normal method of operation of the company concerned.

9.34    It will normally be necessary to determine the replacement cost of land and of construction work separately. The replacement cost of land, including land which has been developed or is in the course of development, is the open market value of the bare land, plus estimated attributable acquisition costs, ignoring any development work which has taken place. The replacement cost of the construction work should be calculated as for other stock and work in progress, having regard to the normal method of operation of the company.

9.35    Where it is a company's present practice to include financing costs as part of construction work in progress it may continue to do so. In such cases the value to the business of stocks of land and constructions will include financing costs both for balance sheet purposes and for the purpose of determining the value to the business at the date of consumption.

9.36    If there is evidence indicating that on completion the value to the business of stocks of land and constructions will be materially less than current replacement cost the stock should be written down to its value as if it were a completed construction less the estimated costs, current at the date of the valuation, required to complete the construction.

# 10 The Treatment of Tax in Current Cost Accounts

10.1 Tax in the current cost profit and loss account will not necessarily be the tax related to the current cost operating profit but will be the tax payable (or credited) in respect of the year in question as determined by the then existing tax legislation. Nevertheless, the only portion of the tax charge in respect of corporation tax (deferred or otherwise) on profits and capital gains which should be deducted from the revaluation surplus is that attributed to capital gains on fixed assets and investments. Similarly the tax benefit of losses in respect of fixed asset or investment revaluation deficits should be credited to revaluation surplus. All other such charges or credits will be deducted from or added to current operating profit or extraordinary items as appropriate.

10.2 Differences of either a permanent or temporary nature between a company's reported profit computed on an historical cost basis and its taxable profit have become increasingly widespread in recent years due to various provisions of existing taxation legislation. Permanent differences give rise to a corporation tax charge which is higher or lower than that resulting from the application of the standard rate of corporation tax to the reported profit and are the result of either the disallowance as deductions from taxable income of such items as the cost of entertaining United Kingdom customers or the exclusion from taxable income of such items as the tax repayment supplement.

10.3 Temporary differences, known as 'timing differences' are normally the result of tax regulations and accounting conventions not recognising income or expenditure in the same accounting periods and can arise as follows:

(a) From income and expenditure being taxable or tax deductible in a different period from that in which it is credited or charged to profit and loss account, e.g. accrued interest receivable is not taxable until actually received.

(b) From the acceleration of income or expenditure in the calculation of taxable profit, e.g. the full cost of plant and machinery is allowable in the year of purchase by means of 100% first year allowances whereas only part is charged to profit and loss account as depreciation.

(c) from the deceleration of income or expenditure in the calculation of taxable profit, e.g. capital allowances on cars costing over £5,000 are restricted to £1,250 per annum even though the depreciation charge may be higher.

(d) from special taxation legislation which creates differences substantially unrelated to the income and expenditure for the year (e.g. stock relief).

## DEFERRED TAX

10.4   Taxation legislation which gives rise to temporary timing differences described above defers tax rather than forgives it. Consequently unless new timing differences arise in the future which offset the reversal of current timing differences the deferred tax will eventually become payable. Nevertheless, as taxation legislation stands at present, there is often a strong presumption that new timing differences will arise in future which will preclude any actual liability to tax from arising for an indefinite period. The proposed accounting standard therefore requires that deferred tax should be accounted for, on the liability method, in respect of the tax deferral or 'savings' arising from all timing differences of material amount other than those which can be seen with reasonable probability to continue for the foreseeable future.

10.5   The four main types of timing difference are discussed below.

### 'Short-term' timing differences

10.6   Short term timing differences are usually the result of accruing in the accounts income or expenditure which is treated on a cash basis for taxation purposes. Deferred tax should be provided in the current cost accounts in respect of all temporary tax savings resulting from short term timing differences. Any tax liability that it is known will arise on receipt of income should be provided for in the period in which the income accrues. Deferred tax thus provided for should be included as part of the tax charge against operating profit for the year.

### Example 10.1

Pine Ltd's accounts for 1978 show an operating profit of £130,000 and interest income receivable of £12,000. With a tax rate of 50% Pine Ltd has a tax charge of £71,000, of which £6,000 is deferred and £65,000 is the current liability.

In 1979 the company receives the interest receivable at the end of 1978 but does not earn any more interest. The operating profit for the year is £124,000. The tax charge is £62,000 but the current liability is £68,000, the difference being made good by the transfer of the deferred tax provided in 1978.

171

### Accelerated capital allowances

10.7    In computing taxable income at present companies are granted 100% first year allowances in respect of capital expenditure on plant and machinery. The effect of such an allowance is to reduce the tax written down value to nil in the year of acquisition. As the depreciation charge for the year of acquisition will almost invariably be less than the full cost of the asset it follows that a timing difference will arise in that year and will reverse in subsequent years as a result of further depreciation charges.

### Example 10.2

A company buys plant and equipment for £90,000 and depreciates it over 3 years. During each of those 3 years it makes a profit, before tax and depreciation, of £230,000. It is assumed that there are no changes in the replacement cost of plant and machinery over the 3 years. The tax charge (assuming a rate of 50%) and liability of the company in years 1 to 3 is:

|  | Year 1 | Year 2 | Year 3 |
|---|---|---|---|
|  | £'000 | £'000 | £'000 |
| Operating profit before tax and depreciation | 230 | 230 | 230 |
| less Depreciation | (30) | (30) | (30) |
| Operating profit before tax | 200 | 200 | 200 |
| Tax—current | 70 | 115 | 115 |
| —deferred | 30 | (15) | (15) |
| Current cost profit | 100 | 100 | 100 |
| Originating timing differences | 90 | — | — |
| Reversing timing differences | (30) | (30) | (30) |
| Net originating (reversing) timing differences | 60 | (30) | (30) |
| Deferred tax charge at 50% | 30 | (15) | (15) |
| Balance sheet— |  |  |  |
| Current tax payable | 70 | 115 | 115 |
| Deferred tax | 30 | 15 | — |

In each of years 2 and 3 the balance on deferred tax is after £15,000 has been transferred from deferred tax to current tax payable to account for the overall reversal of timing differences in those years.

10.8    In the situation illustrated in Example 10.2 assuming the company acquires no other assets, provision for deferred tax will need to be made in respect of the timing difference in the year of acquisition because its reversal in subsequent years will give rise to taxable income in excess of book income in those years.

10.9    In more usual situations companies will be involved in a continuing programme of capital expenditure and reversals of timing differences from previous years will be offset or exceeded by new timing differences arising on the current year's capital expenditure. In such cases no provision for deferred tax is necessary to the extent that it can be seen with reasonable probability that no additional tax liability will arise in the foreseeable future due to the reversal of timing differences being offset by future timing differences.

10.10   The test of whether it is probable that no liability will arise in the foreseeable future will differ from company to company. The main consideration however will be the directors' plans for future capital expenditure.

10.11   If, in the past, the company has always incurred capital expenditure eligible for capital allowances of an amount at least equal to historical cost depreciation and the directors can show there is no reason to expect a discontinuance of this practice in future, then *prima facie* there is a reasonable probability that no liability will arise in future and thus no deferred tax provision will be necessary. It is historical cost depreciation that is relevant because the deferment of tax will relate to a first-year allowance based on original historical cost. Insofar as current cost depreciation exceeds historical cost depreciation, a permanent tax difference will arise.

## Example 10.3

Peachtree Limited has prepared the following table of capital expenditure and timing differences for the past four years, the current year (year 0) and for the next four years.

| Year | Actual | | | | | Projected | | | |
|---|---|---|---|---|---|---|---|---|---|
| | −4 | −3 | −2 | −1 | 0 | 1 | 2 | 3 | 4 |
| | £ | £ | £ | £ | £ | £ | £ | £ | £ |
| Capital expenditure and capital allowances | 1,000 | 1,500 | 2,000 | 2,400 | 2,800 | 3,500 | 4,200 | 5,000 | 6,000 |
| Depreciation | 200 | 500 | 900 | 1,380 | 1,940 | 2,440 | 2,980 | 3,580 | 4,300 |
| Timing differences −4 | 800 | (200) | (200) | (200) | (200) | | | | |
| −3 | | 1,200 | (300) | (300) | (300) | (300) | | | |
| −2 | | | 1,600 | (400) | (400) | (400) | (400) | | |
| −1 | | | | 1,920 | (480) | (480) | (480) | (480) | |
| 0 | | | | | 2,240 | (560) | (560) | (560) | (560) |
| 1 | | | | | | 2,800 | (700) | (700) | (700) |
| 2 | | | | | | | 3,360 | (840) | (840) |
| 3 | | | | | | | | 4,000 | (1,000) |
| 4 | | | | | | | | | 4,800 |
| | 800 | 1,000 | 1,100 | 1,020 | 860 | 1,060 | 1,220 | 1,420 | 1,700 |

First year allowances are assumed to be 100%. All assets are depreciated on a straight-line basis over 5 years with a nil residual value at the end of their lives.

173

Only the historical cost depreciation is shown; as explained in paragraph 10.11 current cost depreciation should not be taken into account when considering timing differences on first year allowances.

It can be seen from the table that in the past four years new timing differences have always exceeded reversals of timing differences and the pattern is expected to continue for the next four years. If the directors are able to represent that, on the basis of present knowledge, there is no reason to expect a variation from this pattern in the future it is reasonable to assume that no deferred tax provision is required in the current year (Year 0).

10.12  In Example 10.3 it is assumed that budgets are available for the next four years. The extent to which companies are able to plan capital expenditure forecasts will obviously vary from company to company but it is envisaged that in judging what will happen in the 'foreseeable future' outline capital expenditure forecasts should normally be available for no less than three years. However, if detailed forecasts are available only for a shorter period serious consideration should be given to providing for deferred tax in full, on the basis of prudence, unless the directors are able, despite the absence of detailed forecasts or budgets, to establish a firm intention to invest at the appropriate level, and to continue doing so, and are prepared to make a representation to that effect.

10.13  Example 10.4 illustrates the situation where detailed forecasts are available for four years. It can be seen with reasonable probability that a liability will arise but that this will be reduced by investment two years hence.

### Example 10.4

Peartree Limited, using the same assumptions as in Example 10.3 produces the following table of capital expenditure and timing differences in respect of the previous four years, the current year (Year 0) and the next four years:

| Year | Actual | | | | | Projected | | | |
|---|---|---|---|---|---|---|---|---|---|
| | −4 | −3 | −2 | −1 | 0 | 1 | 2 | 3 | 4 |
| Capital expenditure | 5,000 | 2,000 | 3,500 | 1,500 | 2,500 | 2,000 | 4,000 | 500 | 1,600 |
| Depreciation | 1,000 | 1,400 | 2,100 | 2,400 | 2,900 | 2,300 | 2,700 | 2,100 | 2,120 |
| Timing differences −4 | 4,000 | (1,000) | (1,000) | (1,000) | (1,000) | | | | |
| −3 | | 1,600 | (400) | (400) | (400) | (400) | | | |
| −2 | | | 2,800 | (700) | (700) | (700) | (700) | | |
| −1 | | | | 1,200 | (300) | (300) | (300) | (300) | |
| 0 | | | | | 2,000 | (500) | (500) | (500) | (500) |
| 1 | | | | | | 1,600 | (400) | (400) | (400) |
| 2 | | | | | | | 3,200 | (800) | (800) |
| 3 | | | | | | | | 400 | (100) |
| 4 | | | | | | | | | 1,280 |
| | 4,000 | 600 | 1,400 | (900) | (400) | (300) | 1,300 | (1,600) | (520) |

174

It can be seen that a liability is expected to arise in Years 0, 1, 3 and 4. A provision for deferred tax should be made in the current year (Year 0) at the current rate of tax on the net effect (i.e. £1,520) of reversing and originating timing differences in those years, less the excess investment in Year 2, less any provision made in previous years in respect of these reversals, plus any liability not already provided for in respect of years subsequent to Year 4.

## Stock relief

10.14 Stock relief was first introduced by the Finance Act 1975 as a measure of relief for the rising costs of holding stock in a period of steeply rising prices and has been modified and extended by subsequent Finance Acts. Stock relief is based on the difference between the value of stock in the balance sheet at the year end and the value of stock in the balance sheet at the beginning of the year. It can therefore be given for an increase of stock value due to either volume or price changes or a combination of both.

10.15 The 'foreseeable future' for stock is likely to be a shorter period than that for fixed assets as the year-end value is dependent in part on outside factors not necessarily within the control of the company. These include changes in costs, changes in sales volume, and changes in delivery dates. In view of the uncertainty surrounding the timing and effect of such changes it is suggested that provision should be made for deferred tax unless the directors are able to represent that they see no reason to expect a liability to arise and provide reasonable evidence for that belief.

## Example 10.5

Crabapple Ltd's forecast stock level and trading profit for the coming year show that the stock relief of £20,000, claimed in respect of the current year will be clawed back by £12,000. The company therefore provides deferred tax of £6,000 (50% × £12,000) in the current year.

10.16 Stock relief granted under existing tax legislation is based on stock values calculated in accordance with historical cost conventions (as under SSAP 9). Except in limited circumstances replacement cost has been rejected by the House of Lords as a valid basis of valuation. Consequently when forecasting the value of stock for the purpose of determining whether any deferred tax provision is necessary, the 'historical' cost value of stock holdings at future balance sheet dates (e.g. FIFO values) should be determined if they are likely to be materially different from the current cost values at those dates. For example, if a company's stock holding period is particularly long, the difference between FIFO cost and current cost could be material.

## Revaluation of assets

10.17 The revaluation of assets may give rise to subsequent tax liabilities on their disposal only in the following case:

175

(a) When a revaluation surplus is realised; *and*
(b) When the surplus is a taxable amount; *and*
(c) When no roll over relief is claimed.

Consequently if it is intended to continue to use an asset until the end of its useful life a liability to tax will arise on disposal only if roll over relief is not claimed in respect of any capital gain arising on the ultimate sale proceeds.

10.18 It will be appreciated from the above that an actual tax liability on disposal following a revaluation will only arise in limited circumstances. It is considered unnecessary therefore to provide for any deferred tax in respect of revaluation surpluses if the directors are able to represent that there is no intention to dispose of the asset in such a way as to give rise to a liability.

### The liability method

10.19 From the foregoing paragraphs it is clear that under CCA deferred taxation should be regarded as a liability and not as a deferred credit. It is appropriate therefore to maintain the balance of any provision for deferred tax at the tax rate for the current year thus giving the best estimate available of the future actual liability. An adjustment to opening balances will therefore be necessary where the tax rate changes from that used in previous years. The adjustment should be debited or credited as appropriate to profit and loss account (or revaluation reserve in the case of the revaluation of non-current assets) as a taxation adjustment. This method of accounting for deferred tax is known as the liability method as explained in SSAP 11.

## THE TREATMENT OF TAX IN THE PROFIT AND LOSS ACCOUNT

### Corporation tax

10.20 The corporation tax charge based on the taxable profit for the year should be charged against the operating profit for the year except that corporation tax on extraordinary or prior year items should be deducted from those items.

### Deferred tax

10.21 Deferred tax on timing differences should be charged against operating profit except if it relates to revaluation surpluses on non-current assets in which case it should be deducted in arriving at the net of tax revaluation surpluses.

176

## BIRCHWOOD'S TAX

10.22 The opening balance on Birchwood's deferred tax account is made up of:

|  | £'000 |
|---|---|
| Tax on timing differences arising from accelerated capital allowances and stock relief | 23,292 |
| *Less:* Advance corporation tax recoverable | 3,070 |
|  | £20,222 |

As Birchwood is involved in a continuing programme of capital expenditure and plans to maintain its stock levels, on the introduction of CCA it writes back the balance on deferred tax attributable to these timing differences. The journal entry (F) in columns 3 and 4 of the worksheet (Table 10.1) is, in £'000s:

| F | Dr | Deferred tax | 23,292 | |
|---|---|---|---|---|
|  | Cr | General reserve | | 23,292 |

10.23 The tax liability on the profits for the year is £3,678,000 and again no provision is made for deferred tax. A provision is also made for Advance Corporation Tax (ACT) due at the end of the year. The following journal entries (k to m) are made in columns 9 and 10 of Table 10.1:

|  |  |  | £'000 | £'000 |
|---|---|---|---|---|
| k | Dr | Profit and loss account—tax | 3,678 | |
|  | Cr | Tax payable | | 3,678 |
| l | Dr | Tax payable | 3,070 | |
|  | Cr | Deferred tax (ACT) | | 3,070 |
| m | Dr | Deferred tax | 3,340 | |
|  | Cr | Tax payable (ACT) | | 3,340 |

# Table 10.1

## BIRCHWOOD LIMITED
## CCA Worksheet

| | 1 | 2 | 3 | | 4 | | 5 | 6 |
|---|---|---|---|---|---|---|---|---|
| | Opening balance sheet historical cost | | Opening balance sheet journal | | | | Opening balance sheet current cost | |
| | Dr £'000 | Cr £'000 | Dr £'000 | | Cr £'000 | | Dr £'000 | Cr £'000 |
| Land and buildings | 4,719 | 569 | C 569 D 1,190 | | C 569 | | 5,340 | |
| Plant and machinery | 15,446 | | A 10,261 | | B 4,357 | | 21,350 | |
| | | | | | | | | |
| Investment in subsidiaries and associates | 13,984 | | | | | | | |
| Quoted and unquoted investments | 1,147 | | | | | | | |
| Stock and work in progress | 51,313 | | E 1,560 | | | | 52,873 | |
| Debtors | 32,727 | | | | | | | |
| Cash | 465 | | | | | | | |
| Creditors | | 23,011 | | | | | | |
| Current tax | | 3,582 | | | | | | 3,582 |
| Bank overdraft | | 6,481 | | | | | | |
| Dividend | | 5,700 | | | | | | |
| Deferred tax | | 20,222 | F 23,292 | | | | 3,070 | |
| Ordinary share capital | | 32,185 | | | | | | |
| Reserves – general | | 14,051 | | | F 23,292 | | | |
| Reserves – revaluation | | | B 4,357 | | A 10,261 D 1,190 E 1,560 | | | |
| Preference share capital | | 4,000 | | | | | | |
| 10% Debentures | | 10,000 | | | | | | |
| Realisation of fixed assets | | | | | | | | |
| Revenue income | | | | | | | | |
| Revenue expenditure | | | | | | | | |
| Depreciation | | | | | | | | |
| Interest | | | | | | | | |
| Tax expense | | | | | | | | |
| Dividends received | | | | | | | | |
| Revenue surplus | | | | | | | | |
| | 119,801 | 119,801 | | | | | | |

| 7 | 8 | 9 | 10 | 11 | 12 | 13 | 14 |
|---|---|---|---|---|---|---|---|
| Income and expenditure for 1979 | | Journal entries | | Profit and loss account for 1979 | | Closing balance sheet | |
| Dr £'000 | Cr £'000 | Dr £'000 | Cr £'000 | Dr £'000 | Cr £'000 | Dr £'000 | Cr £'000 |
| | | g 835 | | | | | |
| 6,036 | | a 627 ⎫ | a 1,002 ⎫ | | | | |
| | | c 7,716 ⎭ | d 2,634 ⎪ | | | | |
| | | | e 6,626 ⎬ | | | | |
| | | | f 595 ⎭ | | | | |
| 139 | | | | | | | |
| | | j 1,993 ⎫ | | | | | |
| | | h 6,587 ⎭ | | | | | |
| | 295,290 | | | | | | |
| 1,319 | 465 | | | | | | |
| 283,487 | | | | | | | |
| 3,582 | | l 3,070 | k 3,678 ⎫ | | | | |
| | | | m 3,340 ⎭ | | | | |
| 6,481 | 3,430 | | | | | | |
| 5,980 | | | | | | | |
| | | m 3,340 | l 3,070 | | | | |
| | 8,000 | | | | | | |
| | | d 2,634 ⎫ | c 7,716 ⎫ | | | | |
| | | f 595 ⎭ | g 1,068 ⎪ | | | | |
| | | | h 6,587 ⎬ | | | | |
| | | | j 1,993 ⎭ | | | | |
| | | | b 137 ⎫ | | | | |
| | 238 | a 1,002 | a 627 ⎭ | | | | |
| | | e 6,626 ⎫ | | | | | |
| | | b 137 ⎬ | | | | | |
| | | g 233 ⎭ | | | | | |
| 1,319 | | | | | | | |
| | | k 3,678 | | | | | |
| | 920 | | | | | | |
| 308,343 | 308,343 | | | | | | |

179

# 11 Investments in Subsidiary and Associated Companies

11.1    In this chapter the amounts to be shown in the holding company's accounts in respect of investments in subsidiary and associated companies are considered. The treatment of such investments in the group accounts is considered in Chapter 14, but, inevitably, certain matters regarding the group accounts are considered also in this chapter. Subsidiary companies are defined by the Companies Act 1948 section 154 and associated companies are as defined by SSAP 1.

11.2    It would be usual to assume that at the date of acquisition the consideration paid by a holding company for a subsidiary was the value to the holding company of that subsidiary. That value will normally consist of an element of goodwill and an element equal to the carrying value (which may have been adjusted on acquisition) in the subsidiary's books of its net assets. It is likely that prior to the introduction of CCA the goodwill element in respect of subsidiaries that had not revalued their fixed assets, would be considerable. After the introduction of CCA, when determining the amount to be paid for a subsidiary the prospective holding company will probably value a particular company at no more than it would have done prior to the introduction of CCA. However, because the subsidiary will have revalued its assets on the introduction of CCA the element of goodwill in that value will be less and the carrying value of the net assets will be greater. The principle behind the treatment of investments in subsidiaries in the holding company's accounts under CCA is that as far as possible the holding company's accounts should reflect the investment in subsidiaries as if CCA had been adopted by all subsidiaries prior to, or at the date of, acquisition.

### Shares in subsidiary companies

11.3    The investment in the equity share capital of a subsidiary company should be shown in the holding company's balance sheet at cost plus post-acquisition movements in attributable reserves less amounts written off in respect of goodwill. Post-acquisition movements in reserves will include, where applicable, all movements in reserves resulting from the introduction of CCA.

180

**Example 11.1**

Oakwood Holdings Limited acquires 100% of the equity share capital of Beechtree Limited on 31st December 1977 at a cost of £575,000 which includes an amount for goodwill of £75,000, which Oakwood writes off on acquisition. The current cost balance sheet of Oakwood at 31st December 1977, therefore, will include an investment in subsidiaries of £500,000 in respect of Beechtree. For the year ending 31st December 1978 Oakwood and Beechtree prepare CCA accounts. Beechtree's accounts shown an increase in reserves during the year of £150,000. The investment in Beechtree to be shown in Oakwood's balance sheet at 31st December 1978 is therefore £650,000 being cost of £575,000 plus post acquisition movements in reserves of £150,000 less goodwill written off of £75,000.

11.4    The method used to calculate goodwill in respect of subsidiaries is the same under both CCA and historical cost accounting. The amount of goodwill arising on acquisition is the difference between:

(a) the value of the net assets of the company acquired at the date of acquisition; and

(b) the value of the purchase consideration.

11.5    Under CCA the value of net assets acquired will be their value to the business, i.e. their current cost value. Any goodwill arising on acquisition will be separately identified in the consolidated accounts and treated in accordance with the provisions of the proposed standard, but will not be separately identified in the holding company's accounts and will be treated as part of the investment in the subsidiary to the extent that it is not written off. If any goodwill is written off in the consolidated balance sheet there is no requirement to write a similar amount off the investment in subsidiaries in the holding company's balance sheet except on the first introduction of CCA.

11.6    On first changing from HCA to CCA, accounts for all subsidiaries should be prepared on a CCA basis. Any historical cost goodwill in the consolidated balance sheet in respect of the subsidiary should be netted off against any revaluation surplus arising on the change to CCA to the extent that the revaluation surplus arising on the change relates to the period prior to acquisition. An equivalent write off is required in the holding company's current cost balance sheet.

**Example 11.2**

The CCA net asset value of Grapevine, a subsidiary of Oaktree acquired on 31.12.73 for £400,000, at 1st January 1977 is £700,000 as follows:

|  | £'000 |
|---|---|
| HCA net assets at 31.12.73 | 200 |
| Increase in HCA net assets between 31.12.73 and 1.1.77 | 260 |
| Adjustment to CCA basis at 1.1.77 | 240 |
| (of which it is estimated £150,000 relates | |
| to the period prior to 31.12.73) | |
|  | 700 |

The investment in Grapevine at 1.1.77 in Oaktree's books is therefore:

|                                    | £'000 |
|------------------------------------|-------|
| Shares at cost                     | 400   |
| Post acquisition movement in reserves | 500 |
|                                    | 900   |
| Less goodwill written off          | 150   |
|                                    | 750   |

The accounting entry in Oaktree's books on the assumption that movements on HCA reserves relate to retained profit is:

|    |                        | £'000 | £'000 |
|----|------------------------|-------|-------|
| Dr | Investment in subsidiary | 350   |       |
| Cr | Revalution surplus     |       | 90    |
| Cr | General reserve        |       | 260   |
|    |                        | 350   | 350   |

11.7 The method of accounting for shares in subsidiaries outlined above is analogous to the historical cost method of accounting known as equity accounting. It has the effect of bringing all the gains of subsidiary companies into the books of the holding company.

11.8 The value of shares in a subsidiary to the holding company will increase as the value of the subsidiary's own net assets increases. Similarly the value of the shares will decrease as the subsidiary's net assets decrease. Therefore when the subsidiary pays a dividend the value of the shares in the subsidiary in the holding company's books will decrease by the amount of the dividend, but the decrease will be offset by the dividend received by the holding company.

11.9 Increases in the value of a subsidiary's net assets (other than because of increases in capital) will be the result of either revaluation surpluses or retention of current cost profit. In the holding company's books any such increase in the value of its shares in subsidiaries should similarly be treated as revaluation surpluses or retention of current cost profit as appropriate. The payment of dividends by the subsidiary to the holding company should be credited to the current cost profit of the holding company and deducted from the holding company's reserves reflecting the value of the investment in the subsidiary.

### Example 11.3

Redwood Limited is a 75% subsidiary of Forest Holdings Limited. Both companies account on a CCA basis. In 1977 Redwood pays a dividend of £100,000 in respect of the whole of its equity share capital, of which Forest's share is £75,000. In Forest's books the dividend will be accounted for as follows:

|    |                                   | £      | £      |
|----|-----------------------------------|--------|--------|
| Dr | Cash or amounts due from subsidiaries | 75,000 |        |
| Cr | Dividends received                |        | 75,000 |

The increase in Redwood's net assets during 1977 after accounting for the divi-

182

dend referred to above is £240,000 of which £200,000 represents revaluation surplus and £40,000 represents retained current cost profit. Forest's share of the total increase is £180,000. The accounting entry in Forest's books will be:

|  |  | £ | £ |
|---|---|---|---|
| Dr | Investment in subsidiary | 180,000 | |
| Cr | Revaluation surplus account | | 150,000 |
| Cr | General reserves | | 30,000 |

### Loans, advances and non-equity capital

11.10 Any amounts in the holding company's balance sheet in respect of subsidiaries, other than the investment in equity capital considered above, should be shown at cost less appropriate provisions. All such items are therefore to be treated in the same way as monetary assets and liabilities. Holdings in a subsidiary's non-equity capital or loan stock should therefore not be valued as if they are quoted or unquoted investments but as if they are monetary items.

### Investments in associated companies

11.11 The treatment of investments in associated companies in the accounts of the holding company is similar in most respects to the treatment of investments in subsidiaries. Investments in quoted associated companies however may be shown at mid-market value. The only other differences which might arise would occur on the initial change to CCA. The basic principle is the same as for investments in subsidiaries. The investment in shares in associated companies should normally be included in the holding company's balance sheet at cost plus post-acquisition movements in attributable reserves less amounts written off in respect of goodwill.

11.12 Under HCA goodwill is not normally separately distinguished in respect of associated companies. Under CCA however, goodwill should be calculated for the purposes of the consolidated balance sheet and be subject to the company's normal accounting policy in respect of goodwill. The goodwill in respect of associated companies acquired prior to the introduction of CCA should be calculated as at the date of acquisition in the same way as for subsidiaries but if this proves impracticable it may be calculated at the date of change to CCA. Consequently, on the introduction of CCA, there may be circumstances in which the value of the associated company in the holding company's accounts could be materially overstated if the second method of calculating goodwill described above is employed without correction. In such cases therefore the associated company may need to be shown in the holding company's balance sheet at a lower figure.

### Example 11.4

Pineforest Limited holds 30% of the equity share capital of Crabtree Limited and regards Crabtree as an associated company. In Pineforest's historical cost balance sheet at 31st December 1976 Crabtree is shown as an investment in an associated company at cost of £500,000. At the date of acquisition the historical cost net assets of Crabtree were £900,000, but it is not practicable to calculate net assets on a CCA basis at that date. Both Pineforest and Crabtree change to CCA for the year ended 31st December 1977. Crabtree's opening current cost balance sheet at 1.1.77 shows CCA net assets of £4·5 million of which £1,350,000 relates to Pineforest's holding. The value of the investment in Crabtree in Pineforest's opening CCA balance sheet at 1.1.77 would therefore initially be calculated as:

|  | £ |
|---|---|
| Cost | 500,000 |
| Add post acquisition movement in attributable reserves: | |
| (£4,500,000 − £900,000) × 30% = | 1,080,000 |
| | £1,580,000 |

Any goodwill in respect of the investment is calculated at the date of the change to CCA. On the change to CCA there is no goodwill in respect of Crabtree because Pineforest's share of Crabtree's CCA net assets at 1.1.77 exceeds the cost of the investment.

Following the normal valuation principle therefore the value of the investment in Crabtree to be shown in Pineforest's CCA balance sheet at 1.1.77 would be £1,580,000. This value, however, is materially greater (by £230,000) than the value of Crabtree's net assets attributable to Pineforest's shares and the value of the investment is therefore reduced to net asset value. The figure of £230,000 is deemed to represent the difference between the cost of acquisition (£500,000) and Pineforest's share of Crabtree's net historical cost assets at the date of acquisition (£270,000).

11.13 The effect of the accounting treatment illustrated in Example 11.4 is to assume that the excess of the book value as initially calculated over the attributable net assets of the associated company represents goodwill *at the date of acquisition* which can be netted off against revaluation surplus deemed similarly to have arisen prior to acquisition.

## BIRCHWOOD'S INVESTMENT IN SUBSIDIARY AND ASSOCIATED COMPANIES AT 1.1.79

11.14 At 31st December 1978 Birchwood's investment in subsidiary and associated companies in its historical cost balance sheet was made up as follows:

|  | % | £'000 |
|---|---|---|
| Subsidiaries | | |
| Brinkwells Limited | 100 | 8,436 |
| Forli Limited | 75 | 1,500 |
| Craeglea Inc. | 100 | 1,406 |
| | | 11,342 |
| Associated Company | | |
| Severn House Limited | 30 | 444 |
| | | 11,786 |
| Amounts owing from subsidiaries | | 2,198 |
| | | 13,984 |

184

11.15 All Birchwood's UK subsidiaries and the UK associated company changed on to a CCA basis on 1st January 1979. The overseas subsidiary did not change to a CCA basis for the purposes of its statutory accounts but it did provide Birchwood with CCA accounts for consolidation purposes. (The CCA accounts in sterling of the subsidiaries are shown in Tables 11.2 to 11.7. (The translation of the overseas subsidiary's accounts is covered in Chapter 12.)

11.16 The CCA values of net assets at 1.1.79 of Birchwood's subsidiary and associated companies, and the share of their net assets attributable to Birchwood's investment is set out below:

| Company | CCA net assets | Birchwood's share | |
|---|---|---|---|
| | £'000 | % | £'000 |
| Brinkwells | 11,365 | 100 | 11,365 |
| Forli | 3,208 | 75 | 2,406 |
| Craeglea | 1,942 | 100 | 1,942 |
| Severn House | 1,510 | 30 | 453 |
| | | | 16,166 |

11.17 Birchwood retained purchased goodwill in its historical cost consolidated balance sheet at cost which, at 31.12.78, was as follows:

| | £'000 |
|---|---|
| Brinkwells Limited acquisition cost of shares | 8,436 |
| Historical cost net assets at date of acquisition | 7,392 |
| | 1,044 |

The remaining subsidiaries were all formed by Birchwood.

11.18 The directors of Birchwood estimate that the amount of the goodwill shown above which it is required should be written off in the consolidated balance sheet on the change to CCA is £840,000, being that portion of the revaluation surplus arising on the change to CCA that is estimated to be applicable to the period prior to acquisition. Birchwood decides however, on the introduction of CCA, to write off the full amount of the historical cost goodwill.

11.19 At the date of Birchwood's acquisition of shares in its associated company the historical cost of net assets of the associated company was £1,210,000 of which £363,000 was attributable to Birchwood. The initial calculation of the value of Birchwood's investment in the associated company is therefore:

| | £'000 |
|---|---|
| Cost | 444 |
| Plus movements in attributable post acquisition reserve (1,510 − 1,210) × 30% | 90 |
| | 534 |

185

11.20 It can be seen that the value calculated above exceeds Birchwood's share of CCA net assets of the associated company at 1st January 1979 by £81,000 (£534,000 − £453,000) and Birchwood decides to write-off this amount against revaluation surpluses.

11.21 Birchwood's investment in subsidiary and associated companies at 1st January 1979 can now be calculated as follows:

| Subsidiaries | Cost | Goodwill written-off | Share of post acquisition reserves | Value at 1.1.79 |
|---|---|---|---|---|
| | £'000 | £'000 | £'000 | £'000 |
| Brinkwells Ltd | 8,436 | (1,044) | 3,973 | 11,365 |
| Forli Ltd | 1,500 | — | 906 | 2,406 |
| Craeglea Inc | 1,406 | — | 536 | 1,942 |
| Associate Severn House Ltd | 444 | (81) | 90 | 453 |
| | 11,786 | (1,125) | 5,505 | 16,166 |
| Amounts owing from subsidiaries | | | | 2,198 |
| | | | | 18,364 |

11.22 It will be noted that the effect of Birchwood's accounting treatment is to value all investments in shares in subsidiary and associated companies at the CCA value of the underlying attributable net assets.

11.23 No adjustment to the amount owing by subsidiaries is required for CCA purposes. This amount is shown at net realisable value in both the historical cost balance sheet and the current cost balance sheet.

11.24 The journal entry (G) required in Birchwood's books to reflect the value of its investment in subsidiary and associated companies are as follows:

| | | | £'000 | £'000 |
|---|---|---|---|---|
| G | Dr | Investment in subsidiaries | 4,371 | |
| | Dr | Investment in associate | 9 | |
| | Dr | General reserves | 876 | |
| | Cr | General reserves | | 781 |
| | Cr | Revaluation surplus | | 4,475 |
| | | | 5,256 | 5,256 |

The distinction between general reserves and revaluation surpluses reflects the movement on the individual companies' reserves and has been

186

calculated as follows:

| | Brinkwells | Forli | Craeglea | Total |
|---|---|---|---|---|
| | £'000 | £'000 | £'000 | £'000 |
| Birchwood's share of general reserves at: | | | | |
| Date of acquisition | 3,392 | — | — | 3,392 |
| 1st January 1979 | 2,516 | 681 | 90 | 3,287 |
| Increase (decrease) | (876) | 681 | 90 | (105) |

All the increase in the associated company is attributable to revenue reserves.

| | Brinkwells | Forli | Craeglea | Total |
|---|---|---|---|---|
| Birchwood's share of revaluation reserves at: | | | | |
| Date of acquisition | — | — | — | — |
| 1st January 1979 | 4,849 | 224 | 205 | 5,278 |
| Increase | 4,849 | 224 | 205 | 5,278 |
| *Less* goodwill | (1,044) | | | (1,044) |
| *Plus* translation gain on share capital (1,647 – 1,406) | | | 241 | 241 |
| | 3,805 | 224 | 446 | 4,475 |

11.25 The above journal entry has been made in columns 3 and 4 of the CCA worksheet shown in Table 11.1.

## BIRCHWOOD'S INVESTMENT IN SUBSIDIARY AND ASSOCIATED COMPANIES AT 31.12.79

11.26 The investment in shares in subsidiary and associated companies at 31st December 1979 is tabulated below. The figures incorporate the movements during 1979 in the attributable reserves, after payment of dividends of the companies concerned.

*Acquired subsidiary*

| | £'000 | £'000 |
|---|---|---|
| Brinkwells Limited | | |
| Cost | 8,436 | |
| Post acquisition movement in reserves (7,816 – 3,392) | 4,424 | |
| | 12,860 | |
| *Less* goodwill written off | 1,044 | |
| | | c/f 11,816 |

*Subsidiary companies that were formed by Birchwood*

Forli Limited

| | | |
|---|---|---|
| Cost | 1,500 | |
| Movement in attributable reserves since incorporation $(1,632 - 0) \times 75\%$ | 1,224 | |
| | | 2,724 |

Craeglea Inc.

| | | | |
|---|---|---|---|
| Cost | | 1,406 | |
| Movement in reserves since incorporation including translation surpluses, calculated as: | | | |
| Equity at 31.12.79 | 2,009 | | |
| Equity at incorporation | 1,406 | | |
| | | 603 | |
| | | | 2,009 |

| | |
|---|---|
| Total value of subsidiaries | 16,549 |

Severn House Limited

| | | |
|---|---|---|
| Cost | 444 | |
| Post acquisition movement in attributable reserves $(1,590 - 1,210) \times 30\%$ | 114 | |
| | 558 | |
| *Less* amount written off | 81 | |

| | |
|---|---|
| Value of associated company | 477 |
| Total investment in shares of subsidiary and associated companies at 31st December 1979 | 17,026 |

11.27 Dividends received by Birchwood in 1979 were as follows:

| | £'000 |
|---|---|
| Brinkwells Limited | 700 |
| Severn House Limited | 40 |
| | 740 |

11.28 The accounting entries required to record the receipt of dividends and the increase in value of Birchwood's investment in subsidiary and associated companies to reflect the movement in reserves are set out below and have been entered in the CCA worksheet (Journal entry n in Table 11.1, columns 9 and 10).

| | | £'000 | £'000 |
|---|---|---|---|
| Dr | Investment in subsidiaries | 836 | |
| Dr | Investment in associate | 24 | |
| Cr | General reserves | | 103 |
| Cr | Revaluation surplus | | 757 |
| | | 860 | 860 |

The amounts have been calculated as follows:

|  | £'000 |
|---|---|
| **Increase in general reserves** | |
| Brinkwells | 73 |
| Forli | 22 |
| Craeglea | (16) |
|  | 79 |
| Severn House | 24 |
|  | 103 |
| **Increase in revaluation reserves** | |
| Brinkwells | 378 |
| Forli, less minority | 296 |
| Craeglea—revaluation reserve | (137) |
| translation gain on share capital | 220 |
|  | 757 |

11.29 The presentation of Birchwood's investments in subsidiary and associated companies will appear in the annual accounts as follows:

*Investment in subsidiaries*

At cost, plus movement in attributable post acquisition reserves, less goodwill written off

|  | £'000 |
|---|---|
| Brinkwells Limited | 11,816 |
| Forli Limited | 2,724 |
| Craeglea Inc. | 2,009 |
|  | 16,549 |
| Amounts owing by subsidiaries | 2,337 |
|  | 18,886 |

*Investment in associated company*

At cost, plus movement in attributable post acquisition reserves, *Less* goodwill written off:

|  | £'000 |
|---|---|
| Severn House Limited | 477 |

## Table 11.1

## BIRCHWOOD LIMITED
## CCA Worksheet

| | 1 | 2 | 3 | 4 | 5 | 6 |
|---|---|---|---|---|---|---|
| | Opening balance sheet historical cost | | Opening balance sheet journal | | Opening balance sheet current cost | |
| | Dr £'000 | Cr £'000 | Dr £'000 | Cr £'000 | Dr £'000 | Cr £'000 |
| Land and buildings | 4,719 | 569 | C 569 } D 1,190 } | C 569 | 5,340 | |
| Plant and machinery | 15,446 | | A 10,261 | B 4,357 | 21,350 | |
| Investment in subsidiaries and associates | 13,984 | | G 4,380 | | 18,364 | |
| Quoted and unquoted investments | 1,147 | | | | | |
| Stock and work in progress | 51,313 | | E 1,560 | | 52,873 | |
| Debtors | 32,727 | | | | | |
| Cash | 465 | | | | | |
| Creditors | | 23,011 | | | | |
| Current tax | | 3,582 | | | | 3,582 |
| Bank overdraft | | 6,481 | | | | |
| Dividend | | 5,700 | | | | |
| Deferred tax | | 20,222 | F 23,292 | | 3,070 | |
| Ordinary share capital | | 32,185 | | | | |
| Reserves – general | | 14,051 | G 95 | F 23,292 | | |
| Reserves – revaluation | | | B 4,357 | A 10,261 ⎫ D 1,190 ⎪ E 1,560 ⎬ G 4,475 ⎭ | | |
| Preference share capital | | 4,000 | | | | |
| 10% Debentures | | 10,000 | | | | |
| Realisation of fixed assets | | | | | | |
| Revenue income | | | | | | |
| Revenue expenditure | | | | | | |
| Depreciation | | | | | | |
| Interest | | | | | | |
| Tax expense | | | | | | |
| Dividends received | | | | | | |
| Revenue surplus | | | | | | |
| | 119,801 | 119,801 | | | | |

| 7 | 8 | 9 | 10 | 11 | 12 | 13 | 14 |
|---|---|---|---|---|---|---|---|
| Income and expenditure for 1979 | | Journal entries | | Profit and loss account for 1979 | | Closing balance sheet | |
| Dr £'000 | Cr £'000 | Dr £'000 | Cr £'000 | Dr £'000 | Cr £'000 | Dr £'000 | Cr £'000 |
| | | g 835 | | | | | |
| 6,036 | | a 627 ⎫ c 7,716 ⎭ | a 1,002 ⎫ d 2,634 ⎪ e 6,626 ⎪ f 595 ⎭ | | | | |
| 139 | | n 860 | | | | | |
| | | j 1,993 ⎫ h 6,587 ⎭ | | | | | |
| | 295,290 | | | | | | |
| 1,319 | 465 | | | | | | |
| 283,487 | | | | | | | |
| 3,582 | | l 3,070 | k 3,678 ⎫ m 3,340 ⎭ | | | | |
| 6,481 | 3,430 | | | | | | |
| 5,980 | | | | | | | |
| | | m 3,340 | l 3,070 | | | | |
| | 8,000 | | | | | | |
| | | | n 103 | | | | |
| | | d 2,634 ⎫ f 595 ⎭ | c 7,716 ⎫ g 1,068 ⎪ h 6,587 ⎬ j 1,993 ⎪ n 757 ⎭ | | | | |
| | | | b 137 ⎫ a 627 ⎭ | | | | |
| | 238 | a 1,002 | | | | | |
| | | e 6,626 ⎫ b 137 ⎬ g 233 ⎭ | | | | | |
| 1,319 | | | | | | | |
| | | k 3,678 | | | | | |
| | 920 | | | | | | |
| 308,343 | 308,343 | | | | | | |

**Table 11.2**

BRINKWELLS LIMITED

CURRENT COST BALANCE SHEET
AT 31st DECEMBER 1979

|  | 1979 | | 1978 | |
|---|---|---|---|---|
|  | £'000 | £'000 | £'000 | £'000 |
| Fixed assets |  |  |  |  |
| Land and buildings |  | 6,143 |  | 5,985 |
| Plant and machinery |  | 4,818 |  | 4,319 |
|  |  | 10,961 |  | 10,304 |
| Current assets |  |  |  |  |
| Stock and work in progress | 14,648 |  | 12,814 |  |
| Debtors | 9,219 |  | 6,438 |  |
| Cash | 102 |  | 219 |  |
|  | 23,969 |  | 19,471 |  |
| Current liabilities |  |  |  |  |
| Creditors | 19,422 |  | 15,552 |  |
| Current tax | 369 |  | 682 |  |
| Bank overdraft | 1,262 |  | 434 |  |
|  | 21,053 |  | 16,668 |  |
| Net current assets |  | 2,916 |  | 2,803 |
| Net assets |  | 13,877 |  | 13,107 |
| Ordinary share capital |  | 4,000 |  | 4,000 |
| General reserve |  | 2,589 |  | 2,516 |
| Revaluation reserve |  | 5,227 |  | 4,849 |
|  |  | 11,816 |  | 11,365 |
| Owing to holding company |  | 2,061 |  | 1,742 |
|  |  | 13,877 |  | 13,107 |

**Table 11.3**

BRINKWELLS LIMITED

CURRENT COST PROFIT AND LOSS ACCOUNT
FOR THE YEAR ENDED 31st DECEMBER 1979

|  | £'000 | £'000 |
|---|---|---|
| Sales |  | 72,964 |
| Cost of sales (historical cost) | 34,296 |  |
| Cost of sales adjustment | (185) |  |
|  |  | 34,101 |
|  |  | 38,863 |
| Administration | 36,445 |  |
| Depreciation | 1,194 |  |
| Interest paid | 82 |  |
|  |  | 37,721 |
| Current cost profit before tax |  | 1,142 |
| Tax |  | 369 |
| Current cost profit |  | 773 |
| Dividends paid |  | 700 |
| Profit retained—increase in revaluation reserve |  | 73 |
| Revaluation surpluses |  |  |
| Fixed assets |  | 563 |
| *less* stock deficit |  | 185 |
| Increase in revaluation reserve |  | 378 |

**Table 11.4**

FORLI LIMITED

CURRENT COST BALANCE SHEET
AT 31st DECEMBER 1979

|  | 1979 | | 1978 | |
|---|---|---|---|---|
|  | £'000 | £'000 | £'000 | £'000 |
| Fixed assets | | | | |
| Land and buildings | | — | | — |
| Plant and machinery | | 2,141 | | 1,648 |
|  | | 2,141 | | 1,648 |
| Current assets | | | | |
| Stock and work in progress | 2,214 | | 2,182 | |
| Debtors | 1,059 | | 1,182 | |
| Cash | 46 | | 189 | |
|  | 3,319 | | 3,553 | |
| Current liabilities | | | | |
| Creditors | 1,528 | | 1,411 | |
| Current tax | 24 | | 126 | |
|  | 1,552 | | 1,537 | |
| Net current assets | | 1,767 | | 2,016 |
| Net assets | | 3,908 | | 3,664 |
| Ordinary share capital | | 2,000 | | 2,000 |
| General revenue | | 939 | | 909 |
| Revaluation reserve | | 693 | | 299 |
|  | | 3,632 | | 3,208 |
| Owing to holding company | | 276 | | 456 |
|  | | 3,908 | | 3,664 |

194

**Table 11.5**

FORLI LIMITED

CURRENT COST PROFIT AND LOSS ACCOUNT
FOR THE YEAR ENDED 31st DECEMBER 1979

|  | £'000 | £'000 |
|---|---|---|
| Sales |  | 14,109 |
| Cost of sales (historical cost) | 8,642 | |
| Cost of sales adjustment | 289 | |
|  | | 8,931 |
|  | | 5,178 |
| Administration | 4,713 | |
| Depreciation | 401 | |
| Interest paid | 10 | |
|  | | 5,124 |
| Current cost profit before tax | | 54 |
| Tax | | 24 |
| Current cost profit | | 30 |
| Dividends paid | | — |
| Profit retained—increase in general reserve | | 30 |
| Revaluation surpluses | | |
| Fixed assets | | 105 |
| Stock | | 289 |
|  | | 394 |

**Table 11.6**

CRAEGLEA INC.

CURRENT COST BALANCE SHEET
AT 31st DECEMBER 1979

|  | 1979 | | 1978 | |
| --- | --- | --- | --- | --- |
|  | £'000 | £'000 | £'000 | £'000 |
| Fixed assets | | | | |
| Plant and machinery | | 1,586 | | 1,548 |
| Current assets | | | | |
| Stock | 877 | | 835 | |
| Debtors | 1,076 | | 1,096 | |
| Cash | 73 | | 129 | |
|  | 2,026 | | 2,060 | |
| Current liabilities | | | | |
| Creditors | 456 | | 666 | |
| Current tax | 14 | | — | |
|  | 470 | | 666 | |
| Net current assets | | 1,556 | | 1,394 |
| Net assets | | 3,142 | | 2,942 |
| Ordinary share capital | | 1,867 | | 1,647 |
| General revenue | | 74 | | 90 |
| Revaluation reserve | | 68 | | 205 |
|  | | 2,009 | | 1,942 |
| Medium term loan | | 1,133 | | 1,000 |
|  | | 3,142 | | 2,942 |

**Table 11.7**

CRAEGLEA INC.

CURRENT COST PROFIT AND LOSS ACCOUNT
FOR THE YEAR ENDED 31st DECEMBER 1979

|  | £'000 |
|---|---|
| Sales | 5,165 |
| Cost of sales | 5,168 |
| Current cost loss before tax | 3 |
| Tax | 13 |
| Current cost loss—reduction in general reserve | 16 |
| Revaluation deficit | |
| Fixed assets | 250 |
| *less* Stock surplus | 87 |
| | 163 |
| Translation gain | 26 |
| Reduction in revaluation reserve | 137 |

# 12 Overseas Assets and Operations

12.1 There are no differences of principle between the treatment of assets and operations in the United Kingdom and the treatment of assets and operations overseas. There are provisions in the proposed standard which deal with the translation of foreign currencies into sterling but, apart from these, the only differences in approach result from practicalities.

12.2 The general principles with regard to overseas assets and operations are as follows:

(a) Assets and liabilities which are located overseas or denominated in overseas currency should be valued at their value to the business in the countries concerned in accordance with the provisions of the proposed standard and translated into sterling using the rate of exchange at the balance sheet date.
(b) Revenue items may be translated either using the rate of exchange at the closing balance sheet date or the average rate of exchange for the accounting period.
(c) Translation differences arising from exchange movements should be treated as revaluation surpluses or deficits.
(d) Any receipts and payments should be translated at the actual rate of exchange; any resulting translation differences should be reflected in the profit and loss account.

## ASSETS AND LIABILITIES OTHER THAN INVESTMENTS IN SUBSIDIARY AND ASSOCIATED COMPANIES

12.3 As stated in paragraph 12.1, it is the practicalities of valuing overseas assets and liabilities which may result in differences between their treatment and the treatment of similar items located in the United Kingdom. There is no difference in principle. For example, land and buildings both in the United Kingdom and overseas may be valued at open market value for their existing use but valuers in different countries may have various methods of arriving at such a valuation. Equally, the concept of market value for existing use may not be recognised in some countries and some other market value may need to be adopted.

198

**12.4** In the case of assets held overseas which attract dollar premium the full amount of the premium (on the basis that replacement cost is the value to the business) may be added to the overseas valuation of the asset but only the amount recoverable on disposal would be included if the asset were valued at its net realisable value.

### Example 12.1

Forest Ltd. owns 1,000 shares of Mango, which are quoted on the X-land exchange. At Forest Ltd's balance sheet date, the mid-market price of Mango's shares was X120. The exchange rate at that date was X4 = £1 and the effective dollar premium was 50%. Forest Ltd. values its investment in Mango at £45,000, i.e.

$$(1,000 \times \frac{120}{4} + 50\%).$$

**12.5** It would normally be appropriate, where the full dollar premium is added to the value of overseas assets, to show by way of note the amount of the dollar premium that would be lost on realisation.

## RECEIPTS AND PAYMENTS IN FOREIGN CURRENCIES

**12.6** Receipts and payments in foreign currencies (e.g. the receipt of dividends) will be recorded at the sterling amounts actually received or paid. Differences on translation in respect of transactions of a capital nature (e.g. the settlement of long term debt) should be treated as revaluation surpluses or deficits. Differences on revenue transactions should be added to or deducted from operating profit.

### Example 12.2

Sap Ltd. purchases goods for $85,000 at a time when the exchange rate is $1·70 = £1. The liability and cost of the goods is recorded at £50,000. When payment is made the exchange rate has fallen to $1·60 = £1, so that £53,125 is actually paid. The entry on payment is:

|    |                  | £      | £      |
|----|------------------|--------|--------|
| Dr | Creditors        | 50,000 |        |
| Dr | Operating profit | 3,125  |        |
| Cr | Cash             |        | 53,125 |

## FOREIGN SUBSIDIARIES

**12.7** The accounts of foreign subsidiaries should be prepared for consolidation purposes on a CCA basis in the country of operation in accordance with the provisions of the proposed standard. Where it is not possible for a foreign subsidiary itself to prepare accounts on a CCA basis the holding company should convert the subsidiary on to a CCA basis for consolidation purposes.

## TRANSLATION INTO STERLING OF SUBSIDIARIES' ACCOUNTS

**The balance sheet**

12.8    All items in a foreign subsidiary's balance sheet should be translated into sterling at the exchange rate ruling at the balance sheet date. Translation differences arising from exchange rate movements since the previous balance sheet date should be treated as surpluses or deficits arising on revaluation. The general method of translation is no different from that used to translate historical cost balance sheets to sterling.

12.9    The difference on translation is the difference between:

(a) opening share capital and reserves translated at the opening rate of exchange; and

(b) opening share capital and reserves translated at the closing rate of exchange.

**Example 12.3**

Fir Inc. is the subsidiary in X-Land of a UK company. Its current cost accounts for 1976 and 1977 show the following:

|  | 1976 | 1977 |
|---|---|---|
| Net assets | 10,000 | 14,000 |
| Share capital | 1,000 | 1,000 |
| Reserves | 9,000 | 13,000 |
|  | X10,000 | X14,000 |
| Closing rate of exchange: |  |  |
| £1 = | X2 | X4 |

The 1977 balance sheet in sterling to be consolidated is:

|  | 1977 | | 1977 |
|---|---|---|---|
|  | X | | £ |
| Net assets | 14,000 | ÷4 | 3,500 |
| Share capital | 1,000 | ÷4 | 250 |
| Reserves | 13,000 | ÷4 | 3,250 |
|  | X14,000 | | £3,500 |

The loss on translation to be debited to revaluation surplus, is the difference between the opening share capital and reserves (X10,000) at the opening and closing exchange rates i.e.

$$\frac{X10,000}{2} - \frac{X10,000}{4} = £2,500$$

200

### The profit and loss account

12.10  As with the balance sheet there is no difference in principle between the translation of an overseas HC profit and loss account and an overseas current cost profit and loss account. The overseas current cost profit and loss account may be translated into sterling either by using the rate of exchange at the closing balance sheet date (i.e. the same rate of exchange used to convert the balance sheet) or by using an average rate of exchange for the accounting period. In the latter case any difference on translation arising from using an average rate of exchange instead of the closing rate of exchange should be treated as a revaluation surplus or deficit.

### Example 12.4

Continuing Example 12.3 the increase in Fir's reserves during 1976 comprised:

|  | X |
|---|---|
| Current cost profit | 3,000 |
| Revaluation surplus | 1,000 |
|  | X4,000 |

Using the average rate method of translation to sterling the exchange rate is

$$\frac{X2 + X4}{2} = X3 = £1$$

The translation is therefore:

|  | X |  | £ |
|---|---|---|---|
| Current cost profit | 3,000 | ÷3 | 1,000 |
| Revaluation surplus | 1,000 | ÷3 | 333 |
|  |  |  | £1,333 |

If translated at the year end rate the movement would be X4,000 ÷ 4 = £1,000 so there is a loss on translation of £333.

|  | X |  | £ |
|---|---|---|---|
| Opening share capital and reserves | 10,000 | ÷2 | 5,000 |
| Closing share capital and reserves | 14,000 | ÷4 | 3,500 |
| Net fall in reserves |  |  | £(1,500) |

|  | £ |
|---|---|
| Made up of: |  |
| Opening balance (from Example 12.3) | (2,500) |
| Movement | 1,333 |
| Loss on translation | (333) |
|  | (1,500) |

**Overseas tax**

12.11 All overseas tax except tax specifically assessed on capital gains on non-current assets should be shown as part of the tax charge in the profit and loss account. Overseas tax specifically assessed on capital gains on non-current assets should be treated as tax on revaluation surpluses and accordingly deducted from such surpluses in the appropriation account.

12.12 Where overseas tax has been based on historical cost profits the situation may arise, as a result of the treatment explained in the previous paragraph, in which the overseas tax charge exceeds the related overseas current cost operating profit. It is also possible for the overseas tax charge to exceed the total current cost profit for the year before tax. Nevertheless, it is considered that in such circumstances the proposed treatment does, in fact, properly reflect the effects of foreign taxation and consequently no part of the overseas tax should be treated as tax on revaluation surpluses.

## ASSOCIATED COMPANIES

12.13 As with overseas subsidiaries the treatment of overseas associated companies should be the same as that for United Kingdom associated companies.

## BIRCHWOOD'S OVERSEAS SUBSIDIARY

12.14 It will be recalled from Chapter 11 that Birchwood holds 100% of the issued share capital of Craeglea Inc., a company incorporated in USA. Craeglea Inc. has been able to prepare current cost accounts for consolidation purposes and these are set out in Tables 12.1 and 12.2 which show respectively the CCA balance sheet at 31st December 1979, and CCA profit and loss account for the year ended 31st December 1979. Column 1 in each table shows the figures in US $ and Column 2 shows the figures translated into £s. The balance sheet has been translated at the year end rate of exchange of £1 = $1·50 and the profit and loss account has been translated at the average rate of exchange for 1979 of £1 = $1·60. The rate at the beginning of 1979 was £1 = $1·70.

12.15 Table 12.3 sets out the calculation of Birchwood's 'ranslation gain. Table 12.3 (a) shows the share capital and reserves at 1st January 1979 being translated at the opening and closing exchange rates respectively (see paragraph 12.9). Table 12.3 (b) shows the movement in the reserves for the year being translated from the average rate for the year to the year end rate (see paragraph 12.10). The resulting exchange gain from (a) and (b) has been included in the sterling revaluation deficit on Table 12.2

It can be seen that Craeglea Inc. has calculated:

(a) The effect on the opening balance sheet, of a change in the exchange rate.

(b) The effect on the movement on the reserves of being translated at the average rate for the period as opposed to the year-end rate.

**Table 12.1**

CRAEGLEA INC.
CURRENT COST BALANCE SHEET AT
31st DECEMBER 1979

| | US Dollars | | £ Sterling | |
|---|---|---|---|---|
| | $'000 | $'000 | £'000 | £'000 |
| Fixed assets | | | | |
| Plant and machinery | | 2,379 | | 1,586 |
| Current assets | | | | |
| Stock | 1,316 | | 877 | |
| Debtors | 1,614 | | 1,076 | |
| Cash | 109 | | 73 | |
| | 3,039 | | 2,026 | |
| Current liabilities | | | | |
| Creditors | 684 | | 456 | |
| Current tax | 21 | | 14 | |
| | 705 | | 470 | |
| Net current assets | | 2,334 | | 1,556 |
| Net assets | | 4,713 | | 3,142 |
| Ordinary share capital | | 2,800 | | 1,867 |
| Revenue reserve | | 126 | | 74 |
| Revaluation reserve | | 87 | | 68 |
| | | 3,013 | | 2,009 |
| Medium term loan | | 1,700 | | 1,133 |
| | | 4,713 | | 3,142 |

203

**Table 12.2**

CRAEGLEA INC.

CURRENT COST PROFIT AND LOSS ACCOUNT
FOR THE YEAR ENDED 31st DECEMBER 1979

| | US Dollars $'000 | £ Sterling £'000 |
|---|---|---|
| Sales | 8,264 | 5,165 |
| Cost of sales | 8,269 | 5,168 |
| Current cost loss before tax | 5 | 3 |
| Tax | 21 | 13 |
| Current cost loss reduction in general reserve | 26 | 16 |
| Revaluation deficit | | |
| Fixed assets | 401 | 250 |
| *less* Stock surplus | 140 | 87 |
| | 261 | 163 |
| Translation gain on revenue and revaluation reserves (see Table 12.3) | — | 26 |
| Reduction in revaluation reserve | 261 | 137 |
| Total reduction in reserves | 287 | 153 |

**Table 12.3**

CRAEGLEA INC.

TRANSLATION LOSS FOR YEAR ENDED
31st DECEMBER 1979

| | Opening balance sheet | | | Translation |
| --- | ---: | ---: | ---: | ---: |
| | | at 1.70 | at 1.50 | gain (loss) |
| | $'000 | £'000 | £'000 | £'000 |
| (a) Share capital | 2,800 | 1,647 | 1,867 | 220 |
| Reserves—revenue | 152 | 90 | 102 | 12 |
| —revaluation | 348 | 205 | 232 | 27 |
| | 3,300 | 1,942 | 2,201 | 259 |
| | | at 1·60 | at 1·50 | |
| | $'000 | £'000 | £'000 | £'000 |
| (b) Current cost loss | (26) | (16) | (18) | (2) |
| Revaluation deficit | (261) | (163) | (174) | (11) |
| | (287) | (179) | (192) | (13) |

**Summary of translation gain**

| | Revenue | Revaluation | Share capital |
| --- | ---: | ---: | ---: |
| | £'000 | £'000 | £'000 |
| Opening balance sheet effect | 12 | 27 | 220 |
| Movement during year | (2) | (11) | — |
| | 10 | 16 | 220 |

**Summary of reserves**

| | Revenue | Revaluation | Share capital |
| --- | ---: | ---: | ---: |
| | £'000 | £'000 | £'000 |
| B/f at 1·70 | 90 | 205 | 1,647 |
| Year at 1·60 | (16) | (163) | — |
| Translation gain on revenue reserves | — | 10 | — |
| Translation gain on revaluation reserves | — | 16 | — |
| Translation gain on share capital | — | — | 220 |
| C/f at 1·50 | 74 | 68 | 1,867 |

# 13 Other Balance Sheet Items and Completion of the CCA Worksheet

13.1     Stock and fixed assets are probably the two balance sheet items the treatment of which will be most affected by the adoption of CCA. In this chapter some other commonly found balance sheet items are considered which, as a result of the adoption of CCA principles, may be recorded in the balance sheet at values different from those that would be recorded in an historical cost balance sheet.

13.2     It will be recalled that, at least on its introduction, CCA will normally require liabilities and monetary assets to be shown in the CCA balance sheet at their historical cost. Consequently this chapter deals only with non-monetary assets. For the convenience of the reader the topics covered in this chapter together with paragraph references are set out below:

| | Paragraphs |
|---|---|
| Investments | 13.3–13.10 |
| Research and development expenditure | 13.11–13.12 |
| Intangible assets | 13.13–13.14 |

Once the balance sheet items covered in this chapter applicable to Birchwood have been considered the CCA Worksheet will be finalised. The procedure for completing the Worksheet is explained in paragraphs 13.25 to 13.30 below.

## INVESTMENTS

13.3     Investments in subsidiary and associated companies were considered in Chapter 11 and such investments are excluded from the following discussion. Similarly the following paragraphs do not deal with investment dealing companies; these were considered in Chapter 9 (paragraph 9.29).

### Quoted investments

13.4     Quoted investments should normally be valued at their closing mid-market price at the year end. If the year end happens not to be a trading day the closing mid-market price for the last trading day prior to the balance sheet date should be used.

13.5     In certain circumstances the directors may consider the mid-market price to be unrealistic and in such cases they may use another method of valuation. Such circumstances may arise, for example, when:

(a) The investing company has a large holding in a company.

(b) The investing company (e.g. a bank) holds gilt-edged stocks or other redeemable securities with the declared aim of holding them until maturity (or until market price exceeds the price at maturity).

(c) The investing company holds the securities as trade investments as a means of securing trading benefits (e.g. where a retailer holds a significant number of shares in the company that manufactures some of his trading stock).

13.6     Where the directors decide that the use of the quoted mid-market price would lead to an unrealistic value being placed on the investment they should value the investment at its value to the business, normally using the valuation criteria applicable to unquoted investments.

### Unquoted investments

13.7     Unquoted investments should be valued at their value to the business by the directors. The directors' valuation would normally be related to:

(a) the applicable proportion of the net assets of the company as determined on a CCA basis; and/or

(b) the value of the stream of income from the investment.

13.8     Where the company invested in has not prepared current cost accounts the investing company should value its investment as best it can by reference to the value of the stream of income from the investment and, if possible, an estimate of CCA net asset value.

13.9     The stream of income to be valued should be dividend income plus any trading benefits secured by holding the investment (e.g. favourable terms for the supply of materials). It would not normally be appropriate to attribute a value to a trading benefit which does not result in an established stream of income (or reduction in expenditure). For example no stream of income can normally be established in respect of an investment made to secure the availability of raw materials unless the raw materials will be made available at below market price.

### Treatment of gains and losses on investments

13.10    The treatment of gains and losses on investments depends on whether the investing company holds its investments for the long term or whether it holds them merely as a means of profitably utilising temporarily available liquid funds. In the former case, any gains or losses should be treated as revaluation surpluses or deficits. Where however the investment is liquid

207

funds temporarily invested the gains or losses should be treated as arising as a result of operations and should be included in operating profit.

An investment can only be classified as liquid funds temporarily invested if:

(a) the investment can readily be converted into cash; and
(b) the investment is identified as liquid funds temporarily invested at the time of purchase or is subsequently identified as liquid funds temporarily invested in which case only gains or losses subsequent to the investment being so identified should be included in the operating profit.

**Example 13.1**

Willow Limited has a long term investment in Leather Limited which was valued on a CCA basis at the beginning of 1978 at £140,000 and at the end of 1978 at £155,000. It also invests any funds which are temporarily surplus to requirements in equity shares. During 1978 it invested £40,000 which at the end of the year was worth £35,000.

The following entries are made in Willow's books at the end of the year:

|     |                                                      | £      | £      |
| --- | ---------------------------------------------------- | ------ | ------ |
| Dr  | Investment in Leather Limited                        | 15,000 |        |
| Dr  | Revaluation surplus                                  |        | 15,000 |
|     | with the surplus on the long term investment and     |        |        |
| Dr  | Operating profit                                     | 5,000  |        |
| Cr  | Short term investments                               |        | 5,000  |
|     | with the deficit on the short term investment.       |        |        |

## RESEARCH AND DEVELOPMENT EXPENDITURE

13.11   Research and development expenditure is as defined in ED 17. Any development expenditure which may be deferred under the terms of ED 17 may be carried forward in the current cost accounts to be written off *pro rata* to the benefits expected to arise in future periods. In all cases the research and development expenditure should only be carried forward to the extent that it can be recovered against future attributable revenue. Any amounts carried forward should be valued at current cost at each balance sheet date using the valuation methods which are most appropriate in the particular circumstances. It is expected that where development expenditure includes charges for the company's own labour and for purchased materials these would be valued in a way similar to that used for revaluing stock and work in progress. Where fixed assets are involved these should be revalued in the same way as other fixed assets and depreciated accordingly. The depreciation charge should be included in development expenditure to be carried forward, and written off subsequently against attributable revenue. Alternatively, the fixed assets may be charged to research and development expenditure on acquisition and revalued each year effectively as if they were materials.

208

## Example 13.2

Mushroom Limited carries out research and development expenditure which it carries forward and amortises over five years. At the end of 1976 it was carrying forward the following amounts at historical cost:

| Year in which expenditure was incurred | Purchased materials | Own labour | Depreciation | Total |
|---|---|---|---|---|
| | £'000 | £'000 | £'000 | £'000 |
| 1974 | 40 | 25 | 15 | 80 |
| 1975 | 95 | 40 | 15 | 150 |
| 1976 | 145 | 110 | 15 | 260 |
| Total | 280 | 175 | 45 | 490 |

The relevant indices for purchased materials and labour are:

| | Purchased materials | Labour |
|---|---|---|
| 1974 (average) | 60 | 75 |
| 1975 (average) | 75 | 85 |
| 1976 (average) | 90 | 95 |
| 1976 (end) | 100 | 100 |

Purchased materials and labour are revalued as follows:

| | Purchased materials | | Labour | |
|---|---|---|---|---|
| | £'000 | | | £'000 |
| 1974 | $40 \times \dfrac{100}{60}$ | 66·7 | $25 \times \dfrac{100}{75}$ | 33·3 |
| 1975 | $95 \times \dfrac{100}{75}$ | 126·7 | $40 \times \dfrac{100}{85}$ | 47·1 |
| 1976 | $145 \times \dfrac{100}{90}$ | 161·1 | $110 \times \dfrac{100}{95}$ | 115·8 |
| | | 354·5 | | 196·2 |

All the fixed assets used were purchased at a cost of £60,000 in 1974 when the relevant index was 75. The index at the end of 1976 was 112·5. The depreciation is revalued as follows:

The GRC at the end of 1976 is:

$$£60,000 \times \frac{112·5}{75} = £90,000$$

The assets expected remaining useful life is 2 years at the end of 1976 and therefore its total life is expected to be 5 years. At the end of 1976 accumulated depreciation should therefore equal 60% of the GRC, i.e. £54,000.

The revised amount of R & D carried forward is:

| Year | Purchased materials | Own labour | Total |
|---|---|---|---|
| | £'000 | £'000 | £'000 |
| 1974 | 66·7 | 33·3 | 100·0 |
| 1975 | 126·7 | 47·1 | 173·8 |
| 1976 | 161·1 | 115·8 | 276·9 |
| | 354·5 | 196·2 | 550·7 |
| *Add* Depreciation | | | 54·0 |
| Total | | | 604·7 |

13.12  When development expenditure which was originally deferred is eventually written off against operating profit it will not normally be necessary to calculate revaluation surpluses up to the date of the write off or to arrive at the average value of the expenditure for the period in which it is written off. It is considered that in most cases it will be sufficient simply to write off the appropriate proportion of the amount brought forward from the previous period.

**Example 13.3**

Bark Limited has carried forward and revalued development expenditure relating to one particular project. Nothing had been written off prior to the 31st December 1975 when the revalued balance was £185,000. The project was completed in December 1975 and no expenditure was incurred thereafter. One fifth of the balance at 31st December 1975 is to be written off in 1976 and the remaining balance is valued on a CCA basis by means of appropriate indices:

| | Purchased materials | Own labour | Depreciation | Total |
|---|---|---|---|---|
| | £'000 | £'000 | £'000 | £'000 |
| Brought forward | 70 | 90 | 25 | 185 |
| Written off—20% | 14 | 18 | 5 | 37 |
| | 56 | 72 | 20 | 148 |
| Revaluation adjustment by reference to appropriate indices | 12 | 7 | 5 | 24 |
| Balance at 31st December 1976 | 68 | 79 | 25 | 172 |

## INTANGIBLE ASSETS (EXCLUDING RESEARCH AND DEVELOPMENT AND GOODWILL)

13.13  The theory of CCA would require that all assets, including intangible assets, should be shown in the balance sheet at their value to the business. In the case of tangible assets their value to the business can normally be

210

ascertained with sufficient accuracy without too much subjective assessment. The value of many intangible assets, however, such as patents and copyrights is rather uncertain. For this reason, except where the value of an intangible asset can be readily established, it should be attributed no value in the current cost balance sheet.

13.14 A value may be established for an intangible asset such as a licence where the asset yields from third parties, a flow of income, the timing and amount of which can be foreseen with a reasonable degree of certainty. It would not be expected that a value would be attributed to a patent which was being exploited by the company that owned it. Once the value of intangible assets has been established it should be revalued each year and depreciated in the same manner as fixed assets. The revaluation should be only in respect of changes in the expected income flow. It is suggested that normally the discount rate should not be adjusted.

### Example 13.4

Brown Limited has granted rights to Green Limited to exploit a patent which Brown had registered. Under the terms of the agreement Brown is entitled to minimum royalties of £10,000 p.a. for five years. It seems likely that the minimum will be paid for the first two years and in the third and subsequent years larger royalties are likely. Brown decides that the only value that can be established for the patent is one calculated by reference to the minimum royalties. Brown's money cost of capital is 15% and it uses this rate to discount a stream of £10,000 per annum receivable at the end of each of the next five years:

$$£10,000 \times 3 \cdot 3522 = £33,522$$

equals the value of the rights under the agreement. The value of £33,522 should be depreciated over the life of the asset.

## BIRCHWOOD'S BALANCE SHEET

13.15 The items dealt with in this chapter which are applicable to Birchwood are considered below. The resulting accounting entries required to adjust Birchwood's balance sheet onto a CCA basis have been recorded in the Worksheet set out in Table 13.1.

### Birchwood's investments

13.16 Investments, appearing in Birchwood's historical cost balance sheet at 31st December 1978, other than investments in subsidiary and associated companies, were as follows:

|  | £'000 |
|---|---|
| UK quoted investments | 1,105 |
| Unquoted investments | 42 |
|  | 1,147 |

211

**Quoted investments**

13.17 The mid-market price of Birchwood's quoted investments at 31st December 1978 was £1,468,000.

13.18 None of Birchwood's share holdings represent a significant proportion of the issued share capital of the companies invested in and a review of mid-market prices for the investments for the two weeks either side of 31st December 1978 has shown that the price at that date was not significantly affected by any unusual short term fluctuations.

13.19 Birchwood has held its quoted investments for a number of years and does not regard them as liquid funds temporarily invested. There are no special trading benefits which accrue to Birchwood as a result of holding the shares.

13.20 Based on the information contained in the preceding paragraphs Birchwood's directors decide to value quoted investments at mid-market price. The necessary journal entry (H in Table 13.1, Columns 3 and 4) to adjust from historical cost to mid-market price at 31st December 1978 is:

|    |                      | £'000 | £'000 |
|----|----------------------|-------|-------|
| Dr | Quoted investments   | 363   |       |
| Cr | Revaluation surplus  |       | 363   |

being the difference between mid-market price and historical cost (1,468 − 1,105).

13.21 At 31st December 1979 Birchwood holds the same investments as at 31st December 1978. The circumstances are the same at the end of 1979 as they were at the end of 1978 and therefore quoted investments are again valued at mid-market price, which at 31st December 1979 produced a total value of £1,482,000.

The necessary journal entry (p in Table 13.1, Columns 9 and 10) is:

|    |                      | £'000 | £'000 |
|----|----------------------|-------|-------|
| Dr | Quoted investments   | 14    |       |
| Cr | Revaluation surplus  |       | 14    |

being the difference between mid-market price at 31.12.78 and mid-market price at 31.12.79 (1,482 − 1,468).

**Birchwood's unquoted investments**

13.22 Birchwood's unquoted investment consists of a holding of 10,000 £1 ordinary shares in Ashtree Limited a public unlisted company with an issued share capital of £100,000 in £1 shares. Birchwood originally purchased the shares because its products were sold by Ashtree's retail shops. Ashtree now manufactures its own products however and Birchwood's holding can no longer be said to secure any trade benefits. Ashtree's financial year end is 31st March and at the time of preparing Birchwood's current cost accounts for the year ended 31st December 1979 Ashtree had not produced any CCA information and its latest published accounts were for the year ended 31st March 1979.

13.23 Birchwood's directors decide that in the absence of CCA information regarding Ashtree they should value the holding of Ashtree's shares on a dividend yield basis. Based on the average dividend yield of listed companies engaged in similar activities to those of Ashtree, and making adjustments considered necessary because Ashtree is not listed, the directors consider that a yield of 18% would be reasonable at both the end of 1978 and the end of 1979.

Birchwood has, since 1975, received an annual dividend from Ashtree of £9,900. The directors of Birchwood see no reason to suppose that the dividend will be reduced in the foreseeable future and at the same time see no justification for assuming an increased dividend. Consequently, based on a dividend yield of 18% the directors value their shares in Ashtree at £55,000. The accounting entry required to record the valuation at 31st December 1978 (journal entry J in Table 13.1, Columns 3 and 4) is:

|  |  | £'000 | £'000 |
|----|----|----|----|
| Dr | Unquoted investments | 13 |  |
| Cr | Revaluation surplus |  | 13 |

being the difference between the valuation and the historical cost (55 − 42) at 31st December 1978.

No adjustment to the valuation is required at 31st December 1979.


**The CCA Worksheet**

13.24 The above journal entries are recorded in the CCA worksheet set out in Table 13.1.


## COMPLETION OF THE CCA WORKSHEET

13.25 All the items in Birchwood's accounts which are affected by the introduction of CCA have now been considered and entered on the Worksheet. It remains now only to complete the Worksheet in respect of the remaining monetary items, i.e. those not affected by the introduction of CCA, and to deal with some closing journal entries before the Worksheet can be completed and totalled. The following paragraphs explain the procedure.

13.26 In order to complete the Worksheet it is necessary first to enter the closing debtors, creditors, dividends payable and stock and work in progress in

Columns 13 and 14 as appropriate. The amounts are:

|  | £'000 |  |
|---|---|---|
| Debtors | 47,332 | (column 13) |
| Creditors | 34,832 | (column 14) |
| Dividends payable | 6,200 | (column 14) |
| Stock and work in progress | 68,650 | (column 13) |
| (from paragraph 8.98) | | |

Final journal entries are then necessary to transfer the balance on the debtors' row to revenue income (sales).

|  |  |  | £'000 | £'000 |
|---|---|---|---|---|
| q | Dr | Debtors | 309,895 | |
|  | Cr | Revenue income (sales) | | 309,895 |

and on the creditors' row to revenue expenditure

|  |  |  | £'000 | £'000 |
|---|---|---|---|---|
| r | Dr | Revenue expenditure | 295,308 | |
|  | Cr | Creditors | | 295,308 |

This last amount represents:

| | £'000 |
|---|---|
| Material, labour and overheads | 269,661 |
| Administrative and selling expenses | 32,643 |
| | 302,304 |
| Current cost depreciation (including loss on disposals) | 6,996 |
| | 295,308 |

13.27 The worksheet can now be cross-cast, entering the total for each row in the profit and loss account or balance sheet columns as appropriate. As with Columns 9 and 10, Columns 11 and 12 are effectively reversed.

13.28 Most balances are self-evident but some need explanation. The balance on the stock and work in progress row is a credit of £7,197,000 which comprises:

| | £'000 | £'000 |
|---|---|---|
| Closing stock at historical cost | | 66,657 |
| Less opening stock at historical cost | 51,313 | |
| cost of sales adjustment | 8,147 | |
| | | 59,460 |
| | | 7,197 |

In the interest of clarity these amounts have been shown separately in columns 11 and 12.

13.29 The balance on the dividend row is a debit of £6,480,000 which comprises the proposed ordinary dividend of £6,200,000 and the preference dividend of £280,000 which was paid during the year.

**13.30** Once each row has been cross-cast the profit and loss account, Columns 11 and 12, can be balanced by inserting the balancing figure, being the current cost profit, after distributions, for the year. This figure is then entered in the balance sheet, Column 14, which can then be cast and will balance.

**Table 13.1**

## BIRCHWOOD LIMITED
## CCA Worksheet

| | 1 | 2 | 3 | 4 | 5 | 6 |
|---|---|---|---|---|---|---|
| | Opening balance sheet historical cost | | Opening balance sheet journal | | Opening balance sheet current cost | |
| | Dr £'000 | Cr £'000 | Dr £'000 | Cr £'000 | Dr £'000 | Cr £'000 |
| Land and buildings | 4,719 | 569 | C 569<br>D 1,190 | C 569 | 5,340 | |
| Plant and machinery | 15,446 | | A 10,261 | B 4,357 | 21,350 | |
| Investment in subsidiaries and associates | 13,984 | | G 4,380 | | 18,364 | |
| Quoted and unquoted investments | 1,147 | | H 363<br>J 13 | | 1,523 | |
| Stock and work in progress | 51,313 | | E 1,560 | | 52,873 | |
| Debtors | 32,727 | | | | 32,727 | |
| Cash | 465 | | | | 465 | |
| Creditors | | 23,011 | | | | 23,011 |
| Current tax | | 3,582 | | | | 3,582 |
| Bank overdraft | | 6,481 | | | | 6,481 |
| Dividend | | 5,700 | | | | 5,700 |
| Deferred tax | | 20,222 | F 23,292 | | 3,070 | |
| Ordinary share capital | | 32,185 | | | | 32,185 |
| Reserves – general | | 14,051 | G 95 | F 23,292 | | 37,248 |
| Reserves – revaluation | | | B 4,357 | A 10,261<br>D 1,190<br>E 1,560<br>G 4,475<br>H 363<br>J 13 | | 13,505 |
| Preference share capital | | 4,000 | | | | 4,000 |
| 10% Debentures | | 10,000 | | | | 10,000 |
| Realisation of fixed assets | | | | | | |
| Revenue income | | | | | | |
| Revenue expenditure | | | | | | |
| Depreciation | | | | | | |
| Interest | | | | | | |
| Tax expense | | | | | | |
| Dividends received | | | | | | |
| Revenue surplus | | | | | | |
| | 119,801 | 119,801 | 46,080 | 46,080 | 135,712 | 135,712 |

| 7 | 8 | 9 | 10 | 11 | 12 | 13 | 14 |
|---|---|---|---|---|---|---|---|
| Income and expenditure for 1979 | | Journal entries | | Profit and loss account for 1979 | | Closing balance sheet | |
| Dr £'000 | Cr £'000 | Dr £'000 | Cr £'000 | Dr £'000 | Cr £'000 | Dr £'000 | Cr £'000 |
| | | g 835 | | | | 6,175 | |
| 6,036 | | a 627 ⎫<br>c 7,716 ⎭ | a 1,002 ⎫<br>d 2,634 ⎪<br>e 6,626 ⎬<br>f 595 ⎭ | | | 24,872 | |
| 139 | | n 860 | | | | 19,363 | |
| | | p 14 | | | | 1,537 | |
| | | j 1,993 ⎫<br>h 6,587 ⎭ | | | 8,147 | | |
| | | | | 66,657 | 51,313 | 68,650 | |
| | 295,290 | q 309,895 | | | | 47,332 | |
| 1,319 | 465 | | | | | 1,319 | |
| 283,487 | | | r 295,308 | | | | 34,832 |
| 3,582 | | l 3,070 | k 3,678 ⎫<br>m 3,340 ⎭ | | | | 3,948 |
| 6,481 | 3,430 | | | | | | 3,430 |
| 5,980 | | | | | 6,480 | | 6,200 |
| | | m 3,340 | l 3,070 | | | 3,340 | |
| | 8,000 | | | | | | 40,185 |
| | | | n 103 | | | | 37,351 |
| | | d 2,634 ⎫<br>f 595 ⎭ | c 7,716 ⎫<br>g 1,068 ⎪<br>h 6,587 ⎬<br>j 1,993 ⎪<br>n 757 ⎪<br>p 14 ⎭ | | | | 28,411 |
| | | | | | | | 4,000 |
| | | | | | | | 10,000 |
| | | | b 137 ⎫ | | | | |
| | 238 | a 1,002 | a 627 ⎭ | | | | |
| | | | q 309,895 | 309,895 | | | |
| | | r 295,308 | | | 295,308 | | |
| | | e 6,626 ⎫<br>b 137 ⎬<br>g 233 ⎭ | | | 6,996 | | |
| 1,319 | | | | | 1,319 | | |
| | | k 3,678 | | | 3,678 | | |
| | 920 | | | 920 | | | |
| | | | | | 4,231 | | 4,231 |
| 308,343 | 308,343 | 645,150 | 645,150 | 377,472 | 377,472 | 172,588 | 172,588 |

# 14 Consolidated Accounts

14.1 The Companies Act 1948 requires companies with one or more subsidiaries to prepare group accounts. Such group accounts will normally be in the form of consolidated accounts but there are circumstances in which consolidated accounts need not be prepared or in which certain subsidiaries need not be included in the consolidated accounts.

14.2 Where a company with subsidiaries has adopted CCA as the basis of its annual accounts, its group accounts should also be prepared using CCA principles.

14.3 For the purpose of preparing consolidated current cost accounts the holding company should require its subsidiaries to produce accounts on a CCA basis. It is recognised, however, that it may not be possible for foreign subsidiaries to prepare accounts using CCA principles and in such circumstances the subsidiary's accounts should be converted to a CCA basis by the holding company.

14.4 The conversion to sterling of accounts drawn up in foreign currencies was considered in Chapter 12. The remainder of this chapter deals with the consolidation of accounts already drawn up in sterling.

## The consolidation procedure

14.5 The methods of preparation of consolidated current cost accounts are no different from those normally used to prepare historical cost consolidated accounts. There are, however, certain aspects of the preparation of consolidated current cost accounts which require special mention.

## Purchased goodwill

14.6 Purchased goodwill is the excess of:

(a) the value of the purchase consideration provided by the acquiring entity, over

(b) the value to the acquiring entity of the tangible and separately identifiable intangible assets acquired, less the liabilities taken over.

218

### Example 14.1

XYZ Limited purchases 100% of the equity share capital of ABC Limited for £100,000. At the date of acquisition XYZ Limited values the tangible and separately identifiable intangible assets less liabilities of ABC Limited at £80,000. The goodwill arising on the acquisition is £20,000 (£100,000–£80,000).

### The value of the purchase consideration

14.7   Where shares in subsidiaries are acquired for cash there will be no problem in determining the value of the purchase consideration. If, however, the purchase consideration or any part thereof is equity, other share capital or loan stock of the acquiring company, the value of the purchase consideration may not be as readily ascertainable. The general principle is that shares or loan stock issued as whole or part consideration are to be valued at their market value at the date of acquisition.

14.8   Quoted shares and loan stock should be valued at their market value at the date of acquisition regardless of whether the acquiring company or the vendor has attributed some other value for the purpose of the sale. Market value in this instance is normally the mid-market quoted price of the shares or loan stock.

### Example 14.2

ABC Limited acquires 100% of the equity share capital of PQR Limited for a purchase consideration of £100,000; the purchase consideration being satisfied by the issue to the vendor of 150,000 50p ordinary shares fully paid in ABC Limited. At the date of acquisition the mid-market quoted price of ABC Limited's ordinary shares was 80 pence. The purchase consideration to be used to calculate the purchased goodwill is £120,000 (150,000 × 80p).

14.9   A similar situation to that illustrated in Example 14.2 arises where the purchase consideration consists of loan stock issued at a discount.

### Example 14.3

ABC Limited acquires 100% of the equity share capital of XYZ Limited for a consideration of £60,000 to be satisfied by the issue of £100,000 5% loan stock. At the date of purchase ABC Limited's 5% loan stock is quoted at 55. Purchased goodwill will be calculated using a value of the purchase consideration of £55,000 (i.e. £100,000 at 55). In ABC Limited's balance sheet the loan stock will be shown at par and a discount on the issue of £45,000 (i.e. £100,000 − £55,000) will be recorded.

### The value to the acquiring company of the subsidiary's net assets

14.10  To ascertain the amount of purchased goodwill arising on an acquisition the value to the acquiring company's business of the tangible and separately identifiable intangible assets acquired less liabilities taken over needs to be established. Where the company being acquired has prepared or can prepare current cost accounts at the date of acquisition no difficulty will normally arise in establishing the required value as, in the majority of cases, the required value will be the value of the acquired company's net assets in its current cost balance sheet at the date of acquisition. There are two circumstances, however, when difficulties may arise:

(a) Where, in the case of an acquisition of shares of a foreign company, no current cost accounts have been prepared by the foreign company.
(b) Where the directors consider that the value to the acquiring company's business of the new subsidiary's net assets is different from that shown in the subsidiary's current cost balance sheet at the date of acquisition.

14.11　In case (a) the situation is the same as that for existing foreign subsidiaries for which current cost accounts have not been produced. In such cases the acquiring company should prepare accounts for the subsidiary on a CCA basis.

14.12　In case (b) in the majority of cases it will normally be permissible to value the net assets in the subsidiary's accounts at the value attributed by the acquiring company. For example, the acquired company may be carrying certain assets in its accounts at economic value. The acquiring holding company might consider that, once the acquired company becomes part of the holding company's group, the assets valued at economic value should be valued for the purposes of valuing purchased goodwill at their net replacement cost. In such a case the assets in the subsidiary's balance sheet should be revalued at net replacement cost, any revaluation surplus being treated as a pre-acquisition amount.

### Example 14.4

Beetroot Limited acquires Carrot Limited for £1,000,000 in cash on 31st December 1979. At the date of acquisition the current cost balance sheet of Carrot Limited shows net assets of £500,000 including a purpose built industrial complex valued on the basis of economic value at £200,000. Beetroot Limited considers that once Carrot Limited joins its group the excess capacity in Carrot Limited's factory will be taken up by work from within the group. Beetroot Limited therefore considers that Carrot Limited's industrial complex should be valued, for the purposes of determining the purchased goodwill, at net replacement cost for the plant and machinery, depreciated replacement cost for the buildings and open market value for existing use for the bare land, amounting in total to £500,000. The purchased goodwill in Beetroot Limited's consolidated balance sheet is therefore £200,000 (£1,000,000 − (£500,000 + £300,000)). The higher value of the industrial complex also may replace the economic value in Carrot Limited's own accounts, the resulting surplus being treated as a revaluation surplus.

### Accounting treatment of purchased goodwill

14.13 Once the amount of purchased goodwill has been established the holding company must decide the accounting policy to be adopted in the consolidated accounts. The main alternatives are:

(a) To write off purchased goodwill immediately on acquisition.
(b) To amortise purchased goodwill over its expected life or an arbitrary shorter period.
(c) To hold goodwill in its accounts at cost until it becomes apparent that cost exceeds current value.

Whichever accounting policy is adopted, any amounts written off should be disclosed on the face of the profit and loss account or appropriation account as appropriate, depending on the policy chosen. Any amounts written off over the last five years (i.e. including the year under review) should be shown by way of note to the accounts. The accounting policy in respect of goodwill should also be disclosed.

### Discounts arising on acquisition

14.14 A discount arises on acquisition when the value of the purchase consideration is less than the value of the net assets acquired. Discounts on acquisition should be treated as negative goodwill and as such the alternative accounting treatments listed in paragraph 14.13 above may be applied as appropriate. The chosen treatment will depend on the company's accounting policy for purchased goodwill.

### Transitional procedures

14.15 On first changing from historical cost accounting to CCA, goodwill retained in the historical cost accounts should be written off against any revaluation surpluses resulting from the revaluation of the relevant assets and liabilities to the extent that such surplus on revaluation is deemed to have existed at the time of the acquisition. Goodwill should not be otherwise revalued because of the transition and may either be written off against available reserves and disclosed in the profit and loss account or appropriation account as appropriate, or carried in the current cost balance sheet at historical cost less amounts written off in accordance with the company's chosen accounting policy.

### Example 14.5

Orange Limited adopts CCA principles on 1st January 1979. At 31st December 1978 the consolidated historical cost balance sheet of Orange Limited included goodwill at cost of £150,000 in respect of a subsidiary purchased on 30th June 1975 for £1·5 m. The directors estimate that the value of the net assets of the subsidiary at 30th June 1975 on a CCA basis would have been £3m and they should therefore write off the historical cost goodwill against revaluation surplus.

14.16 It should be noted that, in the case of Example 14.5, if the relevant revaluation surpluses deemed to have existed at the date of acquisition had been reduced by subsequent revaluation deficits or by distributions, the company could nevertheless write off the goodwill against revaluation surplus even if this would result in a debit balance on revaluation reserve at the date of adoption of CCA. In certain circumstances, if current cost values cannot be produced for the subsidiary at the date of acquisition, it may be necessary to calculate goodwill based on asset values at the date of adopting CCA. In such cases the procedure is similar to that explained in respect of associated companies in Chapter 11.

### Transfers between reserves

14.17 Where, after the introduction of CCA, companies and their subsidiaries make transfers through the general reserve to the revaluation reserve such transfers would be made based on the directors consideration of the circumstances of each individual company. When the consolidated current cost accounts are prepared the directors will need to consider the circumstances of the group as a whole in order to determine the required transfer to revaluation reserve. It is not necessarily to be expected that transfers to the revaluation reserve of a subsidiary will be necessary when looking at the group as a whole and in such circumstances the transfer may be eliminated on consolidation.

### The elimination of intra-group profit

14.18 In preparing historical cost consolidated accounts it is necessary to eliminate from the group's profit for the year any profit which has arisen from the sale of stock (or fixed assets) from one group company to another to the extent that the purchasing company still holds the stock at the end of the accounting period. The required journal entry once the amount of profit to be eliminated has been determined is:

    Dr   Consolidated profit and loss account
    Cr   Consolidated stock
         with the profit to be eliminated.

14.19 Under CCA there are two complications which need to be considered. Firstly, because of the incidence of revaluation surpluses it may be that the amount to be excluded from the value of stock will be less than the amount which should be excluded from operating profit.

### Example 14.6

A Limited and B Limited are two subsidiaries of Group Limited. During an accounting period A sells goods to B (a retail shop) at a fixed price of £100 per item. At the beginning of the period the replacement cost per item to A was £50 but by the end of the period the replacement cost had risen to £70. At the end of the period B held in stock all the items purchased from A during the period and these had cost B £2,000.

The value of B's stock in the consolidated balance sheet at the end of the period should clearly be £1,400 (70/100 × £2,000), i.e. the replacement cost of the stock to the group at the balance sheet date. The operating profit of A to be eliminated on consolidation however will be greater than the £30 per item to be eliminated from the value of stock because in respect of some items sold to B the operating profit recorded was £50. Operating profit per item was reduced to £30 only at the end of the period.

Assuming that the average operating profit per item made by A was £40 the amount to be eliminated from operating profit is £800 (20 × £40). The consolidated adjustment is:

|  |  | £ | £ |
|---|---|---|---|
| Dr | Consolidated operating profit | 800 | |
| Cr | Consolidated stock | | 600 |
| Cr | Consolidated revaluation surplus | | 200 |

The credit to revaluation surplus although being the balancing figure can also be explained logically. When A sold an item to B it stopped registering revaluation surplus in respect of that item. B did not register a revaluation surplus in respect of any items purchased from A because from B's point of view replacement cost did not increase. The stock from the Group's point of view, however, was increasing in replacement cost and the credit to revaluation reserve is to reflect this fact in the consolidated accounts.

14.20 The second complication is that even if stock has been sold to third parties prior to the end of the accounting period there may still be a need to eliminate some operating profit on consolidation.

### Example 14.7

Continuing Example 14.6 assume that on the last day of the accounting period B Limited had sold all of the stock it had purchased from A Limited for £150 per item.

(a) B Limited will have recorded an operating profit of £1,000 in respect of the stock.
(b) A Limited will have recorded an operating profit (as in Example 14.6) of £800.
(c) There is no stock on hand at the period end so there is no stock reduction required.
(d) The group as a whole stopped registering revaluation surplus when A sold the stock to B. In fact it should have stopped registering revaluation surplus only when B sold the items to third parties at the period end. Therefore the group as a whole has overstated operating profit and understated revaluation reserve, in this particular example, by £200.
(e) The required consolidated adjustment is:

|  |  | £ | £ |
|---|---|---|---|
| Dr | Consolidated cost of sales | 200 | |
| Cr | Consolidated revaluation surplus | | 200 |

14.21 It will be appreciated that Examples 14.6 and 14.7 have been much simplified to demonstrate the principles involved. In practice the determination of the amounts to be adjusted could be considerably more difficult. Nevertheless those companies for which the adjustments are likely to be material will need to adopt procedures which will provide them with the necessary information.

### Birchwood's consolidated CCA accounts

14.22 The remainder of the chapter shows the method used to prepare the consolidated CCA accounts of Birchwood Limited and its subsidiary and associated companies. The consolidated accounts being prepared are those for the year ended 31st December 1979. Birchwood Limited's CCA accounts used for this purpose are set out in Table 13.1 (columns 11–14). The accounts of Birchwood Limited's three subsidiaries, Brinkwells, Forli and Craeglea Inc. are set out in Tables 11.2–11.7.

14.23 Tables 14.1, 14.2 and 14.3 are respectively the consolidation of the opening balance sheet, profit and loss account and revaluation surpluses and the closing balance sheets. The majority of items are simply added across. There are, however, certain adjustments which are discussed below. None of the principles involved differ from those applicable to an historical cost consolidation.

### Opening balance sheets

14.24 Two basic adjustments are necessary. First the amount of the investment in subsidiaries in Birchwood's balance sheet needs to be offset against the equity and reserves of the subsidiaries and secondly the minority interest in Forli has to be determined.

14.25 In Birchwood's own balance sheet the investment in subsidiaries was valued at the CCA value of the subsidiaries' net assets (see Chapter 11). Therefore all that is necessary are the following offsetting entries to clear the 'investment in subsidiaries':

**Opening balance sheets**

Brinkwells Ltd (Journal entry A in Table 14.1, Columns 9 and 10)

|  |  | £'000 | £'000 |
|---|---|---|---|
| Dr | Share capital | 4,000 | |
| Dr | Revenue reserves | 2,516 | |
| Dr | Revaluation reserves | 4,849 | |
| Cr | Investment in subsidiary | | 11,365 |

224

Forli Ltd (Journal entry B in Table 14.1, columns 9 and 10)

|     |                         | £'000 | £'000 |
| --- | ----------------------- | ----: | ----: |
| Dr  | Share capital           | 1,500 |       |
| Dr  | Revenue reserves        |   682 |       |
| Dr  | Revaluation reserves    |   224 |       |
| Cr  | Investment in subsidiary |       | 2,406 |
|     |                         | 2,406 | 2,406 |

Craeglea Inc. (Journal entry C in Table 14.1, Columns 9 and 10)

|     |                         | £'000 | £'000 |
| --- | ----------------------- | ----: | ----: |
| Dr  | Share capital           | 1,647 |       |
| Dr  | Revenue reserves        |    90 |       |
| Dr  | Revaluation reserves    |   205 |       |
| Cr  | Investment in subsidiary |       | 1,942 |
|     |                         | 1,942 | 1,942 |

The minority's interest in Forli is one quarter (Journal entry D in Table 14.1, Columns 9 and 10):

|     |                      | £'000 | £'000 |
| --- | -------------------- | ----: | ----: |
| Dr  | Share capital        |   500 |       |
| Dr  | Revenue reserves     |   227 |       |
| Dr  | Revaluation reserves |    75 |       |
| Cr  | Minority interest    |       |   802 |
|     |                      |   802 |   802 |

**Table 14.1**

BIRCHWOOD – CONSOLIDATION

| Opening balance sheets | 1 Birchwood Dr £'000 | 2 Birchwood Cr £'000 | 3 Brinkwells Dr £'000 | 4 Brinkwells Cr £'000 | 5 Forli Dr £'000 | 6 Forli Cr £'000 | 7 Craeglea Dr £'000 | 8 Craeglea Cr £'000 | 9 Adjustments Dr £'000 | 10 Adjustments Cr £'000 | 11 Consolidated Dr £'000 | 12 Consolidated Cr £'000 |
|---|---|---|---|---|---|---|---|---|---|---|---|---|
| Land and buildings | 5,340 | | 5,985 | | — | | — | | | | 11,325 | |
| Plant and machinery | 21,350 | | 4,319 | | 1,648 | | 1,548 | | | | 28,865 | — |
| Investments in subsidiaries | 17,911 | | | 1,742 | | 456 | | | | A 11,365 B 2,406 C 1,942 | | |
| Investments in associate | 453 | | | | | | | | | | 453 | |
| Quoted and unquoted investments | 1,523 | | | | | | | | | | 1,523 | |
| Stock and work in progress | 52,873 | | 12,814 | | 2,182 | | 835 | | | | 68,704 | |
| Debtors | 32,727 | | 6,438 | | 1,182 | | 1,096 | | | | 41,443 | |
| Cash | 465 | | 219 | | 189 | | 129 | | | | 1,002 | |
| Creditors | | 23,011 | | 15,552 | | 1,411 | | 666 | | | | 40,640 |
| Current tax | | 3,582 | | 682 | | 126 | | — | | | | 4,390 |
| Bank overdraft | | 6,481 | | 434 | | — | | — | | | | 6,915 |
| Dividends | | 5,700 | | | | — | | | | | | 5,700 |
| Deferred tax | 3,070 | | | | | | | | | | 3,070 | |
| Ordinary share capital | | 32,185 | | 4,000 | | 2,000 | | 1,647 | A 4,000 B 1,500 C 1,647 D 500 | | | 32,185 |
| Reserves – general | | 37,248 | | 2,516 | | 909 | | 90 | A 2,516 B 682 C 90 D 227 | | | 37,248 |
| Reserves – revaluation | | 13,505 | | 4,849 | | 299 | | 205 | A 4,849 B 224 C 205 D 75 | | | 13,505 |
| Minority interest | | | | | | | | | | D 802 | | 802 |
| Preference share capital | | 4,000 | | | | | | | | | | 4,000 |
| 10% Debentures | | 10,000 | | | | | | | | | | 10,000 |
| Loans | | | | | | | | 1,000 | | | | 1,000 |
| | 135,712 | 135,712 | 29,775 | 29,775 | 5,201 | 5,201 | 3,608 | 3,608 | 16,515 | 16,515 | 156,385 | 156,385 |

226

# Table 14.2

BIRCHWOOD – CONSOLIDATION

| Profit and loss accounts | 1 Birchwood Dr £'000 | 2 Birchwood Cr £'000 | 3 Brinkwells Dr £'000 | 4 Brinkwells Cr £'000 | 5 Forli Dr £'000 | 6 Forli Cr £'000 | 7 Craeglea Dr £'000 | 8 Craeglea Cr £'000 | 9 Adjustments Dr £'000 | 10 Adjustments Cr £'000 | 11 Consolidated Dr £'000 | 12 Consolidated Cr £'000 |
|---|---|---|---|---|---|---|---|---|---|---|---|---|
| Sales | | 309,895 | | 72,964 | | 14,109 | | 5,165 | | | | 402,133 |
| Cost of sales, administrative and selling expenses | 295,107 | | 71,740 | | 14,045 | | 5,168 | | | | 386,060 | |
| Interest paid | 1,319 | | 82 | | 10 | | | | | | 1,411 | |
| Dividends received | | 920 | | — | | — | | | K 40, E 700 | | | 180 |
| Tax | 3,678 | | 369 | | 24 | | 13 | | | | 4,084 | |
| Share of profits of associate | | | | | | | | | | K 40, K 24 | | 64 |
| Dividends | 6,480 | | 700 | | | | | | | E 700 | 6,480 | |
| Minority interest | | | | | | | | | F 8 | | 8 | |
| Difference on exchange | | | | | | | | | | F 8 | | |
| Profit retained | 4,231 | | 73 | | 30 | | | 16 | K 24 | | 4,334 | 8 |
| | 310,815 | 310,815 | 72,964 | 72,964 | 14,109 | 14,109 | 5,181 | 5,181 | 772 | 772 | 402,378 | 402,378 |
| Minority | | | | | | | | | G 98 | | 98 | |
| Revaluation: | | | | | | | | | | | | |
| Fixed assets | | 5,555 | | 563 | | 105 | 250 | | | J 246 | | 5,973 |
| Stock and work in progress | | 8,580 | 185 | | | 289 | | | H 836 | | | 8,771 |
| Subsidiaries | | 836 | | | | | | 87 | | | | 246 |
| Associate | | 24 | | | | | | | K 24 | | | |
| Quoted and unquoted investments | | 14 | | | | | | 163 | | | | 14 |
| Retained revaluations | 14,906 | | 378 | | 394 | | | | J 246 | G 98, H 757, H 79, K 24 | 14,906 | |
| Retained revenue | 103 | | | | | | | | | | | |
| | 15,009 | 15,009 | 563 | 563 | 394 | 394 | 250 | 250 | 1,204 | 1,204 | 15,004 | 15,004 |
| Differences on exchange | | | | | | | | | | | | |
| – revenue | | | | | | | | 10 | J 10 | | | |
| – revaluation | | | | | | | | 16 | J 16 | | | |
| – share capital | | | | | | | | 220 | J 220 | | | |
| Total differences on exchange | | | | | | | 246 | 246 | 246 | J 246 | | |

**Table 14.3**

BIRCHWOOD – CONSOLIDATION

| Closing balance sheets | 1 | 2 | 3 | 4 |
|---|---|---|---|---|
| | Birchwood | | Brinkwells | |
| | Dr £'000 | Cr £'000 | Dr £'000 | Cr £'000 |
| Land and buildings | 6,175 | | 6,143 | |
| Plant and machinery | 24,872 | | 4,818 | |
| Investments in subsidiaries | 18,886 | | | 2,061 |
| Investments in associate | 477 | | | |
| Quoted and unquoted investments | 1,537 | | | |
| Stock and work in progress | 68,650 | | 14,648 | |
| Debtors | 47,332 | | 9,219 | |
| Cash | 1,319 | | 102 | |
| Creditors | | 34,832 | | 19,422 |
| Current tax | | 3,948 | | 369 |
| Bank overdraft | | 3,430 | | 1,262 |
| Dividends | | 6,200 | | |
| Deferred tax | 3,340 | | | |
| Ordinary share capital | | 40,185 | | 4,000 |
| Reserves – general | | 41,582 | | 2,589 |
| Reserves – revaluation | | 28,411 | | 5,227 |
| Minority interest | | | | |
| Preference share capital | | 4,000 | | |
| 10% debentures | | 10,000 | | |
| Loans | | | | |
| | 172,588 | 172,588 | 34,930 | 34,930 |

| 5 Forli Dr £'000 | 6 Cr £'000 | 7 Craeglea Dr £'000 | 8 Cr £'000 | 9 Adjustments Dr £'000 | 10 Cr £'000 | 11 Consolidated Dr £'000 | 12 Cr £'000 |
|---|---|---|---|---|---|---|---|
| — | | — | | | | 12,318 | |
| 2,141 | | 1,586 | | | | 33,417 | |
| | 276 | | | | H 836 | — | |
| | | | | | A 11,365 | | |
| | | | | | B 2,406 | | |
| | | | | | C 1,942 | | |
| | | | | | | 477 | |
| | | | | | | 1,537 | |
| 2,214 | | 877 | | | | 86,389 | |
| 1,059 | | 1,076 | | | | 58,686 | |
| 46 | | 73 | | | | 1,540 | |
| | 1,528 | | 456 | | | | 56,238 |
| | 24 | | 14 | | | | 4,355 |
| | | | | | | | 4,692 |
| | | | | | | | 6,200 |
| | | | | | | 3,340 | |
| | 2,000 | | 1,867 | A 4,000 | | | 40,185 |
| | | | | B 1,500 | | | |
| | | | | C 1,647 | | | |
| | | | | D 500 | | | |
| | | | | J 220 | | | |
| | 939 | | 84 | F 8 | K 24 | | 41,582 |
| | | | | A 2,516 | | | |
| | | | | B 682 | | | |
| | | | | C 90 | | | |
| | | | | D 227 | | | |
| | | | | J 10 | | | |
| | | | | H 79 | | | |
| | | | | K 24 | | | |
| | 693 | | 58 | G 98 | J 230 | | 28,411 |
| | | | | A 4,849 | | | |
| | | | | B 224 | | | |
| | | | | C 205 | | | |
| | | | | D 75 | | | |
| | | | | H 757 | | | |
| | | | | | F 8 | | 908 |
| | | | | | G 98 | | |
| | | | | | D 802 | | |
| | | | | | | | 4,000 |
| | | | | | | | 10,000 |
| | | | 1,133 | | | | 1,133 |
| 5,460 | 5,460 | 3,612 | 3,612 | 17,711 | 17,711 | 197,704 | 197,704 |

229

## Profit and loss accounts and closing balance sheets

14.26 The following entries which are shown in Tables 14.2 and 14.3, Columns 9 and 10 are self explanatory, necessary and in addition to the repeat at the year-end of A to D above:

|   |    |                                                  | £'000 | £'000 |
|---|----|--------------------------------------------------|-------|-------|
| E | Dr | Dividends received                               | 700   |       |
|   | Cr | Dividends payable                                |       | 700   |
|   |    | Inter-company dividend                           |       |       |
| F | Dr | Minority interest (P & L)                        | 8     |       |
|   | Cr | Minority interest                                |       | 8     |
|   |    | Minority's share of Forli's profit               |       |       |
| G | Dr | Minority interest—revaluations                   | 98    |       |
|   | Cr | Minority interest                                |       | 98    |
|   |    | Minority's share of Forli's revaluation surpluses |       |       |

|   |    |                                                  | £'000 | £'000 |
|---|----|--------------------------------------------------|-------|-------|
| H | Dr | Revaluation surplus—subsidiaries                 | 757   |       |
|   | Dr | Retained revenue                                 | 79    |       |
|   | Cr | Investment in subsidiaries                       |       | 836   |
|   |    | Revaluation of investment in subsidiaries        |       |       |
| J | Dr | Differences on exchange                          | 246   |       |
|   | Cr | Revaluation surpluses                            |       | 246   |
|   |    | Gains arising from using closing rate for Craeglea closing balance sheet and average rate for profit and loss |       |       |
| K | Dr | General reserves                                 | 24    |       |
|   | Dr | Dividends received                               | 40    |       |
|   | Cr | Share of profits of associates (revenue reserves) |       | 64    |
|   |    | Share of profits of associated company           |       |       |

# 15 Recording Fixed Assets and Depreciation

## Introduction

15.1    The methods that will be used by a company to record current cost information about its fixed assets will depend on the nature and value of the assets concerned, the management's policy with regard to the level of detail to be recorded and the book-keeping system used by the company. It is not the intention in this chapter to describe a CCA book-keeping system that will be suitable in all cases. It is only possible to consider in outline the elements that should be present in all systems in order to record the information required by CCA. The way in which these elements might be incorporated into a company's existing accounting system can be only suggested.

### General considerations

15.2    The principles of CCA are such that any system for recording CCA information must be flexible. Although, where possible, a consistent approach should be adopted it is not necessarily the case that an asset once valued by one method will continue to be valued by that method until the end of its life. Thus while it may be impractical to obtain estimates of replacement costs based on expert opinion annually it may be possible to obtain such estimates, say, every three years and use a suitable index in the intervening years. Similarly, there will be circumstances in which assets previously valued at their net replacement cost will need to be valued in future at their economic value or net realisable value. Also, estimates of future useful lives may be changed from time to time. Any CCA recording system therefore must be designed to accommodate changes in the following variable factors:

1    The method of valuation.
2    The basis of valuation.
3    The remaining useful life.

### Historical cost information

15.3    For the two years following the introduction of CCA it is likely that companies will be required to publish full historical cost information in their annual accounts. For this purpose companies will be required to calculate a charge for depreciation based on the historical cost of fixed assets.

15.4    For at least two years therefore, and possibly, in the light of taxation and EEC requirements, for the foreseeable future, historical cost information should continue to be recorded by companies which have adopted CCA principles. Furthermore, as the introduction of CCA has clearly demonstrated, even firmly established accounting policies are subject to change and it would be unwise for any company to construct its accounting system so as to make it impossible to produce information other than on one particular basis.

15.5    CCA information and historical cost information can be made available within one book-keeping system in a number of different ways but all systems will probably fall within the following general categories:

1   Systems which are basically historical cost systems with current cost information maintained by way of memorandum.
2   Systems which are basically current cost systems with historical cost information maintained by way of memorandum.
3   Systems which are basically historical cost systems but in which additional current cost information is recorded as an integral part of the double entry so that when the additional information is added to the historical cost information the required CCA information is obtained.

The accounting entries described in this book are primarily those applicable to the second type of system. Companies are encouraged to adopt an accounting system which incorporates current cost information into the double entry and does not regard it only as memorandum information.

### Procedure on the introduction of CCA

15.6    Examples showing the procedure on the introduction of CCA were given in Chapters 5 and 6 in respect of Birchwood Limited. The general procedure is as follows:

1   Value fixed assets at the date CCA is introduced.
2   Calculate backlog depreciation up to the date of introduction.
3   Close any depreciation provision accounts in respect of assets valued other than at their NRC by transferring the balance to the credit of the appropriate asset account.
4   Where applicable provide for deferred tax on the increase in the value of fixed assets.

15.7    In summary the accounting entries are as follows:

1   Dr   Asset accounts
    Cr   Revaluation surplus account
          with the increase in value arising on revaluation
2   Dr   Revaluation surplus account
    Cr   Depreciation provision accounts
          with backlog depreciation

3  Dr   Depreciation provision accounts
     Cr   Asset accounts
          with the balance on depreciation accounts in respect of assets valued at other than their NRC

4  Dr   Revaluation surplus account
     Cr   Deferred tax provision
          with any deferred tax liability expected to arise in the foreseeable future as a result of the revaluation.

### The fixed asset register

15.8 It will be apparent that certain methods of ascertaining GRCs can only be used if assets can be separately identified. Thus while an index can be applied to a large group of assets, the composition of which is known only generally, suppliers' price lists can only be used as a source of price data if individual assets can be identified. Indeed, an inability to identify individual assets or closely-defined groups of assets restricts the useful sources of price data exclusively to indices.

15.9 Even when indices are used as the source of price data their application to large groups of items is undesirable. This is because within a group of assets there may be some assets for which a net replacement cost basis of valuation is inappropriate or for which the GRC of a modern equivalent asset should be used.

Unless these assets can be identified the value of the assets in aggregate may be overstated. In all cases therefore, whether using indices or otherwise, asset values should be ascertained, as far as possible, on an individual basis or on the basis of closely defined groups.

15.10 A fixed asset register will enable the company to arrive at values for individual assets and it is recommended that such a register should be maintained, regardless of the method or basis of valuation, in respect of all but insignificant assets.

### Plant and machinery

15.11 In respect of each identifiable asset or group of assets, the register should include the following information:

(a) A description of the asset(s).
(b) The original (historical) cost and date of purchase.
(c) Expected retirement or scrapping date.
(d) The current basis of valuation.
(e) The source from which price or valuation data is obtained.
(f) The current value of the asset(s).
(g) Where appropriate, the gross replacement cost and accumulated depreciation.

15.12　Wherever it is expected that suppliers' price lists etc. will be used as the source of price data or where the company's own replacement cost estimates are to be used it is important that the description of the asset is sufficiently detailed so that:

(a) it can be identified from the supplier's own description in price lists, catalogues, etc;
(b) an adequately documented estimate can be made of the cost of an alternative replacement;
(c) differences in the specification of alternative replacements can be identified.

15.13　The register should be organised so that, within asset types, assets with the same retirement dates are grouped together. It is suggested that assets valued on the basis of economic value or net realisable value are kept separately from those valued at net current replacement cost. The register might be organised as follows:

Section 1　　Net current replacement cost.
　　　1.1　Plant and machinery analysed by year of expected disposal.
　　　1.2　Furniture and office equipment analysed by year of expected disposal.
　　　1.3　Motor vehicles analysed by year of expected disposal.

Section 2　　Economic value.
　　　2.1　Plant and machinery (together with any associated land and buildings) analysed by year of expected disposal.

Section 3　　Net realisable value.
　　　3.1　Plant and machinery
　　　　　—at scrap value (not depreciated)
　　　　　—others (depreciated), analysed by year of expected disposal.

**Land and buildings**

15.14　Companies should normally include land and buildings in the fixed assets register although it will probably be sufficient simply to maintain a separate ledger account in the general ledger for each property if only a few properties are involved.

15.15　Whichever method is used to record information the following should be separately identifiable:

Freehold land and buildings
　　Open market valuation basis
　　　　—Depreciable amount
　　　　—Residual amount

　　Depreciated replacement cost basis
　　　　—Buildings at depreciated replacement cost
　　　　—Land at open market value

Economic value basis (memorandum)
—Land and buildings valued together with plant and machinery valued on the basis of economic value.

Leasehold land and buildings
Open market valuation basis (for both positive and negative values)
—Depreciable amount
—Residual amount
Depreciated replacement cost basis
—Land
—Buildings
Economic value basis (memorandum).

All amounts on which depreciation charges will be based should be analysed by reference to the year in which the useful life is expected to end.

### Ledger accounts

15.16  To operate a CCA system for recording fixed assets and depreciation the following general ledger accounts will be needed:

1   Asset accounts analysed:
   (a) by asset type (e.g. land and buildings, plant and equipment, etc.) and
   (b) by basis of valuation.
2   Depreciation provision accounts analysed by asset type.
3   Fixed asset revaluation surplus account.

It will be recalled that a depreciation provision account is maintained only in respect of those assets which are valued on the basis of their net current replacement cost. In all other cases net values are recorded in the appropriate asset account.

# 16 Recording the Current Cost of Stock

16.1   The comments in the previous chapter concerning flexibility and reten-tion of historical cost information regarding fixed assets also apply to stock and work in progress. As with fixed assets no more than a guide can be given to the choice of a suitable book-keeping system to account for the current cost of stock. In the following chapter the usefulness of standard costing systems with regard to CCA is considered. In this chapter CCA stock systems in general are considered.

**Accounting for physical quantities**

16.2   The value to the business of stock and work in progress, either for the charge for cost of sales or for balance sheet purposes in most cases can be accurately determined only if the volume of stock is known. In the case of cost of sales the volume required is the number of items sold. Therefore, wherever practicable, companies should maintain records of the physical quantities of stocks as well as a record of stock values. In fact continuously evaluated stock records are not essential. If the quanti-ty of stock consumed during the accounting period and the quantity on hand at the balance sheet date are known the current cost of sales and the balance sheet value of stock can be determined accurately by applying current unit costs to the quantities, e.g. in the case of cost of sales by mul-tiplying the number of items sold in a period by the current cost per item at the date of sale. A stock accounting system, therefore, where stock volumes are known, might in outline be as follows:

1 Perpetual physical stock records are maintained.
2 A record is maintained of the current unit cost of stock (either on an item by item basis or by means of an index applied to historical costs).
3 The cost of sales for a period will be the volume of stock consumed (i.e. the number of items sold) multiplied by the current cost per item at the date (or in the period) of consumption.
4 The current cost of stock at the balance sheet date will be the volume of stock multiplied by the current unit price at the balance sheet date.

**Accounting for values**

16.3   It can be seen that to operate a system such as that described above there is no need to maintain continuously evaluated stock records. If the value of stock is required at any particular date it can be determined by multiplying volumes by current unit costs.

16.4 There are in fact considerable problems involved in maintaining a system which provides a meaningful continuously evaluated balance. In a FIFO system stock is debited with the actual cost of purchases and credited with the FIFO cost of stock consumed. At any point in time therefore the balance on the stock account will represent the FIFO cost of stock on hand. In a current cost system stock is debited with the actual cost of purchases and credited with the current cost of stock consumed. The balance remaining will therefore only represent the current cost of stock if there has been no change in replacement costs during the period. For example, if 100 units are debited to stock at their purchased cost of £2 per unit and are credited to stock when sold at a replacement cost of £2.10 there will be a negative stock balance of £10. In order to maintain a meaningful evaluated current cost stock balance it would be necessary to adjust stock values each time there is an adjustment to replacement costs by debiting stock and crediting revaluation surplus.

### Example 16.1

The following is a summary of the movement of the stock of components for a company in the first quarter of 1976:

|  | Volume | | |
| --- | --- | --- | --- |
|  | January | February | March |
| Opening balance | 200 | 400 | 200 |
| Purchases | 300 | 100 | 200 |
|  | 500 | 500 | 400 |
| Transfer to work in progress | 100 | 300 | 250 |
| Closing balance | 400 | 200 | 150 |

The current replacement cost per unit increased from £100 to £150 on 1st February.

If no adjustment to stock accounts is made for the effect of the change in price the movement in the evaluated records for the stock of components would be:

|  | January | February | March |
| --- | --- | --- | --- |
|  | £ | £ | £ |
| Opening balance | 20,000 | 40,000 | 10,000 |
| Purchases | 30,000 | 15,000 | 30,000 |
|  | 50,000 | 55,000 | 40,000 |
| Transfer to work in progress (at current cost at the date of transfer) | 10,000 | 45,000 | 37,500 |
|  | £40,000 | £10,000 | £ 2,500 |

The balance at the end of March is therefore evaluated incorrectly at a unit price of £16·66 (£2,500 ÷ 150). This situation would not have occurred if the

237

necessary adjustment had been made at the time of the increase in unit cost. The increase per unit was £50 so the effect at the 31st January, when 400 units are in stock was £20,000. The entry needed on 1st February was therefore:

|     |                     | £      | £      |
|-----|---------------------|--------|--------|
| Dr  | Stock               | 20,000 |        |
| Cr  | Revaluation surplus |        | 20,000 |

The balance at the end of March would then be £22,500, i.e. £150 per unit as it should be under CCA.

### Periodic stock valuation

16.5    To avoid the complications that would arise if an evaluated CCA system is adopted companies may decide to continue using their existing systems and to make COSAs and adjustments to stock values for balance sheet purposes as appropriate. In such cases it is suggested that any adjustments made to stock values for balance sheet purposes should be reversed at the beginning of the following period so that a company's existing accounting routines are not disrupted unduly. For example, if a FIFO system is in operation the FIFO cost of stock might be adjusted to current value at the end of period 1 for balance sheet purposes by debiting stock and crediting revaluation surplus. Without further adjustment the balance carried forward in period 2 will be the current cost of stock and not the FIFO cost of stock and the company's normal method of arriving at cost of sales during period 2 would need to be changed to take this into account. So that the company's normal FIFO accounting procedures can be applied without change therefore the stock balance carried forward to period 2 should be adjusted back to a FIFO basis by crediting stock and debiting revaluation surplus in period 2 with the amounts that were debited to stock and credited to revaluation surplus at the end of period 1.

### Example 16.2

If the Company in Example 16.1 used a FIFO system the movement in the value of components in January and February (before making the correcting adjustment) would be:

|                                    | January | February |
|------------------------------------|---------|----------|
|                                    | £       | £        |
| Opening balance                    | 20,000  | 40,000   |
| Purchases                          | 30,000  | 15,000   |
|                                    | 50,000  | 55,000   |
| Transfer to work in progress at FIFO | 10,000 | 30,000   |
| Closing balance                    | £40,000 | £25,000  |

If the adjustment calculated in Example 16.1 is made for balance sheet purposes at 31st January and not reversed the February movement is:

|  |  | £ |
|---|---|---|
| Opening balance | | 60,000 |
| Purchases | | 15,000 |
| | | 75,000 |
| Transfer to work in progress (at FIFO) | | 30,000 |
| Closing balance | | £45,000 |

giving a closing cost per unit of £225 instead of £150. To correct the situation the company on 1st February must either reverse the correcting adjustment made at the end of January or change from its FIFO method of recording transfers to a CCA method.

## A simple system of accounting for stock

16.6   It will have been appreciated that for companies which are unable to continuously update to current cost the evaluated balance of stock a CCA system of accounting for stock which will provide a reasonably accurate evaluated stock balance is impracticable. Such companies should therefore either continue using their existing systems and make COSAs and balance sheet adjustments as appropriate or adopt a simple CCA system as outlined in paragraph 16.2 above. It is appreciated that many manufacturing companies will be unable to adopt a system which requires a 'volume' of purchases to be calculated in the way suggested herein. Nevertheless the system as outlined may be capable of adaption to meet the needs of many companies. The mechanics of such a system might be as set out below:

1  Physical stock records are maintained showing stock movements in quantity only.
2  A record is maintained of current replacement costs for each item of stock (or an average uplift of historical unit prices is calculated, e.g. by means of an index).
3  The cost of purchases is debited to a purchases account, creditors (or cash) being credited.
4  When sales are made, or at the end of each accounting period, the cost of sales is calculated by multiplying the number of items sold by their current cost at the date of sale. This amount is debited to cost of sales and credited to a 'stock reconciliation' account. The current cost can be some form of index or, for example, where one basic product is produced with only relatively minor variations (e.g. motor cars) the current cost can be for a 'typical' item.
5  At the end of each period:

   (a)  The balance on the purchases account is transferred to the stock reconciliation account.
   (b)  The physical stock balances are multiplied by current unit costs to arrive at the current value of stock at the balance sheet date. The difference between the period end current value of stock and the opening stock balance is debited (or credited) to stock and credited (or debited) to the stock reconciliation account.

239

(c) The balance on the stock reconciliation account is transferred to revaluation surplus.

**Example 16.3**

Redwood Ltd. has the following stock movements in an accounting period:

|  | Volume (expressed in numbers of finished goods) |
|---|---|
| Opening balance | 300 |
| Purchases (i.e. all input to stock) | 150 |
|  | 450 |
| Sales | 180 |
| Closing balance | 270 |

The current replacement cost for each unit at the beginning and end of the period was respectively £48 and £50. Purchases at historical cost amounted to £7,350.

$$\text{Cost of sales is } 180 \times \frac{(£50 + £48)}{2} = £8,820$$

Stock movement during the period is:

|  | £ |
|---|---|
| Opening stock 300 × £48 | 14,400 |
| Closing stock 270 × £50 | 13,500 |
| Decrease—debit to stock reconciliation account | £ 900 |

**Stock Reconciliation Account**

|  | £ |  | £ |
|---|---|---|---|
| Purchases | 7,350 | Cost of sales | 8,820 |
| Stock movement | 900 | Balance— |  |
|  |  | revaluation surplus | 570 |
|  | £9,390 |  | £ 9,390 |

The balance of £570 represents the increase in replacement cost per unit during the period of £2 (£50 − £48), multiplied by the average stock holding of 285 units, i.e:
$$\frac{(300 + 270)}{2}.$$

16.7 It should be noted that in the above system no COSA is calculated. The system could in fact be made simpler by eliminating the cost of sales account and the stock reconciliation account and by using the averaging method applied to purchases to arrive at a COSA. The accounting entries would then be:

Dr   Profit and loss account (purchases)
Cr   Creditors (or cash)
      with the cost of purchases

Dr Profit and loss account
Cr Stock
    with the decrease in the value of stock between the beginning of
    the period and the end of the period
Dr Profit and loss account
Cr Revaluation surplus
    with the COSA.

**Example 16.4**

Redwood Ltd. in Example 16.3 has opening stock of £14,400 and closing stock
of £13,500, a decrease of £900.

Redwood calculates cost of sales as follows:

|  | £ |
|---|---|
| Opening stock | 14,400 |
| Purchases | 7,350 |
|  | 21,750 |
| Closing stock | 13,500 |
| Cost of sales | £8,250 |

Redwood calculates a COSA for the period as follows:

|  | £ |
|---|---|
| Decrease in volume during the period 30 (300 − 270) |  |
| Average current value of the decrease | 30 × £49 = 1,470 |
| Purchases | 7,350 |
|  | 8,820 |
| Cost of sales | 8,250 |
| COSA | £ 570 |

The following entries are therefore necessary:

|  |  | £ | £ |
|---|---|---|---|
| Dr | Profit and loss account | 900 |  |
| Cr | Stock |  | 900 |
|  | with the decrease in stock |  |  |
| Dr | Profit and loss account | 570 |  |
| Cr | Revaluation surplus |  | 570 |
|  | with the COSA. |  |  |

The profit and loss account would be debited with purchases to arrive at the
current cost of sales of £8,820 (£7,350 + £900 + £570).

## CONCLUSIONS

16.8    In this chapter we have outlined only one method of accounting for the
current cost of stock and we acknowledge that it may not be practicable
for all companies. We believe however that companies will be able to
develop systems which will suit their particular circumstances, but we
also believe that the development of suitable systems will take time.

16.9    The choices open to companies adopting CCA are broadly as follows:

1 Continue using the existing system and make COSAs and adjustments to the value of stock for balance sheet purposes as appropriate.
2 Adopt a simple CCA system such as that outlined above.
3 Adopt a full evaluated CCA system.

16.10   In determining the approach to be adopted management will need to assess the extent and accuracy of the CCA information they require and weigh the cost of obtaining that information against its usefulness.

# 17 Current Cost Accounting and Standard Costing

17.1    The usefulness of standard costing in the context of historical cost accounting has been proved over a number of years and many systems of varying complexity have been developed. Companies with standard costing systems should find that with a minimum of adjustment their existing system can be used to calculate the current cost of sales and the current cost of stock for balance sheet purposes.

17.2    A standard costing system is a means of recording and monitoring the level of costs and the level of activity and efficiency within a business by recording and analysing variances from pre-determined levels.

17.3    Standard costs are calculated for each element of cost of sales based on a particular level of cost. Actual costs are then compared with standard costs and variances are analysed by cause (e.g. price, volume, etc.). Any individual variance therefore is simply the effect of changes from a predetermined level; the greater the individual variance, the greater the change.

17.4    Thus the level of variances acts in a similar manner to an index. An increase in the level of price variance therefore can be regarded as the equivalent to an increase in a price index with the standard cost as the base. If, for example, the material content of stock is initially evaluated at standard cost and then increased by the percentage that recent material price variances bear to the standard cost of purchases (the 'uplift percentage') the resulting value should normally be an acceptable approximation to the current cost of the material element of stock.

### Example 17.1

Stock on hand at 31st December evaluated at standard cost amounts to £1,200,000. During December the cost of purchases was £840,000 of which £760,000 represented standard cost and £80,000 was purchase price variance. Purchase price variance therefore represents approximately 10·5% of the standard cost of purchases for December and if the percentage is applied to the standard cost of stock on hand at 31st December, giving a value of stock of £1,326,000, that value should be an acceptable approximation to the current value of stock at that date.

243

17.5    There are two cautionary points to bear in mind. Firstly, uplift percentages must be based on variances that are relevant to the current cost of the items to which they are applied. For example, if stock at the balance sheet date consists of a large number of different items but only a few items are purchased in the month immediately prior to the balance sheet date, the purchase price variance for that month may not be representative of the variance from standard of the current purchase price of the stock as a whole. Secondly, the variances used must relate to current prices. If, in order to obtain a price variance that will be representative of the change in price of the stock as a whole, it is necessary to use a period of longer than a month there is a likelihood that the total purchase price variance for the period will approximate, not to the variance at the balance sheet date, but to the average variance over a period before the balance sheet date.

### Example 17.2

(i) Oakwood Limited uses a standard costing system. Purchases for the month of December are representative of the stock balance at the end of December. Although the purchase price variance for December probably reflects prices current in the middle of December the directors decide that they can reasonably assume that prices have not changed materially between the middle of December and the end of December. Oakwood therefore uses the purchase price variance for December as the basis for the uplift percentage.

(ii) Larch Limited uses a standard costing system but finds that a period of four months prior to the balance sheet date is required to be used to establish a mix of purchases which is representative of the mix of stock at the year-end. The purchase price variance for a four month period can be assumed to reflect current prices at the middle of the period, i.e. two months before the year-end. Consequently Larch Limited cannot use the purchase price variance as a basis for the uplift percentage.

### The analysis of stock

17.6    To maximise the usefulness of variances in the determination of the appropriate uplift percentage it is recommended that stocks (and variances) are analysed into suitable categories, e.g. by product type, and that an uplift percentage is calculated for each category. Also there still remains the necessity to analyse stock into its different elements (material, labour and overhead). A percentage uplift calculated with reference only to purchase price variances arising on the purchase of raw materials and components can only be used to ascertain the current cost of the materials element of stock. Labour cost variances and overhead cost variances would need to be used as appropriate for those elements of stock.

### Periodical updating of standards

17.7    Where standard costs are revised at the balance sheet date based on actual costs at that date, or on estimates of actual costs at that date, the new standards can be used to evaluate stock at current cost. The difference between the stock balance evaluated at the old standard (adjusted for historical cost variances from standard in respect of stock on hand as appropriate) and the stock balance evaluated at the new standard will be a revaluation surplus or deficit. This method of valuation however may not be used for balance sheet purposes when standard costs are based on estimated average current costs for the forthcoming accounting period (unless it is the average of only the one month after the balance sheet date) or when the standards are based on actual costs at a date significantly earlier than the balance sheet date.

### The elements of a current cost/standard cost system

17.8    The following is an outline of a system of accounting for the current cost of stock using a standard costing system. It is appreciated that what follows is not the only method of adapting an existing standard costing system to account for current cost and that it may not be suitable for all companies. Nevertheless it is a method which some companies may find practicable and useful.

17.9    In simplified outline the procedure is as follows:

(a) Stock is analysed into appropriate categories, (e.g. by product).
(b) Variances are analysed in the same way as stock and are also analysed between those which reflect current cost levels and those which do not.
(c) Input to stock and cost of sales are recorded at standard cost.
(d) All variances are charged against operating profit.
(e) For each category of stock an uplift percentage is calculated based on those variances which reflect current cost levels (i.e. excluding variances caused by 'abnormal' activity).
(f) At the end of each month accounting entries are made as follows (assuming increasing costs):

    (i) Revaluation surplus is credited with an amount equal to that percentage which reflects the increase in the uplift percentage for the period applied to the opening standard cost of stock (e.g. if the uplift percentage has increased from 5% to 8% revaluation surplus will be credited with 3% of the opening balance of stock at standard cost.)
    (ii) A 'stock valuation adjustment account' is debited with an amount which will increase the balance on the account so that it represents the total uplift percentage applied to the closing stock at standard cost.
    (iii) The double entry is completed by debiting or crediting operating profit with the difference between (i) and (ii).

17.10   At the end of each period, after making the above accounting entries cost of sales will have been charged with the standard cost of stock consumed ((c) above) and the applicable variances from standard ((d) above plus or minus (f) (iii) above) and the balance sheet value of stock will be stock at standard cost plus the balance of the stock valuation adjustment account. At regular intervals (e.g. annually) the balance of stock valuation adjustment account should be eliminated by incorporating it into new standard costs. Example 17.3 demonstrates the application of the system.

## Example 17.3

| | Cost of purchases | Stock at standard price | Profit and loss account | Stock valuation adjustment account | Revaluation surplus |
|---|---|---|---|---|---|
| **January** | £ | £ | £ | £ | £ |
| Opening stock | | 1,000 | | | |
| Purchases | 2,060 | 2,000 | Dr 60 | | |
| Sales | | (1,500) | Dr 1,500 | | Cr 30 |
| Adjustments | | | Cr 15 | Dr 45 | (3% on £1,000) |
| Closing stock | | 1,500 | 1,545 | 45 | |
| **February** | | | | | |
| Purchases | 1,050 | 1,000 | Dr 50 | | |
| Sales | | (1,200) | Dr 1,200 | | Cr 30 |
| Adjustments | | | Dr 10 | Dr 20 | (2% on £1,500) |
| Closing stock | | 1,300 | 1,260 | 65 | |
| **March** | | | | | |
| Purchases | 1,620 | 1,500 | Dr 120 | | |
| Sales | | (1,800) | Dr 1,800 | | Cr 39 |
| Adjustments | | | Dr 24 | Dr 15 | (3% on £1,300) |
| Closing stock | | 1,000 | 1,944 | 80 | |

*Notes:*
(1) Credits to revaluation surplus are based on the opening stock and the movement in the uplift percentage in the month concerned.
(2) The debits to stock valuation adjustment account are the amounts required to increase the balance on that account to the required uplift percentage on closing stock at standard cost.
(3) The adjustment to cost of sales each month represents the total uplift percentage at the end of the month applied to the increase (credit) or decrease (debit) in the value of stock at standard cost.
(4) Closing stocks are valued at standard price plus uplift percentage:

$$\text{Jan.} = £1,500 + £45 \quad (3\%)$$
$$\text{Feb.} = £1,300 + £65 \quad (5\%)$$
$$\text{Mar.} = £1,000 + £80 \quad (8\%)$$

(5) Cost of sales is standard cost plus uplift percentage:

$$\text{Jan.} = £1,500 + £45 \quad (3\%)$$
$$\text{Feb.} = £1,200 + £60 \quad (5\%)$$
$$\text{Mar.} = £1,800 + £144 \quad (8\%)$$

## CONCLUSION

17.11 The introduction of CCA should be regarded by those companies which do not already operate a standard costing system as an opportunity to assess the merits of such a system compared with other systems suitable for use in the context of CCA. Companies which already operate standard costing systems will need to consider the modifications, if any, required in the light of the introduction of CCA. Standard costing is no less compatible with CCA than other historical cost recording systems and is probably more compatible than many because it is geared to identifying cost changes. Nevertheless research will be required to determine how to get the best out of standard costing systems which were designed primarily for use under historical cost accounting.

# 18 The Form of Published Accounts

18.1    This book has been concerned so far only with the preparation of current cost information. In this chapter however the presentation of this information in the published annual accounts is considered.

18.2    The annual audited accounts of a company, and the consolidated accounts of a group of companies should consist of:

(a) a profit and loss account;
(b) an appropriation account;
(c) a balance sheet;
(d) notes to the accounts including, except for wholly owned subsidiaries, a statement of change in the proprietors' interest after allowing for the change in the value of money;
(e) a statement of the source and application of funds (where required by SSAP 10).

## BIRCHWOOD'S ACCOUNTS

18.3    The consolidated profit and loss account, consolidated appropriation account and balance sheet of Birchwood Limited and its subsidiaries for the year ended 31st December 1979 are set out in Tables 18.1 and 18.2. The figures shown in these tables have been extracted from the *consolidation* worksheets in Chapter 14. The presentation of Birchwood's accounts is shown for illustrative purposes only and they are in no way prescriptive. Other methods of presentation may equally comply with the proposed accounting standard. Only extracts from Birchwood's accounts are shown in this chapter as a fuller example of the presentation of a set of current cost accounts is shown at Appendix 1 to ED 18 which details matters arising from the application of the proposed accounting standard which should be included in notes to the accounts.

## THE PROFIT AND LOSS ACCOUNT

18.4    The format of the current cost profit and loss account is similar in most respects to that of a historical cost profit and loss account. The main difference is that the current cost profit and loss account ends with a figure for current cost profit (after tax and where applicable, after

248

extraordinary items) whilst an historical cost profit and loss account would continue by showing distributions. In the current cost accounts distributions are shown in the appropriation account.

### Operating profit for the year

18.5    A small but important point to note is that, whereas in historical cost accounts the profit from trading operations may be described variously as 'trading profit', 'operating profit', or simply 'profit', in the current cost accounts the term 'operating profit' should be used in order to emphasise that it represents only the company's profit from operations. Interest payable (less interest receivable) should not be included in arriving at the operating profit for the year but should be shown separately.

**Table 18.1**

BIRCHWOOD LTD. AND ITS SUBSIDIARIES
CONSOLIDATED PROFIT AND LOSS ACCOUNT
FOR THE YEAR ENDED 31st DECEMBER 1979

(Comparatives are not shown in this example although they would normally be shown as stated in the previous year's account).

|  | £'000 |
|---|---|
| Turnover | 402,133 |
| Operating profit for the year | 16,253 |
| Interest payable less receivable | 1,411 |
|  | 14,842 |
| Share of profits of associated company | 64 |
| Current cost profit before taxation | 14,906 |
| *Less* taxation | 4,084 |
|  | 10,822 |
| *Less* minority interest | 8 |
| Current cost profit for the year | 10,814 |

CONSOLIDATED APPROPRIATION ACCOUNT
FOR THE YEAR ENDED 31st DECEMBER 1979

|  | £'000 | £'000 |
|---|---|---|
| Current cost profit for year |  | 10,814 |
| Net surplus for year on revaluation of assets | 14,906 |  |
| Appropriated to revaluation reserve | 14,906 |  |
|  |  | — |
| Available for distribution and general reserve |  | 10,814 |
| Dividends |  | 6,480 |
| Added to general reserve |  | 4,334 |

249

**Taxation**

18.6    The amount of £4,084,000 in Birchwood's consolidated profit and loss account represents tax on the consolidated current cost profit and is required to include all tax, including overseas tax, other than tax relating to revaluation surpluses on non-current assets. Had Birchwood been required to provide deferred tax, the amount provided would also need to be included in the figure for taxation except for any part attributable to revaluation surpluses on non-current assets. Tax attributable to such revaluation surpluses should be deducted in arriving at the figure for surpluses arising from the revaluation of assets in the appropriation account. Similarly, tax on extraordinary items, if any, should be deducted in arriving at the amount to be shown in respect of such items in the profit and loss account.

**Extraordinary items**

18.7    Changes in value which have to be included in the profit and loss account which are of unusual size and incidence and which have arisen outside the ordinary activities of the company should be treated as extraordinary items, and shown separately in the profit and loss account net of tax and minority interest. Material items of an unusual size and incidence which have arisen within the ordinary activities of the company and which have been charged or credited in arriving at operating profit for the year may also require separate disclosure in order to show a true and fair view.

## THE APPROPRIATION ACCOUNT

18.8    The appropriation account should show:

(a) the current cost profit (or loss) from the profit and loss account;
(b) the surpluses (or deficits) arising during the year from the revaluation of assets;
(c) the amount appropriated by the directors to or from revaluation reserve;
(d) distributions;
(e) the amount taken to or from general reserve.

The appropriation to or from revaluation reserve should be deducted from or added to the net surplus arising from the revaluation of assets with the resulting sub-total being added to or deducted from current cost profit for the year to arrive at the amount either to be distributed or to be taken to general reserve. Any amount transferred to the revaluation reserve represents that part of current cost profit and revaluation surpluses not regarded by the directors in the first instance as currently available for distribution having regard to their assessment of the needs of the business.

18.9    Appendix 2 to ED 18 provides general guidance on the appropriation to or from revaluation reserve. There is an initial presumption that the surplus on the revaluation of assets will need to be appropriated to the revaluation reserve but it is recognised that the directors, on whose shoulders the decision must rest, will sometimes wish to appropriate more, and sometimes less, than that amount. The directors should explain the bases and the reasons for the amount of the appropriations which they make.

### Amount available for distribution and general reserve

18.10 The balance arrived at after deducting from, or adding to, the current cost profit the revaluation surpluses or deficits and the amounts appropriated to or from revaluation reserve is the amount considered by the directors to be available for distribution or retention in a general reserve. From this amount are deducted the distributions made and proposed and the balance remaining is the amount to be added to (or, if distributions exceed the surplus, deducted from) general reserve. In deciding upon the amount to be distributed as dividend the directors should have regard to the company's short and longer run cash planning. The directors also have to act within the constraints imposed by the legal rules relating to distributions.

### Example 18.1

Mapletree Limited's current cost profit for the year ended 31st December 1979 is £1,550,000 and revaluation surpluses for the year amount to £2,570,000 of which £1,500,000 relates to fixed assets.

Included in the balance sheet at 31st December 1979 are fixed assets (all at net current replacement cost) of £6,000,000 and loan stock 1995/1998 of £2,000,000. The directors consider that the company's loan stock will be replaced by further loan stock on redemption and that it has all been utilised in the purchase of fixed assets. The revaluation surpluses on fixed assets financed by the loan stock (i.e. one third) is therefore considered by the directors to be currently available for distribution. Mapletree's appropriation account for 1979 will appear as follows:

MAPLETREE LIMITED
APPROPRIATION ACCOUNT
FOR THE YEAR ENDED 31st DECEMBER 1979

|  | £'000 | £'000 |
| --- | --- | --- |
| Current cost profit |  | 1,550 |
| Net surplus for the year on the revaluation of assets | 2,570 |  |
| Appropriated to revaluation reserve | 2,070 |  |
|  |  | 500 |
|  |  | 2,050 |
| Dividends |  | 1,800 |
| Amount taken to general reserve |  | 250 |

**Table 18.2**

BIRCHWOOD LTD. AND ITS SUBSIDIARIES
BALANCE SHEET AT 31st DECEMBER 1979

| | Group £'000 | Company £'000 |
|---|---|---|
| ASSETS EMPLOYED: | | |
| Fixed assets | 45,735 | 31,047 |
| Investment in subsidiaries | — | 18,886 |
| Investment in associated company | 477 | 477 |
| Quoted and unquoted investments | 1,537 | 1,537 |
| Net current assets | 75,130 | 68,891 |
| Stock and work in progress | 86,389 | 68,650 |
| Debtors | 58,686 | 47,332 |
| Cash | 1,540 | 1,319 |
| | 146,615 | 117,301 |
| Creditors | 56,238 | 34,832 |
| Current taxation | 4,355 | 3,948 |
| Short-term borrowings | 4,692 | 3,430 |
| Dividend | 6,200 | 6,200 |
| | 71,485 | 48,410 |
| ACT recoverable | 3,340 | 3,340 |
| | 126,219 | 124,178 |
| FINANCED BY: | | |
| Issued share capital | 37,185 | 37,185 |
| Share premium account | 3,000 | 3,000 |
| Revaluation reserve | 28,411 | 28,411 |
| General reserve | 41,582 | 41,582 |
| | 110,178 | 110,178 |
| Preference share capital | 4,000 | 4,000 |
| Minority interests | 908 | — |
| | 115,086 | 114,178 |
| Long-term loans | 11,133 | 10,000 |
| | 126,219 | 124,178 |

252

### Example 18.2

Pricefreeze Supermarkets Limited's current cost profit for the year ended 30th June 1980 is £15,600,000 and revaluation surpluses for the year amounted to £6,400,000 of which £5,500,000 relates to the revaluation of stock and the cost of sales adjustment. The directors of Pricefreeze consider that at any time during the year at least 80% of stock is financed by trade creditors and they foresee no change in this percentage in future. Consequently, the directors consider that 80% of the revaluation surplus on stocks is currently available for distribution, and they decide to appropriate to revaluation reserve only £2,000,000 (£6,400,000 − (80% × £5,500,000)) of the net surplus for the year on the revaluation of assets, the remaining £4,400,000 being added to general reserve.

### Example 18.3

Topfruit Jams Limited's current cost profit for the year ended 31st March 1981 is £3,500,000 and revaluation surpluses for the year amounted to £1,200,000. Topfruit's purchases are mainly of fresh soft fruits such as strawberries and raspberries and because of their seasonal nature these items when sold are included in cost of sales at historical cost. The directors consider that, in order to retain sufficient funds to purchase the following season's crop, £1,000,000 of the current cost profit for the year is not currently available for distribution. Topfruit's appropriation account will appear as follows:—

TOPFRUIT JAMS LIMITED
APPROPRIATION ACCOUNT
FOR THE YEAR ENDED 31st MARCH 1981

|  | £'000 | £'000 |
|---|---|---|
| Current cost profit |  | 3,500 |
| Net surplus for the year on the revaluation of assets | 1,200 |  |
| Appropriated to revaluation reserve | 2,200 |  |
|  |  | (1,000) |
|  |  | 2,500 |
| Dividends |  | 2,300 |
| Amount taken to general reserve |  | 200 |

## THE BALANCE SHEET

18.11 The balance sheet presentation requires little comment. The makeup of each item has already been considered elsewhere in this book and the general format is no different from that of an historical cost balance sheet. It is worth noting that the revaluation reserve is regarded as part of total shareholders' funds. The balance on the revaluation reserve is an indicator of that part of reserves not regarded by the directors as currently available for distribution having regard to their assessment of the needs of the business.

## NOTES TO THE ACCOUNTS

18.12   Many of the notes to the accounts are required to satisfy the requirements of the Companies Acts or the requirements of applicable SSAP's and, therefore, are necessary whether current costs accounts or historical cost accounts are being presented. Certain notes, however, relate specifically to features of the accounts unique to CCA while some others will be different for current cost accounts and historical cost accounts. Only those notes requiring special comment are considered below. Appendix 1 to ED 18 provides a comprehensive summary of the disclosure requirements contained in the proposed accounting standard.

### Taxation

18.13   A note is required showing the total tax charge or credit for the year analysed between:

(a) the amount shown separately as taxation in the profit and loss account;

(b) the amount deducted from (or added to) extraordinary items;

(c) the amount deducted (or added) in arriving at the surplus (or deficit) arising from revaluation of assets in the appropriation account.

### Table 18.3

BIRCHWOOD LIMITED AND ITS SUBSIDIARIES
SURPLUS/(DEFICIT) ARISING FROM
REVALUATION OF ASSETS
FOR THE YEAR ENDED 31st DECEMBER 1979

|  | Total £'000 | Minority interest £'000 | Net £'000 | Breakdown of net figure Surplus £'000 | (Deficit) £'000 |
|---|---|---|---|---|---|
| Revaluation of fixed assets | 5,973 | 26 | 5,947 | 6,197 | (250) |
| Revaluation of investments | 14 | — | 14 | 14 | — |
| Revaluation of stocks | 8,771 | 72 | 8,699 | 8,884 | (185) |
| Translation differences | 246 | — | 246 | 246 | — |
|  | 15,004 | 98 | 14,906 | 15,341 | (435) |

**Table 18.4**

BIRCHWOOD LIMITED AND ITS SUBSIDIARIES
FIXED ASSETS
FOR THE YEAR ENDED 31st DECEMBER 1979

**Land and buildings**

| | Freehold land and buildings | | Leasehold land and buildings | Total |
|---|---|---|---|---|
| | At open market value £'000 | At depreciated replacement cost £'000 | At open market value £'000 | £'000 |
| At 1st January 1978 | 1,510 | 8,695 | 1,120 | 11,325 |
| Additions during year at cost | — | — | — | — |
| Disposals during year at book value | — | — | — | — |
| Depreciation charge for the year | (39) | (242) | (93) | (374) |
| Revaluation surplus | 79 | 1,250 | 38 | 1,367 |
| At 31st December 1979 | 1,550 | 9,703 | 1,065 | 12,318 |

| **Plant and machinery** | £'000 |
|---|---|

**Valued at net current replacement cost**

| | £'000 |
|---|---|
| Gross current replacement cost | |
| At 31st December 1978 | 48,920 |
| Additions during year at cost | 8,592 |
| Disposals during year | (1,111) |
| Revaluation surplus (including translation gains of £389) | 8,378 |
| At 31st December 1979 | 64,779 |
| Depreciation | |
| At 31st December 1978 | 20,055 |
| Eliminated on disposals | (680) |
| Charge to profit and loss account for year | 8,422 |
| Backlog depreciation arising on revaluation (including translation loss of £182) | 3,565 |
| At 31st December 1979 | 31,362 |
| Net current replacement cost | |
| At 31st December 1978 | 28,865 |
| At 31st December 1979 | 33,417 |

255

### Surplus arising from revaluation of assets

18.14 An analysis of the surpluses and deficits arising from revaluation of assets should be shown. The analysis of the Birchwood Group's surpluses for the year is shown in Table 18.3. Surpluses and deficits should be shown separately under each category of asset and, similarly, any exceptional surpluses or deficits should be separately disclosed.

### Fixed assets

18.15 An analysis of fixed assets should be provided showing on which bases the land and buildings and plant and machinery have been valued. The analysis of the Birchwood Group's fixed assets is shown in Table 18.4.

18.16 Where authorised external indices have been used to value any fixed assets their source should be disclosed. In years when a full scale professional valuation of land and buildings has been undertaken the name(s) and qualifications of the professional valuer(s) should be disclosed. Where full scale professional valuations have been carried out by employees of the company their names need not be disclosed.

### Goodwill

18.17 In any year in which an acquisition gives rise to a material amount of goodwill, such goodwill should be disclosed in the accounts, separate amounts being shown for each acquisition. Goodwill arising on the acquisition of an associated company is included in this provision. The amount written off goodwill in each of the last five years prior to the current year should be shown in a note to the accounts. The company's accounting policy relating to goodwill should be disclosed in a note to the accounts.

### Deferred tax

18.18 Where the provision for deferred tax is lower than that which would have been made has the full requirements of SSAP 11 been complied with (on the liability method), a note of the potential amount of deferred tax calculated as if the original text of SSAP 11 were in full operation should be shown, distinguishing between the various principal categories of deferred tax and showing for each category the amount that has been provided for.

### The statement of change in the net equity interest

18.19 This statement will be discussed fully in the following chapter and Birchwood's statement of change in the net equity interest after allowing for the change in the values of money will be set out in that chapter.

**Table 18.5**

BIRCHWOOD AND ITS SUBSIDIARIES
STATEMENT OF SOURCE AND APPLICATION OF FUNDS
FOR THE YEAR ENDED 31st DECEMBER 1979

|  | £'000 | £'000 |
|---|---|---|
| Current cost—profit before tax and less minority interest |  | 14,898 |
| *Add:* Items not involving the movement of funds |  |  |
| Minority interest in retained profit | 8 |  |
| Depreciation | 8,933 |  |
|  | 8,941 |  |
| *Less:* Profit retained by associate | 24 |  |
|  |  | 8,917 |
| Realised revaluation surplus on stocks |  | 8,338 |
|  |  | 32,153 |
| *Less:* Exchange difference in current cost profits for the year |  | 13 |
|  |  | 32,140 |
| Other sources: |  |  |
| Sale of fixed assets | 294 |  |
| Proceeds of rights issue | 8,000 |  |
|  |  | 8,294 |
|  |  | 40,434 |
| Applications: |  |  |
| Tax paid | 4,389 |  |
| Dividends paid | 5,980 |  |
| Purchase of fixed assets | 8,592 |  |
|  |  | 18,961 |
|  |  | 21,473 |
| Increase/(decrease) in working capital: |  |  |
| Stock and work in progress | 17,141 |  |
| Debtors | 17,097 |  |
| Creditors | (15,509) |  |
|  | 18,729 |  |
| Liquid funds—cash | 521 |  |
| overdraft | 2,223 |  |
|  |  | 21,473 |

*Note:* The increase in stock and work in progress excludes £433,000 relating to unrealised revaluation surpluses.

## THE STATEMENT OF SOURCE AND APPLICATION OF FUNDS

18.20   A statement of source and application of funds is required to be included in the accounts of those companies falling within the provisions of SSAP 10. The statement of source and application of funds for Birchwood is shown in Table 18.5. The following problems arise in preparing a statement of source and application of funds from CCA accounts:

(a) Current assets, in particular stocks, may include unrealised revaluation surpluses and these should be deducted from the movement in working capital, as they do not involve the movement of funds.

(b) The realised element of revaluation surpluses and deficits represents a source of funds which may be shown either as an adjustment to the funds generated from operations or as an adjustment to the movement of the related assets. Birchwood has chosen to adopt the former course.

18.21   In addition Birchwood needs to deal with exchange differences, which are included in the revaluation surpluses. These have been eliminated from any movements on assets and liabilities dealt with in the statement of source and application of funds.

18.22   Birchwood's statement of source and application of funds is only one example of possible treatments. Other methods may be equally acceptable.

# 19 The Statement of Change in the Net Equity Interest

19.1    The statement of change in shareholders' net equity interest after allowing for the change in the value of money (called in this chapter 'the statement of net change') should show:

(a) the net equity interest as shown in the current cost balance sheet at the beginning of the period, plus any amount brought into the accounts in respect of new equity capital introduced during the period, plus or minus the amount of the adjustments needed to compensate these amounts for the change in the value of money during the period;

(b) the net equity interest at the end of the period before provision for dividends on the equity capital;

(c) the net gain or loss in the net equity interest during the period, being the difference between the amounts referred to in (a) and (b) above;

(d) the dividends on the equity capital for the year;

(e) an analysis of the gain or loss on holding monetary assets and liabilities during the period, showing separately the figures for (i) long-term liabilities, (ii) bank overdrafts and (iii) non-equity share capital.

19.2    In this chapter two methods of preparing the statement of net change are described. In Part 1, a simple method of preparation is described which will provide only the analysis of the gain or loss on holding monetary assets and liabilities which is required by ED 18. Part 2 of this chapter describes a method of preparation which will provide a full analysis of the gain or loss in the shareholders' net equity interest which management may find useful. Both methods are demonstrated by using Birchwood's consolidated accounts for 1979 as an example.

19.3    The change in the value of money during the period is measured by the application of the general index of retail prices (RPI). The figures for the RPI for 1979 are set out in Table 19.2.

## PART 1—THE SIMPLIFIED METHOD

19.4    It is considered easier first to calculate the figures required for the first section of the Statement.

The general method of preparation is as follows:

1  Convert the opening net equity interest, by applying the RPI, to arrive at the adjusted net equity interest at the beginning of the year.
2  Convert any new equity capital introduced during the period by applying the RPI.
3  Add the amounts arrived at in 1 and 2 above and deduct the result from the net equity interest at the year-end before provision for dividends on the equity capital.
4  The amount arrived at in 3 above, if positive, will represent the gain in value for the year in the net equity interest after allowing for the change in the value of money. If it is negative it will represent a *loss* in value.

### Step 1: Conversion of the opening net equity interest

19.5  The conversion is made by multiplying the opening net equity interest by a factor calculated by dividing the RPI for the end of the period by the RPI at the beginning of the period.

19.6  The adjustment factor is therefore:

$$\frac{\text{RPI at December 1979}}{\text{RPI at December 1978}} = \frac{146 \cdot 0}{116 \cdot 9} = 1 \cdot 25 \text{ (rounded)}$$

and, taking the opening net equity interest from Table 14.1 in Chapter 14, the conversion becomes (in thousands of pounds):

$$82,938 \times 1 \cdot 25 = 103,673.$$

### Step 2: Conversion of new equity capital introduced during the period

19.7  The method of converting the increase in equity capital is similar to the method of converting the opening net equity interest. The procedure is:

(a) Multiply the figure for the increase in equity capital in the current cost accounts (i.e. paid up shares plus share premium) by the RPI at the closing balance sheet date.
(b) Divide by the RPI at the date the increase in equity capital was effected.

19.8  The increase in Birchwood's equity capital during 1979 was the result of a rights issue to its shareholders. New ordinary shares were issued, fully paid, on 30th June 1979 as follows:

|  | £'000 |
|---|---|
| Nominal value 20,000,000 shares at 25p = | 5,000 |
| Share premium 20,000,000 shares at 15p = | 3,000 |
|  | 8,000 |

The RPI stood at 137·1 in June 1979.

The conversion of the increase in equity capital is therefore (in thousands of pounds):

$$8,000 \times \frac{146·0}{137·1} = 8,520$$

## Step 3: Calculation of the total gain or loss in the net equity interest after allowing for the change in the value of money

19.9 The total gain or loss in the net equity interest for the year can now be calculated as follows:

|  | £'000 | £'000 |
|---|---|---|
| Adjusted opening net equity interest | | 103,673 |
| *Add:* adjusted increase in equity capital during the year | | 8,520 |
| | | 112,193 |
| Closing net equity interest per current cost balance sheet | 110,178 | |
| *Add:* dividends on equity capital | 6,200 | 116,378 |
| Increase in net equity interest after allowing for fall in the value of money and before dividends on the equity capital for the year | | 4,185 |

19.10 The closing net equity interest shown above is the figure shown in Birchwood's consolidated current cost balance sheet at 31st December 1979 set out in Table 18.2 in Chapter 18.

19.11 The procedure described above is all that is required to complete the first section of the statement of net change.

## Analysis of the gain or loss on holding monetary assets and liabilities

19.12 At first sight it would seem that to arrive at the required figures for net monetary assets it would be necessary merely to deduct the unadjusted closing monetary assets and liabilities from the adjusted opening monetary assets and liabilities. This, however, is an over-simplification. It overlooks the movement of funds during the year between monetary and non-monetary items. For example, suppose a fixed asset (a non-monetary item) is purchased for cash during the year. This purchase constitutes a movement from monetary assets to non-monetary assets. If the total gain or loss on monetary assets and liabilities is analysed by reference only to the opening balance sheet no account will be taken of such movements and the analysis will be incorrect.

19.13 It is necessary, therefore, to convert all monetary income and expenditure, both capital and revenue, as well as the opening net monetary assets for the year by the application of the RPI. The calculation of these figures is set out below.

**Step 4: Net monetary assets at the beginning of the year**

19.14 These are multiplied by the same factor as that calculated for the adjustment of the opening net equity interest in paragraph 19.6.

19.15 The balance sheet figures are as follows:

|  | Opening balance sheet | | Closing balance sheet | |
|---|---|---|---|---|
|  | £'000 | £'000 | £'000 | £'000 |
| Long term liabilities: |  |  |  |  |
| Debentures | (10,000) |  | (10,000) |  |
| Loans | (1,000) |  | (1,133) |  |
|  |  | (11,000) |  | (11,133) |
| Bank overdrafts |  | (6,915) |  | (4,692) |
| Non-equity share capital |  | (4,000) |  | (4,000) |
| Other net monetary liabilities: |  |  |  |  |
| Debtors | 41,443 |  | 58,686 |  |
| Cash | 1,002 |  | 1,540 |  |
| Creditors | (40,640) |  | (56,238) |  |
| Tax | (4,390) |  | (4,355) |  |
| Dividends | (5,700) |  | (6,200) |  |
| ACT recoverable | 3,070 |  | 3,340 |  |
| Minority interest (treat as monetary) | (802) |  | (802) |  |
|  |  | (6,017) |  | (4,029) |
|  |  | (27,932) |  | (23,854) |

The conversion of the opening balance sheet figures is (in thousands of pounds):

$$(27,932) \times 1 \cdot 25 = \quad (34,915)$$

(The closing minority interest is included before making the year-end transfers from revaluation and revenue reserves. Adjustments for these transfers would be made separately in a full analysis of the gain or loss in the net equity interest.)

### Step 5: New equity capital introduced

19.16   The increase in equity share capital introduced during the year has already been converted for the first section of the statement (paragraphs 19.7 and 19.8).

### Step 6: Capital expenditure

19.17   In Birchwood's case this consists only of net expenditure on fixed assets for the year but would also include expenditure on investments where appropriate. The unadjusted figures are obtained from the current cost accounts for the year.

19.18   The figures are adjusted by using a factor calculated by dividing the RPI at the year-end by the average RPI for the year, thus assuming that the expenditure accrued evenly during the year. If, however, the pattern of expenditure throughout the year was erratic, it may be necessary to allocate the expenditure to the appropriate periods in the year and to adjust by applying factors calculated using the appropriate RPI for each specific period in place of the average RPI.

19.19   The calculation is thus:

|  | Unadjusted | | Adjusted |
|---|---|---|---|
|  | £'000 | | £'000 |
| Additions to fixed assets | 8,592 | | |
| Less: sale proceeds of disposals | 294 | | |
| | 8,298 | $\times \dfrac{146 \cdot 0}{134 \cdot 8}$ | 8,987 |

### Step 7: Revenue income and expenditure

19.20   Revenue income and expenditure, with the exception of the tax charge or credit for the year, is treated in the same way as capital expenditure. Taxation in the profit and loss account is deemed to arise at the year-end and therefore requires no adjustment. Dividends paid during the year should be adjusted from their date of payment.

19.21   It is necessary to eliminate non-monetary items from the profit and loss account as only monetary items are dealt with. These non-monetary items are depreciation and the share of retained profits of the associate, only the dividend received from the associate being treated as monetary. The monetary movements on stocks should also be dealt with here, these being the net movement on stock and the revaluation surplus for the year. The latter includes unrealised surpluses which are offset by using the opening and closing current cost stock figures.

263

19.22 The calculation is:

|  | Unadjusted | | Adjusted |
|---|---|---|---|
|  | £'000 | £'000 | £'000 |
| Current cost profit before tax | 14,906 | | |
| *Less:* Share of associate's profit | 64 | | |
|  | | 14,842 | |
| *Add:* Depreciation | | 8,933 | |
| Cost of sales adjustment | | 8,771 | |
| Stock movement: | | | |
| Opening stock | 68,704 | | |
| *less:* Closing stock | (86,389) | (17,685) | |
|  | | 14,861 $\times \dfrac{146 \cdot 0}{134 \cdot 8}$ | 16,096 |
| Dividend from associate— | | | |
| paid 31.12.79 | | 40 | 40 |
| Taxation | | (4,084) | (4,084) |
| Dividends: | | | |
| Preference—paid 31.12.79 | | (280) | (280) |
| Ordinary—proposed | | (6,200) | (6,200) |
|  | | 4,337 | 5,572 |

### Step 8: Gain or loss on monetary assets and liabilities

19.23 All the calculations necessary to produce the total figure for the gain or loss on monetary assets and liabilities have now been made and the final step is to compare them with the closing net monetary assets.

19.24 The requirement to disclose separately the figures for long term liabilities, bank overdrafts and non-equity share capital make necessary the separate calculations which are set out in paragraph 19.26 and 19.27.

19.25 The calculation of the total gain or loss on monetary assets and liabilities can be set out as follows:

|  | Calculation made in paragraph | £'000 |
|---|---|---|
| Adjusted opening balance sheet figures and movements: | | |
| Net monetary liabilities | 19·15 | (34,915) |
| New equity capital introduced | 19·8 | 8,520 |
| Capital expenditure | 19·19 | (8,987) |
| Revenue income less revenue expenditure | 19·22 | 5,572 |
| Exchange differences | | 39 |
|  | | c/f (29,771) |

264

|  | £'000 | Calculation<br>made in<br>paragraph |  |
|---|---|---|---|
|  |  | b/f | (29,771) |
| *Less:* Closing balance sheet net monetary<br>liabilities |  | 19·15 | (23,854) |
| Total gain |  |  | 5,917 |

The exchange differences (treated as monetary) relate to items other than non-current assets and arise as follows:

|  | £'000 | £'000 |  |
|---|---|---|---|
| Total exchange differences |  | 246 | Table 14.2 |
| *Less:* relating to fixed assets |  |  |  |
| —cost | 389 |  |  |
| —depreciation | (182) |  |  |
|  |  | 207 | Table 18.4 |
|  |  | 39 |  |

Exchange differences are deemed to arise at the year-end and thus require no adjustment.

19.26 The general method of producing the individual figures is as follows:
  (a) Multiply the movement for the year in the accounts by a factor calculated by dividing the RPI at the year-end by the average RPI for the year. Differences on exchange should be treated as arising at the year-end.
  (b) Multiply the opening balance by a factor calculated by dividing the RPI at the year-end by the RPI at the beginning of the year.
  (c) Add the figures arrived at in (a) and (b) above and deduct the closing balance from the result.
  (d) If the figure arrived at in (c) is positive it will represent a gain, if negative it will represent a loss.

19.27 The calculations are as follows:

|  | Long-term liabilities | | Bank overdrafts | | Non-equity share<br>capital | |
|---|---|---|---|---|---|---|
|  | £'000 | £'000 | £'000 | £'000 | £'000 | £'000 |
| Balance 31.12.79 |  |  |  |  |  |  |
|  | 11,133 |  | 4,692 |  | 4,000 |  |
| Balance 1.1.79 | 11,000 |  | 6,915 |  | 4,000 |  |
| Movement for<br>year | 133 | = 133 | $(2,223) \times \frac{146 \cdot 0}{134 \cdot 8} = (2,408)$ | | — | — |
| Balance 1.1.79 | 11,000 × 1·25 = 13,750 | | 6,915 × 1·25 = 8,644 | | 4,000 × 1·25 = 5,000 | |
|  | 13,883 |  | 6,236 |  | 5,000 |  |
| Balance 31.12.79 | 11,133 |  | 4,692 |  | 4,000 |  |
| Gain | 2,750 |  | 1,544 |  | 1,000 |  |

The difference of £133,000 on long-term liabilities relates only to an exchange difference which is deemed to arise at the year-end and therefore requires no adjustment.

19.28   Table 19.1 sets out the statement of net change for the Birchwood Group, which would appear as a note to the accounts, and indicates the source of the figures.

**Table 19.1**

**BIRCHWOOD LIMITED AND ITS SUBSIDIARIES**

Statement of change in shareholders' net equity interest after allowing for fall in the value of money for the year ended 31st December 1979

|   |   | £'000 | Source |
|---|---|---|---|
| 1 | Net equity interest at beginning of year | 82,938 | Paragraph 19.6 |
| 2 | New equity capital introduced during year | 8,000 | Paragraph 19.8 |
| 3 |   | 90,938 | 1 + 2 |
| 4 | Increase required to compensate for fall in the value of money during year | 21,255 | 5 − 3 |
| 5 |   | 112,193 | Paragraph 19.9 |
| 6 | Net equity interest at end of year before dividends on equity capital | 116,378 | Paragraph 19.9 |
| 7 | Gain for year after allowing for fall in the value of money | 4,185 | 6 − 5 |
| 8 | Dividends on equity capital for year | 6,200 | Paragraph 19.22 |
| 9 | Loss for year after allowing for fall in the value of money and after dividends | (2,015) | 7 − 8 |

Analysis of the gain on monetary assets and liabilities after allowing for the fall in the value of money:

|   |   | £'000 | Source |
|---|---|---|---|
| 10 | Long-term liabilities | 2,750 ⎫ | |
| 11 | Bank overdrafts | 1,544 ⎬ | Paragraph 19.27 |
| 12 | Non-equity share capital | 1,000 ⎭ | |
| 13 | Other | 623 | 14 − 12 − 11 − 10 |
| 14 |   | 5,917 | Paragraph 19.25 |

The adjustments for the fall in the value of money were made by applying the general index of retail prices, based on January 1978 = 100. At 1.1.1979 the index stood at 116·9, and at 146·0 at 31.12.1979.

19.29 It is important to appreciate the significance of the figure which is the difference between the gain or loss for the year in the net equity interest and the gain or loss on monetary assets and liabilities, after adjusting both for the change in the value of money. This figure is made up partly of the amount by which non-monetary assets have failed to change in value to offset the change in the value of money and partly of the amount of the current cost profit for the year needed to compensate for the change in the value of money during the year. Part 2 of this chapter demonstrates how these two elements might be separated.

19.30 In Birchwood's case a gain is shown on monetary liabilities, which is greater than the gain in the net equity interest for the year. This is an indication that the rise in value of the non-monetary assets, together with the profit, is below the amount required to offset the fall in the value of money, but that this has been partly compensated by the gearing effect of the liabilities and preference shares: without the latter there would have been a loss after allowing for the fall in the value of money of 1,732 (5,917 − 4,185). Table 19.4 gives the detailed analysis.

### Table 19.2

INDEX OF RETAIL PRICES FOR 1979

|  | Month | RPI |
|---|---|---|
| 1979 | January | 119·9 |
| ” | February | 121·9 |
| ” | March | 124·3 |
| ” | April | 129·1 |
| ” | May | 134·5 |
| ” | June | 137·1 |
| ” | July | 138·5 |
| ” | August | 139·3 |
| ” | September | 140·5 |
| ” | October | 142·5 |
| ” | November | 144·2 |
| ” | December | 146·0 |
|  | Total | 1,617·8 |

The RPI at 31st December 1978 was     116·9.

The average for the year is $\frac{1,617\cdot8}{12} =$     134·8.

# PART 2—A METHOD FOR PROVIDING A FULL ANALYSIS OF THE GAIN OR LOSS IN THE NET EQUITY INTEREST AFTER ALLOWING FOR THE CHANGE IN THE VALUE OF MONEY

19.31   In the first part of this chapter, a simple method of preparing a partial analysis of the gain or loss in the net equity interest after allowing for the change in the value of money was described whereby only the figure of gain or loss on monetary items was calculated. It is possible, however, to provide a full analysis of the gain or loss and indeed it may be desirable for management to do so. The following paragraphs set out a method for preparing such an analysis.

19.32   The information made available by a full analysis will keep management better informed of the real changes in their business and the areas in which such changes arise. Although the method proposed might appear complicated at first sight the work involved in preparing a detailed analysis is not great once the general method of preparation is understood.

19.33   The figure for the first part of the statement showing total gain or loss in the net equity interest has already been obtained in Part 1 of this chapter and its calculation will not be repeated here.

19.34   As the figures in the statement of net change are not recorded in the books of account, the analysis is best prepared using a columnar worksheet in which each step is recorded in self balancing columns so that the risk of carrying errors from one step to the next is minimised. This completed worksheet is set out in Table 19.3 and the method of completion is explained below.

### Step 1: Conversion of the opening current cost balance sheet

19.35   This conversion is shown in the first four columns of the worksheet in Table 19.3. The first pair of these columns contains the unadjusted current cost consolidated balance sheet of Birchwood Limited and its subsidiaries as at 31st December 1978 from Table 14.1 in Chapter 14. The second pair of columns contains the current cost balance sheet adjusted by means of the RPI into pounds of year-end purchasing power. These figures are arrived at by multiplying all the figures in columns 1 and 2 by a factor calculated by dividing the RPI for December 1979 by the RPI for December 1978.

$$\frac{\text{December 1979 RPI}}{\text{December 1978 RPI}} = \frac{146 \cdot 0}{116 \cdot 9} = 1 \cdot 25 \text{ (rounded)}$$

268

WORKSHEET FOR PREPARATION OF THE STATEMENT OF NET CHANGE

| | 1 Unadjusted Dr £000 | 2 Cr £000 | 3 Balance sheet at 31.12.78 adjusted Dr £000 | 4 Cr £000 | 5 Net monetary assets Dr £000 | 6 Cr £000 | 7 Journal Dr £000 | 8 Cr £000 | 9 Profit and Loss account Dr £000 | 10 Cr £000 | 11 Statement of net change Dr £000 | 12 Cr £000 | 13 Balance sheet at 31.12.79 Dr £000 | 14 Cr £000 |
|---|---|---|---|---|---|---|---|---|---|---|---|---|---|---|
| Fixed assets | 40,190 | | 50,238 | | | 8,987 | | 4,557 (a) | 8,933 | | | | 45,735 | |
| Investment in associate | 453 | | 566 | | | | | 89 (b) | | | | | 477 | |
| Quoted and unquoted investments | 1,523 | | 1,904 | | | | | 367 (b) | | | | | 1,537 | |
| Stock and work in progress | 68,704 | | 85,880 | | 51,804 | 9,654 | | 9,145 (c) | | | | | 86,389 | |
| Debtors | 41,443 | | 51,804 | | | 58,686 | | | | | | | 58,686 | |
| Cash | 1,002 | | 1,253 | | 1,253 | 1,540 | | | | | | | 1,540 | |
| Creditors | | 40,640 | | 50,800 | 56,238 | 50,800 | | | | | | | | 56,238 |
| Current tax | | 4,390 | | 5,488 | 4,355 | 5,488 | | | | | | | | 4,355 |
| Bank overdraft | | 6,915 | | 8,644 | 4,692 | 8,644 | | | | | | | | 4,692 |
| Dividends | | 5,700 | | 7,125 | 6,200 | 7,125 | | | | | | | | 6,200 |
| Deferred tax | 3,070 | | 3,838 | | 3,838 | 3,340 | | | | | | | 3,340 | |
| Share capital + reserves | | 82,938 | | 103,673 | | | | | | | | | | 103,673 |
| Minority interest | | 802 | | 1,003 | 802 | 1,003 | | | | | | | | 908 |
| Preference share capital | | 4,000 | | 5,000 | 4,000 | 5,000 | | | | | | | | 4,000 |
| Debentures | | 10,000 | | 12,500 | 10,000 | 12,500 | | | | | | | | 10,000 |
| Loans | | 1,000 | | 1,250 | 1,133 | 1,250 | | | | | | | | 1,133 |
| New share capital introduced | | | | | 8,520 | | | | | | | | | 8,520 |
| Net revenue income | | | | | 21,706 | | | | | 19,755 | | 1,951 | | |
| Exchange differences | | | | | 39 | | | | | | | | | |
| Dividends | | | | | | 6,480 | 39 (d) | | 6,480 | | | | | |
| Minority interest | | | | | | | | 98 (e); 8 (e) | 8 | | | | | |
| Revaluation surpluses | | | | | | | | | | | | | | |
| – fixed asset | | | | | | | 8 (e); 26 (e); 4,557 | | | | 4,583 | | | |
| – investment | | | | | | | 456 (b) | 39 (a) | | | 417 | | | |
| – stock | | | | | | | 72 (e) | | | | | | | |
| Stock adjustment | | | | | | | 9,145 (c) | | | | 9,217 | | | |
| Monetary surplus | | | | | 5,917 | | | | | | | 5,917 | | |
| P & L surplus | | | | | | | | | 4,334 | | | 4,334 | | |
| Reduction in net equity interest | | | | | | | | | | | | 2,015 | 2,015 | |
| | 156,385 | 156,385 | 195,483 | 195,483 | 180,497 | 180,497 | 14,303 | 14,303 | 19,755 | 19,755 | 14,217 | 14,217 | 199,719 | 199,719 |

## Step 2: Net monetary assets

19.36 The next two columns of the worksheet, headed 'net monetary items', effectively represent a 'net monetary items account' which is:

1  Debited with all adjusted opening monetary assets.
2  Credited with all adjusted opening monetary liabilities.
3  Debited with all closing monetary liabilities and the closing minority interest before their share of the year's gains.
4  Credited with all closing monetary assets.
5  Debited or credited with exchange differences on monetary items.
6  Debited with all 'monetary' income (capital and revenue) adjusted by means of the RPI.
7  Credited with all 'monetary' expenditure (capital and revenue) adjusted by means of the RPI.

The last two entries account for movements of funds between monetary and non-monetary items.

19.37  Non-equity share capital should be treated as a monetary liability.

19.38  The adjusted opening monetary assets and liabilities are copied into Columns 5 and 6 from Columns 3 and 4. The closing monetary assets and liabilities are copied into Columns 5 and 6 from the closing current cost balance sheet which for this example is set out in Table 18.2, in Chapter 18. The figures for capital income and expenditure and revenue income and expenditure adjusted by means of the RPI are calculated below:

(a) The unadjusted figures are obtained from the current cost accounts for the year as follows:

| | | £'000 |
|---|---|---:|
| 1 | Capital expenditure: | |
| | Addition to fixed assets | 8,592 |
| | *Less:* Disposal sale proceeds | 294 |
| | | 8,298 |
| 2 | Revenue income and expenditure: | |
| | Current cost profit before tax | 14,906 |
| | *Less:* share of profit in associate | (64) |
| | *Add:* depreciation | 8,933 |
| | | 23,775 |

(The cost of sales adjustment and stock movement are treated separately in paragraph 19.40 below.)

Depreciation and the retained earnings of the associate have not been adjusted.

| | | |
|---|---|---:|
| 3 | New equity capital introduced | 8,000 |

| | £'000 |
|---|---|
| 4   Dividends on share capital: | |
| Paid 31st December | 280 |
| Proposed | 6,200 |
| | 6,480 |
| 5   Exchange differences—see paragraph 19.25 | 39 |

(b) The figures are adjusted as follows:

(i) **Capital expenditure:**
The figures are adjusted by using a factor calculated by dividing the RPI at the year-end by the average RPI for the year, thus assuming that the expenditure accrued evenly during the year. If, however, the pattern of expenditure throughout the year is erratic, it may be necessary to allocate the expenditure to the appropriate periods in the year and to convert to pounds of year-end purchasing power by applying factors calculated using the appropriate RPI for each specific period in place of the average RPI.

(ii) **Revenue income and expenditure**
Revenue income and expenditure, including the cost of sales adjustment and stock movement but with the exception of the tax charge or credit for the year, is treated in the same way as capital expenditure. Taxation is deemed to arise at the year-end in the profit and loss account and therefore requires no adjustment. The share of profit in the associated company is replaced by the dividends from the associate.

(iii) **New equity capital introduced**
New equity capital introduced is converted by applying a factor calculated by dividing the RPI at the year-end by the RPI at the date the increase was effected.

(iv) **Dividends**
Dividends proposed or declared and unpaid at the closing balance sheet date require no adjustment. Dividends declared and paid during the year are converted by applying a factor calculated by dividing the RPI at the year-end by the RPI at the date of payment.

(v) Exchange differences are deemed to arise at the year-end and so require no adjustment.

19.39   The adjustments required to convert Birchwood's consolidated profit and loss account and dividends are described below. The calculation of the average RPI number for 1979 is shown in Table 19.2.

19.40 The adjusted figures for income and expenditure are therefore:

1 Capital expenditure:

$$8,298 \times \frac{146\cdot0}{134\cdot8} = 8,987$$

2 Profit and loss account:

| | £'000 | £'000 |
|---|---|---|
| Adjusted income | $23,775 \times \frac{146\cdot0}{134\cdot8} =$ | 25,750 |
| Dividends from associate | 40 | 40 |
| Taxation | ( 4,084) | ( 4,084) |
| | 19,731 | 21,706 |

3 New equity capital introduced

$$8,000 \times \frac{146\cdot0}{137\cdot1} = 8,520$$

4 Cost of sales adjustment

$$8,771 \times \frac{146\cdot0}{134\cdot8} = 9,500$$

Stock movement

$$(17,685) \times \frac{146\cdot0}{134\cdot8} = (19,154)$$

|  | (8,914) | (9,654) |
|---|---|---|

5 Dividends

| | | |
|---|---|---|
| Paid 31.12.79 | 280 | 280 |
| Proposed | 6,200 | 6,200 |
| | 6,480 | 6,480 |

| 6 Exchange differences | 39 | 39 |
|---|---|---|

19.41 These figures are entered in Columns 5 and 6 of the Worksheet, income being debited and expenditure being credited.

19.42 All the entries in the net monetary assets account have now been made and the balance on the account represents the monetary gain for the year.

19.43 In this example it will be seen that there has been a gain of £5,917,000 after allowing for the change in the value of the money, from holding net monetary liabilities.

**Step 3: Closing journal entries**

19.44 The adjusted revaluation surpluses and deficits on non-monetary items should now be calculated. As all tax is treated as monetary, any deferred tax amounts that arise in the current cost accounts will be those used in the statement of net change. These are deemed to arise at the year-end and require no adjustment. Only the revaluation surplus or deficit net of deferred tax, therefore is subject to change. Each journal entry made in Columns 7 and 8 of the worksheet set out in Table 19.3 is explained below. The figures in the Worksheet resulting from each journal entry are distinguished by the letter in brackets to the right of each figure.

### Journal entry (a) Fixed assets

19.45  The adjusted revaluation deficit is calculated as follows:

|  | £'000 |
|---|---|
| Adjusted opening net value (Column 3) | 50,238 |
| Adjusted net additions (Column 6) | 8,987 |
|  | 59,225 |
| *Less:* Profit and loss account depreciation charge for the year | 8,933 |
|  | 50,292 |
| Net book value at the year-end | 45,735 |
| Adjusted deficit for the year, after allowing for the change in the value of money | 4,557 |

19.46  The journal entry is therefore:

|  | £'000 | £'000 |
|---|---|---|
| Dr  Fixed asset revaluation surplus | 4,557 | |
| Cr  Fixed assets | | 4,557 |

### Journal entry (b) Investments

19.47  There have been no additions to investments during the year. The adjusted revaluation deficit is therefore:

|  | Associate £'000 | Others £'000 |
|---|---|---|
| Adjusted opening balance (Column 3) | 566 | 1,904 |
| Closing balance (Column 13) | 477 | 1,537 |
| Adjusted deficit for the year after allowing for the change in the value of the money. | 89 | 367 |

The journal entry is therefore:

|  | £'000 | £'000 |
|---|---|---|
| Dr  Investments revaluation surplus | 456 | |
| Cr  Investments—other | | 367 |
| —associated company | | 89 |
|  | 456 | 456 |

### Journal entry (c) Stock

19.48  It will be recalled that the calculation of revenue expenditure for the year in paragraph 19.38 above eliminated the COSA and the stock movement during the year as being non-monetary items. To complete the profit and loss account for the year these items must be reinstated. Also, to arrive at

273

the adjusted revaluation surplus arising on stock held at the year end the adjusted opening stock balance must be deducted from the closing stock balance. The required calculation is:

|  | £'000 |
|---|---|
| Adjusted opening stock | 85,880 |
| Adjusted movement for year | 19,154 |
|  | 105,034 |
| Closing stock per current cost accounts | 86,389 |
|  | 18,645 |
| Adjusted cost of sales adjustment | (9,500) |
| Adjusted stock deficit | 9,145 |

|  | £'000 | £'000 |
|---|---|---|
| The journal entry is therefore: | | |
| Dr    Stock revaluation surplus | 9,145 | |
| Cr    Stock movement (profit and | | |
| loss account) | | 9,145 |

### Journal entry (d) Exchange differences

19.49    Having accounted for the exchange differences on monetary items in paragraph 19.36 it is necessary to ensure that they are not double-counted.

|  | £'000 | £'000 |
|---|---|---|
| The journal entry is therefore: | | |
| Dr   Exchange differences | 39 | |
| Cr   Investments—revaluation surplus | | 39 |

since the exchange differences have been included in the revaluation reserve for investments. (see paragraph 14.26 journal entry J.)

### Other non-monetary assets

19.50    There are no non-monetary assets in Birchwood's consolidated balance sheet that have not now been adjusted. If other categories of non-monetary asset had been included in the balance sheet (e.g. deferred expenditure) they would require adjustments similar to that made to investments (see paragraph 19.47 above).

### Journal entry (e) Minority interest

19.51 The minority's share in the surpluses for the year is unaffected by the recalculations. Journal entry (e) therefore shows the same minority interest in operating profit and revaluation surpluses as was shown in the original consolidated accounts:

|  |  | £'000 | £'000 |
|---|---|---|---|
| Dr | Minority interest—P/L | 8 | |
| Cr | Minority interest | | 8 |
| | with the minority's share of the profit | | |
| | for the year | | |
| *and* | | | |
| Dr | Revaluation surplus—fixed assets | 26 | |
| | Revaluation surplus—stocks | 72 | |
| Cr | Minority interest | | 98 |
| | with the minority's share of revaluation | | |
| | surpluses for the year. | | |

### Step 4: profit and loss account

19.52 All the closing journal entries have now been made and to complete the worksheet it remains only to extend the recorded entries as appropriate into the columns headed profit and loss account, statement of net change and balance sheet at 31.12.79. The profit and loss account columns (Columns 9 and 10) are completed as follows:

1 Enter as a credit the unadjusted revenue income, used in paragraph 19.40 above, adding back the share of the associate's retained profit for the year.
2 Enter as a debit the depreciation charged for the year.
3 Enter as a debit the actual dividends on the share capital for the year.
4 Enter as a debit the minority interest in the profit for the year.

19.53 Columns 9 and 10 should now balance by including the profit or loss for the year shown by the CCA profit and loss account, as a debit or credit as appropriate, less any dividends shown in the appropriation account.

### Step 5: The balance sheet

19.54 It will be found that it is convenient to complete partially the balance sheet columns before completing the statement of net change columns. Columns 13 and 14 therefore should be:

1 Debited with assets in the year-end current cost balance sheet.
2 Credited with the liabilities and non-equity share capital in the year-end current cost balance sheet.
3 Credited with the adjusted opening net equity interest from Column 4 of the worksheet.
4 Credited with the adjusted figure of any new equity capital introduced, from Column 5.

19.55 The Balance Sheet will be completed later by transferring the balance on the statement of net change columns to the debit or credit column as appropriate.

### Step 6: The statement of net change

19.56 All the calculations necessary to complete Columns 11 and 12 have been made and the statement of net change columns can be completed as follows:

1 Enter as credits all adjusted surpluses on non-monetary items and enter as debits all adjusted deficits on non-monetary items. These are the figures calculated in paragraphs 19.44 to 19.48 and 19.50 to 19.51 above.
2 Enter as a credit the increase in profit, arising from the adjustments made to revenue income and expenditure. This is the difference between the adjusted figure included in Column 5 and the unadjusted figure in Column 10.
3 Enter, as a debit if an increase or as a credit if a decrease, the adjustments made to equity dividends paid during the year (see paragraph 19.40). The dividend line on the worksheet should now cross-cast.
4 Enter, as a credit if a surplus or as a debit if a deficit, the surplus or deficit on holding monetary assets and liabilities from Columns 5 or 6.
5 Enter, as a credit if positive or as a debit if negative, the retained earnings for the year (i.e. the balancing figure) from Columns 9 or 10. (See paragraph 19.53).

19.57 The statement of net change columns should now balance by including as the balancing figure the total increase or decrease in the net equity interest from the first part of the statement.

19.58 The balancing figure from the statement of net change columns should also be entered in the balance sheet columns (as a credit if a surplus or as a debit if a deficit) and the balance sheet columns can then be totalled and should agree.

19.59 It remains now only to prepare the statement of net change in a suitable form. All the necessary figures will be obtained from the current cost accounts, from the worksheet, or by simple addition or subtraction. Table 19.4 sets out a statement of net change for Birchwood Limited and its subsidiaries which analyses fully the gain for the year after allowing for the fall in the value of money and shows the source of each figure.

19.60 The analysis of the gain on monetary assets and liabilities has already been calculated in paragraphs 19.23 to 19.27 in Part 1 and is not repeated here.

276

19.61 The current cost revaluation surpluses should be shown net of minority interests so that they can be compared with the adjusted figure shown on the worksheet.

The calculations are:

|  | Stocks | Fixed assets | Invest-ments |  |
|---|---|---|---|---|
|  | £'000 | £'000 | £'000 |  |
| Current cost revaluation surpluses | 8,771 | 5,973 | 260 | Table 14.3 |
| *Less:* Minority interest | 72 | 26 | — | Paragraph 19.51 |
|  | 8,699 | 5,947 | 260 |  |

**Table 19.4**

BIRCHWOOD LIMITED AND SUBSIDIARY COMPANIES

**Statement of change in value of shareholders' net equity interest after allowing for fall in the value of money during the year to 31st December 1979**

|  |  | £'000 | Figures obtained from |
|---|---|---|---|
| 1 | Net equity interest at beginning of year | 82,938 | Opening current cost balance sheet (Table 14.1) |
|  | *Add:* |  |  |
| 2 | New equity capital introduced during the year | 8,000 | See paragraph 19.38 |
| 3 |  | 90,938 | 1 + 2 |
|  | *Add:* |  |  |
| 4 | Increase required to compensate for fall in the value of money during the year | 21,255 | 5 − 3 |
| 5 |  | 112,193 | Paragraph 19.9 |
|  | *Deduct:* |  |  |
| 6 | Net equity interest at end of year before dividends on equity capital | 116,378 | Paragraph 19.9 |
| 7 | Gain for year after allowing for fall in the value of money | 4,185 | 6 − 5 |
| 8 | Dividends on equity capital for the year | 6,200 | Paragraph 19.22 |
| 9 | Loss for the year after allowing for fall in the value of money and after dividends | (2,015) | 7 − 8 |

277

|  | | £'000 | Figures obtained from |
|---|---|---|---|
| | Made up of: | | |
| 10 | Current cost profit for the year | 10,814 | Table 18.1 |
| 11 | Less preference dividends | 280 | |
| 12 | | 10,534 | 10 + 11 |
| 13 | Addition to compensate for fall in the value of money | 1,951 | See paragraph 19.56 |
| 14 | | 12,485 | 12 + 13 |

**Loss on non-monetary assets**

|  | Stocks £'000 | Fixed assets £'000 | Invest- ments £'000 | | |
|---|---|---|---|---|---|
| 15 Current cost revaluation surplus | 8,699 | 5,947 | 260 | | Paragraph 19.61 |
| 16 *Less:* amount needed to com- pensate for fall in the value of money | 17,916 | 10,530 | 677 | | 15 − 17 |
| | | | | | Table 12.3 |
| 17 | (9,217) | (4,583) | (417) | (14,217) | Columns 11 & 12 |

**Gain on monetary assets and liabilities**

|  | | £'000 | | |
|---|---|---|---|---|
| 18 | Long term liabilities | 2,750 | | |
| 19 | Bank overdraft | 1,544 | | |
| 20 | Non-equity share capital | 1,000 | | Paragraph 19.27 |
| 21 | Other | 623 | | |
| 22 | | | 5,917 | |
| 23 | Gain for year after allowing for fall in the value of money | | 4,185 | 14 + 17 + 22 |
| 24 | *Less:* Dividend on equity capital for year | | 6,200 | Paragraph 19.20 |
| 25 | Loss for the year after allowing for fall in the value of money and after dividends | | (2,015) | 23 − 24 |

# Preface by the Accounting Standards Committee

*This Exposure Draft (ED18) was prepared for the Accounting Standards Committee by the Inflation Accounting Steering Group under the Chairmanship of Mr. Douglas Morpeth. The Steering Group was asked to prepare a draft based on the report of the Inflation Accounting Committee – the Sandilands Committee – taking into account the comments on that report by the Consultative Committee of Accountancy Bodies and other representative bodies. The terms of reference of the Steering Group are set out at the end of this Preface.*

*The formation of the Steering Group was announced on 6 January 1976; it held its first meeting on 12 January 1976 and it reported to us on 29 September 1976. We would pay a warm tribute to the skill and vigour with which the Steering Group, its staff and those co-opted to its working parties have tackled their task and kept to their time-table. We are grateful also to all those whose support made this work possible, including the Government, the City, commerce and industry, accounting firms and the accountancy profession.*

*In our consideration of the Exposure Draft, we have concentrated upon its main principles in an intensive series of meetings, and we believe that the proposals offer a practical and realistic system of Current Cost Accounting. They have been appraised by a representative sample of companies and suggestions made by these companies have been reflected in the draft.*

*Even so, we recognise that details of the proposals may need to be amended as the result of comments made during the exposure period, before a Statement of Standard Accounting Practice is promulgated. To give more adequate time for comment at a particularly busy period for many companies, the exposure period originally planned has been doubled from three months to six months. We hope, however, that those who wish to comment will do so as soon as they reasonably can, instead of waiting until the end of the exposure period is imminent. Collation and consideration of the comments will be a formidable job, and the quicker it can be started, the better.*

*As a consequence of extending the exposure period, it is now
proposed that the Statement of Standard Accounting Practice will
be published on 31 January 1978 instead of 31 October 1977. Its
application will be phased over a three year period, and the first
accounts covered by it will be those of the largest enterprises, for
accounting periods beginning on or after 1 July 1978. The proposals
do not at this stage include a specific date for the application of the
Standard to businesses which do not disclose in their accounts for
the previous period either a turnover or total assets in excess of
£100,000; a decision on this point will be made later, when more
information is available about the time needed by such businesses
to adapt to the new system.*

*To provide continuity of information during the transitional period
before full-scale adoption of CCA it is suggested that for a two year
period companies should publish their results on an Historical Cost
basis in addition to their Current Cost Accounting results. These
historical cost accounts should continue to be prepared in
conformity with Statements of Standard Accounting Practice
based on the historical cost convention.*

*Discussions are being held with Government and the legal
profession to resolve any legal problems which may arise from the
introduction of accounts based on the proposals in ED18.*

*We indicated earlier that details of the proposals in the Exposure
Draft may need modification in the light of comments made during
the exposure period. It may also prove that practical experience in
the working of the Standard will suggest a need for further
modifications and refinements. This would not be surprising, nor
should it be a cause for criticism since it is new territory that is
being explored. What is vitally needed is a generally acceptable
system of accounting both for management purposes and for
reporting which shows the effects of changing price levels and we
believe that the introduction of such a system should not be delayed
by the search for an elusive and probably unattainable degree of
perfection. It is in this belief that we commend the proposals in the
Exposure Draft.*

# Terms of Reference of the
# Inflation Accounting Steering Group

The terms of reference of the Group are:

**1** To prepare for submission to the Accounting Standards Steering Committee a proposal for an exposure draft on Current Cost Accounting, to be based on the proposals of the Inflation Accounting Committee (Cmd 6225), with a view to the implementation of those proposals in company accounts for periods beginning after 24 December 1977 if that proves feasible.

**2** To consult the Secretary of State for Trade as necessary on any general issues arising during that work, and to keep him fully informed of progress.

**3** To report plans and progress to the Accounting Standards Steering Committee.

**4** In preparing these proposals:
(i) to take account of the comments that have been made on the Report, in particular those of the Consultative Committee of Accountancy Bodies;
(ii) to carry out such research as they consider necessary;
(iii) to consider those matters identified in the Report as requiring further study, in particular:
    (a) the practical application of the Committee's recommendations for the valuation of fixed assets, stock and work in progress including the use of published indices, in relation to companies in various classes of business and of various sizes; and
    (b) the need for objective verification of CCA accounts, bearing in mind the requirements of auditors in this respect.
(iv) to test the practicability of draft proposals by 'field tests' on a suitable selection of companies;
(v) to prepare, concurrently, instruction manuals for the guidance of companies;
(vi) to draw ASSC's attention to the impact of the Steering Group's proposals on existing and proposed Statements of Standard Accounting Practice.

# CURRENT COST ACCOUNTING

## CONTENTS                                    Page Numbers

Page numbers

# PART 5 NOTE ON LEGAL IMPLICATIONS 72

# APPENDICES

# Introduction by the Inflation Accounting Steering Group

**1** The continuing and high rate of inflation in the United Kingdom has reduced the usefulness of accounts prepared on the historical cost basis to management, investors, employees and others to such an extent that it is necessary to make a major change in accounting practice. Historical cost accounts have always suffered from the failure to show the impact of changing price levels, but in recent years the rate of inflation has made it essential to remedy this defect. The nature of the necessary change has been debated within the accounting profession for many years and a number of solutions have been put forward. However, the recommendations in the Sandilands Committee's report for the introduction of a system of current cost accounting (CCA) were broadly accepted by the Government and the Consultative Committee of Accountancy Bodies last year, and this Exposure Draft is based on these recommendations.

**2** Management needs up-to-date information on costs and values for the proper running of the business. The system of current cost accounting described in the Exposure Draft will help to provide such information in the management accounts of companies and in their published annual accounts. If more realistic information is to be available to management than is provided by historical cost accounts, the change to current cost accounting needs to be made at the basic management accounting level. It would not be adequate merely to provide once-a-year adjustments in the annual accounts to a basically historical cost system.

**3** As long as industry uses historical costs for management accounts, it may unknowingly undercost with dangerous consequences for the business. It is essential that industry uses immediately for its estimates of cost:
    (a) depreciation calculated on the value to the business of plant and machinery—in most cases this will be replacement cost;
    (b) the estimated cost at the date of sale of materials consumed.
These CCA conventions should be used as soon as possible in compiling all management control figures including monthly profit and loss accounts. It is appreciated that because of the effects of market forces and of the Price Commission, industry may not be able to reflect fully its current costs in the prices it obtains.

**4** The introduction of CCA will lead to five major improvements by comparison with the present historical cost system:

(a) depreciation will be calculated on the value to the business of the assets concerned and not on their historical cost and will thus give a more realistic measure of the cost of resources used;

(b) cost of sales will be calculated in most cases on the cost of replacing the goods sold and not on their original cost;

(c) there will be a new statement in the annual account—the appropriation account—in which there will be brought together the current cost profit, the revaluation surpluses, the amount which the directors consider should be retained within the business having regard to their assessment of its needs, and dividends;

(d) the balance sheet will show current values for most assets and will no longer show their historical cost;

(e) the statement of the change in the equity interest after allowing for the change in the value of money will clearly show how the company has performed in relation to the rate of inflation and will also show its losses or gains from the holding of monetary items.

**5** CCA will provide management, and the users of published accounts, with more realistic information on costs, profits, the value of assets, and the return on capital and on assets. CCA also provides a distinction between the profit earned from the operations of the business and the money gains resulting from changes in the price of a company's assets.

**6** This more realistic information should enable a clearer picture to be obtained of the relative performance of:

(a) managers and products within a company;

(b) different companies; and

(c) different industries

and should help to lead to better decisions being taken in such areas as pricing, cost reduction, levels of remuneration, resource allocation between and within companies, dividends, gearing and borrowing levels.

**7** The essence of the CCA system is simple: the charge against income in arriving at profit for stocks consumed and fixed assets used is based on current replacement costs and not on out-of-date and irrelevant historical costs. Similarly, the balance sheet shows up-to-date values in place of historical costs.

**8** If it is as simple as that, it may be asked, why is the Exposure Draft so long? The answer is that it was decided that it would be more helpful to companies to deal with as many of the known problems of implementing CCA as possible. It should be appreciated, however, that relatively few companies are likely to meet all of the problems in any one year. Much of the Exposure Draft is concerned with putting flesh on the simple system just described.

**9** The Steering Group, however, is conscious that there are a number of areas where it has been able to put forward only an interim solution which will almost certainly require modification in the light of experience. The Steering Group believes that it is more important to produce, as a matter of urgency, a reasonably comprehensive Exposure Draft containing interim solutions in some areas rather than to delay the whole of the Exposure Draft until a final solution is found for all problems. The interim solutions include the treatment of the effects of inflation on the owners' capital and on monetary items, and retentions to maintain the substance of the business. Part of the problem is a lack of consensus on what is the substance of the business (is it the physical assets, or all the assets, or the long-term capital, or the owners' capital, etc?) and whether it should be maintained in money or real terms. It is considered, however, that the suggested treatment, (namely a statement of the change in the equity interest after allowing for the change in the value of money, and a voluntary transfer to or from the revaluation reserve in an appropriation account) forms a basis for further development when a greater degree of consensus becomes evident. The Steering Group also proposes to give further consideration to its interim proposals in the areas of liabilities other than deferred tax, goodwill, and other intangible assets.

**10** Whilst the need to find solutions to the problems of accounting for rapidly changing prices is urgent, the Steering Group was conscious of the burden that changing to a new system might put on companies (running the new system, once installed, may not be materially more difficult than the old) and has, therefore, decided to phase its introduction. There was a choice between phasing by item in the accounts or by size of company. The Steering Group chose the latter because the former had two major disadvantages:

(a) the most important adjustments which would require to be phased in first (depreciation and cost of sales) probably involved the greatest part of the work;

(b) the resulting accounts would have been produced on a mixture of conventions which could hardly be described as true or fair.

**11** Another possibility would be to introduce CCA by means of a supplementary statement. This was rejected because such statements would cause confusion as to which figures were considered to be the right ones.

**12** It should be noted that no starting date has been set for the mandatory use of CCA by small companies. It is intended to develop an appropriate method of CCA for such companies in the light of the experience gained during the first years' operations of CCA by other companies.

**13** It has been necessary in producing this Exposure Draft to balance three requirements:
(a) the need for more useful information;
(b) the need to minimise the extra work required to produce the information;
(c) the need to minimise the opportunity for misleading manipulation of the figures.
The Steering Group believes that it has got the balance about right, and this view is supported by initial reactions from the companies which have appraised the Steering Group's proposals, but it would particularly welcome comments on this point.

**14** It has been argued that CCA will increase the degree of subjectivity in annual accounts. If this is so, then this is part of the price that has to be paid to make accounts more relevant in a period of rapidly changing costs. It will be appreciated that historical cost accounting also contains a degree of subjectivity, particularly in the area of depreciation. Moreover, the amount of subjectivity in CCA should not be exaggerated. With the possible exception of the transfers to or from revaluation reserves, the figures in the accounts will normally be backed by evidence on which both management and the auditors can base their judgement. The Steering Group has maintained close liaison with the Auditing Practices Committee throughout the production of the Exposure Draft and has endeavoured to meet as many as possible of the points raised by that Committee; nevertheless, audit difficulties under CCA will be greater than under historical cost accounting, and the Auditing Practices Committee proposes to issue a booklet early in the new year setting out some of the principal problem areas and recommending ways in which they should be approached.

**15** Many major industrial countries are developing inflation accounting systems. The United Kingdom is amongst the leaders in this field but is developing systems which will not be unique or incompatible. The importance of comparability is recognised and it is hoped that further development of CCA will take place in close consultation amongst interested countries, the EEC and the International Accounting Standards Committee.

**16** The Steering Group is well aware of the importance companies attach to acceptance of CCA by the Inland Revenue and the Price Commission, and is holding discussions with the former and will be with the latter when appropriate. It is also conscious of the need to simplify record keeping, so it is discussing with the appropriate authorities requirements for the retention of historical cost records within the EEC. The legal implications of the introduction of CCA are being discussed with the relevant bodies.

**17** The Steering Group has already modified its proposals in the light of comments and will do so again, if necessary, after studying the comments received during the exposure period when preparing proposals for a Statement of Standard Accounting Practice for consideration by the ASC.

**18** It is appreciated that some organisations and companies in certain industries may need to modify the application of this Standard in order to give a true and fair view. The statement of the change in the equity interest after allowing for the change in the value of money, for instance, presents problems for nationalised industries arising from their special capital structure. There may be different problems in other industries. The Steering Group will give full consideration to reasoned proposals for modification from the relevant trade associations and similar bodies, or from the nationalised industries themselves.

**19** The Steering Group wishes to thank all those who have helped it in its work and, in particular, the "field test" companies and representative bodies which have commented on earlier versions of the proposals in this Exposure Draft.

# Part 1 Proposed standard accounting practice

Several words and phrases used in this part have been given a special meaning. They are defined in Part 2.

## Scope of this standard

**1** It is the intention that this Standard should apply in due course to all financial accounts intended to give a true and fair view of the financial position and profit or loss but, in order to spread the workload on those concerned in its introduction, it has been decided to divide the introduction into four phases:

(a) Phase 1 will apply to:
  (i)  companies listed by The Stock Exchange;
  (ii) limited companies not within category (i), nationalised industries and public trading entities which disclose in their audited accounts for the previous period either:
      (A) a turnover in excess of £10 million; or
      (B) total assets in excess of £10 million.

Phase 1 will *not* apply to companies which have more than 50 per cent of their assets outside the United Kingdom of Great Britain & Northern Ireland and the Republic of Ireland, and which would have difficulty in producing accounts within the Phase 1 time scale. Such companies will be in Phase 2 or 3, depending on their size.

(b) Phase 2 will apply to all limited companies, nationalised industries and public trading entities not included in Phase 1, provided that they disclose in their audited accounts for the previous period either:
  (i)  a turnover in excess of £1 million; or
  (ii) total assets in excess of £1 million.

(c) Phase 3 will apply to all other financial accounts intended to give a true and fair view of the financial position and profit or loss not included in Phases 1 or 2, provided that they disclose in their audited accounts for the previous period either:
  (i)  a turnover in excess of £100,000; or
  (ii) total assets in excess of £100,000.

Phase 3 will, therefore, include all non-trading public entities, trade unions, employers' associations, friendly societies and building societies, provided that they are above the minimum size specified above.

(d)  Phase 4 will apply to all other financial accounts intended to give a true and fair view of the financial position and profit or loss not included in Phases 1, 2 or 3.

**2** For companies producing group accounts, the size criteria in paragraph 1 should apply to the group (see also paragraphs 80 et seq.).

**3** An appropriate method of current cost accounting for companies with an annual turnover and assets below £100,000 (ie companies in Phase 4) is under consideration by the Inflation Accounting Steering Group. The method will be devised in the light of further experience.

## Dates from which effective

**4** The accounting practices set out in this Standard should be adopted as soon as possible and regarded as standard in respect of financial statements relating to accounting periods beginning:
(a)  for organisations included in Phase 1, on or after 1 July 1978;
(b)  for organisations included in Phase 2, on or after 1 January 1979;
(c)  for organisations included in Phase 3, on or after 1 January 1980.

**5** No commencing date for Phase 4 has yet been set. Ample advance notice of the starting date will be given.

## Content of accounts

**6** Annual accounts prepared and presented on the bases set out in this Standard should contain a profit and loss account, an appropriation account and a balance sheet. Except for wholly-owned subsidiaries, there should be included in the notes to the accounts a statement of the change in shareholders' net equity interest after allowing for the change in the value of money. Accounts of enterprises within the scope of SSAP 10 will also include a statement of source and application of funds.

## Profit and loss account

**7** The profit and loss account should show (inter alia)
(a)  the operating profit or loss for the year;
(b)  interest payable less receivable;
(c)  the current cost profit or loss before taxation;
(d)  taxation;
(e)  the current cost profit or loss before extraordinary items;
(f)  extraordinary items; and
(g)  the current cost profit or loss for the year.

2

The operating profit or loss is arrived at after charging depeciation and the cost of sales on the basis of the current value to the business of the physical assets consumed during the year.

## Depreciation: plant and machinery

**8** The charge to the profit and loss account for depreciation should equal the value to the business of the assets consumed during the period. (For a discussion of the concept of value to the business see paragraphs 183 et seq.) When assets are valued on the basis of their net current replacement cost, the value consumed increases as the replacement cost of the asset increases, but since it will not normally be possible to identify individual price movements within an accounting period, the charge may be based on average values for the period, calculated before charging depreciation for the current period. It may be based on end-of-period values if this basis does not produce a materially different charge from one calculated on average values.

**9** Where average values are used, the charge for depreciation is obtained by apportioning the asset's average value over a period equal to the expected remaining useful life of the asset at the beginning of the period.

**10** A review of asset lives should be regularly undertaken on a consistent basis so that the depreciation charge is realistic in relation to the expected life of the asset.

**11** Backlog depreciation (see paragraph 110) should be charged against the related revaluation surpluses, rather than to the profit and loss account.

**12** In a period when the basis of valuing an asset is changed from its net current replacement cost to its economic value or net realisable value, depreciation should first be calculated by the normal method adopted by the company on the assumption of the continuing application of a net current replacement cost basis of valuation. The further write down required should be treated in accordance with the provisions of paragraph 28.

3

## Depreciation: land and buildings

**13** Depreciation is not normally required for freehold land, but is required for freehold buildings. Depreciation should be based on:
    (a) the depreciable amount (see paragraph 111);
    (b) the estimated remaining economic useful life of the buildings at the year end,
both of which will be advised by the valuer, after consultation with the directors.

**14** Depreciation of leasehold land and buildings will be required on both the depreciable amount and the residual amount. If the valuer, after consultation with the directors, estimates that the remaining economic useful life of the buildings exceeds the remaining term of the lease, the entire value of the land and buildings should be depreciated over the remaining term of the lease. Where the remaining economic useful life of the buildings is estimated to be less than the remaining term of the lease, the depreciable amount should be depreciated over the estimated remaining economic useful life of the buildings, and the residual amount should be depreciated over the remaining term of the lease.

## Cost of stock and work in progress consumed

**15** The amount charged to the profit and loss account for the period for stock and work in progress consumed should be the value to the business, at the date of consumption, of the stock and work in progress consumed during the period.

**16** Where a cost of sales adjustment is calculated (see appendix 3) to revise to current cost a cost of sales determined on another basis, the adjustment should be added to or, where appropriate, deducted from the cost of sales charged to the profit and loss account for the period and included as part of the surplus or deficit arising on revaluation of stock.

## Interest

**17** The net amount of interest paid and interest received should be shown separately in the profit and loss account as a deduction from, or addition to, the operating profit for the period. The separate amounts of interest paid and received should be disclosed in a note to the accounts.

# Taxation

**18** All current taxation other than any chargeable on revaluation of non-current assets should be included in the taxation charge for the year with the exception of taxation attributable to extraordinary items and prior year adjustments which should be dealt with in accordance with SSAP 6—Extraordinary items and prior year adjustments.

**19** Any provision for deferred taxation should also be included in the taxation charge for the year with the exception of that attributable to revaluation surpluses on non-current assets which should be charged against such surpluses.

**20** The treatment to be followed is thus that laid down in SSAP 8 —The treatment of taxation under the imputation system in the accounts of companies—which requires that:
"The following items should be included in the taxation charge in the profit and loss account and, where material, should be separately disclosed:
   (a) the amount of the United Kingdom corporation tax specifying:
       (i) the charge for corporation tax on the income of the year (where such corporation tax includes transfers between the deferred taxation account and the profit and loss account these also should be separately disclosed where material);
       (ii) tax attributable to franked investment income;
       (iii) irrecoverable ACT;
       (iv) the relief for overseas taxation;
   (b) the total overseas taxation relieved and unrelieved, specifying that part of the unrelieved overseas taxation which arises from the payment or proposed payment of dividends.
If the rate of corporation tax is not known for the whole or part of the period covered by the accounts, the latest known rate should be used and disclosed".

**21** An analysis of the taxation charge should be shown in a note to the accounts detailing amounts debited or credited in arriving at (a) current cost profit for the year, (b) extraordinary items and (c) surpluses or deficits arising from revaluation of assets.

## Appropriation account

**22** The appropriation account should show:
   (a) the current cost profit or loss for the year;
   (b) the amount of:
       (i) the surpluses or deficits for the year (net of minority

interests) arising from the revaluation of assets; plus or minus
(ii) the amount appropriated by the directors to or from revaluation reserve;
(c) the dividends for the year; and
(d) the balance, being a transfer to or from general reserve.

**23** The net surplus or deficit for the year arising from the revaluation of assets should be analysed according to whether the revaluation arose from:
(a) fixed assets;
(b) investments;
(c) stock and work in progress; and
(d) exchange translation differences.
The total surpluses and the total deficits should be shown in arriving at the net surplus or deficit under each of the above headings.
Exceptional surpluses or deficits should be disclosed separately.

**24** The directors should explain the basis and the reasons for the amounts appropriated to or from revaluation reserve.

## Classification of changes in the value to the business of an asset

**25** The change in the value to the business of an asset should be dealt with either in the profit and loss account or as a revaluation surplus or deficit in accordance with the following paragraphs.

### Land and buildings

**26** A change in the value of land and buildings held as fixed assets should normally be treated as a revaluation surplus or deficit except that:
(a) depreciation should be charged to the profit and loss account; and
(b) where the basis of valuing land and buildings is changed from:
(i) the open market value for their existing use, or
(ii) the depreciated replacement cost for the building and the open market value for existing use for the bare land,
to the open market value for any alternative use, then the surplus or deficit should be shown in the profit and loss account as an extraordinary item;
(c) where land and buildings are written down to be included in a group of assets for which an economic value is calculated, this write-down should be charged to the profit and loss account (paragraph 284).

## Plant and machinery and other fixed assets

**27** A change in the value of an item of plant and machinery or other fixed asset such that the old and new values are both based on its gross current replacement cost should normally be credited or charged, net of backlog depreciation, as a revaluation surplus or deficit.

**28** A change in the value of an item of plant and machinery or other fixed asset, other than one arising directly from a movement in the gross replacement cost of the asset, should be credited or charged to the profit and loss account, disclosed if appropriate as an exceptional or an extraordinary item.

## Government grants

**29** Any change in the value of a fixed asset resulting from a change in the rate of Government grant receivable should be treated as a revaluation surplus or deficit.

## Stock and work in progress

**30** A change in the value of an item of stock and work in progress such that the old and new values are both on a replacement cost basis should normally be treated as a revaluation surplus or deficit.

**31** A change in the value of an item of stock and work in progress, other than a change resulting from a movement in replacement cost, should be credited or charged to the profit and loss account, disclosed if appropriate as an exceptional or extraordinary item.

## Investments

**32** A change in the value of an investment should be treated as a revaluation surplus or deficit except either:
    (a) where the investment represents liquid funds temporarily invested in which case it should be credited or charged to the profit and loss account; or
    (b) where the treatment of the investment is covered by the section on stocks (paragraph 299).
The exception in (a) relating to liquid funds temporarily invested does not apply to organisations a principal part of whose business is the holding of investments.

## *Inclusion of certain revaluation surpluses and deficits in the profit and loss account*

**33** The profit and loss account should be credited or charged with revaluation surpluses or deficits which can be clearly shown to have arisen as a result of:

(a) the purchase or holding of an asset solely with a view to gaining the benefit of an increase in its market value (paragraph 299 and 179);

(b) a decision to make a significant departure from a normal buying pattern by purchasing stock in advance of normal requirements in order to avoid an expected increase in price (paragraph 300);

(c) the purchase of stock at a price substantially different from the relevant market buying price at the date of purchase (paragraph 301).

The composition of amounts so treated, and the reason for including the amounts as part of the operating result, should be disclosed in a note to the accounts.

## Balance sheet

### Land and buildings

**34** The following paragraphs relate to land and buildings held by both property and non-property companies except where property companies are specifically excluded. The procedures peculiar to property companies are outlined in Part 4 of this Standard.

**35** The value to the business of land and buildings in owner occupation will normally be the open market value for their existing use, plus estimated attributable acquisition costs.

**36** If in the valuer's opinion an open market valuation cannot be made, the value to the business should be the total of the depreciated replacement cost of the buildings and the open market value plus estimated attributable acquisition costs of the bare land for its existing use. This value must be reviewed in the context of the overall profitability of the business activity for which the buildings are used, and if appropriate the land and buildings should be included in the group of assets for which an economic value is calculated.

**37** Land and buildings owned by non-property companies should be valued by a professionally qualified valuer at intervals of not more than five years, and more frequently if:
(a) the assets represent a major proportion of the company's gross assets; or
(b) there have been considerable market variations or major changes in the property assets since the previous professional valuation.

**38** In the years between full-scale professional valuations, the directors should estimate the value of land and buildings after consultation with their professional valuers, taking into account, inter alia, market variations and changes in construction costs.

**39** Where leasehold land and buildings have a negative value (eg because of the onerous provisions of the lease), this should be reflected in the balance sheet either as a provision or as a deduction from the positive value of other leasehold interests.

**40** Any land and buildings owned by companies but not for their own occupation (eg rental producing properties) should be valued at their open market value plus estimated attributable acquisition costs. Land and buildings which have become surplus to the company's requirements and for which there is an intention to sell, should be valued at their open market value less estimated disposal expenses.

## Plant and machinery

**41** Plant and machinery should be shown in the accounts at its value to the business at the balance sheet date. This will be its net current replacement cost except where this is greater than both the economic value and the net realisable value, in which case the value to the business will be the higher of the economic value and the net realisable value.

**42** Where the gross current replacement cost of plant and machinery is estimated by reference to the cost of a substantially identical asset, that cost should be calculated by reference to one or more of the following sources of data. Those listed higher in the order are likely to give a closer approximation to the required figure:
(a) suppliers' official price lists, catalogues etc., with appropriate deductions for trade discounts;

9

(b) the company's own replacement cost estimates, based on expert opinion;

(c) an index compiled by the company from its own purchasing experience;

(d) authorised external price indices analysed by asset type;

(e) authorised external price indices analysed by using industry.

## Disclosure requirements relating to plant and machinery and land and buildings

**43** The statement of accounting policies should disclose the bases on which the company has valued its fixed assets, and the basis on which depreciation has been provided.

**44** There should be separate disclosure of plant and machinery valued at net current replacement cost, economic value, and net realisable value respectively. The gross current replacement cost and the accumulated depreciation to date should be shown for those assets that are valued on the basis of their net current replacement cost. For assets valued at their economic value or their net realisable value, only this net figure should be shown; no attempt should be made to construct and disclose any related gross value.

**45** The value of land and buildings valued at open market value should be disclosed separately from the value of land and buildings which includes buildings valued on a depreciated replacement cost basis.

**46** The tabulated statement of fixed assets should show the assets at their value to the business (disclosing gross values where appropriate) at the beginning and end of the year, additions at cost, the disposal of assets at their value to the business, the depreciation charge for the year and the transfers to and from the revaluation reserve.

## Capital-based Government grants

**47** Methods of accounting for capital-based Government grants which have been established by SSAP 4 should continue to be operated, with certain amendments, under CCA.

**48** Where the assets are shown net of the related grant, the grant receivable at the rate applicable at the date of the valuation should be deducted from the gross current replacement cost of the asset; depreciation should be based on this net-of-grant value. Any surplus or deficit arising on revaluation will also be net of the related grant.

**49** If the grant receivable is credited to a deferred credit account, the remaining balance on this account should be adjusted by transfer to or from revaluation surpluses in line with the revaluation of the related assets or changes in the rate of grant receivable. The deferred credit will be released to the operating profit over the lives of the related assets; this has the effect of reducing the charge for depreciation based on gross asset values to the level of a charge based on net-of-grant asset values.

## Intangible assets (including research and development expenditure but excluding goodwill)

**50** Intangible assets should be shown in the balance sheet at their value to the business only where this value can be established. Where such a value cannot be established, the intangible assets should be written off in the profit and loss account.

**51** Where intangible assets are shown in the accounts, they should be revalued each year and depreciated through the profit and loss account in the same manner as other fixed assets.

**52** The existence of assets for which a quantifiable value cannot be established should be noted in the accounts although no value should be placed on them.

**53** Research and development expenditure carried forward should be valued on a current cost basis. This will normally involve revaluing at current costs the constituent elements of the expenditure in accordance with the appropriate provisions of this Standard. Any excess of this value over the amount which it is expected can be recovered out of future earnings should be written off in the profit and loss account.

# Goodwill

**54** In determining the amount of goodwill arising on a purchase:
(a) the net assets acquired are to be valued at their value to the acquiring entity according to the principles of CCA; and
(b) any shares or loan stock issued as whole or part consideration are to be valued at their market value.

**55** In any year in which an acquisition gives rise to a material amount of goodwill, such goodwill should be disclosed in the accounts, separate amounts being shown for each such acquisition.

**56** No account should be taken of any increase after acquisition in the value of purchased goodwill. No value should be placed in accounts on internally generated goodwill.

**57** The policy adopted by companies for accounting for purchased goodwill should be disclosed and consistently applied.

**58** Goodwill should be shown separately in the balance sheet at cost less amounts written off. Any amount written off should be shown on the face of the profit and loss or appropriation account. The amount written off goodwill in each of the last five years should be shown in a note to the accounts.

**59** It has been a common practice under historical cost accounting to calculate goodwill by reference to the book value of the assets acquired. If, at the time of purchase, the assets had a higher value to the business than their book value the revaluation of these assets and the inclusion of goodwill at the amount recorded in the historical accounts would result in double counting. On changing to CCA any goodwill which is brought forward from the historical cost accounts and which arose initially from a difference between the value to the business of the acquired assets at the date of acquisition and the value used in the computation of such goodwill should be written off against surpluses arising on revaluation. Where this is not practicable and where it is still possible to identify the business originally acquired, the goodwill element may be calculated by reference to:
(a) the net assets of the subsidiary, as shown in the current cost accounts at the time of changeover;
(b) the carrying value of the investment in the subsidiary at the time of changeover.

Where (a) exceeds (b) the balance should be treated as a surplus arising on revaluation. Where (b) exceeds (a) the balance should be deemed to be purchased goodwill and treated accordingly. Any other goodwill brought forward from the historical cost accounts should be treated in accordance with paragraph 58. Any write off of goodwill required by this section should be made in both the consolidated and the holding company's accounts.

**60** On first changing from historical cost accounts to current cost accounts the goodwill element in the purchase price of an investment in an associated company should be calculated by reference to the value to the business of the attributable portion of the net assets of an associated company at the time of the acquisition and the value to the business of the consideration. Where this is not practicable the goodwill element should be calculated by reference to:
(a) the net assets of an associated company, as shown in the current cost accounts at the time of changeover;
(b) the carrying value of the investment at the time of changeover.
Where (a) exceeds (b) the balance should be treated as a surplus arising on revaluation. Where (b) exceeds (a) the balance should be deemed to be purchased goodwill and treated accordingly.

## Investments

**61** For the purpose of the following paragraphs investments include trade investments but exclude subsidiary and associated companies.

**62** The following paragraphs do not deal with businesses which trade in investments with the purpose of making a trading profit on increases in market value. The treatment of investments in this case should be in accordance with the provisions of this Standard on stock and work in progress.

**63** Quoted investments should be valued at their mid-market price. In exceptional circumstances when the directors consider mid-market price to be unrepresentative of the value to the business the directors may use another method of valuation, in which case there must be shown in a note to the accounts:
(a) the value at mid-market price and the reasons the directors consider it to be unrepresentative of the value to the business;
(b) the basis that they have used to value the investment.

13

**64** Unquoted investments should be stated at their value to the business as determined by the directors. This would normally be related to:

(a) the net asset value of the company on a CCA basis; and/or
(b) the value of the stream of income from the investment.

Where in the opinion of the directors, the above is unrealistic they should explain the bases they have used.

Where a material amount of unquoted investments is held the basis of valuation should be stated in a note to the accounts.

**65** A gain or loss in value of an investment which is classified as liquid funds temporarily invested should be credited or charged in arriving at the operating profit.

**66** A gain or loss in value of an investment which is not classified as liquid funds temporarily invested should be included in surpluses and deficits arising from revaluation of assets.

**67** Income from investments should be included in operating profit. The Companies Act 1967 requires that there shall be shown the amounts respectively of income from quoted investments and income from unquoted investments.

## Non-current debtors

**68** Non-current debtors should be valued as hitherto, that is, normally at face value less a provision for any expected losses. Where discounting is the present practice, this should be continued.

## Stock and work in progress

**69** The amount at which stock and work in progress is stated in the balance sheet should be the total of the value to the business, at the accounting date, of the separate items of stock and work in progress or of groups of similar items.

## Liabilities (excluding deferred tax)

**70** (a) Liabilities should continue to be shown on the same basis as hitherto, that is, normally at face value.
(b) Where a liability is also a listed security the value of the outstanding amount, based on the mid-market price at the balance sheet date, should be shown by way of note.

# Taxation

**71** (a) Amounts due in respect of current taxation should be separately disclosed as current liabilities as is the usual practice. (b) Advance Corporation Tax considered to be recoverable should continue to be deducted where possible from the deferred tax account.

# Deferred taxation

**72** Deferred taxation should be accounted for, on the liability method (see paragraph 128), in respect of the tax reduction arising from all originating timing differences of material amount other than any tax reduction which can be seen with reasonable probability to continue for the foreseeable future, either by reason of recurring or continuing timing differences or in the case of revalued assets by the continuing use of the assets or the postponement of liability on their sale.

**73** The potential amount of deferred tax for all timing differences, calculated on the liability method, should be disclosed by way of note, distinguishing between the various principal categories of deferred tax and showing for each category the amount that has been provided for.

**74** Companies which have heretofore taken account of timing differences in the deferred taxation account should, at the time when they change over to current cost accounting, release to a general reserve any part thereof which is not required under paragraph 72.

**75** After a company has changed over to current cost accounting, increases or decreases in the deferred tax provision in respect of accelerated capital allowances, stock relief or rates of tax, should be debited or credited to the current cost profit for the year, where appropriate as an exceptional or extraordinary item. Increases or decreases in deferred tax provisions in respect of revaluations of non-current assets should be debited or credited to the relevant revaluation account.

# Statement showing effect of change in the value of money

**76** The accounts should include a statement, by way of note, setting out prominently the gain or loss for the period of account in the shareholders' net equity interest after allowance has been made for the change in the value of money during the period. In the case of a holding company the note should relate to the group accounts only.

**77** The statement should show:
(a) the net equity interest as shown in the balance sheet at the beginning of the period, plus any amount brought into the accounts in respect of new equity capital introduced during the period, plus, or minus, the amount of the allowance needed to compensate these amounts for the change in the value of money during the period;
(b) the net equity interest at the end of the period before provision for dividends on the equity capital;
(c) the net gain or loss in the net equity interest during the period, being the difference between the amounts referred to in (a) and (b);
(d) the dividends on the equity capital for the year.

**78** An analysis of the gain or loss on holding monetary assets and liabilities during the period should also be provided, showing separately the figures for:
(a) long-term liabilities;
(b) bank overdrafts;
(c) non-equity share capital.

**79** The allowance for the change in the value of money should be made by applying a general price index as follows:
(a) for companies registered in the United Kingdom; the general index of retail prices;
(b) for companies registered in the Republic of Ireland; the official consumer price index.
The name of the relevant index, the figures of the index at the beginning and end of the period, and the base date of the index, should be stated.

# Group accounts, etc.

## Group accounts

**80** Companies should produce consolidated accounts on the basis of CCA as outlined in this Standard. This should be achieved by the subsidiary producing accounts on a CCA basis or if this is not possible by the holding company adjusting the subsidiary's accounts to a CCA basis.

**81** CCA consolidated accounts should not include the accounts of any subsidiary on an historical cost basis unless the effect is not material to a consideration of the total group.

**82** The investment in CCA consolidated subsidiaries should be shown in the holding company's balance sheet at cost plus post-acquisition movements in reserves, less amounts of goodwill written off. There should be shown separately in the balance sheet, or a note to the balance sheet:
(a) the cost of investments in subsidiaries;
(b) the attributable post-acquisition movements in reserves, less amounts written off goodwill.
For this paragraph post-acquisition movements in reserves include, where appropriate, the result of the revaluation on changing to CCA.

**83** The attributable reserves held by subsidiaries should be shown separately either on the face of the holding company's balance sheet or by way of note. The make up of the attributable reserves should be shown, eg revaluation reserve, share premium account etc. Only the dividend receivable from a subsidiary should be included in the holding company's current cost profit as available to be dealt with by the holding company.

## Associated companies

**84** An investment in an associated company should be shown in the consolidated accounts at the applicable proportion of net assets of the associated company shown by its CCA accounts. Where the associated company does not prepare CCA accounts the investing company should adjust the associated company's historical cost accounts to a CCA basis.

17

**85** The goodwill element of the purchase price of an investment in an associated company should be aggregated with goodwill arising on the purchase of subsidiary companies and be treated in accordance with the provisions of this Standard on goodwill and the company's accounting policy for goodwill as stated in the notes to the accounts.

**86** There should be shown separately in the group accounts or a note to the accounts the applicable portion of associated companies':
    (a) operating profit and surpluses and deficits arising on revaluation for the year;
    (b) retained post-acquisition reserves.

**87** In the accounts of the holding company, an investment in an associated company should be shown at cost plus the applicable portion of post-acquisition movements in the reserves of the associated company, less amounts written off goodwill.

**88** The attributable reserves held by associated companies should be shown separately either on the face of the holding company's balance sheet or by way of note. The make up of the attributable reserves should be shown, eg revaluation reserve, share premium account etc. In respect of the current cost profit or loss for the period under review of an associated company only dividends receivable by the holding company should be included in the holding company's current cost profit.

**89** The operation of paragraphs 88 and 60 could result in overstating the value of the investment as it is possible for the goodwill element to be double counted. The necessity of writing down the investment should be reviewed on changing to CCA.

**90** Where an associated company is a quoted company the investment may be valued for the consolidated balance sheet and the holding company's balance sheet at mid-market value at the balance sheet date.

# Overseas assets and operations

**91** The value to the business of assets and liabilities which are located overseas or denominated in an overseas currency should be ascertained in the countries concerned in accordance with the provisions of this Standard and translated into sterling using the rate of exchange at the date of the balance sheet. Translation differences arising from exchange rate movements should be treated as surpluses or deficits arising on revaluation.

**92** Revenue items may be translated using either the closing rate of exchange or the average rate of exchange for the period. Where the average for the period is used the difference arising between the average and closing rate should be treated as a surplus or deficit arising on revaluation.

**93** Overseas tax should be charged to the profit and loss account unless covered by paragraph 75.

**94** Any receipts or payments should be translated at the actual rate of exchange.

## Corresponding amounts

**95** In all published annual accounts prepared in accordance with this Standard, all corresponding amounts for the preceding year should be stated as shown in the previous year's accounts, ie, there should be no adjustments for changes in prices since last year.

## Published information other than annual accounts

**96** The first presentation of figures produced in accordance with this Standard should be in the company's annual accounts. Interim accounts are not suitable for the first presentation of such figures as they do not provide an adequate opportunity to explain their significance. However interim accounts should where relevant include a prominent note indicating that the figures have been calculated on an historical cost basis and that the annual accounts will be on a CCA basis.

19

**97** While the Standard applies only to annual accounts, it is desirable, where practical and as the relevant figures become available, that the practice of providing this information should be extended to include other financial statements such as interim accounts, preliminary announcements of figures of the year, ten year summaries, profit forecasts and prospectuses.

**98** Figures in ten-year summaries should be those shown in the annual accounts for the years in question. The conventions on which they have been prepared (eg historical cost or current cost) should be clearly indicated. It is desirable that for the first year in the summary for which current cost figures are shown, historical cost figures for the same year should also be shown. Any adjustments to these figures for subsequent inflation or changes in prices should be shown separately. Any figures for dividends per share should be shown both as originally stated in the annual accounts for the year in question and also in terms of the purchasing power of the pound at the end of the last year in the summary.

## Transitional arrangement

**99** During the period between the coming into operation of this Standard and the consequential revision of other Standards issued by the ASC, and where there is a conflict between this Standard and other Standards issued by the ASC, organisations whose accounts are within the scope of this Standard at the time should follow this Standard and disclose in a note that they have departed from other Standards (which should be specified) because they have followed this Standard. The appropriate place for disclosure of any such departures from Standards is in the company's statement of accounting policies.

## Special situations

**100** It should be noted that all companies to which this Standard applies are expected to comply with the provisions of Part 4 which contains material thought to apply relatively seldom.

# Part 2 Definitions

## Fixed assets

### Plant and machinery

**101**  In this Standard the term plant and machinery should be taken to include motor vehicles, office equipment, fixtures and fittings, ships and aircraft.

### Gross current replacement cost

**102**  The gross current replacement cost of an asset is the lower of:
(a)  the cost that would have to be incurred to obtain and install at the date of the valuation a substantially identical replacement asset in new condition; and
(b)  the cost of a modern equivalent asset.

### The cost of a modern equivalent asset

**103**  The cost of a modern equivalent asset is the gross current cost of a modern piece of plant and machinery adjusted by the present value of any material differences, compared with an identical replacement, in:
(a)  operating costs over its whole life;
(b)  output capacity, provided that any additional output is usable by the company; and
(c)  total expected useful life.

### Net current replacement cost

**104**  The net current replacement cost of an asset is that part of the gross current replacement cost which reflects its unexpired service potential.

### Economic value

**105**  The economic value of a group of assets is the value of the assets in use in the business and is related to the capital value of their future earning potential.

## Net realisable value

**106**  The net realisable value of a fixed asset is the estimated proceeds from its sale in the open market, less all the costs expected to be incurred in realising the proceeds.

## Professionally qualified valuer

**107**  In the United Kingdom, a professionally qualified valuer is one who is a corporate member of the Royal Institution of Chartered Surveyors, the Incorporated Society of Valuers and Auctioneers or the Rating and Valuation Association, and in the Republic of Ireland, a corporate member of the Irish Auctioneers and Valuers Institute, and has appropriate post-qualification experience of valuing properties in the location and category of the subject properties.

## Property company

**108**  A property company is one whose main business is the holding of property:
    (a)  as an investment to earn rental income at arm's length; or
    (b)  for development and resale or holding after development to
    earn rental income at arm's length,
but if a group of companies, which is not principally a group of property companies, includes a company which owns properties which are let to other group companies, that company should not be regarded as a property company for the purposes of this Standard.

## Depreciation

**109**  Depreciation is the measure of the wearing out, consumption or other loss of value of a fixed asset whether arising from use, effluxion of time, or obsolescence.

## Backlog depreciation

**110**  Backlog depreciation is the additional amount required to raise the sum of the accumulated depreciation at the beginning of any accounting year and the charge for depreciation for that year to the amount required to equal the difference between the gross and the net current replacement cost of an asset at the end of the year.

## Depreciable amount

**111** The depreciable amount is that part of the value of land and buildings which should be subject to depreciation. It is normally equal to the depreciated replacement cost of the buildings, but where the land and buildings are valued at their open market value, the depreciable amount is equal to the lower of:
(a) the depreciated replacement cost of the buildings; and
(b) the open market value plus acquisition costs of the land and buildings together.

## Residual amount

**112** The residual amount is the total value of the land and buildings together, less the depreciable amount.

## Stock and work in progress

### Stock and work in progress

**113** Stock and work in progress comprises:
(a) raw materials and components purchased for incorporation into products for sale;
(b) consumable stores;
(c) products and services in intermediate stages of completion, including labour and overhead costs;
(d) finished goods;
(e) goods and other assets purchased for resale.

### Contract work in progress

**114** Contract work in progress is that which is specific to the requirements of a particular customer as a result of a contract. For this to apply it is necessary for there to be in existence a contract or other documentary evidence, such as a letter of intent, which establishes a contractual relationship between the company and the customer for the provision of the finished products or services concerned. Such work in progress includes:
(a) materials specifically purchased for, or specifically allocated to, the contract work in progress;

(b)  any relevant products or services in intermediate stages of completion, including labour and overhead costs;
(c)  any relevant finished items related to the contract which have not been delivered to the particular customer.

## Value to the business

**115** The value to the business of an item of stock and work in progress is the lower of current replacement cost and net realisable value.

## Current replacement cost

**116** The current replacement cost of an item of stock and work in progress is the cost at which the stock and work in progress could be replaced, at the costs existing at the valuation date, by purchase and processing or manufacture according to the normal method of operation of the company. Where there is normally a material time lag between the placing of an order for purchased materials or services and the date of delivery to the company, the cost of such purchased materials or services to be included in the calculation of current replacement cost is the cost at which they were, or could have been, ordered in the normal course of business for delivery at the valuation date.

## Net realisable value

**117** The net realisable value of an item of stock and work in progress is the actual or estimated selling price of the finished product (net of trade but before settlement discounts) less:
    (a)  all further costs to completion; and
    (b)  all costs to be incurred in marketing, selling and distributing.

## Date of consumption

**118** The date of consumption of stock and work in progress is the date at which the stock or work in progress becomes specific to the requirements of a particular customer as a result of a contract and will therefore usually be the date of delivery to a customer.

## Authorised external price index

**119** An authorised external price index is:
(a) for assets in the UK, a price index published by the UK
Government Statistical Service; or
(b) for assets in the Republic of Ireland, a price index published
by the Central Statistics Office of the Republic of Ireland; or
(c) a price index approved for use in CCA by the Accounting
Standards Committee.

## Statement showing effect of change in the value of money and Monetary assets and liabilities

### Net equity interest

**120** The net equity interest is the equity share capital plus reserves.
Equity share capital is the issued share capital excluding any
part thereof which, neither as respects dividends nor as respects
capital, carries any right to participate in a distribution beyond a
specified amount.
Convertible loan stocks should be treated as liabilities until their
conversion.

### Change in the value of money

**121** The value of money changes in relation to the change in the
quantity of goods or services which can be purchased for a pound.
A measure of this change is the general index of retail prices which
measures the price level of the goods and services purchased by
most households, with respect to a given date, in the form of an
index number.

### Monetary items

**122** These are assets, liabilities, or capital, the amounts of which
are fixed by contract or statute in terms of numbers of pounds
regardless of changes in the value of money.

### Non-monetary items

**123** These are all items which are not monetary items, with the
exception of the net equity interest.

## Long-term liabilities

**124** These are liabilities which are due for settlement more than one year after the balance sheet date.

## Non-current debtors

**125** These are debtors which are not due to be, or likely to be, collected within a year of the balance sheet date.

# Deferred taxation

## Timing differences

**126** Timing differences are differences between profits as computed for taxation purposes and profits as stated in financial accounts which result from the inclusion of items of income and expenditure in taxation computations in periods different from those in which they are included in financial accounts. Timing differences originate in one period and are capable of reversal in one or more subsequent periods. In addition the revaluation of an asset is regarded as creating a timing difference when it is incorporated in accounts.

## Deferred taxation

**127** Deferred taxation is the taxation attributable to timing differences.

## Liability method

**128** The liability method of accounting for deferred taxation is a procedure whereby the taxation effects of timing differences are regarded as liabilities for taxes payable in the future or as assets representing recoverable taxes. These liabilities or assets are subject to future adjustment if taxation rates change or new taxes are imposed.

# Sundry

## Operating profit or loss for the year

**129** The operating profit or loss for the year of a company is its revenue less current expenses, including in those expenses the value to the business of the physical assets consumed during the year, but before interest, taxation, or extraordinary items.

## Current cost profit or loss for the year

**130** The current cost profit or loss for the year is the operating profit or loss for the year after accounting for interest payable and receivable, taxation and extraordinary items.

## Goodwill

**131** Purchased goodwill arises on the purchase by an entity either of a business or of shares in a company which, following the purchase, is a subsidiary or associated company of the acquiring entity. Purchased goodwill is the excess of:
(a) the value of the purchase consideration provided by the acquiring entity over
(b) the value to the acquiring entity of tangible and separately identifiable intangible assets acquired, less the liabilities taken over.
In the event that the transaction involves the purchase of shares, the assets and liabilities referred to in (b) above are those attributable to the shares acquired by the acquiring entity.

## Quoted and unquoted investments

**132** The Companies Act 1967, 2nd Schedule, section 28, defines quoted and unquoted investments as follows:
" 'quoted investment' means an investment as respects which there has been granted a quotation of permission to deal on a recognised stock exchange, or on any stock exchange of repute outside Great Britain, and the expression 'unquoted investment' shall be construed accordingly."
This definition is adopted for this Standard.
Sections 28 of Schedule 6 of the Companies Acts (Northern Ireland) 1960 and (Republic of Ireland) 1963 are consistent with the above section with the exception of the words "Great Britain". The definition should be construed accordingly.
In 1972, The Stock Exchange adopted the nomenclature "listed investment" in place of "quoted investment".

**133** Liquid funds temporarily invested should only include investments which:
(a) can readily be converted into cash; and
(b) were identified at the time of purchase as liquid funds temporarily invested or were identified subsequently as liquid funds temporarily invested.

# Part Three
# Explanatory note

## Profit and loss and appropriation account

### Introduction

**134** The current cost profit for the year is arrived at after charging the current value to the business of the physical assets consumed during the year. It is important when interpreting the results of a company, to consider the surpluses or deficits arising during the year from the revaluation of assets, as well as the current cost profit. These surpluses or deficits are of significance because:

(a) the amounts of revaluations significantly affect the costs used in the calculation of current cost profit;

(b) some companies may be more successful than others in anticipating changes in prices;

(c) the amounts of revaluations will vary in different industries and according to the types of assets held;

(d) gains or losses on foreign exchange translations are included in revaluation changes.

These considerations suggest that the surpluses or deficits in question should be shown as prominently in the accounts as the current cost profit.

**135** The need under CCA to take into consideration the revaluation surpluses and deficits when interpreting the accounts has been recognised by providing that the profit and loss account should be accompanied by an "appropriation account" which brings together: the current cost profit for the year; the net surplus arising from the revaluation of assets; the amount which the directors have decided to appropriate to revaluation reserve; the dividends paid or proposed for the year; and the net balance transferred to or from general reserve.

**136** This treatment recognises that, while the current cost profit provides a more realistic indicator than historical cost profit of the results of the business and of the amount that could be distributed without eroding the capital of the business, it cannot, as the Sandilands Committee accepted, be the final determinant of either. There will be occasions when to distribute the whole of the current cost profit would be to erode the capacity of the business to continue on its existing scale, because, for example, this profit measure makes no allowance for the effect of inflation on monetary assets. There will be other occasions when to restrict dividend distribution to the current cost profit would be unduly conservative, because, for example, a company has its stock effectively financed wholly or partly by trade creditors so that the stock revaluation adjustment is in excess of that required to finance the replacement of stock.

**137** It follows that while there is an initial presumption that the surplus on the revaluation of assets will need to be retained in the business, the directors, on whose shoulders the decision must rest, will decide sometimes to appropriate more or less than this figure to the "revaluation reserve"—the name chosen to indicate that part of the reserves regarded by the directors as not being currently available for distribution having regard to their assessment of the needs of the business. The directors should give their reasons for the amount of the appropriations which they make. The considerations likely to enter into their decisions are discussed in Appendix 2, under the heading of 'Guidelines'.

**138** The distinction made in historical cost accounting between realised and unrealised gains and losses loses much of its significance under CCA, since all assets are carried at their current value to the business. However, it is desirable that a note be provided showing the total surpluses and total deficits included in revaluations arising during the year for each main category of asset. In this way, a major drop in the value of an asset or a group of assets is not obscured by increases in the values of others. Similarly it is desirable that exceptional surpluses or deficits arising on revaluation of assets should be separately disclosed.

**139** The directors naturally have to act within the constraint imposed by the legal precedents relating to distributions and will also have regard to the company's cash position. The relationship between the existing legal precedents and the CCA system of accounting is under consideration.

**140** An example showing how the profit and loss account, appropriation account and the balance sheet could appear under CCA is set out in Appendix 1. These statements will be supplemented by a note to the accounts showing the change in shareholders' net equity interest after allowing for the change in the value of money, an example of which appears in the same appendix.

# Earnings per share

**141** The Accounting Standards Committee, in conjunction with other bodies, is considering the appropriate figure of earnings which would form the basis of the earnings per share calculation.

## Depreciation

**142** The charge to the profit and loss account for depreciation should equal the value to the business of the assets consumed during the period under review. When an asset is valued on the basis of its net current replacement cost, the charge for depreciation for that asset should increase as its gross current replacement cost increases, but it will not normally be practicable to identify within an accounting period each individual price movement and relate the charge for depreciation to such movements. It will therefore normally be necessary for the depreciation charge to be based on average asset values during the period (calculated before charging depreciation for the current period).

**143** Other bases of providing depreciation will be acceptable if they produce a reasonable approximation to the correct charge. For example, where monthly accounts are prepared and the charges for depreciation are based on a monthly updating of asset values, the aggregate of the monthly charges will closely approximate to the theoretically correct charge for depreciation for the year.

**144** Depreciation may be based on the end-of-year values if this is considered to be easier in practice and will not produce a materially different charge for depreciation from one calculated on the basis outlined in paragraph 142. It is not normally appropriate to base annual depreciation charges on asset values at the beginning of the year, because in times of rising prices this would understate the correct charge.

**145** Whichever method is adopted for calculating the charge for depreciation, it should be disclosed in the notes to the accounts, and should be consistently applied.

**146** Where depreciation is based on average values, the charge for depreciation for a period is obtained by apportioning, in accordance with the company's depreciation policies, the asset's average value for the period over the expected remaining useful life of the asset at the beginning of the period. It is important in this context that a realistic assessment is made of the remaining useful lives of a company's assets; for this purpose the estimated lives of its assets should be reviewed regularly—for major assets, preferably annually—so that physical wear and tear and changes in the commercial environment and technology are taken into account on a consistent basis.

## Backlog depreciation

**147** In times of rising prices, the amounts charged in the profit and loss account for depreciation will not be sufficient to accumulate a total provision for depreciation equal to the asset's gross current replacement cost at the end of its useful working life. The accumulated depreciation at the beginning of each year and the charge for depreciation for the year are both likely to be based on values which are lower than the value at the end of the year. The sum of the accummulated depreciation brought forward and the charge for the year will therefore not equal the accumulated depreciation required at the end of the year. The shortfall is called "backlog depreciation" and is charged against the related revaluation surpluses.

## Change in basis of valuation

**148** In a period when the basis of valuing an asset of a group of assets is changed from their net current replacement cost at the beginning of the period to the higher of their economic value or net realisable value at the end of the period, depreciation should first be calculated by the normal method adopted by the company on the assumption of the continuing application of a net current replacement cost basis of valuation. The further write-down required to reduce the resulting net current replacement cost to economic value or net realisable value should either be charged against the operating profit, disclosed if appropriate as an exceptional item, or if more appropriate to the particular circumstances, charged as an extraordinary item. The accounting treatment for the writing down of fixed assets is discussed further in paragraph 175.

## Depreciation of land and buildings

**149** Depreciation will not normally be provided on freehold land, except in special circumstances which will include situations where land is exploitable, as for extractive industries, where it has a limited special use, for example as a chemical waste dump, or where it has a high existing use value on the basis of planning consent for a limited period of time.

31

**150** Depreciation should however be provided on freehold buildings. The amount of depreciation charged against the operating profit should be the estimate of the decline in value attributable to operations. Changes in the value of land and buildings should be dealt with in accordance with the principles laid down in paragraph 177.

**151** Depreciation should be provided on an amount to be advised by the valuer and called the depreciable amount. This will normally be equal to the depreciated replacement cost of the buildings, but where the land and buildings have been valued at their open market value plus costs, the depreciable amount is the lower of the open market value for the land and buildings together and the depreciated replacement cost of the buildings. In the years between full professional valuations, the directors will need to estimate the depreciable amount. This may be estimated by the application of an authorised index of construction costs to the latest figure for the depreciable amount advised by the professional valuer.

**152** To be consistent with the treatment of depreciation of plant and machinery, the charge for depreciation should be based on the average depreciable amount for the period. The situation is complicated by the fact that for buildings no gross current cost is estimated, backlog depreciation is not calculated, and the value on which depreciation is based does not itself necessarily appear in the balance sheet. For simplicity, the depreciation charge may be based on the depreciable amount at the accounting date and a period equal to the expected economic useful life of the buildings at that date. This period is taken in contrast to the corresponding period for plant and machinery (see paragraph 146) because the depreciable amount is already net of the depreciation charge for the current accounting period. The valuer, after consultation with the directors, will advise on the expected economic useful life of the buildings.

**153** Depreciation of leasehold land and buildings will be required on both the depreciable amount and the residual amount. If the valuer, after consultation with the directors, estimates that the remaining economic useful life of the buildings exceeds the remaining term of the lease, the entire value of the land and buildings should be written off over the remaining term of the lease. Where the remaining economic useful life of the buildings is estimated to be less than the remaining term of the lease, the valuer will advise on his view of that remaining life and on a depreciable amount for the buildings. The depreciable amount should be written off over the estimated remaining economic useful life. The residual amount—i.e. the total value of the leasehold land and buildings less the depreciable amount, should be written off over the remaining term of the lease.

**154** For both freehold and leasehold buildings, repairs and maintenance expenditure should be charged to the profit and loss account in the normal way. Expenditure on the improvement of buildings should be charged to the asset account; to the extent that such expenditure does not enhance the value of the buildings, it will effectively be charged against the revaluation surpluses when the buildings are next revalued. The division between capital and revenue of expenditure on buildings should be made on the basis of accepted principles.

## Disposals

**155** The strict application of the principles of CCA would require that when an asset is sold or scrapped, the profit and loss account should be charged with depreciation, where applicable, for the period from the previous balance sheet date to the date of disposal and that an adjustment should be made through the fixed asset revaluation reserve for other changes in value. Where this adjustment is not material, the difference between the sale proceeds and the value to the business at the previous accounting date may be charged or credited, as appropriate, to the profit and loss account within the charge for depreciation. If the sale proceeds are materially different from the asset's value at the previous accounting date, depreciation should be calculated for the period to the date of sale, and the remaining balance on the asset account should be treated in accordance with the provisions of paragraph 179.

## Cost of sales

**156** The charge for cost of sales for a period should include the value to the business, at the date of consumption, of stock and work in progress consumed during the period. As a result of the application of this general principal the profit and loss account for the period will normally be charged with the replacement costs which would be incurred in replacing the stock and work in progress consumed.

**157** The date of consumption of stock and work in progress is the date at which the stock or work in progress becomes specific to the requirements of a particular customer as a result of a contract and will therefore usually be the date of delivery to a customer.

**158** The value to the business of an item of stock and work in progress should normally be measured as the lower of the cost at which it could be replaced (current replacement cost) and the net realisable value. In order to match current costs and current revenue, the current replacement cost of stock and work in progress should normally be the cost at which at the date of consumption it was, or could have been, replaced by the normal method of operation of the company. The current replacement cost will therefore comprise the current cost of purchased items together with the current cost of manufacture, processing and other expenses incurred in the normal course of business in bringing the product or service to its location and condition at the date of consumption. Such current costs will include all related production overheads even though these may accrue on a time basis.

## Calculation of the current cost of sales

**159** The charge for cost of sales for a period should include the value to the business, at the date of consumption, of stock and work in progress consumed during the period. The method adopted to calculate the value to the business of stock and work in progress consumed will depend upon the nature of the stock and of the accounting system. The most accurate calculation will be obtained by valuation of each item of stock and work in progress consumed at its current value to the business. For this purpose similar items may be grouped together.

**160** If a standard costing system is in force it may be possible to derive the current value to the business by updating the standard costs to current costs by reference to the current level of cost variances from the standard; the current replacement costs thus obtained should then be compared with net realisable values.

**161** Where the current value of stock and work in progress can be determined accurately at the time of consumption and is charged to cost of sales no further adjustment to the cost of sales is necessary. The difference between the current value and the recorded value of stock and work in progress consumed should normally be recorded as a revaluation surplus or deficit.

**162** However, where stock includes a large number of different items, or where work in progress comprises numerous different elements of material, labour and overhead, the detailed valuation of each item at the lower of current replacement cost and net realisable value may cause considerable difficulties. In these circumstances it may be necessary to adopt a simpler method of calculation which will result in an acceptable approximation to the current cost of sales and this may involve the use of an index of cost movements to revise to current cost a cost of sales determined on another basis. Where the current cost of sales is determined by use of an index of cost movements it is recommended that the averaging method be used; the averaging method is discussed in paragraphs 165-170.

**163** Where an index of cost movements is employed in the calculation of the current cost of sales it should reflect as accurately as possible the changes in costs experienced by the company. Thus an internal index of current cost may be maintained where this would be more appropriate than an authorised external index of stock prices or where use of the latter could give a misleading result. In this event, the internal index should be used in preference to an authorised external index.

**164** From the above discussion of the possible methods of calculating the current cost of sales it follows that the sources of data used in the calculation of the current replacement cost of stock and work in progress consumed may be set out in descending order of preference as shown below; in principle the nearest possible approximation to the actual current replacement cost should be used but in selecting the appropriate method and sources of data consideration should be given to materiality and the cost of the calculation:

(a) the costs currently being incurred by the company at the date of consumption for the various cost elements, ie purchased materials and services, labour and overheads;
(b) for purchased items where no relevant materials or services have been purchased at or near the date of consumption, suppliers' official price lists, catalogues etc., with appropriate deductions for trade discounts;
(c) an index compiled by the company from information on its cost of purchases and on its labour and overhead costs; where the costs of identifiable elements of stock and work in progress have changed at materially different rates a separate index should be prepared for each element;
(d) an authorised external price index for the costs of each type of stock used by the company or for the costs of stocks of companies in the relevant industrial category.

## The averaging method

**165** The objective of the averaging method of calculating the current cost of sales is to charge stock consumed at the average current cost during the period. For this purpose the value of opening stock is converted to the average current cost during the period; the total of purchases and other costs incurred during the period is left unaltered; the value of closing stock is converted to the average current cost during the period. By using the converted values to calculate the cost of sales any increase, or decrease, in stock volume between the beginning and end of the period will be credited or charged to the cost of sales for the period at the average current cost during the period.

**166** The average current cost during the period may be estimated as the average of the unit cost at the beginning and end of the period; however, where the change in unit costs has not occurred evenly throughout the period, it will be more appropriate to calculate the average current cost during the period more accurately.

**167** This method will produce an acceptable approximation to the current cost of sales where stock volumes have been reasonably constant, or have changed at a fairly steady rate, throughout the period. Therefore, where this method is used, the charge to cost of sales should be calculated at the most frequent intervals practicable, for example on a monthly basis, since the inaccuracies which may result when this condition does not hold will thereby be minimised.

**168** Where the average current cost of stock can be determined from the accounting system it should be used, but where this cannot be done the changes in the current cost of stock should be determined by reference to the most appropriate authorised external price index. Where the costs of identifiable elements of stock and work in progress have changed at materially different rates during the period the calculation should, where possible, be made separately for each element using the cost index movements appropriate to each element.

**169** The current costs of stock consumed determined by this method should be compared with the net realisable values of the stock consumed.

**170** An example of a calculation using the averaging method is included for illustrative purposes in Appendix 3.

## Accounting treatment of the cost of sales adjustment

**171** Where a cost of sales adjustment is calculated to revise to current cost a cost of sales determined on another basis, it should be added to or, where appropriate, deducted from the cost of sales charged to the profit and loss account for the period and included as part of the surplus or deficit arising on revaluation of stock.

## Interest

**172** It has been argued that interest on borrowing implicitly assumes an element to compensate the lender for the effect of inflation on his interest and capital and that this element should be matched in the borrower's accounts against the benefit he obtains during inflation from capital gearing by being charged to the revaluation reserve. It can similarly be argued that an element of interest received should be credited to revaluation reserve.

**173** The logic behind these arguments is recognised but their practical application would raise the problem of determining how much of a particular interest payment (if any) reflected compensation for inflation and would also be inconsistent with the proposed treatment of gains and losses on monetary items.

**174** It is considered, therefore, that the net figure of interest paid and interest received should be shown separately in the profit and loss account as a deduction from, or addition to, the operating profit for the year, and that the separate amounts of interest paid and received should be disclosed in a note to the accounts.

## Changes in the value to the business of fixed assets

### Plant and machinery

**175** In accordance with existing practice, changes in the value of plant and machinery, other than changes resulting from a movement in the gross current replacement cost of the asset, should be credited or charged to the profit and loss account, disclosed if appropriate as exceptional or extraordinary items. These changes will include those resulting from:
    (a) the depreciation charge;

(b) a change in the basis of valuation—eg from net current replacement cost to economic value or net realisable value;
(c) subsequent changes in the economic value or net realisable value.

**176** Changes, net of backlog depreciation, in the gross current replacement cost of plant and machinery should normally be treated as revaluation surpluses or deficits. Such changes will include those resulting from:

(a) the adoption as the gross current replacement cost of the cost of a modern equivalent asset;
(b) the introduction or withdrawal of a Government grant, or a change in the rate of grant.

## Land and buildings

**177** Changes in the value of land and buildings held as fixed assets should normally be treated as revaluation surpluses or deficits except:

(a) those resulting from depreciation, which should be charged to the profit and loss account;
(b) where the basis of valuing land and buildings is changed from:

(i) the open market value for their existing use, or
(ii) the depreciated replacement cost for the buildings and the open market value for existing use of the bare land, to the open market value for any potential use, in which case the revaluation surplus or deficit should be shown in the profit and loss account as an extraordinary item.

## Other fixed assets

**178** The same general rules as those which underlie the particular rules for plant and machinery and land and buildings should be applied to the changes in value to the business of other fixed assets. The depreciation of these assets will always be charged to the profit and loss account; changes in value to the business as a result of movements in the gross replacement cost should be treated as revaluation surpluses or deficits; other changes in value should be charged or credited to the profit and loss account, disclosed if appropriate as exceptional or extraordinary items.

## Profits and losses on disposal

**179** Any material balance, representing a profit or loss on disposal, left on an asset account after following the procedure outlined in paragraph 155 should be credited or charged to the profit and loss account, disclosed if appropriate as an exceptional or extraordinary item, except where the profit or loss can be shown to have arisen as a result of a movement in the replacement cost of the asset since its previous revaluation, in which case the balance should be treated as a revaluation surplus or deficit. However, if a fixed asset is taken out of service and held by the company with the intention of taking advantage of expected movements in its net realisable value, the surplus or deficit eventually arising on disposal should be credited or charged to the profit and loss account.

## Stock and work in progress

**180** A change in the value to the business of an item of stock and work in progress such that the old and new values are both based on replacement cost should normally be treated as a revaluation surplus or deficit.

**181** A change in the value to the business of an item of stock and work in progress, other than a change resulting from a movement in replacement cost, should be credited or charged to the profit and loss account, disclosed if appropriate as an exceptional or extraordinary item. Therefore a change in the value to the business of an item of stock and work in progress resulting from wastage, losses, damage, obsolescence or a write-down from current replacement cost to net realisable value, should be charged to the profit and loss account for the period in which it arises.

## Balance sheet

### Fixed assets: general

**182** Current cost accounting requires that assets be stated in the accounts at their value to the business and that the operating profit be struck after charging the value to the business of assets consumed in earning that profit. It is thus necessary to revalue fixed assets and to base depreciation charges on the revalued amounts. The accounting treatment of the changes in value arising from the revaluation of fixed assets is discussed in paragraphs 175 to 179.

**183** The value to the business of assets is their deprival value—
ie the maximum amount of the loss that would be suffered by the
company if it were deprived of the assets concerned.

**184** The loss suffered by a company on being deprived of an asset
can be estimated from three viewpoints:
  (a) the cost of replacing the asset in its existing condition (its
  net current replacement cost);
  (b) the loss of the future earning potential of the asset (its
  economic value); and
  (c) the loss of the estimated net sales proceeds (its net
  realisable value).

**185** In the absence of evidence to the contrary, it may be assumed
that an asset will continue in profitable use for the remainder of its
useful working life. In such circumstances, the economic value will be
the greatest value, but the deprival value will not be the economic
value since the earning potential can be maintained by the
replacement of the asset in its existing condition. The maximum loss
in these circumstances is therefore the net current replacement cost,
and this will be the most common method of arriving at an asset's
value to the business. The circumstances in which it is appropriate to
value assets at their economic value or net realisable value are
considered in Part 4 of this Standard.

## Land and buildings

**186** Land and buildings are normally held by companies for one or
more of the following reasons:
  (a) for owner occupation, to be used in earning the profits of
  the business;
  (b) as an investment to earn rental income at arm's length;
  (c) for development and resale or holding after development to
  earn rental income at arm's length.
A company which is substantially engaged in the second or third of
the above activities is defined for the purpose of this Standard as a
"property company". The general rules outlined in the paragraphs
which follow relating to the valuation of land and buildings
also apply, except where specifically excluded, to the land
and buildings owned by property companies. The procedures
peculiar to property companies are considered in Part 4 of this
Standard. If a group of companies, which is not principally a group of
property companies, includes a company which owns properties

which are let to other group companies, that company should not be regarded as a property company as defined.

**187** In this Standard, "land" is not accorded its strict legal definition, but means bare, undeveloped land; "buildings" is taken to mean any structural (as distinct from agricultural) improvement to bare land, and this will include, for example, hard standing or sewers even though these would not normally be considered to be "buildings".

**188** It is acknowledged that a number of the terms used in this Standard in relation to land and buildings differ from those familiar to valuers of property in Scotland, but no difficulty should be encountered in recognising the equivalent in Scottish practice. As there is no freehold property in Scotland, the division corresponding to that between freehold and leashold will be between feuhold and leasehold.

**189** As with plant and machinery, the deprival value of land and buildings can also be considered from the viewpoint of their net current replacement cost, economic value or net realisable value, although owner-occupied land and buildings in isolation cannot normally be accorded an economic value as discussed in Part 4 of this Standard, since they do not give rise to a separate identifiable cash flow. The net current replacement cost of land and buildings should not normally be considered to be the cost of rebuilding in the existing state the existing buildings on the same plot of land, but should be regarded as the cost of buying a similar property on the open market, since this would be the likely course of action if the owner were to be deprived of the property.

**190** Thus in normal cases the value to the business of land and buildings will be the open market value for their existing use plus the estimated attributable acquisition costs, which should be taken to include stamp duty, legal costs and any agents' fees. Land and buildings should be valued free and clear of any mortgage liability attaching to them. In these Explanatory Notes the term "open market value plus costs" should be understood to include the estimated attributable acquisition costs.

**191** "Open market value", "existing use", "alternative use" and "depreciated replacement cost" have the meaning given in the draft guidance notes issued by the Royal Institution of Chartered Surveyors to its members in November 1976. This statement may be consulted as it gives the explanatory background to these terms.

**192** "Existing use" does not necessarily require that the property be valued on the basis of the actual trade being carried on in the buildings. Many buildings are general-purpose structures capable of being used, virtually unaltered, for a number of different trades; such buildings should be valued on the basis of their common use— eg as a light industrial factory, or as office accommodation.

**193** Where an open market valuation for a property cannot be prepared owing to the specialised nature of the buildings, their particular use, their location, or otherwise, the value of the property should be calculated as the sum of:

    (a) the open market value plus costs of the bare land for its existing use, and

    (b) the depreciated replacement cost of the buildings.

The depreciated replacement cost of the buildings will be based on the valuer's estimate of the current replacement cost of the buildings and of the extent to which this should be reduced to take into account the physical wear and tear of the existing buildings and their obsolescence. An estimate will need to be made of the remaining economic useful life of the buildings, and to this end the valuer will need to consult with the directors because the maximum physical life of the buildings might be greater than the technological life of the process being carried out within them; in such cases the shorter life should be used in the calculation of the depreciated replacement cost.

**194** Where land and buildings are valued on the basis outlined in paragraph 193, the value should be reviewed by the directors in the context of the overall profitability of the activity in which the land and buildings are employed. This is comparable with the economic value of plant and machinery, and is discussed in Part 4 of this Standard.

**195** The valuation of land and buildings owned by non-property companies should be prepared by a professionally qualified valuer at intervals of not more than five years and more frequently if:

    (a) these assets represent a major proportion of the company's gross assets, or

    (b) there have been considerable market variations or major changes in the property assets since the previous professional valuation.

**196** A company which employs professionally qualified internal valuers will not need to commission a full external valuation of all its land and buildings in order to satisfy the requirement of a periodical professional valuation, although an external valuation of at least a sample of the land and buildings will be required, except in some cases of buildings valued on a depreciated replacement cost basis, in order to substantiate the internally prepared valuation.

**197** In a year when a professional valuation of particular properties is not undertaken, the directors should estimate their value after consultation with their professional valuers. Estimates of the value of groups of properties will have to take into account not only market variations, but also the value of additional properties acquired, additions to and the refurbishment of existing buildings, changes in use, demolition, abandonment and disposal. These estimates should be supported by evidence which can be independently verified of such matters as changes in local property values or in construction costs.

**198** Any land and buildings which have become surplus to the company's requirements and for which there is an intention to sell, should be valued at their net realisable value—ie their open market value less disposable expenses. Land and buildings owned by companies but not for their own occupation, should be valued at their open market value, which will include their value for any potential use, plus costs. These holdings will include income-producing properties and properties acquired against possible but uncertain future requirements.

**199** The valuer should state in his report his opinion of the alternative use value of the land and buildings where this is materially different from the existing use value. An alternative use value normally implies a net realisable value—ie the estimated sale proceeds less all disposal costs. Where material, an estimate of these costs should be made and deducted from the valuation advised by the valuer, and the resulting net value should be reported in the Directors' Report (in accordance with Companies Act 1967 Section 16(1)(a)) where it materially exceeds the existing use value.

## Leasehold land and buildings

**200** Leasehold land and buildings should be valued on the same principles as freehold land and buildings. Where material, their value should be introduced into the accounts even where no premium was originally paid for the leasehold interest, or where there has been no other capital expenditure incurred. A negative value should be reflected in the balance sheet either as a provision or as a deduction from the positive value of other leases.

## Land and buildings in the course of development

**201** Land and buildings in the course of development should be valued at the lower of:
(a) the aggregate of the open market value plus costs of the bare land and the current replacement cost of the construction work completed at the date of valuation, and
(b) the estimated open market value at the date of the valuation, plus costs, of the land and buildings as if the development were complete, less the estimated costs, current at the date of the valuation, required to complete the development.

**202** Where, because of the nature of the buildings, the land and buildings will not have an open market value when completed, the second of the alternative methods of valuation in paragraph 201 will not be appropriate, and the land and partially completed buildings should be valued on the basis of the first alternative.

**203** As noted in paragraph 194, where land and buildings are valued on the basis of the depreciated replacement cost of the buildings plus the open market value of the bare land, rather than the open market value of the land and buildings together, their value should be reviewed in the context of the overall profitability of the activity in which they are employed. This review should also be extended to land and buildings in the course of development valued on the basis of the first of the above alternatives.

## Plant and machinery

**204** The term "plant and machinery" should be taken to include motor vehicles, office equipment, fixtures and fittings, and, where the context allows, ships and aircraft.

## Gross current replacement cost

**205** The net current replacement cost of an asset is derived from its gross current replacement cost, which is the lower of:
(a) the current cost of a substantially identical asset in new condition; and
(b) the cost of the modern equivalent asset.

**206** Normally it will be appropriate to calculate the gross current replacement cost on the basis of the cost of a substantially identical asset. However where there has been marked technological advance so that it would in practice be more economical for a company to replace the existing asset with an alternative replacement rather than a substantially identical one, it will be appropriate to reflect the effect of the advent of a technologically improved alternative asset on the value of the existing asset owned and to reduce the gross current replacement cost to the lower cost of the modern equivalent asset.

**207** The cost of the modern equivalent asset is obtained by adjusting, as explained in Part 4 of this Standard, the gross cost of an alternative replacement which incorporates modern technology, for material differences, compared with a substantially identical asset, in potential output, operating costs and useful life.

**208** Companies should aim to establish the actual gross cost of a substantially identical asset as precisely as is reasonably practicable; this will involve giving consideration to the use of the following data sources. Those listed higher in the order are likely in most cases to give a closer approximation to the required figure. In selecting the appropriate methods, companies should have regard to the materiality and cost of valuation; it is expected that in valuing their various fixed assets most companies will wish to use more than one of the data sources:
   (a) suppliers' official price lists, catalogues, etc, with appropriate deductions for normal trade discounts;
   (b) the company's own replacement cost estimates, based on expert opinion;
   (c) an index compiled by the company from its own purchasing experience;
   (d) authorised external price indices analysed by asset type;
   (e) authorised external price indices analysed by using industry.
Whichever methods are adopted, they should be based on documented objective evidence and be capable of independent verification.

**209** As regards methods (d) and (e) above, in the Republic of Ireland separate indices for asset types or using industries are unlikely to be available.

**210** If price indices are used, their source should be disclosed in the notes to the accounts.

## Net current replacement cost

**211** The net current replacement cost will be gross current replacement cost less the sum of the accumulated depreciation at the beginning of the period, backlog depreciation (see paragraph 147) and the depreciation charge for the period under review. The net current replacement cost therefore reflects the diminution in the gross current replacement cost of an asset due to wear and tear and obsolescence, so that it represents the value of the unexpired service potential of the asset.

## Plant and machinery in the course of construction

**212** Plant and machinery in the course of construction by a company for its own use should be valued at the current replacement cost of the work completed at the date of the valuation. If there is evidence indicating that on completion the value to the business of the asset will be considerably less than its gross current replacement cost, it should be written down to its value as if it were complete less the estimated costs, current at the date of the valuation, required to complete its construction.

## Capital-based Government grants

**213** SSAP4 requires that grants relating to fixed assets be credited to revenue over the expected useful life of the related assets either:
    (a)  by reducing the cost of acquisition of a fixed asset by the amount of the grant, or
    (b)  by treating the amount of the grant as a deferred credit, a portion of which is transferred annually to revenue.

**214** It is consistent with the concept of deprival value for a grant potentially receivable at the date of a valuation to be taken into account in arriving at the value to the business of an asset at that date.

**215** The first of the two methods outlined in paragraph 213 of treating Government grants can be more easily modified to take into account the requirements of CCA, and for this reason it is recommended. Under this method, the gross current replacement cost will effectively be net of the grant receivable at the rate applicable at the date of the valuation; depreciation should be based on this net-of-grant value. Any surplus or deficit arising on revaluation will also be net of the related grant.

**216** The same result may also be achieved if grants receivable are credited to a deferred credit account, although this method of accounting is more complicated in practice. Adjustments to the remaining balance on the deferred credit account arising through the revaluation of the related assets or changes in the rate of grant should be treated as revaluation surpluses or deficits. Depreciation will be based on the gross value of the asset, but this charge will effectively be reduced to a charge based on the net-of-grant value by releasing the deferred credit to the operating profit over the life of the related asset.

**217** Any change in the value to the business of an asset as a result of a change in the rate of grant receivable should be transferred to or from the revaluation reserve. If the rate of grant falls, resulting in an increase in the value to the business of the affected assets, it may be necessary to consider whether the net current replacement cost is still the appropriate basis of valuation and whether the assets' values should be written down to their economic value. This consideration is necessary whichever method of accounting for the grant has been adopted.

## Procedure in the year of introducing CCA

**218** On the initial introduction of CCA there may be assets still in use which have been fully written off and others where the remaining book value does not reflect a realistic estimate of the remaining useful life. CCA requires a realistic value to be placed on these assets, the requisite net adjustment to the gross value of the assets and their accumulated depreciation being treated as a revaluation surplus.

## Intangible assets (including research and development expenditure but excluding goodwill)

**219** CCA requires a current value to be placed on all assets, tangible or intangible, owned by a business, and for the profit and loss account to be charged with the value of those assets consumed during the year.

**220** Owing to the uniqueness of each intangible asset, the replacement cost approach to its valuation is not appropriate; it would have to be valued, if at all, on the basis of its economic value or net realisable value.

**221** If a value for an intangible asset can be established, this should be reported in the balance sheet, revalued each year and depreciated through the profit and loss account in the same way as is appropriate for tangible fixed assets which are valued on the basis of their economic value or net realisable value.

**222** There will be some intangible assets for which a current value cannot be established. Since it is inappropriate to include such assets in current cost accounts at their historical cost as this cost may bear no relationship to their current value, they should be written off to the profit and loss account.

**223** If a value for intangible assets cannot be introduced into the accounts because of the lack of objective evidence of their value, the existence of the assets should be noted in the accounts although a value should not be placed on them.

**224** Research and development expenditure which it is permissible to carry forward under the provisions of ED17 should be revalued at current cost, so that the profits of subsequent accounting periods are charged with the current cost of the research and development expenditure previously undertaken. The constituent elements of the research and development expenditure—normally fixed assets, materials and labour costs—should be revalued according to the guidelines laid down in this Standard. Where the resulting value is higher than the amount which it is expected can be recovered out of future revenues, it should be written down to that amount by way of a charge to the profit and loss account.

## Goodwill

**225** The appropriate accounting treatment of goodwill has been continually debated. This Standard does not attempt to resolve this debate, but limits itself to giving guidance on the adjustments made necessary by the introduction of current cost accounting.

**226** The CCA concept implies that all assets should be shown in the balance sheet at their value to the business. It could therefore be argued that:

(a) any goodwill arising on purchase should be shown in all subsequent balance sheets at its current value to the acquiring business;

(b) internally generated goodwill should be included in accounts at its value to the business.

The balance sheet would then be a full statement of the value to the business of all assets both tangible and intangible. The total net assets would therefore represent the directors' estimate of the value of the business. This would represent a major change from established accounting practice and has been rejected on the grounds that it would introduce too great a degree of subjective judgement into the preparation of the balance sheet.

**227** Following the rejection of (a) and (b) in paragraph 226 this Standard excludes the revaluation of purchased goodwill and requires that internally generated goodwill should not be valued in the accounts. The value to the acquiring entity at the time of purchase of the assets acquired and the consideration given should be used to calculate the value of purchased goodwill. Purchased goodwill should be shown in the balance sheet at cost less amounts written off.

## Investments

**228** For the purpose of the following paragraphs investments include trade investments but exclude subsidiary and associated companies. The treatment of businesses which trade in investments for the purpose of making a trading profit from increases in market value is covered in paragraph 299 of this Standard.

**229** The general principle underlying the valuation of investments is that they should be included in the balance sheet at their value to the business. In the case of quoted investments this would normally be the mid-market price, on the grounds that this is normally a reasonable estimate of economic value. There will be exceptions to this general rule where it is apparent the mid-market price does not give a reasonable representation of the value to the business. In these cases the directors should value the investment at its value to the business stating by way of note the mid-market value, the reasons why they do not regard this as representing the value to the business, and the basis that they have used to value the investment.

**230** In principle unquoted investments should be valued in the same manner as quoted investments. This would be at their estimated market price less a discount for non-marketability. Such an estimate would normally be determined by reference to:

    (a) the applicable proportion of the net assets of the company as determined on a CCA basis, and/or

    (b) the value of the stream of income from the investment.

**231** Changes in the value of an investment should be treated as a surplus or deficit arising on revaluation, unless the investment represents liquid funds temporarily invested. An investment can be classified as liquid funds temporarily invested only if the investment:

    (a) can readily be converted into cash; and

    (b) was identified either at the time of purchase or subsequently as liquid funds temporarily invested.

Gains or losses on liquid funds temporarily invested should be credited or charged to the operating profit.

## Non-current debtors

**232** Whether discounting should be applied to non-current debtors as a general rule raises questions which cannot be settled quickly. It is therefore considered that non-current debtors should be valued as hitherto, that is, normally at face value less a provision for any expected losses. Where discounting is the present practice, this should be continued.

## Stock and work in progress

**233** Stock and work in progress should be stated in the balance sheet at its value to the business at the balance sheet date.

### Value to the business

**234** The value to the business of an item of stock and work in progress should normally be measured as the lower of the cost at which it could be replaced (current replacement cost) and its net realisable value. Economic value is not normally appropriate as a separate criterion for the value to the business because stock and work in progress is not normally used in the business over a period of time to generate a flow of income but is held for sale or for incorporation into a finished product to be sold at a future date. Therefore the net realisable value will normally represent the economic value.

**235** The comparison of current replacement cost and net realisable value needs to be made separately in respect of each item of stock and work in progress. Where this is impracticable, groups or categories of items which are similar will need to be taken together. To compare the total net realisable value of stock and work in progress with the total current replacement cost could result in an unacceptable setting off of amounts by which net realisable value falls short of current replacement cost against current cost operating profits which have not yet been earned; as a consequence the value to the business of stock and work in progress could be overstated.

## Current replacement cost

**236** The current replacement cost of stock and work in progress should normally be the cost at which it could be replaced at the balance sheet date by the normal method of operation of the company.

## Net realisable value

**237** The net realisable value of an item of stock and work in progress is the estimated proceeds of sale of the finished product less all further costs to completion and less all costs directly related to the item in question to be incurred in marketing, selling and distributing; future costs should be included in this calculation at the actual amounts expected to be incurred.

**238** Thus where an item of stock is stated at net realisable value, if the estimate of sale proceeds and further costs is accurate no profit or loss or surplus or deficit will arise in future periods.

## Calculation of the value to the business for balance sheet purposes

**239** The order of preference of sources of data for the calculation of the current cost of sales which is listed in paragraph 164 applies also for the calculation of the value to the business at the balance sheet date. Where the current cost of sales is determined by a method using an index of cost movements it will normally be appropriate to use a similar method to determine the balance sheet value.

**240**  Where a standard costing system is in force it may be possible to determine the current replacement cost at the balance sheet date by updating the standard costs to current costs by reference to the current level of cost variances from the standard. Alternatively, the current replacement cost may be estimated by applying an appropriate index of cost movements to an initial valuation on another basis; for example, stock recorded on a first in, first out basis using actual historical costs incurred can be restated by indexation to its current cost. The current replacement costs obtained should be compared with net realisable values.

## Liabilities (excluding deferred tax)

**241**  The problems of applying a value to the business approach to liabilities include such matters as the determination of the value of non-marketable debentures and loans; whether rises or falls in the value of liabilities caused by changes in the market interest rate structure should be differentiated from those due to alterations in the market's assessment of the company's earnings expectations and risk, and, if so, how the two effects can be separated; whether a discounting procedure should be applied to trade creditors and other short-term liabilities; and to what extent unrealised gains and losses arising from changes in the value of liabilities should be shown in the profit and loss account and to what extent in reserves as revaluation surpluses or deficits.

**242**  These matters call for extended study and this, together with the view that simplicity of treatment is important, has led to the conclusion that on practical grounds no change should be made, for the time being at least, in existing practice of showing liabilities.

**243**  It is considered, however, that the value of those liabilities which are listed securities should be calculated on the basis of the current mid-market quotation and shown by way of note. This would provide an approximate indication, on an objective basis, of the amount for which the company could rid itself of the liability.

## Deferred taxation

**244**  Corporation tax in the UK is at present based on profits calculated by reference to historical cost. There are however certain allowances (such as capital allowances of up to 100% in the first year and stock relief) which, although in form are related to historical cost profits, may be regarded by a going concern as being in substance something different. For example, a going concern with a continuing programme of capital expenditure exceeding its depreciation charges may argue that the capital allowances are more akin to replacement cost or current cost depreciation than historical cost depreciation. Likewise a going concern may argue that stock relief allows a cost of sales adjustment in the tax assessment somewhat akin to the adjustment under current cost accounting rather than a transitory and refundable relief. In such a going concern, the probability that receipt of these allowances or reliefs will give rise to a subsequent liability may be argued to be small or remote (except in the case of a change in tax law which itself could be argued to be an event to be accounted for at the time of change). This probability decreases in a period of rapid inflation. Current cost accounting differs in principle from historical cost accounting in being a current value system of accounting, in which the aim is to represent as fully as reasonably possible the commercial reality of the situation to which it refers. With a change to current cost as the basis of accounting there is, therefore, a narrowing of the difference between the basis of accounting and the substance of the tax allowances and reliefs. It has been concluded that for current cost accounting under the present tax system, or under one where assessments are based more closely on current cost concepts, SSAP 11 requires modification so as to give recognition to the substance of the allowances and reliefs. The modifications are explained in more detail below but, broadly speaking, provisions for deferred taxation should not be required where a future liability is not reasonably foreseeable.


**245** Having regard to the principle of value to the business involved in current cost accounting, it is also a matter for consideration whether amounts provided for deferred taxation should be discounted. If SSAP 11 were to apply without other modification (ie full application to all timing differences) then discounting would be an important matter for consideration having especial regard to the large amounts involved and the remoteness of liability. However, in view of the conclusion that SSAP 11 should be modified for CCA purposes to a probability basis rather than a comprehensive basis, the importance of discounting deferred tax is reduced. Having regard also to the conclusion elsewhere in this Standard that liabilities should not normally be discounted at this stage of development of CCA, it is likewise concluded that deferred tax balances (arising from SSAP 11 as now modified for current cost accounting by this Standard) should not be discounted.

**246** With UK and Irish tax law as they stand at present, the following broad types of timing differences emerge:

(a) 'Short-term' timing differences usually arising from the receipts and payments basis adopted in the determination of taxable profits compared with the accruals basis applied in accounts; examples are the temporary disallowance of a provision until such time as the relevant liability arises or expenditure is incurred, and the taxing of interest when received rather than as accrued;

(b) differences from accelerated capital allowances available at the option of the taxpayer;

(c) differences from stock relief;

(d) differences from revaluation of non-current assets—of especial significance under CCA which requires the revaluation of assets on the basis of value to the business.

## 'Short-term' timing differences

**247** Deferred taxation should continue to be provided for in full on 'short-term' timing differences. SSAP 11 requires no modification in this respect.

## Accelerated capital allowances

**248** In many businesses timing differences arising from accelerated capital allowances are of a recurring nature, and reversing differences are themselves offset, wholly or partially, or are exceeded, by new originating differences, thereby giving rise to continuing tax reductions or the indefinite postponement of any liability attributable to the tax benefits received. An example of a recurring timing difference situation is that arising when a company having a relatively stable or growing investment in depreciable assets takes tax relief year by year on capital expenditure of an amount which equals or exceeds the additional tax which would otherwise have been payable in consequence of the original timing difference. There may on the contrary be cases where timing differences are not recurring, mainly because of a spasmodic or highly irregular pattern of capital expenditure, which may indicate that a liability in subsequent years should be provided for in full.

**249** It is therefore appropriate that in the case of accelerated capital allowances, provision be made for deferred tax except in so far as the tax benefit can be expected with reasonable probability to be retained in consequence of recurring timing differences of the same type. The assessment of reasonable probability in these cases should be made in the light of the current intentions of the directors and of the company's expectations and plans for the future viewed in relation to the historical pattern of capital expenditure.

## Stock relief

**250** Under CCA, if the current price level of stock held rises, the relevant part of the rise in value is included in the charge to the profit and loss account as the stock is used. The corresponding credit is to a revaluation reserve. If the tax system were to be based on the method of CCA, tax would be chargeable on the CCA profit and no timing difference would arise. Where the price level of stock falls, the cost of sales adjustment is a credit to the profit and loss account, withdrawn from the revaluation reserve, and again the tax remains in step with the profit.

**251** Under the existing tax system, stock relief, while not exactly matched with this rise or fall in the cost of sales, will tend to move with it when stock price levels change, so that tax will be approximately matched with profit. This suggests that a deferred tax provision is not appropriate under CCA.

**252** This match of tax with profit under CCA may not always hold under the existing tax system since volume changes can also give rise to relief or withdrawals of relief. It is considered however that it is not consistent with the CCA approach to impose a requirement to provide for deferred tax in all cases such that tax charges would normally fail to match profit.

**253** However, circumstances may arise where a fall in stock volume can be expected. It is considered, therefore, that provision should be made for deferred tax on stock relief to the extent that the tax saving cannot be expected with reasonable probability to continue. (It is noted in this context that a volume change in stock which leads to a withdrawal of relief automatically generates a cash flow sufficient to provide for the tax in question.)

**254** In the case of companies registered in the Republic of Ireland, stock relief claimed under the Finance Act 1976 (Republic of Ireland) should be regarded as a deferral of taxation.

## Revaluation of non-current assets

**255** Where non-current assets are written up in the accounts a subsequent sale may give rise to a tax charge consisting of either or both of the following:

(a) a capital gain, taxed at the effective rate applicable to chargeable gains;

(b) a balancing charge, or the restriction by an equivalent amount of future claims for capital allowances on other assets—this would represent a tax charge or forfeiture of tax relief at the rate applicable to income.

In the case of a going concern these liabilities will generally be remote because of the continuing replacement of the assets in the business and the availability of roll-over and similar relief on realisation of the gain.

**256** It is considered, therefore, that the general principle of reasonable probability should apply. Provision for tax on the revaluation surplus should be made on this basis where the asset or assets concerned are expected to be disposed of within the foreseeable future and an ensuing liability to taxation will arise.

## Liability method

**257** The practical effect of these rules, based on probability and the value to the business basis of CCA, is for the deferred tax balance to be regarded as a liability rather than a deferred credit.
Accordingly the balance should be maintained at current rates of tax.

## Monetary assets and liabilities

**258** Any profit concept carries with it a concept of maintenance of "capital" or "substance" of the enterprise. The fact that the system recommended by the Sandilands Committee does not provide for the real maintenance of the associated monetary working capital or of any liquid resources held while awaiting investment or to meet contingencies, has led to a view that the system is inadequate and that the results of enterprises with different mixes of assets and liabilities, and different capital gearings, will not be comparable under it. A particular objection is that the system will lead to a serious overstatement of the profits of institutions such as banks that by their nature must always have a net surplus of monetary assets, and, on the other hand, will understate the profits of companies which finance a large part of their stock by trade credit. It is also argued that the system is defective because it does not distinguish the effect of the change in the value of money.

**259** These criticisms have been countered by the argument that, unlike the corrections for depreciation and cost of sales under CCA, the above matters can be detected, and their effects calculated or estimated, by those who use the published accounts, and that the introduction into the main accounts of adjustments for them will bring undue complications into the interpretation of the new system and prevent an effective trial of the latter.

**260** Proposals considered have included the indexation of net monetary assets, the indexation of all monetary items but excluding from current profit any resultant "gains" on long-term liabilities, the application of a "stock adjustment" to trading debtors and creditors (including cash in the case of banks), and the crediting to current profit of holding gains in proportion to the gearing of the company. It has however been found impossible to achieve a reasonable degree of agreement on these matters, all of which have been put to a wide range of field testers.

**261** It is evident that there is a widespread difference of opinion. It has been decided to adopt a simplified version of the system outlined in the CCAB "Initial Reactions" to the Sandilands recommendations which provides for a supplementary statement to be annexed to the main accounts. It compares total opening and closing net assets as valued on the current cost basis after putting both on to the same basis in real terms (ie allowing for the change in the value of money) by use of a general price index. Insofar as these valuations give a satisfactory assessment of the net assets at their respective dates the statement thus provides a final figure of total growth or decay in terms of net assets that is comparable for different companies with the same accounting dates and can be rapidly adjusted for comparisons where the accounting dates differ. It is a combination of all gains and losses whether realised or unrealised with respect to historical cost. It is proposed that the statement should take the form of a prominent note to the accounts (see Appendix 1).

**262** This solution is proposed as a working method which is likely to secure the greatest measure of common support for the immediate future until further experience has been obtained, and on the more specific grounds that the required statement:

(a) is relatively easily prepared;

(b) provides information on profitability that is considered by a substantial body of opinion to be relevant and important;

(c) does not compromise the effective trial of the new system;

(d) incorporates figures for any gain or loss on net monetary liabilities or assets, analysed into its main constituents.

**263** It is considered that the adoption of this system should be regarded as a step in the development of accounting practice and not as a final stage. The Accounting Standards Committee will maintain continuing study in this area. In particular, regard will be had to the possibility of further development of the form in which the information in the statement is presented, or alternatively of its abandonment, according to what the evidence on its merits and demerits may in due course suggest.

# Group accounts, etc.

## Group Accounts

**264** No new principles are involved in the preparation of consolidated accounts for a group on a CCA basis. Under historical cost accounting the consolidated accounts are produced by aggregating the historical cost accounts of the subsidiaries and the holding company and eliminating intra-group balances and profits. The same procedure should be adopted for CCA. The problems arising are of a practical nature. It may not be possible or practicable for the subsidiary to produce current cost accounts. In these circumstances the holding company should adjust the historical cost accounts of the subsidiary to a CCA basis for consolidation purposes.

**265** The accounts of the holding company are often regarded as being relatively unimportant. However, the Companies Act 1948 requires that the balance sheet of the holding company be included in the published accounts. It is one of the fundamental principles of CCA that assets should be shown at their value to the business at the balance sheet date. The investment in a subsidiary should be shown at its cost plus or minus post-acquisition movements in the applicable portion of the reserves of the subsidiary less amounts of goodwill written off.

# Associated Companies

**266** The accounting treatment of investments in associated companies under historical cost accounting is laid down in SSAP 1. The basic principles underlying SSAP 1 are appropriate to current cost accounting, and the relevant paragraphs in the Standard on current cost accounting should be interpreted as adapting SSAP 1 to CCA.

**267** It is inappropriate to include historical cost figures in current cost accounts. Where the associated company cannot produce current cost accounts the investing company should adjust the associated company's historical cost accounts to a CCA basis.

# Overseas assets and operations

**268** Based on the principle that assets should be shown in the balance sheet at their value to the business at the balance sheet date, the most appropriate method of dealing with overseas assets and operations is to ascertain their value in the country concerned in accordance with the provisions of this Standard and then translate at the closing rate of exchange. Differences arising on the translation should be treated as surpluses or deficits arising from revaluation. Where a branch or subsidiary cannot produce current cost accounts, the head office or holding company should adjust the historical cost accounts to a CCA basis and then translate.

**269** It is suggested that there are two main alternative methods of translating revenue items:
    (a) the closing rate;
    (b) the average rate for the period, the resulting difference being treated as a surplus or deficit arising on revaluation.
It is thought that the adoption of either method is consistent with CCA, and this Standard therefore leaves the choice of method to each organisation.

**270** The requirement in paragraph 37 that a valuer should be professionally qualified does not mean that a valuer of overseas assets should necessarily be qualified as defined in paragraph 107.

**271** As noted in ED16 the subject of foreign currency translation is one "on which conflicting opinions are strongly held and it must be expected that some time will elapse before a standard is issued which will describe the method or methods of accounting to be applied". Paragraphs 91 to 94 of this Standard should be regarded as an interim measure.

## Corresponding amounts

**272** When introducing a new system of accounting it is prudent to have a period of parallel running during which figures under the old and new system are both produced. Two questions need to be settled:

(a) for how long should historical cost figures be published; and

(b) which historical cost figures should be published.

**273** It is the Steering Group's view that the period of parallel running should be kept to as short a period as possible in order to minimise the work-load of companies and the possible confusion as to which are the true figures. It believes, therefore, that full historical cost figures should be published for the first two years that an organisation's accounts are published in accordance with this Standard. Such historical cost figures should be prepared in conformity with Statements of Standard Accounting Practice based on the historical cost convention and should be audited.

**274** It is however probable that the EEC's Fourth Directive will require historical cost figures to be published for the indefinite future. In the last published draft (Supplement 6/74—Bulletin of the European Communities) it is proposed that the differences should be disclosed between the revalued and historical cost amounts for fixed assets and stock together with the resulting additional value adjustments, eg additional depreciation provisions. The Steering Group understands that the current drafts continue to require such detailed disclosure of differences for all items in the balance sheet.

**275** The Steering Group would welcome comments on the usefulness of such historical cost information and on the work-load on companies of producing it in addition to current cost accounts.

# Part 4 Special situations

**276** The material in this Part of the Standard is thought to apply relatively seldom. It has, therefore, been segregated from Parts 1, 2 and 3 in order to make those parts more easily readable. However, all companies and other organisations to which this Standard applies are expected to comply with the provisions in this Part.

## Fixed assets

### Modern equivalent asset

**277** As indicated in Part 3 of this Standard the gross current replacement cost of an asset is the lower of the gross current cost of a substantially identical replacement and the cost of a modern equivalent asset. If there has been marked technological advance so that the current cost of an identical replacement gives an unrealistically high value for the existing asset, it may be appropriate to estimate the cost of a modern equivalent asset.

**278** A modern alternative asset will incorporate current technology which may produce material differences in capital cost, output, operating costs or useful life and therefore cannot be regarded as a direct alternative to the existing asset. To estimate the cost of the modern equivalent asset, the gross capital cost of the modern alternative asset should be adjusted by:

(a) the present value of any material differences in operating costs over its whole life;

(b) any material differences in output capacity, as long as any increased output from the modern machine is usable by the company; and

(c) material differences in the total life of the modern machine, compared with the substantially identical replacement.

It may be appropriate in certain circumstances to consider the cost of a modern piece of machinery which has similar capacity to that of a battery of existing assets, or, more unusually, to consider the cost of a group of modern machines which would replace the capacity of one existing machine.

**279** If no reasonable estimate, supported by actual experience, can be made of the adjustments to the gross cost of the modern asset required to arrive at the cost of a modern equivalent asset, the gross current cost of the existing asset should be considered to be the cost of a substantially identical asset in new condition, or an estimate of what this would be if one were available.

**280** Where the existing machine has considerable excess capacity and this situation is expected to continue indefinitely, eg where there has been a decline in the market for the output of the machine or group of machines being valued, the net current replacement cost of the existing large-capacity machine will be an unrealistic assessment of its value to the business. In these circumstances, the existing machine should be valued at the net current replacement cost of the smallest machine which would provide the business with the capacity which is justified by market conditions foreseeable over the remaining life of the present machine.

## Economic value and net realisable value

**281** In exceptional cases the net current replacement cost basis of valuation may yield unrealistically high figures for the value of some assets. In these circumstances, the maximum loss suffered were the company to be deprived of those assets would be the higher of their economic value and their net realisable value, and this will be their value to the business.

**282** The use of economic value should normally be restricted to the following circumstances:

(a) where there is an intention that a group of assets should continue in use or be available for use in the business;

(b) cash flows applicable to the group of assets can be separately identified; and

(c) the current and foreseeable cash flows are, in the opinion of the directors, insufficient to justify the replacement of the capacity in any form were the company to be deprived of the assets.

**283** In these circumstances, the economic value of the group of assets may be estimated by reference to the present value of expected future cash flows. This value, by its very nature, depends on informed managerial opinion but this must be based on supporting evidence capable of review by the company's auditors. In estimating the present value of future cash flows, regard should be paid to the following guidelines:

(a) the cash flows should be reasonably foreseeable both as to amount and timing and should include appropriate allowances for expected price changes;

(b) an appropriate rate of discount to be applied in arriving at

the present value of future cash flows would be the particular company's money cost of capital ie the estimated or actual rate at which the company could raise finance in the market for the same period as the cash flows are anticipated;
(c) cash flows and the cost of capital should normally be calculated before taking into account the incidence of taxation; this treatment will produce values on a basis consistent with that of other assets valued at net current replacement cost or net realisable value.

**284** As noted in paragraph 194, an economic value approach may be appropriate for land and buildings where an open market value cannot be ascertained. It is necessary in these circumstances for the value of the land and buildings to be reviewed in the context of the profitability of the activity being carried out inside the buildings. The land and buildings should therefore be included in the group of assets for which a cash flow is identified and for which an economic value is calculated. When this occurs, the value of the land and buildings should be added to the net current replacement cost of the plant and machinery with which it is to be grouped, and the aggregate value should be written down to the group's economic value by charging the profit and loss account. The economic value thus embraces both plant and machinery and land and buildings; any apportionment of this value between the constituent items can only be done on an arbitrary basis.

**285** It is expected that there will not be many occasions on which the net realisable value of a group of assets exceeds their economic value. It may occur, however, when:
(a) there is a decision to dispose of an asset before the end of its useful working life; or
(b) the asset is reaching, or has reached, the end of its useful working life, in which case the net realisable value will be its net scrap value.

**286** Depreciation, where appropriate, of assets valued at their economic value or net realisable value should be based on these assets' average value for the period.

## Leased assets

**287** Paragraphs 288 to 296 do not apply to the valuation of leasehold land and buildings which is considered in Parts 1 and 3 of this Standard.

**288** Two types of leases should be distinguished:
(a) a finance lease, or full pay-out lease—under which the asset is leased for a period considered to be the whole useful life of the asset and during which the rentals receivable are sufficient to amortise the lessor's capital outlay and to show a profit; in such circumstances the lessor often has no expertise in the assets being leased;
(b) an operating lease—under which the rentals receivable in the primary rental period are not expected to be sufficient to amortise the lessor's capital outlay, and he is dependent for his profit on the residual value of the asset at the expiry of the lease. He may then dispose of the asset or enter into a new lease, possibly with a different lessee. The lessor in these circumstances often has expertise in the assets concerned.

## Operating leases

**289** No special treatment is considered necessary for operating leases. The asset acquired by the lessor should be revalued each year and depreciated through the profit and loss account in the normal way. The lessee will charge against his operating profit, as an expense, the rental payments under the terms of the lease.

## Finance leases: the lessor

**290** The asset owned by the lessor should not be regarded as the asset which is the subject of the leasing agreement, but as a right to a stream of income represented by the rental payments determined by the lease agreement. The current value of this income stream—the asset's economic value—should be calculated using as the discount rate the rate of return implicit in the lease.

**291** The reduction year by year in the economic value will be determined by the rate of discount used, and should be charged against the rental income received in arriving at the operating profit. It will not be appropriate to provide depreciation on the current value of the asset which is subject to the leasing agreement.

**292** The economic value of the asset at any subsequent accounting date may be calculated by the lessor using either the original rate of discount or the rate of return implicit in leases currently being negotiated. Any change in the economic value as a result of using a different rate of discount from that previously applied, should be treated as a revaluation surplus or deficit.

## Finance leases: the lessee

**293**  Since the lessee has the constructive, if not the legal, ownership of the asset, he should show in his accounts:
  (a)  the net current replacement cost of the asset; and
  (b)  the liability for the payments due under the lease.

**294**  The asset will be treated in the accounts of the lessee in the same way as other fixed assets; it will be revalued annually and depreciated according to the normal rules.

**295**  As the rental instalments are paid, the liability should be appropriately reduced, the reduction being credited to the operating profit thereby reducing the rental paid to an amount which approximates to the interest element of the instalment. In addition, depreciation based on the current replacement cost of the asset will be charged to the profit and loss account.

**296**  The notes to the accounts on fixed assets should identify the value, where material, attributed to leased assets.

## Property companies

**297**  In view of its significance in the accounts of property companies, it is particularly important that the value at which land and buildings are stated in the accounts is fair. The whole of a property company's property portfolio should therefore be professionally valued every year on a consistent basis and as close as is practicable to the year end, and a full external valuation of all the land and buildings owned should be carried out at least every third year. If in the years between the full external valuations the property portfolio is valued by the company's internal professionally qualified valuers, an external valuation of at least a sample of the land and buildings will be required in order to substantiate the internally prepared valuation.

**298**  A company which is involved in developing, by itself undertaking the construction work, its own land for resale, should be considered as a construction company and not a property company in this context. The property assets of construction companies will normally be held as trading stock and should be dealt with under the provisions of this Standard which relate to stock of land and constructions.

## Stock and work in progress

Inclusion of certain revaluation surpluses and deficits in the profit and loss account

**299** In some cases the whole business of a company, or an identifiable part thereof, consists of the purchase of assets solely with a view to gaining the benefit of an increase in their market value thereby enabling a surplus to be realised; examples of this are investment dealing and certain commodity dealing activities. If the profit and loss account is charged with the current replacement cost of such assets at the date of sale, the result of the operations would be recorded largely, or wholly, as a revaluation surplus or deficit and little or no operating profit or loss would be recorded. Since such treatment would not properly reflect the nature of the activities of the business the relevant amounts should instead be treated as operating profits and losses.

**300** A similar position will arise in the event that a trading or manufacturing company makes a significant departure from its normal buying pattern by purchasing stock in advance of normal requirements in order to avoid an expected increase in price. In these circumstances to charge cost of sales with the current replacement cost at the date of consumption would result in the gain or loss arising from the departure being recorded as a revaluation surplus or deficit and not as part of the operating profit or loss. In order to reflect properly the nature of the gain or loss resulting from the departure it should be included in the profit and loss account. However, this treatment presupposes a departure from normal buying patterns and thus it is essential that such decisions should be clearly recorded by management at the time of purchase together with details of the date(s) at which the purchases would normally have been made.

**301** There may also be instances where stock is purchased at a price substantially below, or above, the relevant market buying price at the date of purchase. In such circumstances, and for the same reasons as set out in paragraph 300 above, the difference between the actual purchase price and that market price at the date of purchase should be reflected as an operating profit or loss and not as a revaluation surplus or deficit. There is a similar requirement as to proper evidence being recorded, at the time of purchase, both of the stock concerned and the price at which, in normal circumstances, it would have been purchased.

**302** Where one or more of the circumstances outlined in paragraphs 299 to 301 can be clearly shown to exist, the total of the relevant surpluses or deficits should be included in the profit and loss account. The composition of the amounts so treated, and the reasons for including the amounts as part of the operating result, should be disclosed in a note to the accounts.

## Goods purchased for resale which are turned over rapidly

**303** Goods purchased for resale should be valued in the balance sheet at the lower of current replacement cost and net realisable value. This requirement may cause difficulties where there is a large number of rapidly changing individual items, for example goods purchased for resale held by merchants, retailers and stockists. In many such cases stock has previously been stated in the balance sheet at current selling price less the normal gross profit margin; this approach is acceptable where it is the only practicable method of arriving at a figure for balance sheet purposes which approximates to the value to the business.

**304** Alternatively, for balance sheet purposes only, if the stock turnover rate is sufficiently fast the FIFO (first in, first out) method of valuation may provide an adequate approximation to current replacement cost, but this should be used only where there has not, on average, been a change of price levels during the period the goods have been held in stock which would be likely to result in a material difference between the FIFO value and the current value to the business.

**305** The requirement to charge cost of sales with the value to the business at the date of consumption may also cause difficulties. It will not normally be practicable to attempt to calculate the revaluation surplus or deficit on each individual item of stock sold where there is a rapid turnover so that each item of stock is held for only a short period. However, the rate of stock turnover will not affect the total revaluation surplus or deficit arising during a period because the total revaluation surplus or deficit depends only upon the volume of stock held and the change in unit value of stock during the period. In these circumstances it may be necessary for the cost of sales adjustment, required to revise to current cost a cost of sales determined on another basis (eg FIFO), to be calculated using the averaging method or a similar method. The indices used in such a calculation should be representative of the changes in current cost of suitable categories of stock.

## Contract work in progress

**306** The date of consumption of stock and work in progress is the date at which the stock or work in progress becomes specific to the requirements of a particular customer as a result of a contract. Therefore the date of consumption will usually be the date the finished goods are delivered to a customer.

**307** Work in progress on standard products: in many cases work in progress represents intermediate stages of production of goods which are standard products of the company and which, when completed, could be sold in the normal course of business to a number of alternative customers. In these circumstances the finished product becomes specific to the requirements of a particular customer, and is therefore consumed, only when it is delivered to the customer. The date of consumption is therefore the date of delivery.

**308** Contract work in progress: for some companies work in progress may represent an intermediate stage of production of a product, or a service, which is specific to the requirements of a particular customer and which is significantly different from any standard product of the company. This work in progress may not be available for inclusion in products which could be sold to customers other than the particular customer concerned; an example of an industry where this situation frequently occurs is the construction industry. In these circumstances, the date of consumption of the work in progress will arise before the completion of the finished product and the treatment described in paragraphs 311 to 316 below should be applied.

**309** Some manufacturing companies produce substantial items which, although incorporating elements which may be specific to the requirements of a particular customer, conform largely to a standard pattern. Work in progress on such items may not fall within the description given in the preceding paragraph because the item may not be significantly different from items being produced for other customers. Where the normal period of manufacture of such items is lengthy it is frequently the case that the majority, if not all, of such work in progress has been undertaken to fulfil contracts with various customers. In these circumstances it is appropriate on practical grounds to treat such work in progress, to the extent that it is covered by contracts with customers, as contract work in progress.

**310**  Where work in progress is specific to the requirements of a particular customer as a result of a contract it is not appropriate to treat the work in progress as part of the trading stock of the company. Such work in progress possesses the characteristics of a monetary asset, value for which will be received only from the customer to whose requirements the finished product is being produced, and should be treated as contract work in progress.

**311**  In the circumstances described in paragraphs 308 to 310 the date of consumption of the contract work in progress, being the date at which the work in progress becomes specific to the requirements of a particular customer as a result of a contract, will normally arise before completion or delivery of the finished goods or services. In this case the charge for cost of sales should be made when the sale is recorded and not at the date of consumption.

**312**  The value to the business of work in progress incurred before the date of consumption should be determined at the date of consumption in accordance with the normal rules, and costs incurred after that date should be recorded at the actual amounts incurred. Where appropriate, the total resultant value to the business should be reduced to net realisable value.

**313**  Where costs have been incurred prior to the date of consumption a revaluation surplus or deficit may arise. For example, if stock held as part of general stock is specifically allocated to the contract work in progress it should be charged to the work in progress at its value to the business at the date of allocation; a revaluation surplus or deficit will arise where this value to the business differs from the purchase cost of the stock concerned. Otherwise, costs incurred on the contract work in progress, including labour costs and related production overheads, should be charged to the work in progress at the actual costs incurred.

**314**  The intention of the method of accounting defined above for contract work in progress is to treat such work in progress as a monetary asset. No adjustment is to be made to the value of a monetary asset other than to write it down to net realisable value if appropriate.

**315**  Where an item of plant or machinery is purchased specifically for the purpose of undertaking a particular contract, and it is not intended that the item will continue in use by the company after completion of the contract, the accounting treatment of the item should be consistent with that adopted for other elements of the contract work in progress. The value to the business of the contract work in progress should therefore include an amount based on the purchase cost of the item rather than its current value.

**316** The amount at which contract work in progress is stated in the balance sheet should be its value to the business at the accounting date. The charge to cost of sales at the date of sale of the finished product should include the value to the business determined in accordance with the foregoing rules.

## Stock of land and constructions held as trading stock

**317** Stocks of land and constructions comprise land held for development and resale, and completed construction work or sites which are in the course of development. In order to have regard to the normal method of operation of the company it will usually be necessary to determine the value to the business of the land and of the construction work separately.

**318** The current replacement cost of the land, including land which has been developed or is in the course of development, is the open market value of the bare land, plus estimated attributable acquisition costs, ignoring any development work which has taken place. The current replacement cost of the construction work should be calculated by reference to the normal method of operation of the company. In the case of developed sites, or a site in the course of development, the current replacement cost of each plot or separate part of the site should include a relevant proportion of the current replacement cost of any common construction work such as access roads or sewage facilities.

**319** The value to the business of a developed site, or a site in the course of development, should be determined as the total of the open market value of the bare land, plus acquisition costs, and the current replacement cost of the existing construction work or, if lower, the net realisable value based upon an estimate of the open market value of the completed development as at the anticipated date of completion. Where a site constitutes contract work in progress the principles explained in paragraphs 311 to 316 should be applied.

**320** The amount at which stock of land and constructions held as trading stock, and work in progress on such sites, is stated in the balance sheet should be the total of the value to the business, at the accounting date, of the separate sites. When such stock is consumed, the charge for cost of sales should be the value to the business at the date of consumption.

## Purchased seasonal agricultural produce

**321** Where stock includes purchased agricultural produce which becomes available only on a seasonal basis it may not be possible to determine an appropriate current replacement cost if such stock is consumed over a lengthy period following the date of purchase. In some cases it may be possible to purchase the produce at the date of consumption in a preserved form, or to purchase the produce from a later crop which may have different characteristics or emanate from a different geographical area. However, if such purchases do not conform to the normal method of operation of the company, the current replacement cost should not be determined by reference to the cost at which such purchases could be made. In these circumstances the value to the business of the produce stock should be calculated at the lower of the unit cost of bulk purchases made from the most recent relevant harvest and net realisable value.

**322** This treatment may not adequately reflect any changes in the cost of such produce from one crop to the next. Where this is so, consideration may be given at the year end by the directors of the company to the retention of additional amounts based on an estimate of the replacement costs which will be incurred.

**323** The amount at which purchased seasonal agricultural stock is stated in the balance sheet should be its value to the business at the accounting date. The charge for cost of sales for consumption of such stock should be the value to the business of the stock at the date of consumption.

## Consumable stores

**324** The revaluation of consumable stores to current replacement cost would not normally result in a material adjustment. Unless the adjustment would be material they should be valued at cost (or net realisable value if this is likely to be lower). Consumable spares, jigs, fixtures and loose tools are sometimes treated as stock. Where such items are not of substantial value in relation to the business they should normally be valued at cost (or net realisable value if this is likely to be lower). Where major items of substantial value are concerned these should be valued at their value to the business.

## Stock sold on hire purchase or credit sale terms

**325** Where stock is delivered to customers on hire purchase or credit sale terms it is subject to the terms of the hire purchase or credit sale contract and becomes specific to the particular customer from the date of delivery. Therefore the date of consumption is the date of delivery and the value to the business of stock sold under such agreements is that ruling at the date of delivery. The amount stated in the balance sheet for stock sold on hire purchase or credit sale terms, and the charge to cost of sales for consumption of such stock, should be based on the value to the business of the stock at the date of consumption.

# Part 5 Note on legal implications

## United Kingdom

**326** The Steering Group is discussing with the Department of Trade and with the legal profession the legal implications of the introduction of CCA for Company Law and the Law of Contract.

**327** The disclosure requirements of this Standard are not intended to override exemptions from the disclosure requirements of the Companies Acts, available to and utilised by special classes of company under Part III of the Second Schedule of the Companies Act 1967, under Part III of the Sixth Schedule of the Companies Act (Northern Ireland) 1960, and applicable to companies incorporated outside the United Kingdom under Section 4(3) of the Companies Act 1967.

## Republic of Ireland

**328** Discussions are taking place with the Department of Industry and Commerce and with the legal profession on the legal implications of the introduction of CCA for Company Law and the Law of Contract.

**329** The disclosure requirements of this Standard are not intended to override exemptions from disclosure requirements of the Companies Act available to and outlined by special classes of company under Part III of the Sixth Schedule of the Companies Act 1963.

## Appropriation to revaluation reserve with respect to Irish companies

**330** In the case of companies registered in the Republic of Ireland or Northern Ireland, the appropriation to revaluation reserve will have to take into account any amounts to be transferred to capital reserve as defined in the Sixth Schedules of the Companies Act 1963 (Republic of Ireland) and the Companies Act (Northern Ireland) 1960.

## EEC

**331** Discussions are taking place as to the compatibility of the requirements of this Standard with the proposals of the draft Fourth and other relevant Directives.

## Other overseas countries

**332** The Steering Group is exploring the question of the compatibility of the requirements of this Standard with the requirements of the SEC of the USA, and of other overseas countries.

# Appendix 1. Example of presentation of set of CCA statements

This appendix does not form part of the Statement of Standard Accounting Practice. The methods of presentation used are illustrative only and in no way prescriptive and other methods of presentation may equally comply with the Standard.

(Comparatives are not shown in this example although they would normally be shown as stated in the previous year's accounts).

# X. Ltd. and its Subsidiaries
# Year ended 31st December, 197 .
# Consolidated Profit and Loss Account

|  | See Note | £000s | Paragraph in Standard |
|---|---|---|---|
| Turnover |  | X |  |
| Operating profit/(loss) for the year | 1. | X | 129 |
| Interest payable less receivable |  | X | 17 |
|  |  | X |  |
| Share of profits/(losses) of associated companies |  | X | 86 |
| CURRENT COST PROFIT/(LOSS) BEFORE TAXATION AND BEFORE EXTRAORDINARY ITEMS |  | X |  |
| Taxation | 2. | (X) | 20 |
|  |  | X |  |
| Minority interest |  | (X) |  |
| Current cost profit/(loss) before extraordinary items |  | X |  |
| Extraordinary items (net of tax and minority interest) | 3. | X |  |
| CURRENT COST PROFIT/(LOSS) FOR THE YEAR |  | X | 130 |

(Paragraph in Standard: } 7 spanning from turnover through to current cost profit for the year)

# Consolidated Appropriation Account

| | | | |
|---|---|---|---|
| Current cost profit/(loss) for the year |  | X |  |
| Net surplus for year on revaluation of assets | 4. | X |  |
| Appropriated to revaluation reserve* | (X) | X |  |
| Available for distribution and general reserve |  | X |  |
| Dividends |  | (X) |  |
| Added to/(deducted from) general reserve |  | X |  |

(Paragraph in Standard: } 22)

* This transfer is the amount of the net surplus that the directors consider should be retained having regard to the needs of the business: it may exceed or be less than the net surplus. The directors should explain the basis and the reasons for amounts transferred, (see paragraph 24 and Appendix 2).

# X Ltd. and its subsidiaries
# Balance Sheet at 31st December, 197 .

|  | See Note | Group £000s | Company £000s | Paragraph in Standard |
|---|---|---|---|---|
| ASSETS EMPLOYED: |  |  |  |  |
| Fixed assets | 5. |  |  | 44/46 |
| Interest in subsidiaries | 6. |  |  | 82 |
| Interest in associated companies | 7. |  |  | 84 |
| Other investments | 8. |  |  | 63/64 |
| Intangible assets (including goodwill) | 9. |  |  | 50-53/58 |
|  |  |  |  |  |
| Net current assets |  |  |  |  |
| Stock and work in progress |  |  |  | 69 |
| Debtors |  |  |  | 68 |
| Cash |  |  |  |  |
|  |  |  |  |  |
| Creditors |  |  |  | 70 |
| Current taxation |  |  |  | 71 |
| Short-term borrowings |  |  |  | 70 |
| Dividends |  |  |  |  |
|  |  |  |  |  |
| FINANCED BY: |  |  |  |  |
| Issued share capital |  |  |  |  |
| Share premium account |  |  |  |  |
| Revaluation reserve | 10. |  |  |  |
| General reserve |  |  |  |  |
|  |  |  |  |  |
| Minority interests |  |  |  |  |
| Deferred taxation | 11. |  |  | 72-75 |
| Long-term loans | 12. |  |  | 70 |

# Matters arising from application of the Standard which should be included in notes to the accounts

Paragraph
in Standard

ACCOUNTING POLICIES:
The statement of accounting policies should refer to:
(a) the basis of valuation of fixed assets;   43
(b) the basis on which depreciation is provided;   43
(c) the basis of accounting for purchased goodwill.   57

(1) OPERATING PROFIT:
The composition and reasons for including certain
revaluation surpluses or deficits as operating
profits or losses should be disclosed.   33

(2) TAXATION:
The note, in addition to providing the information required by
the Companies Acts, should also give an analysis of the taxation
charge showing the amounts debited/credited in arriving at:

              Current cost profit    £000s    21/75

              Extraordinary items

              Surplus on revaluation of
              non-current assets

(3) EXTRAORDINARY ITEMS AND EXCEPTIONAL ITEMS:
These should be disclosed as required by SSAP6.

## (4) SURPLUS (DEFICIT) ARISING FROM REVALUATION OF ASSETS:

|  | Total £000s | Minority Interest £000s | Net £000s | Surplus £000s | Breakdown of net figure in (Deficit) £000s | Paragraph Standard |
|---|---|---|---|---|---|---|
| Revaluation of fixed assets |  |  |  |  |  | ⎫ |
| Revaluation of investments |  |  |  |  |  | ⎬ 23 |
| Revaluation of stock and work in progress |  |  |  |  |  | ⎭ |
| Exchange translation differences |  |  |  |  |  | 91/23 |
| Associated companies |  |  |  |  |  | 86 |
| Total |  |  |  |  |  |  |

Exceptional surpluses/deficits arising on the revaluation of assets should be disclosed separately.                                               23

## (5) FIXED ASSETS:
*Land and Buildings*

|  | 1 £000s | 2 £000s | 3 £000s | 4 £000s |  |
|---|---|---|---|---|---|
| At 1st January 197 |  |  |  |  | ⎫ |
| Additions during year at cost |  |  |  |  | ⎪ |
| Disposals during year at book value |  |  |  |  | ⎬ 45/4 |
| Depreciation charge for the year |  |  |  |  | ⎪ |
| Revaluation surplus/(deficit) |  |  |  |  | ⎭ |
| At 31st December 197 |  |  |  |  |  |

*1=Freehold land and buildings at open market value*
*2=Freehold land and buildings at depreciated replacement cost*
*3=Leasehold land and buildings at open market value*
*4=Total*

*Plant and equipment*                                       £000s    Paragraph
(a) *Valued at net current replacement cost*                         in Standard
   *Gross current replacement cost*
   At 1st January 197 .
   Additions during year at cost
   Disposals during year
   Amounts eliminated in respect of assets now valued
     at their economic value
   Revaluation surplus/(deficit)                  ——————
   At 31st December 197 .
                                  44/46

   *Depreciation*
   At 1st January 197 .
   Eliminated on disposals
   Charge to profit and loss account for year
   Backlog depreciation arising on revaluation
   Amounts eliminated in respect of assets now valued
     at their economic value

   At 31st December 197 .

                                       £000s

   *Net current replacement cost*
   At 31st December 197 .

   At 31st December 197 .

(b) *Valued at economic value*              £000s  £000s    Paragraph
   At 1st January 197 .                               in Standard
   Disposals
   Depreciation charge for year
   Revaluation surplus/(deficit)
   Assets previously valued at NRC

   NRC                                                 44/46
   Further write-down required

   Economic value at 31st December
     197 .

   At 31st December 197 .

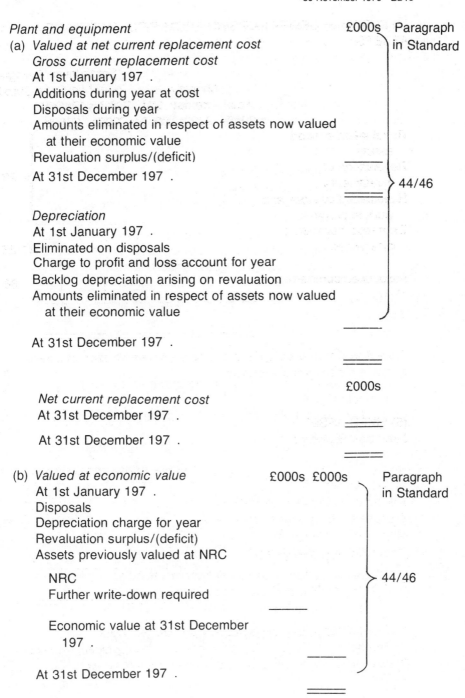

(c) *Total*             Paragraph
  At 31st December 197 .       in Standard

  At 31st December 197 .

N.B. A further section of the table would also be required for any
fixed assets shown at net realisable value.         44

(6) INTEREST IN SUBSIDIARIES:
There should be shown separately in the accounts of
the holding company:
    (a) the cost of investments in subsidiaries;
    (b) the attributable post-acquisition movements
    in reserves, less any goodwill written-off.   82/83
An analysis of the attributable post-acquisition
reserves should also be shown.

(7) INTEREST IN ASSOCIATED COMPANIES:
There should be shown separately in the accounts of
the holding company:
    (a) the cost of investments in associated
    companies;                   87/88
    (b) the attributable post-acquisition movements
    in reserves, less any goodwill written-off
An analysis of the attributable post-acquisition
reserves should also be shown.

(8) OTHER INVESTMENTS:
    (a) If quoted investments are not valued at
    mid-market price the reasons for adopting
    another basis and the basis used should be
    stated.                       63
    (b) The basis of valuation used for unquoted
    investments should be stated if the amount is
    material.                  64

(9) INTANGIBLE ASSETS (including goodwill):      Paragraph
The existence of intangible assets for which a      in Standard
quantifiable value cannot be established should be
noted in the accounts although no value should be
placed on them.      52
The following information should be supplied in
respect of goodwill:
    (a) separate amounts for each material
    acquisition (including associated companies) for
    the year;      55
    (b) amounts written off goodwill in each of the
    last five years.      58

(10) REVALUATION RESERVE:

|  | Group £000s | Associated Companies £000s |
|---|---|---|
| As at 1st January 197 . | | |
| Transfers during year | | |
| As at 31st December 197 . | | |

(11) DEFERRED TAXATION:

|  | Gross £000s | Provided in accounts £000s |
|---|---|---|
| Short-term timing differences | | |
| Accelerated capital allowances | | |
| Stock relief | | |
| Revaluation of non-current assets | | |
| Contingent liability | | |

73

(12) LONG-TERM LOANS:
If the loans take the form of
listed securities their market
value should be shown.      70

(13) STATEMENT OF CHANGE IN                         Paragraph
SHAREHOLDERS' NET EQUITY INTEREST                in Standard
AFTER ALLOWING FOR THE CHANGE IN
THE VALUE OF MONEY                          £000s          76

| | | |
|---|---|---|
| Net equity interest at beginning of year | X | 77(a) |
| New equity capital introduced during year | X | 77(a) |
| | X | |
| Amount required to compensate for the change in the value of money during year | X | |
| | X | |
| Net equity interest at end of year before dividends on equity capital | X | 77(b) |
| Gain/(loss) for year after allowing for the change in the value of money | X | 77(c) |
| Dividends on equity capital for year | X | 77(d) |
| Gain/(loss) for year after allowing for the change in the value of money and after dividends | X | |

(14) ANALYSIS OF THE GAIN/(LOSS) ON
MONETARY ASSETS AND LIABILITIES AFTER
ALLOWING FOR THE CHANGE IN THE VALUE
OF MONEY:                                                       78

| | |
|---|---|
| Long-term liabilities | X |
| Bank overdrafts | X |
| Non-equity share capital | X |
| Other | X |
| Total gain or loss | X |

The allowance for the change in the value of money
was made by applying the general index of retail
prices, based on January 1974=100. At 1.1.197
the index stood at X, and at Y at 31.12.197 .          79

# Appendix 2. Guidelines for appropriations to or transfers from revaluation reserve

(This appendix is for general guidance and does not form part of the Statement of Standard Accounting Practice.)

**1** The following are examples of matters which may call for appropriation to revaluation reserve of amounts greater than the net surplus on revaluation of assets having regard to the directors' assessment of the needs of the business:

(a) *Provision for the maintenance of net monetary assets.* This might arise in the following circumstances:

(i) An increase in the current value of stock resulting from higher prices may call for the financing of a corresponding increase in the amount of trade debtors less trade creditors.

(ii) A company may expect that additional reserves will be needed to finance contract work in progress as a result of higher prices. As contract work in progress is treated as a monetary asset in the calculation of current cost profit after it becomes specific to the requirements of a particular customer as a result of a contract, the stock revaluation adjustment will not lead to the retention of amounts for the financing of similar work in progress at a higher value.

(iii) Banks and some other financial institutions by the nature of their business have an excess of net monetary assets and need to finance an increased holding of these assets if they are to maintain the same real level of business during a period of inflation. A similar situation may arise with other institutions holding cash.

(b) *Provision for backlog depreciation.* Directors may take the view that the backlog depreciation set against revaluation surpluses for the year should be taken into account in determining amounts transferred to revaluation reserve. This may be considered necessary in the case of a company operating a limited number of major assets and where the nature of the replacement cycle of those assets results in amounts set aside by way of depreciation being insufficient for their replacement.

(c) *Additional provision for the replacement of seasonal agricultural produce.* The stock revaluation adjustment in any one year may not provide for the anticipated replacement cost of seasonal agricultural produce.

(d) *Maintenance of shareholders' equity.* The directors may wish to show what retentions would be consistent with the maintenance of the purchasing power of the shareholders' equity. In this case the total amount to be transferred to revaluation reserve should be equal to the figure described as the amount required to compensate for the change in the value of money during the year in the statement showing the change in shareholders' net equity interest after allowing for the change in the value of money.

**2** The following are examples of situations in which the directors may consider that amounts less than the net revaluation surplus should be transferred to revaluation reserve:

(a) *Replacement of assets by creditor financing.* A company may have its stock effectively financed wholly or partly by trade creditors, so that the stock revaluation adjustment is in excess of that required to finance the replacement of stock.

(b) *Replacement of assets by long-term and/or short-term borrowings.* The directors may be able, and intend, to finance the replacement of assets by such borrowings while maintaining a reasonable debt/equity ratio.

**3** Overall contraction or growth of the business.

(a) The directors may decide upon an overall contraction of the business such that the transfer to revaluation reserve can be restricted or that amounts taken to revaluation reserve in prior years are no longer required. In the latter situation a transfer will be called for from revaluation reserve to appropriation account.

(b) Directors may wish to make further retentions to finance the growth of the business. Such retentions would be reflected in the amount added to general reserve.

# Appendix 3. Example of the use of the averaging method for calculation of the current cost of sales

(This appendix is for general guidance and does not form part of the Statement of Standard Accounting Practice. The example of the use of the averaging method for calculation of the current cost of sales is illustrative only and in no way prescriptive and other methods of determining the current cost of sales may be preferred and may comply with the Standard.)

**1** The objective of the averaging method of calculating the current cost of sales is to charge stock consumed at the average current cost during the period. In the illustrative example shown below the calculation is made for a period of one year. The averaging method will produce an acceptable approximation to the current cost of sales where stock volumes have been reasonably constant, or have changed at a fairly steady rate, throughout the period. Therefore where this method is used, the charge to cost of sales should be calculated at the most frequent intervals practicable, for example on a monthly basis, since the inaccuracies which may result when this condition does not hold will thereby be minimised.

**2** In the simple example which follows, changes in current costs of stock have been determined from movements in an index of stock costs for each type of stock used by the company. In practice it may be necessary to use an index which represents changes in the current cost of a group of different types of stock taken together, using an appropriate pattern of weighting for the different types of stock concerned. The index of cost movements used should be appropriate to the costs incurred by the company. An index may be compiled by the company from information on the costs it has incurred and such an index may be more appropriate than an authorised external index for each type of stock or for stocks of companies in the relevant industrial category.

## Example

**3** A company uses two materials, A and B; labour costs and overheads are ignored here although such elements of the cost of stock can be dealt with in a similar way to that shown below for the

materials. The company records stock on a first in, first out (FIFO)
basis using actual historical cost incurred.
The following information is available:

|  | Material A | Material B |
|---|---|---|
| Opening stock at 1st January 1979 on a FIFO basis | | |
| Material A (representing 3 months' purchases) | £367,200 | |
| Material B (representing 3 months' purchases) | | £210,000 |
| Purchases during the year | £1,684,800 | £1,161,100 |
| Closing stock at 31st December 1979 on a FIFO basis | | |
| Material A (representing 3 months' purchases) | £453,600 | |
| Material B (representing 5 months' purchases) | | £499,500 |

**4** The movements in the current cost of the stock are represented
by the following index series. (Note: each index number is
appropriate to the middle of the month concerned*.)

|  |  | Material A | Material B |
|---|---|---|---|
| 1978 | October | 100.2 | 98.9 |
| | November | 102.0 | 100.0 |
| | December | 103.8 | 101.1 |
| 1979 | January | 106.2 | 101.9 |
| | February | 108.2 | 103.2 |
| | March | 109.9 | 103.9 |
| | April | 111.8 | 105.0 |
| | May | 113.6 | 106.2 |
| | June | 116.1 | 106.7 |
| | July | 118.1 | 108.1 |
| | August | 120.2 | 109.1 |
| | September | 121.9 | 110.2 |
| | October | 123.8 | 111.0 |
| | November | 126.0 | 111.7 |
| | December | 128.2 | 113.0 |
| 1980 | January | 129.8 | 114.0 |

* The index series published by the Government Statistical Service in the booklet "*Price index numbers for Current Cost Accounting*" can be taken to be appropriate to the middle of the months concerned. The third edition of the booklet, to be published in December 1976, will include price indices for the stocks of different industries together with a list of the price indices which are available for specific types of stock. Details of the movements in the indices for specific types of stock are available from the Central Statistical Office; depending upon the demand for these indices, they may be included in future editions of the booklet.

**5** The cost of sales for the period on an historical cost basis (using FIFO values) may be stated as follows:

|  |  |  | £ | £ |
|---|---|---|---:|---:|
| Opening stock | — Material A | | 367,200 | |
| | Material B | | 210,000 | 577,200 |
| add Purchases | — Material A | | 1,684,800 | |
| | Material B | | 1,161,100 | 2,845,900 |
| | | | | 3,423,100 |
| deduct Closing stock | — Material A | | 453,600 | |
| | Material B | | 499,500 | 953,100 |
| Cost of sales on an historical cost basis (using FIFO values) | | | | £2,470,000 |

**6** To apply the averaging method it is necessary to convert the value of opening and closing stock to the average current cost during the period. As a first step it is necessary to determine from the index of cost movements the index number relevant to the initial value of the stock (in this case the FIFO value):

*Opening stock at 1st January 1979*

Stock of Material A represents 3 months' purchases, therefore the average FIFO value may be taken as the cost at mid-November 1978, for which the index number is—                                                                                              102.0

Similarly, stock of Material B also represents 3 months' purchases and the appropriate index number (mid-November 1978) is—                                                          100.0

*Closing stock at 31st December 1979*

Stock of Material A represents 3 months' purchases, therefore the average FIFO value may be taken as the cost at mid-November 1979, for which the index number is—                                                                                              126.0

Stock of Material B represents 5 months' purchases and the appropriate index number (mid-October 1979) is—                                           111.0

**7** The average current cost of stock during the year may be represented by the average of the index numbers for the beginning and end of the year, which is:

For Material A:
$$\frac{105.0+129.0}{2} = 117.0$$

For Material B:
$$\frac{101.5+113.5}{2} = 107.5$$

Where the full index series for the period is available (as shown in paragraph 4) and the rate of change in the current cost has been markedly uneven, it will be more appropriate to calculate the average current cost using the arithmetic average of the twelve monthly index numbers. This method will also be more appropriate where the final index number for the month following the end of the period, or for the last month in the period, is not known at the time the calculation is made, because any error in the estimates of these index numbers used in the calculation will cause less distortion to the index number used to represent the average current cost during the year.

**8** The conversion of opening and closing stock values from the initial (FIFO) basis to the average current cost for the period is calculated as:

$$\text{FIFO value} \times \frac{\text{index number for the average current cost (paragraph 7)}}{\text{index number appropriate to the FIFO value (paragraph 6)}}$$

Therefore the opening and closing stock may be expressed at average current cost for the year as follows:

£

*Opening stock*
Material A
$$367,200 \times \frac{117.0}{102.0} = 421,200$$

Material B
$$210,000 \times \frac{107.5}{100.0} = 225,750$$

*Closing stock*                                                            £
Material A                    $\dfrac{453,600 \times 117.0}{126.0}$ = 421,200

Material B                    $\dfrac{499,500 \times 107.5}{111.0}$ = 483,750

**9** The current cost of sales is calculated using the average current cost values for the opening and closing stock obtained in paragraph 8, and may be stated as follows:

|  |  | £ | £ |
|---|---|---|---|
| Opening stock | — Material A | 421,200 | |
| | Material B | 225,750 | 646,950 |
| add Purchases | — Material A | 1,684,800 | |
| | Material B | 1,161,100 | 2,845,900 |
| | | | 3,492,850 |
| deduct Closing stock | — Material A | 421,200 | |
| | Material B | 483,750 | 904,950 |
| Current cost of sales | | | £2,587,900 |

The index numbers used in the calculations are stated to four figures. Indices prepared by a company and those published by the Government Statistical Service may not always be accurate to within one decimal place. An index of cost movements will normally be only an approximation to the changes in costs incurred by the company. Therefore it is prudent to regard as significant only the first three figures in the resultant calculations of the converted opening and closing stock values. In this example, these converted values, and hence the current cost of sales, should therefore be rounded to the nearest £1,000. Thus the current cost of sales is stated as £2,588,000.

**10** The cost of sales adjustment required to restate to current cost the cost of sales determined on an historical cost basis using FIFO values is therefore:

|  | £ |
|---|---|
| Current cost of sales (paragraph 9) | 2,588,000 |
| less, Cost of sales on historical cost basis (paragraph 5) | 2,470,000 |
| Cost of sales adjustment | £118,000 |

The cost of sales adjustment of £118,000 should be debited to the cost of sales charged to the profit and loss account and included as part of the revaluation surplus arising during the period which is to be shown separately in the appropriation account.

**11** The averaging method is discussed in more detail, together with examples of different applications of the method, in Chapter 8 of the Inflation Accounting Steering Group's *Guidance Manual on Current Cost Accounting* published by Tolley Publishing Company Ltd and the Publications Department of the Institute of Chartered Accountants in England and Wales.

# Appendix 4. Sources of indices—U.K. and Overseas

## United Kingdom

A periodical entitled *"Price index numbers for Current Cost Accounting"* is published for the Central Statistical Office by HMSO, P.O. BOX 569, London SE1 9NH, Telephone 01/928 6977, to whom enquiries should be directed.

## Republic of Ireland

A periodical entitled *"Irish Statistical Bulletin"* includes some indices relevant to the application of current cost accounting and is issued by the Central Statistical Office, Ardee Road, Dublin 6, Telephone Dublin 977144, to whom enquiries should be directed.

## Overseas

Enquiries should be addressed to the Central Statistical Office, Branch 6, Great George Street, London SW1P 3AQ, Telephone 01/233 7718 or 7661.

# Appendix 5. Recommended reading

1. The Inflation Accounting Steering Group's *Guidance Manual on Current Cost Accounting*
2. The Inflation Accounting Steering Group's *Brief Guide to the Exposure Draft on Current Cost Accounting*
3. The Inflation Accounting Steering Group's *Background Papers to the Exposure Draft on Current Cost Accounting*
4. *Report of the Inflation Accounting Committee (The Sandilands Report) (Cmd 6225)*
5. The Consultative Committee of Accountancy Bodies' *"Initial Reactions to the Report of the Inflation Accounting Committee (The Sandilands Report)"*
6. The Consultative Committee of Accountancy Bodies' *"Inflation Accounting—The Interim Period"*
7. *"Inflation Accounting—Auditors' Reports during the Interim Period"*
8. *"Guidance Notes on the Valuation of Assets"* (Royal Institution of Chartered Surveyors)

The above are available from:
The Institute of Chartered Accountants in England and Wales,
Chartered Accountants' Hall,
P.O. Box 433,
Moorgate Place,
London EC2P 2BJ
    (Items 1, 2, 3, 5, 6, 7)

The Institute of Chartered Accountants of Scotland,
27 Queen Street,
Edinburgh EH2 1LA
    (Items 1, 2, 5, 6, 7)

The Institute of Chartered Accountants in Ireland,
Fitzwilliam Place,
Dublin 2
    (Items 1, 2, 3, 5, 6, 7)

The Association of Certified Accountants,
22 Bedford Square,
London WC1
    (Items 1, 2, 6, 7)

The Institute of Cost and Management Accountants,
63 Portland Place,
London W1N 4AB
    (Items 1, 2, 3, 5, 6, 7)

The Chartered Institute of Public Finance and Accountancy,
1 Buckingham Place,
London SW1
    (Items 1, 2, 3, 5, 6, 7)

Her Majesty's Stationery Office,
P.O. Box 569,
London SE1 9NH
    (Item 4)

Tolley Publishing Company Ltd.,
44a High Street,
Croydon,
Surrey CR9 1UU
    (Items 1, 2, 3)

R.I.C.S. Publications,
Norden House,
Basing View,
Basingstoke, Hants RG21 2HN
    (Item 8)

Comments should quote reference ED18 and be addressed to:

C. A. Westwick,
The Secretary,
Inflation Accounting Steering Group,
First National House,
119, Finsbury Pavement,
London EC2P 2HJ

and should be despatched so as to be received not later than
**31 May 1977.**

It would greatly assist the Steering Group's work if comments are submitted as early as possible within the exposure period, are in the same order as the topics are dealt with in the Exposure Draft and are referenced to the relevant paragraph(s) of the Exposure Draft. All replies will be regarded as on public record unless confidentiality is requested by the commentator.

This draft is issued for comment only by the

**Accounting Standards Committee** of

**The Institute of Chartered Accountants in England and Wales**
**The Institute of Chartered Accountants of Scotland**
**The Institute of Chartered Accountants in Ireland**
**The Association of Certified Accountants**
**The Institute of Cost and Management Accountants and**
**The Chartered Institute of Public Finance and Accountancy**

and does not necessarily represent the views of the Councils of these bodies. It should be noted that the draft may be modified in the light of comments received before being issued in the form of an accounting standard.

NOTE: This is a draft of an initial standard. The Accounting Standards Committee will review the resulting Statement of Standard Accounting Practice in the light of experience of its operation.

# Draft Guidance Note: Current Cost Accounting The Valuation of Fixed Assets

## 1 Introduction

This Draft Guidance Note has been prepared by the Assets Valuation Standards Committee in order to advise members of the valuation principles and procedures which they should follow when instructed to value fixed assets of companies and other organisations for incorporation in Reports and Accounts prepared on the basis of Current Cost Accounting. The Accounting Standards Committee has published Exposure Draft No. 18 of an Accounting Standard for Current Cost Accounting and the Inflation Accounting Steering Group has published the Guidance Manual and the Background Papers to the Exposure Draft. This, the RICS Guidance Note, should assist members in preparing valuations so as to meet the requirements of the proposed Standard. It should be noted that when the Standard is finally issued, all companies are required to observe its provisions; members in receipt of valuation instructions are, therefore, advised not only to acquaint themselves with the Exposure Draft but also to discuss with their clients and their advisers any relevant matters or points requiring clarification.

Current Cost Accounting requires that assets be stated in a company's accounts at their value to the business. For fixed assets this is regarded as deprival value of the assets, that is, the loss that would be suffered by the company if it were deprived of the assets, and this loss can be estimated from three viewpoints, namely:

(a) **Net current replacement cost** i.e. the current cost of purchasing a new asset less a deduction to reflect wear and tear and obsolescence.
(b) **Net realisable value** i.e. open market value less the expenses of sale.
(c) **Economic value** i.e. the present value of:

  (i) the net income the asset can generate over its working life; and
  (ii) any residual value.

These notes are concerned with the valuers' role in assessing depreciated replacement costs and open market values of 'land and buildings' and the value to the business of 'plant and machinery', these being particularly relevant in determining figures under (a) and (b) above. They apply to the

1

valuation of assets within the United Kingdom and whilst drawn in terminology to reflect English property law, valuers of land and buildings in Scotland should have no difficulty in following the text and feuhold should be referred to instead of freehold.

It should be noted that 'land' is not used in the legal context, but is bare land without any buildings, other structures or site works.

Para. 18 draws attention to the application of the Standard to overseas assets. The AVS Committee of the Irish Branch of the RICS will publish a Draft Guidance Note applicable to the Republic of Ireland.

A 'property company' is one whose main business is the holding of property:

(a) as an investment to earn rental income at arm's length; or
(b) for development and resale or holding after development to earn rental income

except where such a company is:

(i) one of a group of companies, which is not principally a group of property companies; or
(ii) a 'construction company' i.e. a company undertaking construction work on its own land for resale.

All other companies are 'non-property companies'.

The proposed Standard sets out four phases for its introduction commencing with accounting periods beginning on and from 1st July 1978. The first phase applies to:

(i) all companies listed on the Stock Exchange, and
(ii) companies outside (i), nationalised industries and public trading entities which disclose for the previous accounting period either

(a) a turnover in excess of £10m or
(b) total assets in excess of £10m.

Companies having more than 50% of their assets outside the UK and Ireland are excluded from Phase I.

The second phase beginning on and from 1st January 1979 will apply to all limited companies, nationalised industries and public trading entities not within Phase 1 providing they disclose either a turnover or total assets in excess of £1m. The remaining companies, unincorporated businesses and all other financial accounts will become subject to the Standard in two further phases.

Organisations may introduce CCA earlier if they wish and members should consider, in appropriate cases, advising their clients to adopt the basis of valuation for land and buildings as set out in paras. 4, 5 and 6 as soon as practicable ahead of the requirement to introduce CCA as the basis is generally in accordance with earlier Guidance Notes:

2

Guidance Note No. A.2 will be withdrawn in due course.

The recently developed practice by which a member reviews an internal valuation in whole or in part and expresses his opinion thereon, or comments on certain valuation criteria, is considered undesirable and not in conformity with professional standards. Accordingly members are advised to suggest to client companies during the interim period before the CCA Standard is in force that the sampling procedure set out in para. 10 is adopted.

## LAND AND BUILDINGS

### 2 The valuer

The valuer should be professionally qualified, which means he must be a corporate member of the RICS or ISVA or RVA and have post-qualification experience and knowledge of valuing properties in the location and category of the subject properties. (This follows the City Code and is somewhat similar in intention to the Regulations issued under the Insurance Companies Act 1974). (Para. 9 discusses the circumstances when internal and external valuers should or may be employed).

### 3 Division of types of asset

Land and buildings will generally be held as fixed assets by a company for one or more of the following purposes:

(a) Owner occupation
(b) As investments to earn rental income
(c) For future development either for resale or to earn rental income.

Land and buildings may also be held as trading stock as opposed to fixed assets.

As the CCA Standard requires to some degree a different approach to each category of property holding, each is the subject of individual comment.

In all cases it should be noted that the valuer should include with the valuation of the land and buildings such plant and machinery which it is customary to regard as an integral part of the ownership of the property and which are generally identified in Guidance Note No. F.1 in the Guidance Notes Handbook entitled 'Valuation of Assets'.

Land and buildings which are subject to a debenture, mortgage or are otherwise charged as security are to be valued as if free and clear and this assumption should always be stated in the Valuation Certificate whether or not the existence of a charge is known to the valuer.

If the valuer is aware of any restriction or a charge which might give the lender an opportunity to delay a disposal or require a fine or penalty on the repayment of the loan he should draw attention to its existence but he is not responsible for its verification or evaluation as a possible contingent liability which might arise in certain circumstances if the asset were to be realised.

## 4    Land and buildings in owner occupation

The normal basis for the valuation of owner-occupied land and buildings will be open market value for the existing use assuming vacant possession. Value to the business will be open market value plus acquisition costs. Existing use does not here necessarily mean the particular trade currently being carried on in the building; many buildings are general purpose structures, suitable for a variety of different trades, e.g. light industrial buildings, warehouses, retail units. Neither is it intended that the words 'existing use' be given precisely their same meaning as in planning law as the existing use value of land and buildings for Current Cost Accounting would include development value for the purposes of the business to the extent to which this would be reflected in the price that would be paid in the open market. A definition of 'open market value' will be found in Guidance Note No. D.1 in the Guidance Notes Handbook.

No regard should be paid to any inter-company leasing arrangements by which rental payments may or may not pass from one company to another in the same group. When these arrangements exist the properties should be valued as if owner-occupied. By the same token it would not be correct to value on an assumed sale and leaseback transaction.

There are some kinds of property which are rarely (if ever) sold except by way of a sale of the business in occupation, due to the specialised nature of the buildings, site works, location or otherwise. In these cases existing use valuations can only be made by reference to depreciated replacement costs and such valuations should be expressed as being subject to the adequate potential profitability of the business compared with the value of the total assets. It is the responsibility of the directors of the company to determine whether and by how much the depreciated replacement cost as advised by the valuer should be reduced in the event of the business having insufficient potential profitability. It is stressed that depreciated replacement cost basis of valuation is a method of last resort but nevertheless one which will need to be adopted in the case of some specialised properties.

A 'depreciated replacement cost' basis of valuation normally requires an estimate of the open market value of the land for the existing use, plus acquisition costs and an estimate of the new replacement cost of the buildings and site works, plus Architects', Engineers', Quantity Surveyors' and other fees, these estimated figures to be reduced on account of age, condition, layout and restricted life due to lease terms, planning consents, environmental factors and functional obsolescence. The discount for functional obsolescence should be assessed in consultation with the directors as the useful life of the buildings may be affected by the

4

expected life of the plant or processes carried on in the buildings, which may therefore become obsolete before the end of their physical life. When the valuation has been made on this basis the valuer should state that in his opinion it is not possible to assess the existing use value with vacant possession in the open market.

In the event of the land and buildings being valued on a depreciated replacement cost basis and the alternative use value being materially different, the amount of this valuation should be reported. Where land and buildings are valued on an open market value for the existing use and there is a relevant alternative use value which is materially different, then the amount of the alternative use value should also be reported. It is to be noted that the alternative use value will only be disclosed in the Directors' Report if it is above the open market value for existing use.

In the case of owner occupied properties an alternative use value is not suitable for incorporation in the accounts as this would assume that the business was no longer occupying and using the land and buildings and had in fact either ceased or removed elsewhere. (See para. 5 for comments on the application of alternative use values to investment and development properties).

Any land and buildings which are owned and are being made ready for occupation by the company or which the company intends to occupy within the next accounting period should be valued at the relevant date on open market value for the intended use of the business. In these cases the valuer should consult with the directors as to the treatment of the cost of the works being carried out. It may be appropriate to value the property in its state before the commencement of the work, for the company to record the work being undertaken at its current cost and for the whole to be valued at the end of the accounting period during which completion takes place. Alternatively the basis of valuation described in para. 6 may be adopted.

The directors should indicate to the valuer any properties which are surplus to the requirements of the company and such surplus properties will be valued on an open market value basis with potential for any alternative use. The total value of surplus properties must be shown separately in the Valuation Certificate as the company will need to make a deduction for the estimated expenses of sale in order that the properties can be incorporated in the accounts at their net realisable value. Such surplus properties will be valued as stated in para. 5.

5    **Land and buildings held as investments or for development**

Such properties will be valued on an open market value basis subject to existing tenancies, other than those between companies within a group of companies, and will take account of existing or alternative uses. It would not be correct to assume any other basis or to qualify the basis, e.g. as between a willing buyer and a willing seller. Due regard must be had to the existence or otherwise of planning and superior landlords' consents for development, redevelopment or changes of use. It would be wrong to value on the assumption that all necessary consents had already been obtained when this is not in fact the case. The value to the business of such properties is the open market value as described above plus acquisition costs.

6       **Properties in course of development**

The basis of valuation for properties in course of development, and intended to be held as fixed assets for owner occupation or investment to earn rental income, should be:

(i) Properties which on completion will be valued on an open market value basis: the lower of

    (a) the estimated open market value of the land and buildings when completed assuming market conditions prevailing at the valuation date less the estimated total expenditure at costs current at the date of valuation to be incurred in completing the development; or

    (b) the estimated depreciated replacement cost, namely the open market value of the land for its existing use plus acquisition costs plus the estimated current replacement cost of the partly completed building in its condition at the valuation date.

(ii) Properties which on completion will be valued on a depreciated replacement cost basis:
as in para. (i) (b) above.

In arriving at the value under para. (i) (a) the building will be assumed to be vacant except to the extent of any contracted lettings. It will be noted that in para. (i) (b) the partly completed building is not taken at actual cost but at the estimated replacement cost current at the date of valuation.

7       **Land and buildings held as trading stock**

Members may be called upon to value land and buildings held as trading stock and not as fixed assets. The same principles will apply as those to be used when valuing land and buildings held for development but the valuer should first consult with the directors as it is likely that he will be required to give:

(i) the open market value at the relevant date of the land together with any buildings in existence at the date of acquisition and still remaining, i.e., as if no development work other than demolition had taken place subsequent to acquisition; and

(ii) where applicable, his estimate of the open market value of the land and buildings at the anticipated date for completion of the development which is in hand.

8       Frequency of valuations

(a) **Non-Property Companies**
The Exposure Draft requires that valuations should be carried out at intervals of not more than five years and more frequently if land and buildings represent a major proportion of the company's gross assets or there have been considerable market variations or major changes in the property assets since the last full valuation.

In the intermediate years the directors should estimate the value of the land and buildings after consultation with their professional valuers, either internal or external. Account must be taken not only of market variations but also the value of additional properties or interests acquired, changes in planning consents, additions to and the refurbishment of existing buildings, demolitions, abandonments and disposals.

(b) **Property Companies**
Valuations should be carried out annually of all properties.


9       **Internal and external valuers and valuations**

An internal valuer, whether a director or an employee, may carry out valuations, providing he is professionally qualified (see para. 2) with the necessary experience and knowledge, has no significant financial interest in the company, and, having regard to any particular circumstance, the auditors do not require an external valuer to make a valuation.

Members who act as internal valuers must ensure that they disclose to the auditors any financial interest, e.g., shareholding or participation in a share incentive scheme, they might have in a company and should consider in the light of the actual circumstances whether it is proper for them to undertake the internal valuation so that no question of a conflict of interest can arise and the member's professional integrity be brought into question.

In those cases where an external valuer is required to provide a valuation it is not permissible for either him or any of his partners or co-directors to be also a director or employee of the company or of another company within a group of companies or to have a significant financial interest in the company or group, or the company or group to have a significant financial interest in the valuer's firm or company.

Internal and external valuers should be employed under the following circumstances and conditions on those occasions when a valuation is required of all properties of a company:

**Non-Property Companies**
Internal or external valuers may be employed at the directors' discretion but if internal valuers are employed a sample in accordance with para. 10 shall be valued by an external valuer.

7

**Property Companies**

All the properties owned by property companies should be valued by external valuers at least every three years. In the years between full external valuations, internal or external valuers may be employed at the directors' discretion, but if the former are employed then a sample, in accordance with para. 10, shall be valued by an external valuer.

Subject to the requirements of company law the name and qualifications of an internal valuer need not be stated in the company's accounts but a statement will be made to the effect that the valuation has been carried out by a qualified valuer employed by the company. If the valuation of the entire property holding is made by an external valuer, the name and qualifications will be stated, but when a sample is valued the name and qualifications of the external valuer will not be stated.

10   **Valuations of samples**

As stated in para. 9 valuations of a sample by an external valuer will be required when all the company's properties have been valued by an internal valuer.

It will be the responsibility of the company's directors, after consultation with the auditors, to select the properties to form the sample and this will be done when the internal valuation has been made.

The external valuer, who will be appointed by the directors, will have no responsibility for the selection of the sample, although he may be consulted thereon.

The external valuer will be required to undertake a full-scale valuation of the sample and, except with the prior concurrence of the auditors, must not rely on any facts which may be provided to him, e.g. floor areas, and should state any matters, e.g. term of leasehold tenure, which may require verification by lawyers or other parties. (See Guidance Note No. G.1 entitled 'Verification of Information Supplied to or Adopted by a Valuer', in course of publication).

The external valuer will supply his Valuation Certificate to the company and should state therein that he accepts no responsibility in respect of the unsampled balance of the portfolio and maintains a neutrality of opinion as to the value of that balance and the applicability thereto of his valuation of the sample.

It will be noted that the above procedure is designed to provide the company with a means to satisfy the auditors that an internal valuation is corroborated by a valuation of a sample by an external valuer. The external valuer cannot be drawn into any discussion regarding the value of properties not included in the sample dealt with by him.

11   **Negative values**

Leasehold interests under which the rent paid exceeds the open market rental value will have a negative value. In some cases the ownership of even freehold land and other leasehold interests may be a liability, e.g., due to expenses of reclamation or dilapidations, and valuers should provide a negative valuation. It is incorrect to advise a 'nil' valuation amount.

Negative values should be reported separately.

## 12    Taxation

Whilst the valuer has regard to the effect of taxation generally on market value he should take no account of any liability for taxation which may arise on a disposal, whether actual or notional, and in particular he should make no deduction for Capital Gains Tax, Development Gains Income Tax or Development Land Tax. He should make this clear in his Valuation Certificate. If at the date of valuation a property is subject to a Compulsory Purchase Order, the valuer should draw attention to this as any compensation will henceforth be on a net basis after deduction for Development Land Tax, if any.

## 13    Acquisition and sale costs

It will be noted that the value to the business of land and buildings is to include acquisition costs and net realisable value is arrived at after deduction of the expenses of sale. The valuer in his Valuation Certificate will provide only the open market value (the figure which would appear in a contract for sale) but he may be asked to assist in an estimate being made of the acquisition costs and/or the expenses of sale, which can vary according to company arrangements. In a depreciated replacement cost approach the valuer will have to make his own assessment of the expenses associated with acquiring the land and erecting the buildings in his overall appraisal.

## 14    Depreciation

In normal circumstances depreciation will not be provided on freehold land. Exceptions will include land the exploitation of which has a limited life, e.g., extractive industries or a disused quarry used for refuse disposal, or a use authorised by a planning permission for a limited time.

Depreciation should be provided on freehold buildings over the period of their future economic useful life as estimated by the valuer after consultation with the directors. In many instances it may not be possible to judge precisely the life of buildings and in these cases banding may be appropriate but in that event care should be taken to ensure a consistent approach at subsequent revaluations. The useful life should be the period of time arising from a number of circumstances after which it is unlikely to be economic to maintain the building. The valuer will need to consider all the relevant circumstances which will include functional and economic

9

obsolescence; costs of maintenance and repairs; the likelihood and practicability of alternative uses; and environmental factors.

The amount to be depreciated will be the depreciated replacement cost of the buildings or, if less, the open market value for existing use plus acquisition costs of the land and buildings and will be termed 'the depreciable amount'. The valuer will normally be required to advise on the depreciable amount. If open market value plus acquisition costs exceeds depreciated replacement cost the difference if any will be called the 'residual amount' but it should be noted this does not necessarily represent the value of the land.

The sample principles will apply to leaseholds except that the period over which depreciation is calculated will be the shorter of the estimated economic useful life or the unexpired term of the lease and if there be a 'residual amount' this will be amortized over the unexpired term of the lease.

It should be noted that the provisions for depreciation apply to all land and buildings owned by both non-property and property companies.

## 15   Authorised indices of building costs

In assessing depreciated replacement cost it is necessary to start from the current replacement cost. It will be a matter for the valuer's judgement whether he requires this to be re-assessed by an appropriately qualified surveyor or if he up-dates an earlier assessment or an actual cost. In updating, the valuer may, particularly at intermediate years when consulted by directors, use an authorised building cost index. The indices which are authorised and should be used in these circumstances are currently restricted to those published by the Central Statistical Office. The following index comes within the authorised category:

'Cost of New Construction Index'—To be published by the Central Statistical Office in 'Price Index Numbers for Current Cost Accounting' from HMSO.

(It is expected that an agency will be established to authorise other indices which are currently prepared and published by professional institutions, trade associations and other bodies).

## 16   Dilapidations

Buildings should be valued in their state of repair and condition as at the valuation date. If the valuer is requested to prepare a valuation on the assumption that the buildings are in an acceptable state of repair and condition, e.g. for the reason that the company maintains a deferred repairs reserve, he should also advise on their value in their existing condition.

## 17    Mineral bearing land

The valuation approach to mineral bearing land used by the extractive industries, e.g. quarries, sand and gravel pits, should be the same as described in the preceding paragraphs pending the outcome of any separate study which may be made concerning the application of Current Cost Accounting to wasting assets. This Note is not concerned with rights to oil and similar specialised operations.

Plant and machinery used in connection with the operation should be valued separately as described later in this Note.

## 18    Overseas assets

It is intended that the provisions of the Standard should apply to overseas assets and wherever possible the provisions and procedures for the valuation in the UK of 'land and buildings' and 'plant and machinery' should be applied.

It should be noted that the valuations are required for incorporation within the UK company's group accounts and will not necessarily be incorporated in the accounts of the overseas company—in some countries if this were done and the valuations were above cost a tax liability could arise.

Where difficulties are encountered in applying the Standard it can be anticipated that companies may wish to consult with their UK professional advisers on the basis of valuation and/or selection of suitable qualified and experienced valuers.

## 19    Valuation certificate

The Valuation Certificate should follow the general format as appended to Guidance Note No. A.1 in the Guidance Notes Handbook; it may be abbreviated as appropriate. If the Certificate does not specifically identify the properties but refers, for example, to 'all the Company's properties', a Letter of Comfort should be obtained from the directors confirming the accuracy of the statement, otherwise it may be desirable to append an appropriate Schedule of Properties.

Apart from the method of sub-totals recommended on the standard format, the Valuation Certificate should contain separate totals, with any negative values totalled separately, for:

(a) Open market value for the existing use.
(b) Depreciated replacement cost.
(c) Open market value for an alternative use as applied to (a) and (b).
(d) Land and buildings held as trading stock.

The Certificate should include a statement that the valuer is qualified to undertake the valuation within the definition of para. 2 (and/or the

11

Exposure Draft No. 18). The Certificate should be signed in accordance with Guidance Note No. E.2 in the Guidance Notes Handbook.

20 **Non-publication clause**

The Valuation Certificate should contain a non-publication clause (see Guidance Note No. A.2 in the Guidance Notes Handbook) so that the valuer can approve any reference to the valuation either in the Report and Accounts or in any other published document.

The valuer, when accepting instructions, should only do so on the basis that the Valuation Certificate will contain a non-publication clause and any other caveats which he considers necessary.

## PLANT AND MACHINERY

21 **General**

When a valuer is asked to make a valuation of plant and machinery for inclusion in a company's accounts it is essential that there should be a clear understanding by all concerned of what is being valued and the date of valuation. It is also essential that there should be a clear understanding of the basis of valuation and the proposed treatment of that valuation in the accounts.

22 **Basis of valuation**

In the absence of evidence to the contrary, it should be assumed that it would be worthwhile for the company to replace the asset in substantially its existing form if it were deprived of it, and therefore it should be valued on the basis of its net current replacement cost, which is derived from its gross current replacement cost. Replacement cost includes the costs of installation.

The Exposure Draft acknowledges that the incidence of technological advance may require the gross current replacement cost of an asset to be estimated by reference to the cost of a modern equivalent asset—i.e., the cost of a replacement asset which incorporates current technology and may enable the total costs of producing the existing level of output to be reduced—where this is expected to be below the cost of an identical asset. For further discussion on this subject reference should be made to the Exposure Draft and the Inflation Accounting Steering Group's Background Papers to the Exposure Draft; the following comments relate solely to the valuation of a substantially identical replacement to the asset owned.

The methods of ascertaining the gross replacement cost in the order of probable accuracy are:

(i) Suppliers' official price lists, catalogues, etc., with appropriate deductions for trade discounts.

12

(ii) The company's own replacement cost estimates based on expert opinion.

(iii) An index compiled by the company from its own purchasing experience.

(iv) Authorised external price indices analysed by asset type.

(v) Authorised external price indices analysed by using industry.

Whichever method or methods are used they should be based on documental objective evidence capable of independent verification.

Authorised indices are currently restricted to those published by the Central Statistical Office. The CSO proposes to publish monthly indices classified by asset type and by using industry under the title 'Price Index Numbers for Current Cost Accounting' available from HMSO. It is expected that an agency will be established to approve other indices for use in Current Cost Accounting.

The valuer should ascertain the net current replacement cost by reflecting the diminution in value of the gross value of the asset due to wear and tear and functional obsolescence so that the net current replacement cost represents the value of the unexpired service potential of the asset. Functional obsolescence should normally be assessed in consultation with the directors.

Account should be taken of special factors such as the effect on value of the building housing the plant having a limited life, being held on a limited tenure or subject to a limited planning consent. Furthermore, it is necessary to consider the value of individual items in relation to the value of the plant as a whole.

In some cases a net current replacement cost basis will not be appropriate. It would almost certainly be inappropriate to use this basis of valuation where land and buildings in which the plant and machinery are housed are valued on an alternative use basis. When reference is made to a valuation of land and buildings on an alternative use basis (see para. 4 and Note No. A.3 in the Guidance Notes Handbook), consideration needs to be given to the effect on the value of plant and machinery. In these circumstances the following alternatives would be available:

(i) where the plant and machinery could be moved to and used by the company at another site, the valuation would be on a net current replacement cost basis but making an allowance for the costs of removal and reinstallation;

(ii) where the plant and machinery cannot be moved it would be worth little more than scrap value;

(iii) where plant and machinery is to be sold rather than used in the company's business net realisable value would be appropriate based on open market value or, if there is a time limit on the sale, forced sale value.

Definitions of open market value and forced sale value are given in Annexe 'A' to this Draft Guidance Note. These definitions should be used

13

for the purpose of valuations which are to be used in company accounts, but they in no way override any statutory definitions of market value which may have to be adopted, e.g., for the purpose of valuation for capital gains tax, or compensation cases.

23 **Plant and machinery forming part of a building**

Problems have arisen when valuing land and buildings where there are items of plant and machinery which are regarded by the valuer as forming part of the building but which the accountant may wish to segregate for accounting purposes. A valuer when valuing premises will, unless specifically instructed otherwise, include all items of plant and machinery on the premises which provide services to the land and buildings and which are normally regarded in the open market as an integral part of the premises for letting or sale or as security for a loan.

A list of such items is given in Guidance Note No. F.1 in the Guidance Notes Handbook but it is stressed that the list is not comprehensive and merely indicates, as a general guide to valuers, those items that would usually fall to be included with the land and buildings. Normally process plant and machinery should be separately valued.

It is possible that some or all of the items of plant and machinery normally included in the valuation of land and buildings may be needed to be separated for accounting purposes, for instance when it is expected that they have a shorter useful life than the rest of the premises and depreciation is being provided accordingly, or to correspond with the headings adopted by the company in its accounts. In such circumstances the valuer will have to specify which items of plant and machinery are and are not included in his valuation and that it is not practicable to arrive at separate valuations of the individual components. Nevertheless, the valuer may be able to assist in suggesting ways of allocating the overall valuation between the different components. The valuer should clearly state in the report, and it should be explained in any reference thereto in the company accounts, that the valuation is an overall valuation and any split between the components is only an allocation to the components of amounts within the overall valuation figure.

24 **Dies, moulds, patterns and spare parts**

A valuation of plant and machinery must clearly state what is or is not included. Such items as dies, moulds, patterns and spare parts, which are normally excluded from the valuation may or may not be included in headings other than plant and machinery in the company accounts, or be written off. In order to ensure that there is no misunderstanding the valuer should specify in the valuation what items are included in the Valuation Certificate and any exclusion of items of plant and machinery should also be specified.

14

If a value is required for dies, moulds and patterns it should be separately stated. Spare parts would not normally be valued as part of the unit as it is common practice for these to be carried in stock. Auxiliary items necessary for the operation of the unit would be valued with the unit.

## 25 Motor vehicles, ships, aircraft

These are to be treated in the same manner as plant and machinery but it seems unlikely that members will normally become involved in their valuation.

## 26 Plant and machinery register

It is recommended that all companies be encouraged to maintain an up-to-date plant and machinery register showing as a minimum, the location of each item, its date of acquisition, original cost and any further capital expenditure, as this assists considerably in a valuation and its reconciliation with the company accounts.

## 27 Non-publication clause

The Valuation Certificate should contain a non-publication clause. (See para. 20).

Comments on this Draft Guidance Note should be sent before 31st May 1977 to:

The Divisional Secretary
General Practice Division
Royal Institution of Chartered Surveyors
29 Lincoln's Inn Fields
London, WC2A 3ED

Unless confidentiality is requested all comments will be regarded as on public record.

The Guidance Notes Handbook—'Valuation of Assets'—is available from the above address at a price of £5.00 to include amendments up to December 1977.

30th November 1976

ANNEXE 'A'

## PLANT AND MACHINERY

### Definition of the open market value and the forced sale value

**The Open Market Value** is defined as the best price at which the interest in the plant and machinery might reasonably be expected to be sold by either Private Treaty, Public Auction or Tender, as may be thought to be appropriate assuming:

(a) a willing seller;
(b) a reasonable period within which to negotiate the sale, taking into account the nature of the plant and machinery and the state of the market;
(c) values will remain static throughout the period;
(d) the plant and machinery will be offered generally on the market;
(e) no account is to be taken of an additional bid by a special purchaser;
(f) the plant and machinery may be valued, either

   (i) as a whole; or
   (ii) as individual items.

**The Forced Sale Value** is defined as the open market value (as defined in the above paragraph) with the proviso that the vendor has imposed a time limit for completion which cannot be regarded as a reasonable period as referred to in (b) above.

# Index

*References are to paragraph numbers in the manual.*